Anna E. R. and Laura Furness

In memory of their grandfather

Alexander Ramsey

SAMUEL JOHNSON

SAMUEL JOHNSON

A Survey and Bibliography of Critical Studies

JAMES L. CLIFFORD

and

DONALD J. GREENE

UNIVERSITY OF MINNESOTA PRESS, MINNEAPOLIS

PREFACE

THE first version of this list, *Johnsonian Studies, 1887–1950: A Survey and Bibliography*, by James L. Clifford, was published by the University of Minnesota Press in 1951. A continuation for the decade 1950–1960, prepared by the present editors, was published in 1962, as part of a volume of *Johnsonian Studies* collected by Magdi Wahba in Cairo, United Arab Republic. The present volume combines these two, with various additions and corrections, and then provides two major extensions: (1) recent studies, 1960 to 1968 (with partial coverage of works published in 1969), for which James L. Clifford is chiefly responsible, and (2) the period from Johnson's own lifetime up to 1887, for which Donald J. Greene is chiefly responsible. In effect, then, the volume now spans well over 200 years, from Johnson's early career to the present.

This list makes no claim to being exhaustive. Not every discussion of Johnson, every article or note specifically concerned with him, or every reference in books about other people and themes, has been included. Many short items in *Notes and Queries*, the *Times Literary Supplement*, and elsewhere, even though wholly about Johnson, have been omitted. Only those which appear to add something to our knowledge about the man or his works, which contribute some original interpretation or, occasionally, which are outstanding in obtuseness of critical opinion (useful for teachers and historians) have been included. But while there has been selectivity in choosing short articles and notes, we have tried, at least for the period from 1887 on, to list every separately printed pamphlet or book having to do with Johnson. Some have doubtless eluded us—to be the source of continuing embarrassment in years to come; some obviously will be of no use whatever except to the most ardent collector. But at least there will be found here the most complete listing of the mass of privately printed Johnsoniana which has flowed from the presses in modern times.

It should be made clear that this does not also constitute a complete bibliography of Boswell. In the special section devoted to him there are included only items which have a definite connection with Johnson or with the *Life*. Nor has it appeared feasible to include all important works about other members of the Johnson circle, though in Section 5 readers will find many useful references to Mrs. Piozzi, Sir John Hawkins, Edmund Burke, Fanny Burney, Sir Joshua Reynolds, to name only a few, which also provide evidence about their relations with Johnson. Intended to be selective, this section gives only representative standard works which have appeared to us to have some value for students of the Johnson group.

The thousands of miscellaneous references contained in books and articles about other people and topics constitute an even more difficult problem. Obviously it would be futile to attempt to list every mention of Johnson's name, every quotation from Boswell's *Life*, every excerpt in school textbooks, every allusion to his opinions. Even if such a compilation could ever be assembled and published, its usefulness would be doubtful. On the other hand, many of the most interesting criticisms of Johnson may be found in works in which his name does not appear on the title page, or even in a chapter heading. It is hoped that in the present list the more important of these passages will be found, though possibly everyone will wonder why some have been omitted and others included. No full explanation can be given, except that at one time or another we have judged that the reference might be of some use to a hypothetical historical research worker, Johnson collector, or literary critic.

The user should be cautioned, in particular, that the "coverage" of the nearly a century and a half prior to 1887 is only a first approximation to the thoroughgoing investigation of the Johnsonian writings of that period which would be desirable. The difficulties of such an investigation are formidable; they include, as well as the sheer bulk of the material, the rarity and inaccessibility of files of many eighteenth-century newspapers and periodicals and the inadequate indexing of eighteenth- and nineteenth-century journals; and to do a really first-rate job would require many more years of patient research than we have been able to devote to it. It may be useful to note some categories in the early period where we have had to be ruthlessly selective, if the compilation was to remain within manageable proportions:

1. During Johnson's own lifetime, hostile or facetious journalistic squibs. We have included a fair number of the more interesting of these, but the reader who would like to see the whole array should consult the bibliographical appendix to Helen Louise McGuffie's doctoral disserta-

tion (item 10/5:10), a one-hundred-page list of items published between 1750 and 1784. Anyone who works on Johnson's "reception" by his contemporaries must be grateful to Miss McGuffie's devoted labor.

Throughout this period, and most of the nineteenth century, the bibliographer is also plagued by the unacknowledged reprinting of journalistic items in other periodicals. We have detected a good many of these in the course of our work, but we cannot guarantee that an occasional item will not be found listed more than once, under different titles and in different journals. In the later nineteenth and the twentieth centuries, this problem takes the form of the scholar or critic who dashes off a longish review for a journal and some years later reprints it, with a new title and with or without some revisions, as an essay in a collection of his critical writings.

2. In the two or three decades immediately following Johnson's death, a host of small biographical notes, anecdotes (often of dubious authenticity), and the like. Two groups from this period have been drastically pruned: (a) verse epitaphs on Johnson, which proliferated in the newspapers and magazines in the months immediately after his death; (b) early publications in periodicals of letters by Johnson. Important early collections of letters we have tried to include; but, since R. W. Chapman's edition (item 23:14) gives the data of first publication of each letter, it seemed pointless to repeat information so easily available.

3. In the middle and later nineteenth century, short, uncritical appreciative or "inspirational" biographical sketches of Johnson, deriving completely from Boswell and other well-known sources, and appearing in "family magazines" and volumes for the edification of the young. A substantial representation of these do appear in the list, but we have made no great effort to be exhaustive.

Notwithstanding such omissions, we have added approximately a thousand entries from the earlier period, and we believe that their inclusion will make the list of greater use to the student, even if it still falls far short of perfection.

It may also be worth pointing out that, although we have pushed the lower limit of the list back to Johnson's own lifetime, we do not of course attempt to provide a bibliography of Johnson's own writings. We have included some entries giving the details of early publication of a number of his major works, partly to save the inexperienced student the trouble of looking them up in Courtney (item 1/1:19) or elsewhere, partly in order to list some significant contemporary reviews of those early editions. But such entries constitute only a tiny fraction of the bibliography of Johnson himself.

Something should be said about the technical form used. As an aid to librarians and specialized workers, the bibliographical entry is given in fairly full detail. Where, however, volumes have been published in both England and the United States with no change in contents, usually only the original publisher is given. Each entry is numbered (not always consecutively) merely to provide an easy means of reference. Wherever an author's name is known, the work is entered under that name. On the other hand, where a volume is an edition or a compilation it is entered under its title, and the editor's or compiler's name follows.

The index is a combination of (a) a complete author index to the works listed in the Bibliography, and (b) a subject index to topics and persons specifically mentioned in the Survey and in titles and summaries in the Bibliography. A genuinely comprehensive subject index, which would have to be based on careful analysis of every item included in the Bibliography and would necessitate greatly expanded summaries of books and articles, would be desirable, but is a task beyond our present resources of time and scholarly assistance. The compromise given here should, however, be of some help to users. When the name of an author with three or more works in the list is given, we have provided a brief indication of the subject matter of each work. The subject indexing also eliminates the need for the lists of items headed "See also" found at the end of each section in the older list. The cross-referencing function of these is now served by the subject index: for example, anyone looking for items dealing with Boswell other than those included in Section 4 need only consult the entry "Boswell" in the index.

In this edition, we have made two major changes of form from the earlier one. One of these has been to rearrange the entries in chronological order of publication (or, sometimes, composition, where there is a long interval between composition and publication) instead of alphabetically by author. Since the index of authors is alphabetically arranged, anyone wishing to locate a piece by a particular author can easily do so there, and there seems little use in duplicating the alphabetical arrangement in the body of the work. The chronological arrangement, however, will help put into historical perspective the progress of research in various topics of Johnsonian study. The order we have used has normally been, first, publications dated by year only; second, publications dated by month within that year; then publications dated on a specific day within that month. (Pieces bearing identical dates of publication are arranged alphabetically by author's name or, where that is missing, title.) Sometimes, however, this order has not been adhered to, when, as with early biographical accounts, it is well known that a periodical article dated, say, "January 1785" was published earlier than a book dated merely "1785." Items are numbered consecutively within sections: e.g., item 3:25 is the 25th item in Section 3 of the list, and item 10/6:40 is the 40th item in subsection 6 of Section 10. In some sections, breaks in the numbering sequence indicate divisions of the section (generally into "Editions" and "Commentary").

The second change has been to try to minimize the "catch-all" nature of Section 10 ("General and Miscellaneous References") of the older list, partly by introducing a number of subdivisions into the new Section 10 (now called "General Comment on Johnson") and partly by adding a new section (11, "Johnson's Views and Attitudes on Various Subjects"), so that the new list contains a total of 25 sections against the older list's 24. The "various subjects" listed in the new Section 11 may seem a very mixed bag. Their choice, however, was not an arbitrary decision on the part of the compilers, but was dictated by the frequency of occurrence of notes and articles on those subjects. If the section contains a sizable subsection on "Johnson and the occult" but none on, say, "Johnson and food," this does not mean that the compilers feel that the occult is more important than food, or even that Johnson thought that it was ("He who does not mind his belly will hardly mind anything else"), but only that more students have so far chosen to investigate Johnson's attitude toward the occult than toward food. Section 1, "Bibliography," has also been subdivided so as to make it less unwieldy and more useful to the student.

In the past one valid criticism of all bare bibliographical lists has been the fact that there is often no way for a reader to tell what each item is about, or how important it is. To meet this criticism, without expanding the list overmuch and rendering it too expensive to print, we have tried, for titles which are not self-explanatory, to give some short description of the contents. In order to help readers to select the more important recent scholarly references we have resorted to a particularly dangerous device—that of putting an asterisk before each one which appears to us to be of particular use either historically or critically. At the risk of appearing arbitrary or prejudiced, we have felt that the value of some selectivity for many who will casually consult the list outweighs any possible criticism of our choices. The basis of selection has always been usefulness—and we have attempted to include (1) new discoveries; (2) new critical approaches, whether they appear valid to us or not; (3) sound historical summations or literary evaluation. In some instances where discoveries appear in several places, first in articles and later in books, only the last version is starred. For very early works, however, the usefulness of the asterisk is dubious; we have used it sparingly to indicate important earlier works otherwise likely to be overlooked. It seems impertinent to attach it to our listings of Johnson's own works, and we have not done so.

That the present list contains grave faults which might have been mended by further years of patient checking we are fully aware. But it is our hope that, imperfect as it is, it still will prove useful to students of the period. And thus we dismiss it, not with Johnson's "frigid tranquillity," since we have much to fear and hope from censure and from praise. To captious critics, however, we offer one reminder: "In this work, when it shall be found that much is omitted, let it not be forgotten that much likewise is performed."

ACKNOWLEDGMENTS

ORIGINALLY this list was planned in collaboration with James E. Tobin, as one of a projected series of eighteenth-century bibliographies, and he was responsible for much of the early accumulation of material. A similar project had been begun by Richard L. Greene and Robert Metzdorf, then at the University of Rochester. They graciously withdrew and helped in every possible way. Collectors on both sides of the Atlantic have been very generous in allowing researchers to rummage through their libraries for Johnsonian "scrappiana," as Sir Sydney Roberts described much of what appears in the following pages. We think in particular of the kindness of Mary Hyde in placing at our disposal the great collection at Four Oaks Farm, Somerville, New Jersey.

It is obviously impossible to mention everyone who has assisted us in various ways with the project. We do wish to list, with gratitude, the names of those who have at various times given generously of their time and energy to the furthering of our researches: Gellert S. Alleman, O M Brack, Jr., R. W. Chapman, Virginia I. Clifford, Elliott V. K. Dobbie, Irvin Ehrenpreis, Mrs. E. G. Franklin, Lord and Lady Harmsworth, Susan Hawk, Allen T. Hazen, Masahiro Hiwatashi, Mr. and Mrs. Donald F. Hyde, Ralph H. Isham, Paul J. Korshin, N. Lester, A. Lloyd-Jones, Percy Laithwaite, Herman Liebert, E. L. McAdam, Jr., John H. Middendorf, Samuel Monk, Robert B. Orlovich, Frederick A. Pottle, L. F. Powell, A. L. Reade, Sir Sydney Roberts, Robert B. Schwarz, Arthur Sherbo, D. Nichol Smith, J. E. Stockwell, Zenzô Suzuki, Howard Weinbrot, and countless librarians on both sides of the Atlantic.

In particular, we wish to thank J. D. Fleeman, of Pembroke College, Oxford, who has been engaged in a somewhat similar task to ours, and who kindly consented to a mutual exchange of "work in progress," and helped us with many puzzles, especially in the earlier section; and Dr.

Lawrence C. McHenry, Jr., of the Philadelphia General Hospital, an ardent Johnsonian, who for many years has faithfully kept us up to date on medical and scientific publications dealing with Johnson. A special note of gratitude is due to Magdi Wahba, of the University of Cairo, who greatly assisted the progress of the present work by undertaking, in 1962, the publication of our "Additions and Corrections to *Johnsonian Studies, 1887–1950*" and *Johnsonian Studies, 1950–1960: A Survey and Bibliography*. We also wish to express our thanks to the various research and clerical assistants who have worked with us on the project, in particular David Drum, Gertrude Kimbrough, Paul Zagorsky, and Morris and Evelyn Warshawski, and for generous financial assistance provided by the research grants committee of the University of California at Riverside, the William F. Vilas Trust at the University of Wisconsin, and the supporters of the Leo S. Bing Chair of English at the University of Southern California. To the staff of the University of Minnesota Press we are grateful for much skillful and patient editorial assistance.

J. L. C.
D. J. G.

Columbia University
University of Southern California

CONTENTS

Part II. BIBLIOGRAPHY OF INDIVIDUAL WORKS

SAMUEL JOHNSON

ABBREVIATIONS

ELH	*ELH, A Journal of English Literary History*
GM	*Gentleman's Magazine*
JEGP	*Journal of English and Germanic Philology*
JHI	*Journal of the History of Ideas*
JNL	*Johnsonian News Letter*
Life	James Boswell, *The Life of Samuel Johnson, LL.D.*, ed. G. B. Hill, rev. L. F. Powell, 6 vols. (Oxford, 1934–50)
MLN	*Modern Language Notes*
MLQ	*Modern Language Quarterly*
MLR	*Modern Language Review*
MP	*Modern Philology*
N&Q	*Notes and Queries*
PMLA	*Publications of the Modern Language Association of America*
PQ	*Philological Quarterly*
RES	*Review of English Studies*
SP	*Studies in Philology*
SRL or *SR*	*Saturday Review of Literature* (later *Saturday Review*), New York. (*Saturday Review*, not abbreviated, refers to the nineteenth-century London weekly.)
TLS	*Times Literary Supplement*, London
J or SJ	Samuel Johnson
B or JB	James Boswell

For the explanation of the asterisk (*) before certain items, see the Preface, p. ix.

A Survey of
JOHNSONIAN STUDIES

JOHNSON the man is familiar to most of us. Without much stretch of the imagination we can see the great bushy wig, the massive features, the awkward lumbering walk of the Great Cham. We can hear him begin an emphatic remark to Boswell, "Why, Sir—" or even more characteristically, "No, Sir—." And gradually, with our own changing point of view, we are beginning to recapture something of Johnson's vigorous reasoning intelligence, his common-sense critical genius. More and more the man the eighteenth century knew is emerging. What follows is the story of this rediscovery.

Never since his death in 1784 has Johnson been forgotten by the reading public. Acknowledged as a great man of letters by his contemporaries, he became a symbol of reaction to the young poets of the next age. The Romantics, with the exception of Scott and Byron, used him as a whipping boy to advance their own theories of art. The Victorians, although not taking him seriously as a writer or thinker, still found him interesting, but for qualities far different from those we stress today. Indeed, in no other figure can the shift of critical sensibility between the two ages be more clearly shown. This change of emphasis was well advanced as early as 1831, as Macaulay shows in his savage review of Croker (10/6:28). "What a singular destiny has been that of this remarkable man!" wrote Macaulay of Johnson. "To be regarded in his own age as a classic, and in ours as a companion." And it was Macaulay's own brilliant emphasis on Johnson's idiosyncrasies rather than his ideas which set the tone for succeeding generations. Johnson the kindhearted, tea-drinking, bad-mannered eccentric—Johnson reaching down to twitch off a lady's shoe, superstitiously touching every post along the street, doing all manner of foolish things—this was the figure who became familiar to every schoolboy. Even Carlyle, while regarding Johnson as a hero of faith in an age of atheism and doubt, stressed the man,

3

not the writer (10/6:35). For nineteenth-century readers Johnson was essentially an amusing and somewhat lovable eccentric, who had a place in their affections comparable to their favorite Dickens character or to Falstaff.

It was Boswell, of course, who provided most of the evidence, for it was Johnson the erratic talker, so masterfully described in the *Life*, that everyone remembered. Ironically, it was the greatness of his disciple's art which for at least a century tended to obscure Johnson's true stature. A few readers, to be sure, still found delight in Johnson's works: the number of editions of *Rasselas* proves that. But it is significant that since the early nineteenth century there has been no newly edited complete edition of Johnson's works. The Victorians were generally content to take Johnson as a character out of a great book.

Of all the eighteenth-century figures it is easiest to see why Johnson as a man so appealed to the Victorians. His morality and probity of personal conduct were unimpeachable. There were no sexual irregularities or records of drunkenness to suppress. In his talk and writings there was none of the occasional vulgarity and indecency to be found in Pope and Swift. His rough exterior hid a proverbial heart of gold. He was a friendly "clubbable" man, eager for talk for its own sake, drawing into his circle most of the famous men of his day. His weaknesses were those easily understandable and forgivable in a fictional creation. Moreover, they were weaknesses traditionally associated with the English character. Thus in many readers' minds Johnson more and more took on the guise of a mythical John Bull—a symbolic caricature of the nation's rugged strength and bullheadedness, its insular point of view.

To be sure, even when this image of Johnson was at its most powerful, in the late nineteenth century, there were some dissenters—a few people who admired Johnson the writer as much as, or even more than, Johnson the personality, and a number who could abide neither. The history of Johnson's reputation since his own lifetime is in fact complex and needs even more study than it has received (see Section 10/5). It can be argued that from the time his name became widely known in the 1750's, as the author of *The Rambler* and the *Dictionary*, there existed a "double tradition" of Johnson, to use Bertrand Bronson's phrase (10/6:283). On the one hand, there is a tradition of unstinted, sometimes extravagant praise. Early accounts stressed Johnson's personal morality, his integrity in the face of poverty and neglect (e.g., 3:1, 9:9). As his publications increased and his fame grew, even such routine biographical accounts as that in *Biographia Dramatica* (3:2) could speak of him as "no less the glory of the present age and nation, than he will be the admiration of all succeeding ones" and could pray "May it be long before he seeks the place which only can supply a reward adequate to his private merits!" And it is interesting to see how long the tradition of straightforward adulation of Johnson lasted. Here are a few samples of it: in 1805, "He is the great master of moral painting. His high wrought designs have all the gigantic fullness of Michael Angelo" (24:50); in 1829, "A jewel, rough set, yet shining like a star . . . one of the truly great men of England" (10/6:27); in 1842, "Though few or none can hope to emulate his *greatness*, all may, trusting in the same almighty Help, walk in the same *good* path with Dr. Samuel Johnson" (3:77).

As the last quotation suggests, and as might have been expected, this tradition was long preserved in the ranks of the Evangelicals, to whom both Johnson's deep piety and his political conservatism appealed; in the columns of their periodical, the *Christian Observer*, Johnson remains the object of intense, unquestioning devotion well beyond the first half of the nineteenth century. To be sure, it was not long after 1850 that people were beginning to speak of this attitude as a thing of the past: "When I was a boy the most revered name in letters was that of Dr. Johnson. He had been dead nearly fifty years, yet the echoes of his massive voice still vibrated on the ear, and the heave of his long-drawn sentences resounded through our literature" (10/6:52). Yet as late as 1882, another writer—a veteran United States senator, distinguished for his services to American higher education—could sturdily affirm, "The hold that Johnson has on the esteem of mankind, after the lapse of a century, proves that he was no unreal giant, but a hater of shams, and ever striving for the eternal verities" (3:707).

There was enough uncritical praise of Johnson current in the late eighteenth and early nineteenth centuries to make it a plausible hypothesis that some, at least, of the condemnation of him was a reaction to it. Nevertheless, this opposing tradition, that of virulent condemnation of Johnson root and branch—his personality, his appearance, his mannerisms, his prose style, his conversation, and everything he ever wrote—was born at the same time as the tradition of admiration, and developed simultaneously with it. Helen Louise McGuffie (10/5:10) has heroically tabulated all the journalistic abuse heaped on Johnson during his own lifetime: her bibliography of it between the years 1750 and 1784 extends to over one hundred pages (some of it, to be sure, is repetition of the same piece of abuse in different periodicals). The chapter headings of her discussion—phrases quoted from various detractors—indicate its scope: "The Great Corrupter of Our Language" (the periodical essays); "Sir Hercules Nonsense: The Most Unfit Person To Compile a Dictionary"; "Johnsonius Obstinatus: The Ignorant and Inattentive Editor of Shakespeare"; "Pensioner Johnson: The Despicable Tool of a Tory Administration" (the political pamphlets); "Rambling Sam: The Dogmatical Journalist" (*A Journey to the Western Islands of Scotland*); "The Rancorous Biographer and Surly Critic" (*The Lives of the Poets*). If it were worth the space, one could add dozens more: "This literary Caliban . . . his drunken and beastly phrenzies"; "A mean detractor of virtue which he could not appreciate, of principles which he could not comprehend and of piety which he could not imitate; the contracted Tory pensioner, dictionary compiler, high-church bigot, and semi-popish reviler"; "known pensioned advocate of despotism," "old Grub . . . arch-critic caterpillar." "Supercilious," "pomposity," "dogmatical," "dictatorial" are some of the terms most frequently encountered.

Much of this kind of exuberant name-calling, of course, was simply cheap journalism, typical of its day. Johnson was not the only eminent person subjected to it, and it is pleasant to note that occasionally Johnson's admirers could retaliate in kind. A writer in the *St. James's Chronicle* (9:7) had described him as a lion, the prince of beasts, unworried by the "troop of monkies" who chatter at him. In the next issue, "One of the Monkies" replied to the effect that "prince of *beasts*" was indeed a good description of Johnson. The Johnsonian retorted a little later with an onslaught against him and other detractors, concluding "On Parent Dunghill, where begot,/ There let the Toadstool Mushrooms rot,/ Unnoticed and unknown!" Unimportant in itself as most of this crude stuff is, it is nevertheless significant (as Miss McGuffie points out) that the charges here hurled at Johnson become the major themes of serious criticism—or at least criticism which students were taught to take seriously, like Macaulay's and Gosse's—of the nineteenth century: Johnson's prose is abominable, his knowledge of lexicography and Shakespeare editing is inadequate to the tasks he undertakes, as a political writer he can be dismissed as a blind Tory bigot, his criticism and biography suffer from rancor and prejudice. It has been the task of much modern Johnson criticism to investigate such charges carefully, and to show, from a close study of what he actually wrote, how baseless and irresponsible most of them are.

Certainly Johnson managed to tread on a good many toes, as even the more literate early attacks indicate. There were, of course, the fiercely patriotic Scotch—"The most celebrated literary pedant that this age hath produced, hath endeavoured to cast a general obloquy upon a nation that will disdain ever to allow him a place among the literary worthies" (11/5:1). There were the devotees of Romantic poetry, who looked back to Gray, whom Johnson condemned, as their forerunner, and Pope, whom Johnson praised, as their enemy: "The reputation of Dr. Johnson . . . has given to his *Lives of the Poets* a circulation which has beyond all question been injurious to the cause of our imaginative literature. . . . It was a luckless day for the poets when they fell into the hands of Samuel Johnson" (22:82). There were those bemused by Rousseau and late eighteenth-century "optimism" about the nature of man, who were shocked by Johnson's sturdily orthodox belief in original sin: *Idler* 89 is a "frightful caricatura" of human nature—"of what dreadful consequences to society must be the propagation of the system of human depravity disseminated" by Johnson!—and the writer opposes to it Rousseau's "amicable portrait" of human nature (16:50). Another writer commented that a "young mind rising from a perusal of *The Rambler* would conceive the most melancholy ideas of human nature. . . . Mankind would appear to him an undistinguished mass of fraud, perfidy, and deceit" (10/6:21). Those who felt they had a vested interest in Shakespeare were quick to condemn Johnson's treatment of him: "The long-expected edition of Shakespeare by Dr. Johnson and Mr. Steevens"—the great revised edition of 1773, the model for all later variorum editions—"may perhaps attract the notice of the public for a few weeks, but will soon, by general consent, be forgotten, or remembered only to furnish laughter with a subject" (19:52).

Throughout the late eighteenth and early nineteenth centuries, the tradition of praise of Johnson seems on the whole to have had slightly the upper hand over the opposing tradition. At least, it was the dominant one in the more official publications, such as encyclopedias and biographical dictionaries, whereas the tradition of condemnation tended to lead a somewhat more disreputable existence, sometimes in flimsy pamphlets and short-lived magazines. But around 1857 the tradition of disparagement emerged from underground, so to speak, and became the official, majority one. The change is symbolized by the replacement in that year of George Gleig's admirably balanced and judicious article on Johnson in the *Encyclopaedia Britannica* (3:35), which had first appeared in 1797, by Macaulay's much shallower and more limited one (3:92). Though less prejudiced than his notorious review of Croker, it essentially repeats the same distorted picture of Johnson. Recommended by Macaulay's dazzling prose—which, ironically, may have owed a good deal to Johnson's—both it and the essay on Croker were reprinted innumerable times and used as school textbooks for decades all over the world; probably most adult Johnsonians even today were introduced to Johnson by them. And they appeared at just the right time to influence the many popular histories of English literature which were beginning to be produced as textbooks for the newly born study of English literature as a subject in colleges (for instance, 10/6:45, 10/6:48, 10/6:54, 10/6:73).

The sources of Macaulay's prejudice against Johnson were no doubt many. Politics was certainly one, Macaulay being a devout Whig. Perhaps even more important, he was one of the first generation upon which the Romantic writers had a profound impact, and was no doubt affected by the casual and often misconceived slurs on Johnson tossed off by men like Blake, Wordsworth, Coleridge, and De Quincey (9:44, 10/1:2, 10/6:33, 22:83), for whom Johnson was symbolic of the older generation of writers against whom they were revolting. Macaulay's position was facilely adopted by later pundits, such as Edmund Gosse (10/6:82), and in literary circles it became the thing to drop such remarks as this wonderfully supercilious one from the "advanced" *Westminster Review* in 1879: "We cannot refrain from expressing our gratitude that our lot is cast in a time when in society such a man as Samuel Johnson is an impossibility" 10/6:66). The seal of the Establishment may be said to have been set on the anti-Johnson attitude by a leading article in the *Times* on the occasion of the centenary of Johnson's death (10/6:80). Celebrations had been planned in Lichfield; but the *Times* doubts their success. Few read Johnson nowadays: "The infatuated admiration which he inspired . . . is not wholly comprehensible to this generation. . . . He had but little disposition towards abstract thinking and no lively imagination, so that he cannot be ranked high as a philosopher or poet." To this Birkbeck Hill replied, with heat but justice, "He [the writer in the *Times*] knows Johnson through Macaulay's article in the *Edinburgh Review*, than which Hogarth himself never drew a grosser and . . . coarser caricature. . . . If we are to celebrate the centenary, let us begin by destroying the grotesque figure which Macaulay set up" (10/6:81).

That destruction was not to be accomplished in Hill's lifetime; even now it is far from complete. Hill's protest, however, reminds us that there did occur in the middle and later nineteenth century occasional intelligent and searching discussion of Johnson by people who had obviously read his writings with care and responded to them with the amount of thought they require—the astute Lord Chancellor Brougham, for instance (3:79), whose political position as a "radical," though it won him the enmity of the orthodox Whig Macaulay, apparently did not interfere with his appreciation of Johnson; the great constitutional scholar and Vinerian Professor of Law at Oxford, A. V. Dicey (10/6:63); W. J. Courthope (11/9:2), replying to Sir Leslie Stephen's somewhat shallow analysis of Johnson's thought; the anonymous author of an essay in the *Spectator* (14:47), which is very possibly the most acute criticism of Johnson's poetry before T. S. Eliot's famous essay of 1930 (14:73); John Hepburn Millar, displaying a genuine appreciation of Johnson's literary criticism (22:1 [1896]); and, of course, Birkbeck Hill himself, who, though we are now more aware than before of his deficiencies as an editor, must always be held in esteem by Johnsonians as an indefatigable battler for Johnson in that era of uncritical detraction.

But despite these attempts to keep Johnson the writer in the foreground, the Romantic view was predominant. Almost without question Johnson was ignored as a literary artist and critic. His style was thought to be too pompous and heavy, his subject matter too rigidly didactic, his criticism too bigoted and unimaginative. Only his life was interesting. Typical is the attitude of a writer for *Temple Bar* in 1892: "Boswell may be said, without hyperbole, to have unearthed Johnson, and embalmed him. But for Boswell, the man was gone, past power of recall. . . . Our knowledge of Johnson comes to us solely and exclusively through Boswell's spectacles . . . not one man in a thousand . . . has ever dipped into any single thing that Johnson wrote" (10/6:98). The same point of view, sometimes even more strongly expressed, can be found in a host of other writers of the day. It is summed up by Brander Matthews (10/6:148): "Without Boswell, Johnson's fame would have shriveled long ago. His authority as a critic—and it is only as a critic that he has any claim to authority—is now thoroughly discredited. . . . His style, which was once widely admired, long exerted an evil influence upon English literature." Or as a much later writer (4:137) puts it: "How many of Boswell's devoutest readers today ever open the *Idler*, the *Rambler*, the *Lives of the Poets*, *Rasselas*, or any other volume of the Doctor's once-conquering prose? . . . [Johnson] lives today only by his disciple's brilliance." (See also 6:38.)

With this attitude firmly fixed, it is not surprising to find most of the books and articles in the late nineteenth and the early twentieth centuries concentrating on Johnson the talker and his friends. For many people he had become the patron saint of intellectual conviviality. Johnson clubs sprang up everywhere. When papers were read the topics centered on the great man's talk as recorded by Boswell, or upon the ramifications of his large acquaintanceship. The "Johnson Circle" endlessly provided amusement and delight to casual readers and persistent collectors. (See Sections 6 to 8.)

The collectors deserve more than a word, for they have been of major importance in the development of the new Johnsonian approach. The most celebrated of the earlier twentieth century—R. B. Adam and A. Edward Newton—not only carried on the traditional interest in every person and thing connected with the Johnson circle, but increasingly directed attention to Johnson's own works. Moreover, from the start both men showed a commendable desire to share their treasures, to make them available to serious research scholars. Long before the mammoth catalogue of the Adam collection appeared (1/4:19), most of the valuable items in it were well known. A. Edward Newton publicized his finds in a series of delightfully written essays (4:91, 5:152, 7:78, 7:91) which undoubtedly stirred up in the United States more interest in the whole movement than any other single force, with the exception of the personal inspiration of Professor Chauncey B. Tinker for generations of students at Yale University (10/6:273). Tinker's own collection, now in the Yale Library, has been described for students in a sumptuous catalogue prepared by Robert Metzdorf (1/4:49), and there have been valuable catalogues of a number of modern Johnsonian exhibitions (1/4:48, 1/4:50, 1/4:51, 1/4:56).

In later decades the great collectors to be mentioned are Herman Liebert and James M. Osborn of Yale and the Donald F. Hydes of Somerville, New Jersey. Uniting the mammoth Adam collection, a large part of the Newton holdings, and many Johnsonian manuscripts from various Boswell discoveries, the Hyde collection is one of the most comprehensive of books and manuscripts concerned with one literary group (for descriptions, see items 1/4:42, 1/4:46, 1/4:55, 5:400, 10/6:377).

Collectors and amateur littérateurs everywhere were aided by the gradual dispersal early in the twentieth century of large portions of the tremendous horde of Johnsoniana belonging to Mrs. Thrale-Piozzi (1/4:24, 1/4:25, 21:3, 23:52, etc.), and by the appearance in the auction rooms of other mementos of the group. Interest was so aroused that prices rocketed sky-high. To compare prices secured for Johnson's letters, for example, in the 1890's with those in the 1920's is a revelation in shifting market values. For a while Johnson and his friends vied with Shakespeare and the great Romantics in the crowded auction rooms. Prices in the 1960's were even more astonishing. In 1887 a set of the first edition, two volumes folio, of the *Dictionary* was sold for £1.4.0 (around $6); in 1888 Leigh Hunt's copy brought £3.5.0 (around $16); in 1920 a set sold for £7.10.0 ($37). In 1968 the average selling price was £450 —over $1,000.

There is no need to do more than mention the exciting discovery of Boswell's archives—the gradual bringing together of all the new material by another great collector, Lt. Col. Ralph Isham—the expert editing of the papers by the late Geoffrey Scott, Frederick A. Pottle, and other helpers (4:13, 4:19, 4:20, 4:21)—or the final fortunate acquisition of most of the manuscripts by Yale University. The Yale Editions of the Private Papers of James Boswell, in conjunction with McGraw-

Hill and William Heinemann, publishers, have been moving steadily forward. The chief editors are Frederick A. Pottle, F. W. Hilles, and Herman W. Liebert. So far, nine volumes of the so-called trade edition of Boswell's journals have appeared and two of the research edition of Boswell's correspondence (4:21), including Marshall Waingrow's very important edition of Boswell's correspondence concerning the writing of the *Life of Johnson*.

Utilizing all the modern discoveries, F. A. Pottle has now produced what will long be valued as the standard biography of Boswell (4:200) and in collaboration with Frank Brady is at work on the second and concluding volume. For a listing of recent Boswellian scholarship there is now available a check list prepared by Anthony E. Brown (4:2).

One result of all these discoveries is the piling up of evidence concerning the determined efforts of early editors and biographers to suppress various details of Johnson's life. Although many are unimportant, some are really significant. For example, the recent editors of his prayers and religious meditations found that Johnson's original manuscript, now in the library at Pembroke College, had been seriously censored by its first editor, the Reverend George Strahan. Painstaking and ingenious methods of infrared-ray photography have enabled scholars to decipher passages erased because they conflicted with the image of Johnson it was wished to create—the image which to a large extent *was* created and which prevailed in the nineteenth century. It now appears, so the editors of Johnson's diaries write (24:139), that Strahan, their first editor, was "interested in creating and preserving a conventional pattern of Johnson's religion and marriage." In "instances where Johnson is talking about his relations with Tetty or about his religious doubts and scruples, Strahan, with an eye to posterity, has crosshatched Johnson's words so thoroughly that they cannot be read by ordinary means." David Fleeman has recently deciphered more of the excised passages (24:170). And it appears that Boswell, to some degree, seconded Strahan's efforts, for a somewhat unexpected light is cast on Johnson's marital life by the recovery of evidence, suppressed by Boswell, of Johnson's determination to marry again after Tetty's death (3:194), and of Johnson's "innocent" dalliance with Mrs. Desmoulins on (though not in) his bed, with Tetty asleep in the next room (see 3:201, chapter 17, from the Boswell Papers at Yale). Another exciting discovery is the text of Johnson's earliest known English poem (see 3:201 and 14:6). It is difficult not to wonder what Wordsworth, not to mention later Romantic critics, would have said had he known its title—"On a Daffodil." Trivial as such discoveries may appear at first glance, they should at least serve as a warning against attempting oversubtle interpretations of Johnson on the basis of incomplete or censored earlier accounts of his life and work.

Just as major collecting of Johnsoniana began from Boswell's *Life* and gradually widened to concentrate on Johnson's own works, so serious scholarship of the modern period started with the editing of Boswell and other biographical works about Johnson. To be sure, Birkbeck Hill's edition of the *Life* and the *Tour to the Hebrides* in 1887, generally accepted as a landmark, was no isolated event. Hill's work was the culmination of the editing of Boswell for the century. His edition is the most heavily annotated and for its day the most accurate and complete. But although a landmark for its own time, it has manifest deficiencies. According to present standards, Hill was far from a perfect textual editor; his notes, while impressive, are often willfully prejudiced (oversuspicious of Mrs. Piozzi, he accepted many of Baretti's fabrications); and his huge index leaves much to be desired. Nevertheless, these weaknesses were not immediately apparent to Hill's contemporaries, and the work was greeted with a paean of praise (except from Percy Fitzgerald; see 4:67, etc.). Hill's other editions, the *Letters* in 1892, the *Johnsonian Miscellanies* in 1897, and the *Lives of the Poets* in 1905, followed much the same pattern and were of immense importance in bringing to Johnsonian studies a scholarly, serious approach. With time, however, all have needed expert revision.

In 1923 when the Clarendon Press began to make plans for a new printing of the *Life* (4:14 [1934]), it was recognized that Hill's edition had become a standard text; scholars everywhere were referring to it merely by volume and page number, often with no further identification. Any change of pagination would thus produce much confusion in scholarly circles. On the other hand, important information had come to light since 1887, which needed to be incorporated in the footnotes. The decision was finally made, whether rightly or wrongly, to keep to the old pagination and to relegate most of the new discoveries to appendixes. (For an attack on this policy and a defense see C. B. Tinker's review and R. W. Chapman's reply [4:123].) One thing is certain: L. F. Powell, the new editor, showed great skill and ingenuity in revising Hill's notes, bringing in whatever was feasible of the new and cross-indexing what had to go to the rear of the volumes. He verified the text and identified many persons whom Boswell thought it best not to name. His editing of the *Tour to the Hebrides* (volume five) is an outstanding improvement on Hill. All Johnsonians owe him a great debt of gratitude for his thorough, scholarly work.

The first four volumes of Powell's revision of Hill appeared in 1934; volumes five and six (including the index), which were held up because of the war, finally appeared in 1950. But still Dr. Powell labored on, and volumes five and six have been thoroughly reworked, with a second edition published in 1964. The second edition of the first four volumes, now in the process of exhaustive correction and revision, may be expected in a few years.

The revision of Hill's two-volume collection of Johnson's letters was undertaken by R. W. Chapman of the Clarendon Press. After many years of laborious research and brilliant textual study he finally brought out his edition in 1952, in three volumes and containing some five hundred additional letters (23:14). Textually this version is a great improvement over Hill, since Chapman made every effort to collate with original manuscripts every letter he included. Of course, such a goal proved unattainable, but with great pertinacity he followed the trail of individual manuscripts all over the world and was thus able to check the great majority of them. Wisely he did not attempt to retain Hill's arrangement and pagination, although he did keep the numbering of individual letters, a decision which involved the use of decimals (such as 120.1 and 120.2). Chapman tried to include all known Johnson letters, including those in the *Life*, which had been omitted by Hill, but in order to save space, he decided to annotate far less than had his predecessor. As a result, scholars need to have both editions easily available —Chapman's for accurate texts and new discoveries and Hill's for full, illustrative commentary. Moreover, Chapman's notes, with his passion for contractions and his many confessions of things he had not done, are often tantalizing, and his multiple indexes and many appendixes render his volumes difficult to use. Someday we should have a fully annotated modern edition incorporating all the new evidence. Meanwhile, Mary Hyde, in an essay, "Not in Chapman," has brought together a very useful list of additions since 1952 (23:121). The list contains a number of valuable discoveries, including the letters of Johnson to Charlotte Lennox first described by Duncan Isles (23:119).

During the nineteenth century and the early twentieth, the universally acknowledged omnipotence of Boswell's *Life* frightened away many other possible biographers of Johnson. There were, of course, a few short lives—by Sir Leslie Stephen in the English Men of Letters Series (3:104); Francis Grant (3:112); John Dennis (3:126); Sir Sydney Roberts (3:136); Christopher Hollis (3:153); Hugh Kingsmill (3:161)—for the most part intended as introductions to Boswell, not as rivals. Recently there have appeared numerous volumes, by M. J. C. Hodgart (3:208) and others, containing short resumés of Johnson's life, and a vituperative, debunking sketch by C. E. Vulliamy (3:177). Space will permit no more than mention of the score or more delightful appreciative studies of Johnson—by Augustine Birrell, S. C. Roberts, E. S. Roscoe, Harry Salpeter, C. B. Tinker, which may be found listed in Section 10/6. Nor is it possible to discuss the many sections devoted to Johnson in histories of English literature, in student anthologies, collected volumes of essays, and the like. Only the more important are listed in the following check list, since they tend to follow easily recognizable stereotyped patterns, adding little to our real knowledge of Johnson. For the most part these summaries tend to lag behind the trend of the times, being little more than repetitions of nineteenth-century opinions.

The first full-length biography of Johnson to appear in the twentieth century was that by Joseph Wood Krutch in 1944 (3:175), an admirable piece of work. He was able to make an independent, scholarly appraisal in the light of new discoveries and new hypotheses. Boswell and all the other commentators are judiciously used. Having available A. L. Reade's important discoveries, Krutch was able to give an excellent picture of Johnson's childhood and early education; while the recent publication of Mrs. Thrale's diaries and letters (5:264, 5:271) allowed him to present a fairer treatment of the Streatham period. The chief strength of Krutch's volume, however, lies in the critical analyses of Johnson's own works. With no Romantic condescension, Krutch forces the reader to grapple at first hand with Johnson's controlling ideas, to appreciate his achievements within the framework of his own concepts of art, and to understand the true springs of his greatness.

Krutch's concentration on Johnson the writer and thinker, which would have startled and amused Victorian readers, was only the culmination of a steady shift of emphasis. One of the pioneers in this change was Walter Raleigh, whose admirable Six Essays on Johnson in 1910 focused attention on Johnson's criticism and editing (10/6:146). Of even more importance throughout the mid-twentieth century was D. Nichol Smith of Oxford, whose chapter in the Cambridge History of English Literature (10/6:161), work on eighteenth-century Shakespearian criticism (19:4, 19:75), and unrelenting insistence on the merits of Johnson's poetry (14:5, 14:78, 14:85) have exerted an all-pervasive influence on the twentieth-century point of view. Representing the best traditions of accurate, thorough, and penetrating scholarship, Nichol Smith, as teacher and writer, personally enhanced the general reputation of all eighteenth-century research.

In the United States, as well as at Oxford, there have been inspiring teachers, active in pointing out the merits of Johnson. We should certainly be negligent did we not pay more than passing tribute to the labors of Robert K. Root, Charles G. Osgood, Irving Babbitt, Ronald S.

Crane, Lane Cooper, George Sherburn, Bertrand H. Bronson and W. J. Bate, who, with Chauncey B. Tinker, already mentioned, have been personally responsible for a large number of our active younger Johnsonians. And there is the outstanding work of Frederick A. Pottle, who has done, and is doing, so much to reinterpret Boswell for our generation (4:1, 4:135, 4:142, 4:200).

In the twentieth century, interest in Johnson the man found expression not only in heavily annotated and illustrated editions of Boswell, and in a horde of appreciative essays and privately printed brochures, but also in serious biographical research by a number of gifted workers, the chief of whom was Aleyn Lyell Reade, of Blundellsands, Liverpool. Reade was almost without parallel in the annals of scholarship. Beginning early in the twentieth century as a genealogist interested in his own family records (3:127), he soon concentrated all his efforts on the early life of Dr. Johnson. The ten volumes of *Johnsonian Gleanings* and an *Index* which appeared from 1909 to 1952 are a milestone in patient accurate research (3:131). With the added help of Algernon Gissing, Percy Laithwaite, and others (3.142, 3:145, 3:148, 3:157), we now know infinitely more about Johnson's family, his early surroundings and companions, than did Boswell or any of Johnson's contemporaries.

Much of this information was made available in a continuous narrative in James L. Clifford's *Young Sam Johnson* (3:201). As its dedication made clear, this biography owed its very existence to the devoted labors of A. L. Reade, Percy Laithwaite, and the other self-effacing scholars and antiquarians. Through their efforts, and from the Boswellian discoveries of the 1940's, it was at last possible to fashion a portrait of Johnson as a young man.

Reade was able to bring his microscopic and revealing researches to bear on Johnson's life only up to the 1740's. The two decades before Boswell himself appeared on the scene are still relatively unknown. Indeed, one might add that the future happy hunting ground for biographers must be Johnson's middle years—the 1750's and 1760's—the time of his greatest productivity. These were the years of the great essays, of *Rasselas* and the *Dictionary*. But what was Johnson's everyday life like? What, for example, was Johnson doing most of the time in 1760 and 1761, one of the most obscure periods, for which Boswell can offer only scattered guesses? Where are the new Reades and Laithwaites, willing to devote long years to the patient uncovering of minutiae connected with Johnson's friends and colleagues during this dark period? There is still much to search for. Of course, we have had some exciting discoveries—witness Maurice Quinlan's proof of an actual meeting between Johnson and Benjamin Franklin (5:300), the finding of Charlotte Lennox's papers (23:119), Roy Wiles's documentation of the wide distribution of many of the *Rambler* essays through provincial newspapers (16:122), and the puzzling appearances of hundreds of notations of "Mr. Johnson" in Thomas Hollis's unpublished diary (3: 215). And there are many other intriguing problems which require thorough study.

Among the newer approaches, as might be expected, are various attempts to psychoanalyze Johnson. That by W. B. C. Watkins (10/6:242) is shrewd, if oversensational in places; that by Edward Hitschmann (3: 733) is filled with errors, an absurdly mixed-up Freudian analysis made without full knowledge of the facts. Katharine Balderston's bombshell suggestion of certain masochistic tendencies evidenced in Johnson's relations with Mrs. Thrale (3:182) has stirred up much discussion but requires further elaboration and discussion after a decision on the exact meaning of terms. Worthy of high recommendation is an analysis of the great man's character by Herman W. Liebert (10/6:272). Much discussion of Johnson's own remarkable insight in psychological matters will be found in recent studies (see p. 24 below). Physicians seem to have been as much fascinated by Johnson's bodily ailments as psychologists have been by the troubles of his mind; Section 3 below contains a remarkable series of medical studies, to which Lord Brain, the eminent neurologist, MacDonald Critchley, Lawrence C. McHenry, Jr., and Ronald MacKeith have been the most faithful recent contributors. Johnson indeed furnished material for some important pioneering medical research: his loss of speech after a stroke provided a useful case history for the study of aphasia (3:749), and rather grimly, a diagram of one of his lungs, examined postmortem, illustrates the first clinical description of emphysema (8:16, 3:743).

Other important evidence has steadily been made available in fullscale studies concerned with close associates of Johnson at various periods in his life. Of these the most distinguished are Joyce Hemlow's biography of Fanny Burney (5:346) and Roger Lonsdale's of Dr. Burney (5:382), which can surely be called definitive. Both have had access to a wealth of new evidence contained in Burney family papers now in the British Museum, the Berg Collection of the New York Public Library, and the private library of J. M. Osborn of Yale University.

If Clarence Tracy had been able to uncover similar caches of material about the enigmatic Richard Savage (13:44), we should know a great deal more about the obscure years of Johnson's early life. Unfortunately, although Tracy has examined all existing evidence, time has more effectively obscured the solution to the problem of Savage's paternity than it did the scandals of the Burney tribe, despite all Fanny's efforts at suppression. Ralph Wardle's study of Goldsmith (5:343) will be useful for factual details, but critically it leaves much to be desired. Percy Scholes's biography of Sir John Hawkins (5:322) was consistently marred by an irrational animus against its subject. Happily, Sir John's reputation as a biographer has been convincingly defended in an admirable study by Bertram H. Davis (3:207). If lacking in Boswell's sense of drama and his skill in making vivid a particular scene, Hawkins does supply invaluable information, particularly concerning the earlier portions of Johnson's life, and is not as unsympathetic or uncharitable as has been supposed. Davis also has prepared a modern abridged edition of Hawkins's *Life of Johnson* (3:27), and is at work on what will be the standard life of Hawkins. Among other recent works to be mentioned are J. A. Cochrane's life of William Strahan (5:378), F. W. Hilles's printing of important manuscripts of Sir Joshua Reynolds, some concerning Johnson (5:317), J. L. Abbott's researches at the Royal Society of Arts (3:218), the gleanings by Edward Ruhe from the papers of Thomas Birch (5:351, 25:64), Garland Cannon's account of Sir William Jones (5:385), and various essays concerning other relationships of Johnson's contained in the anniversary volume collected by Hilles entitled *New Light on Dr. Johnson* (10/6:306) and in the Festschrift for L. F. Powell, *Johnson, Boswell and Their Circle* (10/6:329).

Despite all this important work, there are still more of Johnson's close friends who would repay serious examination. One need mention only a few—the elusive William Guthrie, who clearly must have been an important influence on Johnson in the early years of his connection with the *Gentleman's Magazine*; Dr. Richard Bathurst, for whom Johnson had such affection; John Payne, the publisher; Topham Beauclerk; Thomas Davies; James Grainger; George Steevens. Any Johnsonian can think of others. If some seem too minor to deserve a whole book to themselves, a volume of shorter biographical studies, done after exhaustive research in manuscript archives, would be a very welcome alternative. It is good to know that serious work is being done on Hawkesworth, George Steevens, and John Nichols.

Before any author can be critically studied, we must be certain of what he wrote and have adequate scholarly editions for our use. Thanks to Boswell, Mrs. Thrale, and others of Johnson's contemporaries, we have a fair idea of what Johnson produced. And thanks to the work of W. P. Courtney, D. Nichol Smith, R. W. Chapman, L. F. Powell, Allen T. Hazen, E. L. McAdam, Jr., and David Fleeman, to name only the more important of modern bibliographers, we have identified most of it. (See Sections 1/1 and 25.) Donald J. Greene has carefully documented just when, and with what authority, each ascription to Johnson has been made (1/1:44).

During the past half century, it should be pointed out, there have been some exciting finds: the realization of the extent of the ghostwriting of the law lectures for Chambers (11/3:10, 11/3:18); the rediscovery of Johnson's translation of Crousaz's attack on Pope (25:33), of various articles in Dr. Robert James's *Medicinal Dictionary* (13:31), of a preface to the 1753 index to the *Gentleman's Magazine* (25:44), of various other dedications and prefaces to other people's works (25:35), and of unsigned essays in the periodicals (25:40, 25:42, 25:43, 25:54). We know much more about Johnson as a writer of sermons (24:105, 24:116, 24:120). Moreover, thanks to F. V. Bernard, Gwin Kolb, Jacob Leed, Arthur Sherbo, and Donald J. Greene (see, for example, 13:61, 25:68, 25:71, 25:73, 25:83) we now have more information about his journalism in the 1740's and 1760's. All in all, the work of the indefatigable bibliographical sleuths has been well done. It may be pointed out that E. A. Bloom's survey of Johnson's work as a journalist (25:69) had been in substance completed before much of this work appeared. Many of the new attributions labor under the disadvantage that almost the only evidence for them is internal, and certainly one would feel happier about them if more corroborative external evidence were forthcoming—just as one would welcome more evidence about similar older ascriptions, made by Boswell and others, which have long formed part of the traditional canon of Johnson's works. Perhaps the most forceful argument that has been advanced in justification of this kind of activity is that in some of the early and middle years when Johnson had nothing to live on but what his pen could provide, the amount of writing hitherto ascribed to him by the traditional canon is so scanty that it is hard to see how he could have survived. Possibly a meticulous biographer, working with the minutiae of Johnson's economic life, together with a historian of journalism, who could provide concrete information about rates of payment and details of the way in which periodicals of the time were conducted, will be able to shed useful light on this problem.

The new preoccupation with matters of canon has stimulated interest in the analysis of Johnson's prose style (Section 12). Many misconceptions concerning the so-called pomposity of his writing have been cleared away by the excellent work of W. K. Wimsatt, Jr. (12:26, 17:104), and others, and many readers are finding to their surprise that the sonorous effects which Johnson often produces are not the result of an excessive use of long, difficult words. For instance, one characteristic sentence from *Rasselas*, containing forty words, has thirty-seven of one syllable. Yet the total effect is unmistakably Johnsonian.

In recent years there have been more and more attempts to analyze the style by statistical methods. One scholar, S. Krishnamurti, has had the enterprise to subject some pieces whose ascription to Johnson has not been entirely certain to a mathematical test, devised by the eminent statistician G. Udny Yule, of the frequency of occurrence of the same nouns (12:31, 12:33–12:35). The results in all cases are consistent with an attribution to Johnson. A beginning has been made in analysis of style by statistical mathematicians working with the formidable aid of electronic computers and the like, which may in time enable some of these questions of the Johnson canon to be satisfactorily cleared up. See, for example, recent discussions by Arthur Sherbo, Louis Milic, and others (12:42, 12:48). The same kind of minute and exact analysis is necessary when a satisfactory text has to be established from variant or dubious readings found in manuscripts and early printed editions of Johnson's writings; and William B. Todd has recently shown how modern techniques of textual criticism may usefully be applied to Johnson's works (20:78; see also 20:84).

The greatest need has long been a complete edition of all of Johnson's works. Although there have been convenient reprints of some individual works (18:1, 21:1) and Allen T. Hazen, in his immensely useful collection of Johnson's prefaces and dedications (25:35) has provided texts and commentary for a large number of the fugitive pieces, there was no new attempt at a complete edition after 1825. Even this set of volumes is now recognized as inferior textually. In 1950 it was possible to say that "it would be difficult to find another major author of the past who stands so desperately in need of a thorough modern re-editing" (1/2:8). Finally, in 1955, some wealthy collectors and enthusiasts provided the necessary financial support and with appropriate fanfare the Yale Edition of the Works of Samuel Johnson was launched (2:8). Herman W. Liebert became chairman of the editorial committee, and Allen T. Hazen, general editor. The latter has now been succeeded by John H. Middendorf. But large group projects inevitably move slowly. After the publication of the first volume, *Diaries, Prayers, and Annals*, edited by E. L. McAdam, Jr., with Donald and Mary Hyde in 1958 (24:7), which had been almost ready to go to press before the larger project was organized, nothing appeared for five years. Then in 1963 came *The Idler* and *The Adventurer*, edited by W. J. Bate, John M. Bullitt, and L. F. Powell (16:1); and the next year the *Poems*, edited by E. L. McAdam, Jr., with George Milne (14:6). If some may wonder why another reprinting of the poems was necessary after the admirable authoritative edition prepared by the late D. Nichol Smith and McAdam for the Oxford University Press in 1941 (14:5), it might be well to point out that in some of the later discoveries of Boswell papers at Malahide Castle there was found important additional evidence—for example, the entire manuscript in Johnson's handwriting of the *Vanity of Human Wishes*, part of *London*, and a number of hitherto unknown juvenile poems. Thus in the new volume there is a surprising amount that is completely new.

In 1968 came two volumes of Johnson's Shakespearian writings, edited by Arthur Sherbo, with an introduction by Bertrand H. Bronson (19: 11). Three volumes of *The Rambler*, under the general supervision of W. J. Bate, with a scrupulously produced text by Albrecht Strauss, were published in 1969. Closely following these will be the *Journey to the Western Islands of Scotland*, edited by Mary Lascelles; the political pieces, edited by Donald J. Greene; the sermons, edited by Jean Hagstrum and James Gray; and the parliamentary debates prepared by Benjamin Hoover. After the long wait, there is now actually a log-jam at the printer's. But many of the most eagerly awaited volumes, for instance those containing *Rasselas* and *The Lives of the Poets*, still remain far in the future. Obviously, when we do have authentic texts, thoroughly annotated and well indexed, of everything which Johnson is known to have written, we will be in a better position to evaluate his total accomplishment.

Even without the help of adequate modern texts, much has already been done to reinterpret Johnson the thinker and man of letters. One group of writers now stresses Johnson the strong teacher—the neglected moralist. Never a philosopher in the strictest sense, and without a purely speculative mind, Johnson was nevertheless a deep thinker. Like Socrates, he was essentially a wise man, a sage who excelled as a teacher of the art of living. Moreover, his sincerity, lucidity, and vigor make a direct appeal to twentieth-century readers. For many perplexed moderns the combination in Johnson of basic skepticism with a firm spiritual faith has a definite fascination. With the reawakening in many educated people of a serious interest in theology, thanks to the work of such great twentieth-century Protestant theologians as Karl Barth, Paul Tillich, and Reinhold Niebuhr and to the widespread publicity given the work of the Second Vatican Council, the bases of Johnson's devout Christianity are being more thoroughly and intelligently explored than in the past—though, to be sure, not without some dispute over the findings (24:127, 24:157, 24:163). There have been two full-length books, by Maurice Quinlan (24:162) and Chester Chapin (24:169), and some simple, erroneous old stereotypes are being abandoned. The Christian pessimism, which the nineteenth century found unsympathetic, does not appear to us quite so unwarranted. Indeed, there is evidence that more and more readers are going to Johnson for spiritual solace. An inspiring appraisal of this side of Johnson may be found in Charles G. Osgood's *Poetry as a Means of Grace,* originally intended for preministerial students at Princeton (10/6:247). The religious appeal of Johnson, to be sure, the Victorians never quite forgot. Our new emphasis is merely on the fundamental values of his belief.

It is with Johnson the man of letters that the greatest shift in opinion has taken place. Most of the earlier general estimates relied largely on Boswell's reporting of Johnson's conversation. To be sure, some of these were of value. Chauncey B. Tinker's *Dr. Johnson and Fanny Burney* (5: 134) was extremely useful in calling attention to the non-Boswellian sources of information about Johnson. John Bailey's *Dr. Johnson and His Circle* (10/6:160) in the Home Library series—pleasantly written for popular consumption—introduced the great man to many new readers, but largely represented the old nineteenth-century approach. As Paul Elmer More pointed out (*ibid.*), Bailey is somewhat obtuse in his estimate of Johnson as a thinker and imperfect in his recognition of his subject's true genius. Percy H. Houston's *Doctor Johnson: A Study in Eighteenth Century Humanism* (11/9:5), a transitional work, grounded in the old prejudices, yet aware of the new implications, is not wholly satisfactory as an analysis of Johnson's thought.

But during the last fifteen years there has been a truly startling change of approach. More and more, Johnson's casual remarks made during social give and take are being ignored, and concentration is being placed on his published writings. This trend is clearly seen in Walter Jackson Bate's *The Achievement of Samuel Johnson* in 1955 (10/6:291), where major emphasis is placed on the *Rambler* and *Idler* essays and other works of the 1750's. Donald J. Greene, in his *The Politics of Samuel Johnson,* 1960 (20:83), goes even farther in his insistence on the great importance of Johnson's early writings for any true understanding of his opinions; and Robert Voitle in *Samuel Johnson the Moralist,* 1961 (11/9:28) concurs. Recently in two challenging books, Arieh Sachs's *Passionate Intelligence: Imagination and Reason in the Works of Samuel Johnson,* 1967 (11/9:45), and Paul Alkon's *Samuel Johnson and Moral Discipline,* 1967 (11/9:44), the process is further expanded. Throughout is stressed a careful reading of all that Johnson saw fit to publish, and the result has been to change materially the old image of Johnson as thinker and moralist. Instead of the proverbial bigoted reactionary, the authoritarian and traditionalist, which the nineteenth century drew out of Boswell's anecdotes, the new critics find him largely a scientific empiricist, moving with his time in the Lockean tradition toward modern skeptical analysis.

To be sure, much depends upon what passages are chosen for quotation. Does one illustrate and stress Johnson's passionate commitment to orthodox Christian doctrines and his firm belief in subordination and hierarchy? Or does one show the skeptical bent of his mind on ordinary matters, his constant struggle to find the truth and to evaluate human actions in the light of the new psychological theories? The older writers took the former approach, the newer critics take the latter. Both present important aspects of Johnson's complex mind.

Certainly the new approach challenges the old view of Johnson as a rigid thinker. In the past scholars tended to think of Johnson as always viewing the intellect and the passions as operating through universal and immutable principles. But, as can easily be proved, much of Johnson's morality was experiential. Johnson works from the premise that all human action originates in the mind, and thus any moralist must be a careful observer of just how the human mind works. After the moralist has made his observations, he then uses them in order to draw from direct experience practical recommendations for confronting moral decisions. Nevertheless, despite the enormous variety in human impulses and motivations, there are moral judgments which can be made. Reason can, through training, control the contrary pleasures of passion and imagination. Thus, for Johnson, moral discipline is scientific and depends upon experience, rather than upon fixed norms. Just the same, he still believes in the possibility of using empirical knowledge as the basis for authoritative instruction.

Not that such an approach necessarily contradicts Johnson's firmly held religious beliefs. He is able to hold to his Christian convictions and at the same time use the new scientific psychology to analyze human imperfections. Nor does the emphasis on Johnson's empirical approach mean that he judged everything by prudential or utilitarian standards. Once he has observed the facts, any final analysis is always upon moral grounds.

It should be stressed that this new critical approach to Johnson need not be considered as basically anti-Boswellian. As the result of all the new discoveries, Boswell is recognized as a great creative artist in his own right. Nor is there any attempt to destroy the traditional image of the older Johnson, the emphatic talker so beloved by generations of readers of the *Life*. Most Johnsonians have two faces—one which they turn to Boswell, and the other to Johnson's works. If, like Janus, the two faces may sometimes appear to be looking in opposite directions, one must remember that they are attached to the same head. The Boswellian face sees Johnson the delightful companion, the patron saint of clubbability; the other sees the deep thinker and moralist so powerfully delineated in the works of his middle period.

In the new appraisal of all of Johnson's works perhaps most surprising is the revival of interest in Johnson's poetry. What the late nineteenth century considered "unmelodious," and at best second-rate, is now finding openly enthusiastic admirers. From the days of Sir Walter Scott, who could scarcely repeat *The Vanity of Human Wishes* without tears starting in his eyes, until the nineteen twenties there were few critics willing to call Johnson a major poet. Yet some now are willing to do just that, though unwilling perhaps to go so far as T. S. Eliot, who calls the imitations of Juvenal "among the greatest verse satires of the English or any other language" (14:8, 14:73). While it is universally recognized that Johnson is a poet of limited range (14:78), the merits of the Latin verses, of a few of the early poems (notably "On St. Simon and St. Jude"), and of many of the light impromptu lines, are becoming more apparent. Even *Irene* is less disdained than formerly (15:33, 15:34). For most readers, however, the two great satires, the prologues, and the lines to Levet will remain the most popular (concerning the latter see 14:69, 14:77, 14:90).

Leading in the new appraisal have been T. S. Eliot, who in several places has stressed Johnson's importance (14:89, 10/1:67), and D. Nichol Smith, who, besides providing several excellent analyses of the poems (14:78, 14:85), has shown convincingly that the whole body of Johnson's verse gives us as true and vivid a picture of his mind as we can gain from his prose (see also 14:92 and Bronson in 14:7). As might be expected, it is *The Vanity of Human Wishes* which is the most acclaimed. "Nowhere else in all our poetry is the theme that 'all is Vanity' given so majestic expression" (14:78); it is "one of the great poems of the language" (14:91). Alfred Noyes (10/6:246) stresses particularly the long-overlooked emotional quality of the lines: "It is customary almost to ignore Johnson as a poet; but, behind all the dignity and formality of those lines, there are tears hidden; pangs of mortal grief, and the passion of an immortal and unconquerable spirit, gazing through Life and Time and Death, into the depths of the Eternal. . . . The language and the manner are far removed from those of our day. Many poets have written couplets which may strike us as more 'brilliant'; but I know of none in the language which, if read with the simple integrity of spirit that is their due, are so likely to fill the reader's eyes with unexpected tears."

It is impossible here to do more than mention some of the important recent studies. The relationship of *London* and *The Vanity of Human Wishes* to the satires of Juvenal has been expertly analyzed by John Butt,

Henry Gifford, and Mary Lascelles (14:109, 14:117, 14:120); and there have been discerning general discussions by Donald Davie, Ian Jack, Susie I. Tucker, Henry Gifford, Edward A. Bloom, F. W. Hilles, and Howard Weinbrot (14:97, 14:98, 14:113, 14:132, 14:134, 14:146). Particular notice should be taken of valuable studies, by Bertrand H. Bronson, Macdonald Emslie, and Chester Chapin, of Johnson's use of personification and his mastery of other metaphoric effects (14:90, 14:106, 14:108). No longer can there be any doubt that Johnson is firmly entrenched as one of the major poets of the Augustan Age in England. Summing up the new attitude, a reviewer in the *Spectator* (14:5) insists: "Johnson is by no means to be disposed of as a minor poet inferior to Dryden or even to Goldsmith. His is a unique, authentic voice, and his genius is evident in his poems, and not only in his prose and his conversation."

What would have astonished older readers more than anything else is the way Johnson's periodical essays are being read by many of our younger readers. As the result of the inspired teaching of such men as Walter Jackson Bate at Harvard and Bertrand H. Bronson at California, students are now devouring the *Rambler* and *Idler* essays with avidity, and finding, to their surprise, that what they had somehow assumed to be hackneyed, ponderous pieces of stale morality are filled with pertinent, exciting observations. Johnson's sturdy independence of thought, his shrewd understanding of human motives, his witty summing up of the basic problems of human relationships, all make an immediate appeal to the members of a generation with few illusions.

One of the most striking of recent claims is that made by Bate in his *The Achievement of Samuel Johnson* (10/6:291) that the writings of Johnson reveal "the closest anticipation of Freud to be found in psychology or moral writing before the twentieth century." Kathleen M. Grange further documents this claim by showing the modernity of Johnson's accounts of certain psychoanalytic concepts (11/9:32). For example, Johnson is shown to be one of the first to use the word "repress" in the modern psychological sense. Chiefly in *The Rambler*, but also in many other works, one can find penetrating studies of human frustration, of the devious effects of blocked wills, and of complex human motivation. In Johnson's life of that strange pretender Richard Savage there is a complete portrait of a masochistic parasite (13:41). Of course, Johnson does not use the technical terms of modern psychiatry, but he unerringly fastens on the basic themes and patterns. He was always curious about quirks of human character, and he tried to probe beneath the surface to the unconscious motivations which are the sources of action. In many of his character sketches, Johnson vividly portrays the tragic errors and frustrations of ordinary life, and it is this aspect of his writing which today proves so fascinating.

It was the *Dictionary* which established Johnson's fame for his contemporaries. "Dictionary" Johnson he was often called; and the two massive volumes were hailed as one of the achievements of the age. Later lexicographers, of course, have far surpassed him in etymological knowledge. And general amusement over certain obviously—sometimes intentionally—distorted definitions has tended to obscure the true merit of the work. Earlier research by Wimsatt, Gove, Watkins, and others (10/1:29, 17:91, 17:104) focused attention on the knowledge of older English literature evidenced in the quotations, and on the methods employed by Johnson in putting the volumes together.

In 1955, for the bicentenary celebration, James Sledd and Gwin J. Kolb produced the most careful and complete assessment of the *Dictionary* (17:136). Together with an important article by the same authors (17:128), it places Johnson where he belongs, in the mainstream of "lexicographical tradition." Johnson obviously was not a great innovator. He naturally relied on the other dictionary makers who preceded him, and actually was first in the field only in his method of historical illustrative quotations. It must be remembered, however, that the application of the historical method was an enormous forward stride. And the significance of his choice of what to quote, as modern critics have been pointing out, is enormous. One can find in the *Dictionary* a perfect example of his own literary, scientific, aesthetic, and moral tastes. Johnson's aim was to teach all kinds of things in addition to grammar and good English usage—something no lexicographers before or since have seriously tried to do. The *Dictionary* was to be a useful anthology of great thoughts, as well as a linguistic tool. But stress on this side of the work should not obscure Johnson's technical linguistic contribution. Modern dictionary makers are not averse to confessing their debt. While still finding much to laugh at in the occasional amusing oddity, we now recognize that in the definitions lies one of the chief strengths of the *Dictionary*.

What can be said of *Rasselas*, that touchstone, as D. Nichol Smith has often insisted (10/6:276), with which to determine a true Johnsonian? If the reactions of recent college students may be accepted as evidence, it continues to be read with interest and delight, for the simple tale of the travelers' search for happiness in our real world of disappointed hopes is ever fresh and stimulating. Yet there still is no scholarly, annotated edition, though we now have a number of inexpensive reprints with good introductions and some with full annotation (in particular, see those by Warren Fleischauer, Charles Peake, and John Hardy [18:1,

2:40]) and new translations into Arabic, Japanese, and Spanish among
other languages (18:2). For the bicentennial in 1959 Magdi Wahba
assembled a volume of *Bicentenary Essays on Rasselas* (18:81), which
contained a number of pleasant and useful pieces and was published,
fittingly enough, in Cairo. Since then there has been a rush of critical
studies, for *Rasselas* is being studied seriously as never before. Instead
of being shrugged off as a formless Eastern tale, with little narrative interest, a kind of huge collection of truisms without much pertinence
today, it is being reexamined with eager delight. We are arguing over
its setting, its structure, over the basic plan of the book, the importance
of Imlac in the development of the themes, the difficult problem of what
happens at the end of the book, and a score of other matters incapable
of easy solution. As a sample of some of the most challenging recent
work, we might mention Donald M. Lockhart's description of the historical background (18:111), Gwin Kolb's investigation of publication
details (18:104), Agostino Lombardo's suggestion about Imlac's importance to the plot (18:85), and Kathleen M. Grange's analysis of
Johnson's account of a schizophrenic illness in the astronomer (18:107);
and there are other useful critical essays by John M. Aden, Sheridan
Baker, F. W. Hilles, Emrys Jones, Ellen Douglas Leyburn, Sheldon
Sachs, W. O. S. Sutherland, Jr., Paul West. Like every masterpiece,
Rasselas is being studied on many levels.

As to the edition of Shakespeare, the most important recent event is
the appearance in the Yale Edition of all of Johnson's Shakespearian
writings (19:11). Obviously this supplants Sherbo's earlier reprinting
of Johnson's notes in the Augustan Reprint series (19:7) and other collections of his criticism (19:4, 19:5). For those who are interested in all
matters concerned with the Shakespeare edition, a lively and no doubt
salutary controversy was stirred up by the publication in 1956 of Sherbo's book on Johnson as editor of Shakespeare (19:103). The *casus belli*
was Sherbo's thesis that the content of the famous preface and of some
of Johnson's notes was not so original as had been formerly assumed, a
thesis which some other students felt to be expressed in a way that made
it almost tantamount to a charge of plagiarism and caused them to retort, with some heat, "in defence of Johnson." If, as we have suggested
in the paragraphs above, there is a healthful tendency in Johnson studies
generally to see Johnson "in the tradition" rather than as idiosyncratic,
it is possible that more such controversies will develop in the future, the
dividing line between immoral plagiarism and laudable traditionalism
being often not easy to determine. (A similar controversy once raged
over Johnson's great musical contemporaries, Bach and Handel, some
nineteenth-century musicologists assiduously calling attention to the

unscrupulous way in which they stole tunes without acknowledgment from their predecessors and their contemporaries, and even from themselves. Nowadays the matter seems to worry scarcely anyone.)

Perhaps the greatest stumbling block to the appreciation of Johnson —particularly for Americans—has always been his political pamphlets, which universally earned him the label of a bigoted Tory. Enthusiastic liberal thinkers, supremely confident in man's ability to perfect human institutions, were horrified by what seemed to them Johnson's servile attitude toward authority and the established order. But mid–twentieth-century political thinkers appear to be more willing to examine sympathetically the bases for Johnson's conservatism. In this regard an excellent beginning was made in a number of studies by B. H. Bronson, J. W. Krutch, and Stuart G. Brown among others (10/6:254, 3:175, 11/9:11).

That Johnson was not merely a subservient party member was seen long ago by G. B. Hill and John Sargeaunt (20:59, 20:60). His political ideas grew out of his moral and ethical judgments, not from any selfish or material considerations. Johnson's deep sympathy for the poor, his hatred of slavery and oppression (we must always remember his toast to the next insurrection of the slaves in the West Indies), his suspicion of government by the financial interests—all tended to make him an independent, rather than a conventional Tory. A basic skepticism kept him, like so many others of his age, wary of Whig optimism. That skepticism, which carried doubt over into the realm of man's reason, produced a disbelief in the possibility of any major sudden improvement in human institutions. It must be remembered that the greatest writers of the day—Dryden, Swift, and Hume—were all political Tories. Johnson was essentially of this tradition (as recent writers have pointed out), except that the violence of his temperament never permitted him to develop the consistent philosophical approach of Hume or the trusting Catholicism of the later Dryden. But he, like them, found the increase of Whig industrial power a threat to individual rights.

A careful study of Johnson's political writings—not merely the irritable remarks drawn out of him by Boswell after annoying probing— shows that from *Marmor Norfolciense* in 1739 to *Taxation No Tyranny* in 1775 Johnson consistently fought what he considered the dangers of self-interest—the greed for wealth and power in individuals and in governments. His overpowering fear was the rising importance of the rich commercial classes, with their ruthless acquisitive instincts. In *Further Thoughts on Agriculture* in 1756 he showed his awareness of the fundamental modern conviction that liberty involves the opportunity to obtain the necessities of life. But such an idea presupposes a powerful central government—one which will be above the rugged individualism of laissez faire economics. To achieve such an end, Johnson placed his faith in a strong executive which would hold the balance of power in the commonwealth and control society for the good of all. Seeing England in the grasp of greedy merchants, and the colonies in the control of men whom he regarded as rabble-rousers avid for commercial gain, he believed the only solution to be not violent revolution, for he distrusted man's potential ability to improve, but an intelligent use of the established traditional order in church and state. Because the rising capitalism of his day was so obviously Johnson's *bête noire*, it is not so surprising really that modern radicals now find his thought more attractive than did the optimistic liberals of the nineteenth century (see, for example, 11/9:11).

In stressing their conception of Johnson as a bigoted and rather stupid old Tory, nineteenth-century writers tended to play down the Rambler's basic interest in political affairs. "He was in no sense a statesman," Macaulay decided. "He never willingly read or thought or talked about affairs of state." Three books published during the last two decades call attention to the fact that he at least *wrote* a very great deal about them. *Dr. Johnson and the English Law* by E. L. McAdam, Jr. (11/3:18) records some of the results of his brilliant discovery of Johnson's collaboration with Sir Robert Chambers in the long series of lectures (1,600 pages in manuscript) that Chambers delivered to the law students of Oxford University as successor to Blackstone as Vinerian Professor. Johnson's ideas about the legal foundations of affairs of state, transmitted through Chambers's students, must have had a considerable influence on the general climate of legal and political opinion in England in the latter part of the eighteenth century. The excerpts McAdam prints contain some of Johnson's most powerful writing and thinking, and the lectures form a document at least as profoundly revealing of the bases of Johnson's ideas about the problems of the human situation as do *Rasselas* and *The Rambler*. Any modern student who ignores them when trying to frame general conclusions about Johnson's controlling ideas does so at his own peril.

The longest continuous single work that Johnson ever wrote is the series of Parliamentary "debates" printed for a number of years in the early 1740's in the *Gentleman's Magazine*, a document at least half a million words in length, a most formidable repository of political and moral wisdom, both theoretical and practical, which has hitherto hardly been studied seriously. Benjamin Hoover has supplied a useful introduction to such study (20:77), in which he demonstrates the untenability of many of the things that used to be said about the *Debates*. Although in some details and in actual wording they come from Johnson's own imagination, they do rest on a solid foundation of fact about what went on in the two Houses. Moreover, they are not grossly prejudiced and partisan. Instead of presenting a collection of faceless individuals delivering colorless truisms, they are full of lively characterization and incisive thinking and expression.

Finally, Donald J. Greene's *The Politics of Samuel Johnson* (20:83) attempts to survey all of the political parts of Johnson's known writings (and there turn out to be a very large number of them, in almost every part of his adult life). More important, perhaps, the author has studied the drastically revised picture of the political structure of eighteenth-century Britain which in the last thirty years has replaced the simple old Whig-versus-Tory myth in responsible modern historiography. His conclusion is that Johnson's political conservatism was the kind that follows naturally from a rigorously skeptical and empiricist turn of mind; it is so far from being bigoted and fearful that it can even accommodate itself, on occasion, to revolutionary ideas—as, for instance, the idea of a rebellion by the Negro slaves in the West Indies. That such forceful claims should arouse active opposition in those who cling to the traditional interpretations is obvious, and there have been a number of replies. Witness, in particular, the controversy over Johnson and "Natural Law" (11/9:36). Honest controversy is always the lifeblood of serious scholarship.

Along with a deeper understanding of Johnson's political beliefs has come further study of the origins of his other "prejudices." In an admirable essay (10/6:254) Bertrand Bronson argues that the inconsistencies and paradoxes in Johnson's remarks come from the opposition in him of two strong forces—the skeptical conservatism of his intellectual attitude and the romantic exuberance of his temperament. Again and again his violent passions carried him away; at the same time his powerful intellect kept him from fully accepting romantic illusions. Of course, many of the outbursts about Scotland were intended only to tease his Scottish friends, but there was also an underlying distrust of the Presbyterian reformers and the bustling business enterprise of the inhabitants north of the Tweed. His famous tour to the Hebrides in 1773 removed some prejudices and settled him more firmly in others. Moreover, it thrust him into one of the most celebrated controversies of his life—over the authenticity of the Ossianic pieces (some excellent discussions of this struggle, as well as commentaries on his trip, will be found listed in Section 21).

In 1950, when preparing the first version of this list, the editor saw no reason to comment on modern criticism of the *Journey to the Western Islands of Scotland*. Recently, however, it has become the center of argument, which might well be noticed. What essentially was Johnson's purpose in describing for the public his Hebridean journey? Was it meant to be merely another factual travel book? Or did it embody basic social and political commentary? Jeffrey Hart has suggested that Johnson had three themes which he meant to stress—the tragic destruction of the pre-Reformation culture in Scotland, the breakdown of the Highland class system in the eighteenth century—also to be lamented—and the rise of middle-class progressive culture, about which Johnson was ambiguous (21:108). To this interpretation Donald J. Greene vehemently objected (21:109), and he was later supported by R. K. Kaul (21:115), Arthur Sherbo (21:124), and Clarence Tracy (21:128). Hart's explanation, they contend, represents a misreading of the work. This kind of explication is based on a preconceived notion of what Johnson must have thought, judging from his other recorded remarks, and not on what he actually wrote. It is false, they insist, to assume that Johnson believed the world was a better place in the days of feudalism, monasticism, and scholasticism. If he saw some things he liked in the old clan system, he thought its disadvantages outweighed any advantages. Elsewhere there has been further discussion of the problems involved (21:129, 21:130). Highly to be recommended is a discussion of the origins of the *Journey* by Mary Lascelles, its newest editor (21:121).

Of other so-called biased judgments and misconceptions, many have recently received thorough examination. There is his dislike of Hume, interestingly analyzed by Ernest Mossner (10/4:27), and of Gray (22:133); his puzzling scorn of history (11/9:18); his supposed contempt for natural scenery (11/7:6); his attitude toward subordination (20:75, 10/6:254). In some instances we can now see that Johnson, according to his own postulates, was right; in others it is evident that his attitude was merely the result of irritated petulance. Interestingly enough, even the notorious refutation of Bishop Berkeley has found a defender in a professional philosopher, H. F. Hallett, who intricately tries to prove that Johnson's point in kicking the stone has never been rightly understood (11/9:17).

Much of our difficulty in understanding and appreciating Johnson stems from his own lack of consistency. Instead of being a rigid doctrinaire, he was often not quite certain of where he stood. As Stuart G. Brown (11/9:11) clearly sees: "The significance of Dr. Johnson is precisely that he was on both sides, in contradiction with himself. He was, in a sense, as his writings reflect, caught between the old order and the new and he did not always know which way to turn." Brown's is only one of many modern analyses of Johnson's thought that tend to stress the complexity of his ideas—the fact that he was certainly not a true reactionary, but a perplexed transitional figure. Perhaps psychologically that is one explanation of his acerbity.

Concerning Johnson's last major work, the *Lives of the Poets*, modern commentary may be considered in two sections—first, Johnson as a biographer, and, second, as a critic. From the early discussions by Walter Raleigh (22:92) to the present there has been much discussion of Johnson's general biographical techniques. He is included in all histories of the genre (see 10/2:6, 10/2:22), and he naturally assumes a major position in those which concentrate on the eighteenth century (22:101, 10/2:15, 10/2:18). Recently, too, there have been a number of important investigations of Johnson's procedure in preparing individual lives. Witness J. H. Leicester's analysis of the sources of the life of Shenstone, and F. W. Hilles's of the life of Pope, which examine surviving original notes in Johnson's handwriting, the holograph manuscript, and corrected proof sheets (22:130, 22:135). Here we are given a revealing glimpse of a biographer's actual methods.

Finally, it is Johnson's literary criticism which is undergoing the most pronounced revival. In sharp contrast to the Romantic point of view, many modern writers are finding more and more to admire in Johnson's common-sense judgments. Everyone is familiar with the typical nineteenth-century approach. De Quincey, perhaps, was the most violent, exploding in a frenzy of anger over what he called the "malignity" of Johnson's treatment of Milton and calling Johnson's interpretations "scandalously false, scandalously misconstructed" (22:83). Most of the Victorian critics who followed tended to agree. Indeed, J. Churton Collins felt that the defects of the *Lives of the Poets* were so great that the work should never be placed in any reader's hands unless properly edited with a good commentary (22:89). Johnson, Collins insisted, appears to have been "abnormally deficient in imagination, in fancy, in all that is implied in aesthetic sensibility and sympathy." Robert Bridges (22:97) and Lytton Strachey (22:87) most delightfully state this widespread opinion. Johnson's aesthetic judgments, Strachey insists, "have always some good quality to recommend them—except one: they are never right." It is Johnson's wit that saves all; "he has managed to be wrong so cleverly, that nobody minds." In other words, we read Johnson only for amusement. Nobody would ever take him seriously as a critic.

But recently many people are taking him seriously. As our own frame of reference more closely approximates that of the eighteenth century and as our unthinking acceptance of Romantic sensibility as absolute dogma begins to waver, our understanding of Johnson's critical position becomes more sympathetic. During the last four decades the turnabout has been overwhelming. Consider this from Alfred Noyes, who in 1940 remarked of Johnson that "In his criticism of the defects both of Shake-speare and of Milton he is far shrewder, far truer and far more inde-pendent of authority than any later critic. Macaulay, when he poured contempt on Johnson's critical powers, was the conventionalist, Johnson the original thinker" (10/6:246). And three years later Yvor Winters, after proclaiming that a great critic is the rarest of all literary geniuses, could casually add that "perhaps the only critic in English who deserves that epithet is Samuel Johnson" (*The Anatomy of Nonsense*, p. 240).

About the same time, F. R. Leavis in *Scrutiny* (10/1:41) remarked that Johnson's criticism is "living literature, alive and life-giving." De-spite certain real limitations, "Johnson is a better critic of eighteenth-century poetry than Matthew Arnold." Even the controversial disap-proval of Gray's pindarics and the attacks on the popular Miltonic imi-tations of the day are defended by Leavis. "Now that we no longer search the eighteenth century for what is congenial to Victorian-roman-tic taste—for poetry from the 'soul,'" we can appreciate Johnson's an-noyance at "the weakness of taste in his age." Indeed, according to Leav-is, the treatment of Gray, "who has not even yet fully emerged from the Arnoldian transfiguration," actually illustrates Johnson's "excellence as a critic of eighteenth-century verse." And the *Life of Cowley* is perhaps the "most striking demonstration of his uninhibited versatility." More-over, we have only to cite other analyses by J. W. Krutch, T. S. Eliot, H. W. Donner, W. J. Bate, S. G. Brown, M. H. Abrams, Jean Hagstrum, W. R. Keast, W. K. Wimsatt, Jr., to name only the more obvious, to show what is going on (10/1:39, 10/1:67, 10/1:60, 10/1:43, 10/1:30, 10/1:35, 10/1:55, 10/1:56, 10/1:68).

Happily, in recent years critics have been carefully examining John-son's specific techniques and explaining the reasons for his various con-troversial decisions. David Perkins, for example, has carefully analyzed the well-known passages on metaphysical poetry in the *Life of Cowley* and is better able to point out just what they mean and what they show about Johnson's judgment (22:123). Even what was once considered to be utterly scandalous, the criticism of *Lycidas*, something to be shrugged off by Johnsonians as an embarrassing faux pas, has found defenders. Warren Fleischauer, in an analysis which should be more widely known, shows that Johnson's evaluation can be justified when considered in the light of his overall attitude toward literature. "It is not, certainly, that Johnson did not understand *Lycidas*; it is rather that modern critics have not understood Johnson's critique of *Lycidas* as an integral part and pith of his *Lives of the Poets*, at one with his norms of criticism. . . . John-son was true to his norms, and therefore not false to *Lycidas*" (22:134). Oliver F. Sigworth goes even farther and boldly proclaims that the critique of *Lycidas* marks the "end of Renaissance criticism. . . . Modern criticism begins with Johnson" (22:150).

However much such generalizations may shock conventional readers, the attitude is symptomatic of a new spirit in modern criticism. The later twentieth century appears to be demanding more of the qualities of Johnson in its own writing. Significantly, an excellent discussion of Johnson by J. B. McNulty, entitled "The Critic Who Knew What He Wanted" (10/1:48), ends with a plea to modern critics to follow the example of the "Great Cham." Johnson's "truly amazing ability to see into the heart of a question and to state his findings clearly and in few words" appeals to present-day readers more than much of the appreciative criticism of the nineteenth century.

The wheel has made a full turn. Yet one must not suppose that the old attitude toward Johnson the writer and thinker has been completely eradicated. Of all nineteenth-century ghosts it is one of the most difficult to lay. But it is significant that today any sneer at Johnson's writings is certain to elicit an immediate rebuttal (see 10/6:250). And even in the popular magazines and anthologies designed for the general reader, the shifting mood is apparent (for example, see item 2:33). "It is time for Johnson's Works to be taken down from the library shelves," pleads Julian Symons in a recent popular selection, ". . . time for an act of justice towards one who was a great writer as well as a remarkable man" (2:32). This from one not openly a professional Johnsonian! Certainly the rehabilitation of Johnson the writer is at full tide.

"To make light of Johnson's writings," as Noël Lewis puts it (10/6: 185), that "old and timeworn habit of thoughtless, prejudiced or half-informed people . . . to say with parrot-like monotony that he existed in conversation alone, that without Boswell he would never have been known, to ask the silly question, Who reads Johnson now-a-days?"—all this is decidedly out of fashion.

If the present list reveals anything significant, it surely is the vitality of Johnson for every changing generation and for every shifting taste. As the various sections testify—in biography, memoirs, editing, criticism, and religious inspiration—Johnson is still alive and vital to many people.

A Bibliography of
JOHNSONIAN STUDIES

A Bibliography of
JOHNSONIAN STUDIES

1. BIBLIOGRAPHY

1/1. JOHNSON's WRITINGS

Includes general discussions of the canon. Items dealing with questions of attribution relating to specific works or classes of works are listed in Part Two. Items 1/1:10, 13, 17, 18, 20, 27, 28, 29, 40, 41, 43, 50 also list writings about Johnson.

*1/1:1. [Notice of Thomas Davies, ed., *Miscellaneous and Fugitive Pieces* —see item 2:10], *GM*, XLIV (November 1774), 524–26. Assigns to Johnson some thirty early journalistic pieces reprinted by Davies. See item 13:20.

*1/1:2. "An Account of the Writings of Dr. Samuel Johnson, including some incidents of his life," *European Magazine*, VI (December 1784), 411–13; VII (January 1785), 9–12; (February), 81–84; (April), 249–50.

1/1:3. [Cooke, William.] "A Catalogue of Dr. Johnson's Works," in item 3:17, pp. 231–40. Highly inaccurate; some corrections in 2nd ed., 1785.

*1/1:4. Boswell, James. "A Chronological Catalogue of Dr. Johnson's Prose Writings," in item 4:14. The 3rd ed., 1799, contains some additions to this list (by Boswell or Malone), and the 5th ed., 1807, some by Alexander Chalmers. See item 1/1:44 for a discussion of its accuracy.

1/1:5. Chalmers, Alexander. Facsimile of MS list of attributions of periodical pieces to Johnson (ca. 1805), in item 1/4:19, III, following p. 56. Reprinted in item 1/1:47.

1/1:6. Nichols, John. "The Rise and Progress of the *Gentleman's Magazine*," *General Index to the Gentleman's Magazine from the Year 1787 to 1818* (1821), III, [iii]–lxxx.

1/1:7. Watt, Robert. "Johnson, Samuel, M.A.," in *Bibliotheca Britannica*, columns 549–50. Edinburgh: Constable, 1824.

1/1:8. Quérard, J. M. *La France Littéraire*, IV, 229–30. Paris: Firmin Didot,

1830. Reprinted, Paris: Maisonneuve et Larose, 1964. Lists French translations of Johnson's works.

1/1:9. Lowndes, William Thomas. "Johnson, Samuel, LL.D.," *The Bibliographer's Manual of English Literature*, II, 1030–33. London: William Pickering, 1834. New ed., rev. and enl. by Henry G. Bohn, V, 1217–21, London: Henry G. Bohn, 1857.

1/1:10. Allibone, S. Austin. [Life and critique of Johnson], *Putnam's Monthly* (New York), III (April 1854), 408–15. Rev. and enl. as "Johnson, Samuel, LL.D.," *A Critical Dictionary of English Literature*, I, 971–82, Philadelphia: Childs and Peterson, 1858. A biographical, bibliographical, and critical account; useful for its large number of quotations of early nineteenth-century judgments. Rep. Detroit: Gale, 1965.

*1/1:11. "The Autobiography of Sylvanus Urban" [Johnson's early association with the *Gentleman's Magazine*], *GM*, CCI (July–December 1856), 1–9, 131–40, 267–77, 531–41, 667–77; CCII (January–April 1857), 3–10, 149–57, 282–90, 379–87.

1/1:12. A., M. "Dr. Johnson's Works" [Oxford, 1825], *N&Q*, 2nd ser., XI (March 9, 1861), 191; also (April 6), 269, and (April 27), 335. Their editorship.

1/1:13. Anderson, John P. "Bibliography," in item 3:112, pp. i–xxvii, following p. 175 of the text.

1/1:14. Harrison, Richard. "The Bibliography of Dr. Samuel Johnson" [addenda to published bibliographies], *Bookworm*, I (1888), 351.

1/1:15. Simms, Rupert. *Bibliotheca Staffordiensis*, pp. 251–54. Lichfield: The Johnson's Head, 1894.

1/1:16. Hill, George Birkbeck. *Talks about Autographs.* London: Fisher Unwin, 1896.

1/1:17. Moulton, Charles W. "Samuel Johnson" [a gathering together of many references], *The Library of Literary Criticism*, III, 720–68. Buffalo, N.Y.: Moulton Publishing Co., 1902.

1/1:18. Smith, D. Nichol. Bibliography, in *Cambridge History of English Literature*, ed. A. W. Ward and A. R. Waller, X, 459–80. Cambridge: Cambridge University Press, 1913.

*1/1:19. Courtney, William P., and D. Nichol Smith. *A Bibliography of Samuel Johnson.* Oxford: Clarendon Press, 1915. Reissued with facsimiles, 1925. Reprinted 1968. Reviewed by A. W. Reed, *RES*, II (January 1926), 105–7. A complete revision by J. D. Fleeman is (1970) in progress.

1/1:20. *Samuel Johnson and Johnsoniana: Being Some Account of the Books by or about Dr. Johnson Published by the Oxford University Press.* Prepared by R. W. Chapman. London: Oxford University Press, 1926.

1/1:21. Chapman, R. W. "The Numbering of Editions in the Eighteenth

Century" [deals with the *Rambler, Idler, Adventurer*, and *Lives of the Poets*], *RES*, III (January 1927), 77–79.

1/1:22. Brett, Oliver. "A Note on Dr. Johnson's First Editions" [prices, etc.], *Life and Letters*, III (October 1929), 366–68.

*1/1:23. Chapman, Robert William. *Cancels*. London: Constable & Co., 1930.

1/1:24. Chapman, Robert William. "Johnsonian Bibliography" [various finds since item 1/1:19], *Colophon*, Pt. XII (December 1932), 13–20; Pt. XVI (March 1934), 1–8. See also *TLS*, January 5, 1933, p. 12.

1/1:25. Pottle, Frederick A. "Printer's Copy in the Eighteenth Century" [problems of Johnson and Boswell bibliography], *PBSA*, XXVII (1933), 2, 65–73.

*1/1:26. Chapman, Robert William, and Allen T. Hazen. "Johnsonian Bibliography: A Supplement to Courtney," *Proceedings of the Oxford Bibliographical Society*, V (1939), 119–66.

1/1:27. Esdaile, Arundell. "Dr. Johnson and His Circle," *Fordwick: The Quarterly List of Books Added to the Brentford and Chiswick Public Libraries*, No. 27 (January 1939), 3–6. Reprinted in *News Notes and Quotations*, No. 35, Enoch Pratt Free Library, Baltimore, Md., 1939.

1/1:28. Dyson, H. V. D., and John Butt. *Augustans and Romantics*, pp. 220–24. London: Cresset Press, 1940. Later rev. editions.

*1/1:29. Smith, D. Nichol. "Samuel Johnson," in *Cambridge Bibliography of English Literature*, ed. F. W. Bateson, II, 613–28. Cambridge: Cambridge University Press, 1940. A revised entry by J. D. Fleeman is (1970) in preparation for a new edition of *CBEL*. See also item 1/1:40.

1/1:30. Stauffer, Donald. Bibliography in item 10/2:15 (1941), II, 134–48.

*1/1:31. Piozzi, Hester Lynch. [An important listing of minor pieces by Johnson in item 5:271, pp. 204–5 and index, pp. 1137–39.]

1/1:32. McAdam, Edward L., Jr. "Pseudo-Johnsoniana" [seven works definitely not by Johnson], *MP*, XLI (February 1944), 183–87.

1/1:33. Weed, Katherine K., and Richmond P. Bond. "Johnson," *Studies of British Newspapers and Periodicals from Their Beginning to 1800: A Bibliography*, *SP*, Extra Series, No. 2 (1946), pp. 89–91.

*1/1:34. Liebert, Herman W. "This Harmless Drudge" [new bibliographical discoveries], *New Colophon*, I, Pt. 2 (April 1948), 175–83.

1/1:35. Hazen, Allen T. "New Styles in Typography" [Johnson's lack of interest in the printing of his works], in item 10/6:273, pp. 403–9.

1/1:36. Brown, T. J. "English Literary Autographs: VI. Samuel Johnson," *Book Collector*, II (Summer 1953), 143.

1/1:37. Sherbo, Arthur. "The Cancels in Dr. Johnson's *Works* (Oxford, 1825)," *PBSA*, XLVII (4th quarter, 1953), 376–78.

1/1:38. Chapman, R. W. "The Congreve Manuscripts" [six early MSS of Johnson], *Bodleian Library Record*, V (1955), 118.

1/1:39. Sherbo, Arthur. "Johnson and J. Roberts, Publisher" [published three books by Johnson, not one, as Boswell says], *JNL*, XV, no. 4 (December 1955), 12.

1/1:40. [Powell, L. F.] "Samuel Johnson," in *Cambridge Bibliography of English Literature*, Vol. V (Supplement), ed. George Watson, pp. 462–68. Cambridge: Cambridge University Press, 1957.

1/1:41. Clifford, James L. "The Eighteenth Century," in *Contemporary Literary Scholarship: A Critical Review*, ed. Lewis Leary, pp. 97–99. New York: Appleton-Century-Crofts, 1958.

1/1:42. Moser, Edwin. "A Critical Examination of the Canon of the Prose Writings of Samuel Johnson" (dissertation, New York University, 1959), *Dissertation Abstracts*, XX (1960), 3283–84.

1/1:43. "Johnson (Samuel), LL.D.," *British Museum Catalogue of Printed Books*, Vol. CXVIII, columns 3–53. Photolithographic edition to 1955. London: British Museum, 1962. Later supplements.

*1/1:44. Greene, Donald J. "The Development of the Johnson Canon," in *Restoration and Eighteenth-Century Literature*, ed. Carroll Camden, pp. 407–27. Chicago: University of Chicago Press for William Rice University, 1963.

1/1:45. Simmons, J. S. G. "Samuel Johnson 'on the Banks of the Wolga,'" *Oxford Slavonic Papers*, XI (1964), 28–37. Russian translations of *The Rambler*, *Rasselas*, and other works.

*1/1:46. Fleeman, J. D. *A Preliminary Handlist of Documents & Manuscripts of Samuel Johnson*. (Occasional Publications, No. 2.) Oxford: Oxford Bibliographical Society, 1967.

1/1:47. Greene, Donald J. "Johnsonian Attributions by Alexander Chalmers," *N&Q*, May 1967, pp. 180–81.

1/1:48. Brack, O M, Jr. "The Ledgers of William Strahan," in *Editing Eighteenth-Century Texts*, ed. D. I. B. Smith, pp. 59–77. Toronto: University of Toronto Press, 1968. Quotes Strahan's records of the printing of Johnson's works.

1/1:49. Greene, Donald. "No Dull Duty: The Yale Edition of the Works of Samuel Johnson," in *Editing Eighteenth-Century Texts*, ed. D. I. B. Smith, pp. 92–123. Toronto: University of Toronto Press, 1968. An account of its origin and progress.

1/1:50. Winans, Robert B. "Works by and about Samuel Johnson in Eighteenth-Century America," *PBSA*, LXII (4th quarter, 1968), 537–46.

1/1:51. McAdam, E. L., Jr. *Johnson and Boswell: A Survey of Their Writings*. (Riverside Studies in Literature.) Boston: Houghton Mifflin, 1969.

1/2. Writings about Johnson

See also the following items in Section 1/1:10, 13, 17, 18, 20, 27, 28, 29, 40, 41, 43, 50.

1/2:1. "Johnsoniana" [Johnsonian publications in the anniversary year of his death], *Book-Lore*, I (January 1885), 39–40.

1/2:2. Pratt Institute, Brooklyn, School of Library Service. "Dr. Johnson and His Friends" [a bound, typewritten bibliography], *Lectures on General Literature*, No. 53, pp. 504–13. 1893–94.

1/2:3. "Memorials of Dr. Johnson" [a discussion of various books about Johnson], *Church Quarterly Review* (London), L (July 1900), 355–70.

*1/2:4. "Samuel Johnson" (annual entries, 1925–1960), in *English Literature, 1660–1800: A Bibliography of Modern Studies Compiled for Philological Quarterly*, ed. R. S. Crane *et al.* 4 vols. Princeton, N.J.: Princeton University Press, 1950–62. Continued annually in July number of *Philological Quarterly*. Further cumulative printings are expected.

1/2:5. Bird, Lois M. "American Criticism of Samuel Johnson, LL.D., 1807–1938: A Contribution to Bibliography" (typewritten). Madison, Wis.: University of Wisconsin Library School, 1938 (in University of Wisconsin archives).

1/2:6. *Johnsonian News Letter* [miscellaneous items about eighteenth-century English literature]. Begun in 1940 at Lehigh University; later issued from Columbia University. Ed. James L. Clifford; William L. Payne, asst. ed. 1946–50; John H. Middendorf, asst. ed. 1950–60, coeditor 1960–. Four issues a year.

1/2:7. *The New Rambler*. Periodical of the Johnson Society of London [see item 6:31]. 2 issues a year, since July 1941. Nos. 1–13 mimeographed; beginning with No. 14 printed in new format. Nos. 1–3, ed. Frederick Vernon; Supplement to 3 and Nos. 4–12, eds. William Kent and A. Lloyd-Jones; Nos. 13–27, ed. A. Lloyd-Jones; June 1957–January 1966, ed. F. N. Doubleday; June 1966–, ed. J. H. Leicester.

*1/2:8. Clifford, James L. *Johnsonian Studies, 1887–1950: A Survey and Bibliography*. Minneapolis: University of Minnesota Press, 1951. Reviewed by Mary C. Hyde, *PBSA*, XLV (4th quarter, 1951), 365–67; H. W. Liebert, *PQ*, XXXI (July 1952), 277–78; R. W. Chapman, *RES*, n.s., III (July 1952), 299–300; E. L. McAdam, Jr., *MLN*, LXVII (November 1952), 498; Gwin J. Kolb, *MP*, L (February 1953), 215–16. See also item 1/2:13.

1/2:9. *Abstracts of English Studies*. Monthly. Boulder, Colo.: National Council of Teachers of English. Vol. I, 1958–. Annual indexes list incidental references to Johnson in (selected) studies of other literary figures and topics.

1/2:10. Davis, Herbert. "Recent Studies of Swift and Johnson," in *Sprache und Literatur Englands und Amerikas*, Vol. III: *Die wissenschaftliche Erschliessung der Prosa*, ed. Gerhard Müller-Schwefe, with Hermann Metzger, pp. 11–25. Tübingen: Niemeyer, 1959. Contains in Johnsonian portion some factual inaccuracies.

*1/2:11. Fabian, Bernhard. "Samuel Johnson: Ein Forschungsbericht," *Die Neueren Sprachen*, 1959, no. 9 (September), 393–407; no. 10 (October), 441–54.

1/2:12. Clifford, James L. "Samuel Johnson," *Later Eighteenth-Century English Literature (English 214): A List of Reference Works and Selected Reading*, pp. 4–11. New York: Columbia University, 1960 (rev. ed.).

*1/2:13. Clifford, James L., and Donald J. Greene. "A Bibliography of Johnsonian Studies, 1950–1960," in item 10/6:316, pp. 263–350. Some copies bound separately.

1/2:14. Bond, Donald F. *The Eighteenth Century*. (Goldentree Bibliographies.) New York: Appleton-Century-Crofts (expected 1970).

1/3. Books Owned by Johnson; Johnson as Book Collector and Bibliographer

*1/3:1. *A Catalogue of the Valuable Library of Books, of the late learned Samuel Johnson, Esq.; LL.D. . . . Which will be Sold by Auction . . . By Mr. Christie . . . on Wednesday, February 16, 1785.* Also facsimile reprint, "for the meeting of the Johnson Club at Oxford, June 11, 1892, by Unwin Brothers . . . London." Facsimile reprint (with names of purchasers and prices) with essay by A. Edward Newton, New York: Hackett; London: Elkin Mathews, 1925.

1/3:2. Hutton, Arthur W. *Dr. Johnson's Library*. Paper read at Oxford, June 11, 1892. Privately printed. Reprinted in item 6:16, pp. 117–30.

1/3:3. Dobson, Austin. "Johnson's Library," *Eighteenth Century Vignettes*, Second Series, pp. 180–91. London: Chatto & Windus, 1894.

1/3:4. "Dr. Johnson on Book Collecting" [letter to Barnard, May 28, 1768], *Bookworm*, VII (1894), 363–66.

1/3:5. Marston, R. B. "Dr. Johnson and Walton's 'Angler' " [a copy of Walton's book purchased on Johnson's recommendation], *Athenaeum*, No. 3487 (August 25, 1894), p. 257.

1/3:6. Wheatley, Henry B. "Dr. Johnson as a Bibliographer," *Transactions of the Bibliographical Society*, VIII (1907), 39–61. Separately reprinted, London: Blades, 1907.

1/3:7. Millar, Eric G. "Dr. Johnson as a Bibliographer," *Library*, 4th ser., II (March 1922), 269–71.

1/3:8. Esdaile, Arundell. "Dr. Johnson the Bibliographer," *Contemporary*

Review, CXXVI (August 1924), 200–210. Reprinted; see item 10/6: 243.

1/3:9. Roberts, Sydney Castle. "Johnson's Books," *London Mercury*, XVI (October 1927), 615–24. Reprinted in item 10/6:216. See also "Dr. Johnson's Library," *TLS*, July 4, 1942, p. 336; July 11, p. 343; July 18, p. 360.

1/3:10. Powell, Lawrence F. "Samuel Johnson: An Early 'Friend of the Bodleian'" [Erse books presented to the library], *Bodleian Quarterly Record*, V (December 1928), 280–81.

1/3:11. Williams, Iolo A. "The Elusive Dr. Johnson" [as subscriber to Boyse's *Poems*, 1757], *Book-Collector's Quarterly*, Pt. VII (July–September 1932), 53–59.

1/3:12. Williams, Iolo A. "A List of Books of Verse to Which Samuel Johnson Was a Subscriber," *Points in Eighteenth-Century Verse*, pp. 111–13. London: Constable & Co., 1934. See item 1/3:22.

1/3:13. Chapman, Robert William. "Johnson's Copy of 'Phillips's Poems,'" *N&Q*, CLXXXIV (January 30, 1943), 76.

1/3:14. Chapman, Robert William. "Johnson as Book-Collector," *N&Q*, CLXXXIV (February 27, 1943), 136.

1/3:15. Chapman, R. W. "Johnson and Baxter's Anacreon," *N&Q*, CLXXXVI (May 20, 1944), 246. Cf. *Life*, V, 376 and *passim*; Johnson owned a copy as an undergraduate.

1/3:16. Gove, Philip B. "Johnson's Copy of Hammond's Elegies," *MLQ*, V (December 1944), 435–38.

1/3:17. Thomas, Alan G. "Dr. Johnson and the Book Trade," *Books and the Man* (Antiquarian Booksellers Association annual), 1953, pp. 31–37.

1/3:18. McAdam, E. L., Jr. "Dr. Johnson as Bibliographer and Book Collector," in item 10/6:306, pp. 163–75.

1/3:19. Mahoney, John L. "Dr. Johnson at Work: Observations on a Columbia Rare Book" [*Poems of Collins*, 1771, with Hammond's *Elegies*, marked by Johnson], *Columbia Library Columns*, X (November 1960), 20–23. See item 1/3:16.

1/3:20. Parish, Charles. "Johnson's Books and the Birmingham Library," *New Rambler*, January 1961, pp. 7–21.

1/3:21. Thomas, Alan G. "Dr. Johnson and the Book Trade," *New Rambler*, June 1961, pp. 22–28.

1/3:22. Fleeman, J. D., W. Rea Keast, and Donald Eddy. "Johnson as a Subscriber" [list of books to which Johnson subscribed], *JNL*, XXV, no. 4 (December 1965), 2–3. An expansion of the list in item 1/3:12.

1/3:23. Fleeman, J. D. [Preliminary list of books dedicated to Johnson], *JNL*, XXVI, no. 2 (June 1966), 7.

1/4:1. *Collecteana Johnsoniana. Catalogue of the Library . . . of Mrs. Hester Lynch Piozzi. At the Emporium Rooms . . . Manchester, by Mr. Broster.* September 17, 1823.

1/4:2. *Bibliotheca Boswelliana* [sale catalogue of the library of James Boswell the younger]. London: Sotheby, May 24, 1825.

1/4:3. Fields, Annie (Mrs. James T.). "A Third Shelf of Old Books," *Scribner's*, XVI (September 1894), 343–52. A description of her and her husband's collection, containing Johnson material. With facsimile of letter to James Compton (Chapman No. 811.1).

1/4:4. *Johnsoniana in the Library of Robert B. Adam.* Buffalo, N.Y.: Privately printed, 1895.

1/4:5. *Catalogue of an Exhibition Commemorative of the Bicentenary of the Birth of Samuel Johnson.* New York: Grolier Club, 1909.

1/4:6. *Samuel Johnson, 1709–1784, a List of Books with References to Periodicals in the Brooklyn Public Library.* Brooklyn, N.Y.: Public Library, 1909.

1/4:7. *Catalogue of an Exhibition of Manuscripts, First Editions, Early Engravings and Various Literature Relating to Samuel Johnson,* arranged by Chauncey B. Tinker. New Haven, Conn.: Yale University Library, November 1–6, 1909.

1/4:8. *List of Books and Articles Relating to Samuel Johnson, 1709–1784, Compiled on the Occasion of the Exhibition Held at the Yale University Library,* November 1–6, 1909.

1/4:9. *Catalogue of the Johnsonian Collection of R. B. Adam,* introduction by Charles G. Osgood. Buffalo, N.Y.: Privately printed for R. B. Adam, 1921 (a single volume). See also item 1/4:19.

1/4:10. "The Johnsonian and Boswellian Collections of Mr. R. B. Adam," *Grosvenor Library Bulletin* (Buffalo, N.Y.), IV (March 1922), 1–23.

1/4:11. [Chapman, R. W.] "A Johnsonian Collection" [Adam Library], *TLS,* April 20, 1922, p. 258.

1/4:12. *Catalogue of Books by or Relating to Dr. Johnson and Members of His Circle,* offered for sale by Elkin Mathews Ltd. Compiled by A. W. Evans; introduction by John Drinkwater. London: Elkin Mathews, 1925.

1/4:13. *Notes on a Loan Collection of Johnsonian Books and MSS. Shown at Amen House, July 1925.* Oxford: Oxford University Press, 1925.

1/4:14. Merritt, E. Percival. "Piozzi on Boswell and Johnson" [description of Amy Lowell collection], *Harvard Library Notes,* II (April 1926), 104–11.

1/4:15. *The Books of a Busted Bibliophile, Alias A. Edward Newton* [sale catalogue]. New York: Anderson Galleries, November 29, 1926.

1/4:16. *The Works of Samuel Johnson . . .* [bookseller's catalogue]. New York: Brick Row Bookshop, 1927.

1/4:17. *The Important Collection of XVIIth and XVIIIth Century Books Formed by Lt. Colonel Ralph H. Isham* [auction sale catalogue]. New York: American Art Association, January 7, 1927.

1/4:18. *Catalogue of an Exhibition of Literary Material Pertaining to Doctor Johnson and James Boswell.* Cambridge, Mass.: Club of Odd Volumes, May 14–23, 1928.

*1/4:19. *The R. B. Adam Library Relating to Dr. Samuel Johnson and His Era.* London and New York: Printed for the author by Oxford University Press, Vols. I–III, 1929; Vol. IV, 1930. Reviewed by F. A. Pottle, *PQ*, IX (April 1930), 195; L. F. Powell, *RES*, VII (April 1931), 230–35.

1/4:20. *The Library of Jerome Kern* [auction sale catalogue, January 7–10, 21, 1929], pp. 232–44, 249. New York: Anderson Galleries, 1929.

1/4:21. "Notes on Sales" [Johnsonian manuscripts], *TLS*, June 13, 1929, p. 480; October 24, 1929, p. 852.

1/4:22. Charnwood, Dorothea, Lady. "Johnsoniana," *An Autograph Collection and the Making of It*, pp. 281–97. New York: Henry Holt & Co., 1930. Reprints most of item 7:84.

1/4:23. *Catalogue of an Exhibition of the Private Papers of James Boswell from Malahide Castle.* New York: Grolier Club, December 18, 1930, to February 7, 1931.

*1/4:24. Tyson, Moses. "Unpublished Manuscripts, Papers and Letters of Dr. Johnson, Mrs. Thrale, and Their Friends, in the John Rylands Library," *Bulletin of the John Rylands Library*, XV (July 1931), 467–88.

1/4:25. Guppy, Henry. "Library Notes and News" [description of Johnson and Thrale MS]. *Bulletin of the John Rylands Library*, XVI (January 1932), 9–15.

1/4:26. *The Renowned Library of Lieutenant-Colonel Ralph H. Isham* [sale catalogue]. New York: Anderson Galleries, May 4, 1933.

1/4:27. *An Exhibition of Original Manuscripts Autograph Letters and Books of and Relating to Dr. Samuel Johnson . . . from the Collection of Dr. A. S. W. Rosenbach.* Free Library of Philadelphia, 1934.

1/4:28. "A Johnson Exhibition," *Bodleian Quarterly Record*, VII (3rd quarter, 1934), 466–71.

1/4:29. "A Johnson Exhibition," *Harvard Library Notes*, III (March 1935), 20–29.

*1/4:30. Hazen, Allen T., and E. L. McAdam, Jr. *A Catalogue of an Exhibition of First Editions of the Works of Samuel Johnson in the Library of Yale University 8 November to 30 December, 1935.* New Haven, Conn., 1935.

1/4:31. Abbott, Claude Colleer. *A Catalogue of Papers Relating to Boswell,*

Johnson and Sir William Forbes Found at Fettercairn House. Oxford: Clarendon Press, 1936. Reviewed by R. L. Greene, *MLN*, LIII (May 1938), 384–87; H. Williams, *RES*, XIV (April 1938), 230–31.

1/4:32. Hazen, Allen T. "First Editions of Samuel Johnson," *Yale University Library Gazette*, X (January 1936), 45–51. Description of Yale exhibition and discussion of discovery of Johnson's translation of Crousaz.

1/4:33. *The Valuable Library of Charles T. Jeffrey* [sale catalogue]. Philadelphia: Freeman, April 14, 1936.

1/4:34. Greene, Richard L. *The R. B. Adam Library Relating to Dr. Samuel Johnson and His Era.* Rochester, N.Y., 1936. Reprinted from *Alumni Review*, University of Rochester, October–November, 1936. A descriptive pamphlet.

1/4:35. Gilchrist, Donald B. "Johnsonian Library in the University of Rochester," *Englische Studien*, LXXI (June 1937), 436–37.

1/4:36. *Dr. Johnson in Texas* [exhibition celebrating Stenberg gift]. University of Texas Library, 1940.

1/4:37. *Rare Books, Original Drawings, Autograph Letters and Manuscripts Collected by the Late A. Edward Newton* [sale catalogue], II, 108–48. New York: Parke-Bernet Galleries, 1941.

1/4:38. Gomme, Laurence. *The Robert B. Adam Library Relating to Dr. Samuel Johnson and His Era.* New York: Privately printed, Richard Ellis, 1945. A descriptive pamphlet.

1/4:39. "The Collection of Books by or Relating to Samuel Johnson and James Boswell Formed by R. W. Chapman," *Sotheby Sale Catalogue*, London, June 1, 1945.

1/4:40. [Geoffrey Madan Sale], *Sotheby Sale Catalogue*, London, June 29, 1948, pp. 30–41.

1/4:41. Abbott, Claude Colleer. "New Light on Johnson and Boswell," *Listener*, XLI (May 19, 1949), 853–54. New discoveries of papers.

1/4:42. Chapman, R. W. "Hyde Collection of Johnsonian Manuscripts," *TLS*, September 23, 1949, p. 624.

1/4:43. Chapman, R. W. "Manuscript Hunting in Two Continents" [with facsimile of restoration of letter "edited" by Mrs. Piozzi], *New Colophon*, II, pt. 8 (1950), 370–78.

*1/4:44. Hyde, Mary C. "The History of the Johnson Papers," *PBSA*, XLV (2nd quarter, 1951), 103–16.

1/4:45. *The Rothschild Library. A Catalogue of the Collection of Eighteenth Century Books and Manuscripts Formed by Lord Rothschild.* 2 vols. Cambridge: Privately printed, 1954.

1/4:46. Hyde, Donald and Mary. "The Hyde Collection," *Book Collector*, IV (Autumn, 1955), 208–16.

1/4:47. Blodgett, Thurston. *The Age of Samuel Johnson, LL.D.: a Book*

Collection. Kent, Conn.: Kent School, 1959. A catalogue of his collection presented to the school.

1/4:48. *Johnson's Books: Catalogue of an Exhibition of Books in the Birmingham Library* [commemoration of 250th anniversary of Johnson's birth]. Birmingham: Birmingham Library, 1959.

*1/4:49. Metzdorf, Robert F. *The Tinker Library: A Bibliographical Catalogue of the Books and Manuscripts Collected by Chauncey Brewster Tinker.* New Haven, Conn.: Yale University Library, 1959.

*1/4:50. *Dr. Samuel Johnson . . .* [catalogue of] *An Exhibition of Books, Manuscripts, Views and Portraits arranged jointly by the Reference Library and the Museum and Art Gallery 14th September to 4th October 1959.* Birmingham: City of Birmingham Public Libraries, 1959.

*1/4:51. *Samuel Johnson, LL.D. (1709–1784). An Exhibition of First Editions, Manuscripts, Letters, and Portraits to Commemorate the 250th Anniversary of his Birth, and the 200th Anniversary of the Publication of his Rasselas. September 22–November 28, 1959.* New York: Pierpont Morgan Library, 1959. Foreword by Herbert Cahoon.

1/4:52. Hyde, Mary C. "A Library of Dr. Samuel Johnson" [description of the Hyde collection], *Vassar Alumnae Magazine,* XLV (May 1960), 2–6.

1/4:53. Powell, L. F. "Johnson Exhibited" [at 1959 celebrations], in item 10/6:316, pp. 9–13.

1/4:54. *Samuel Johnson, Londoner* [catalogue of the Festival of London exhibition, 1964]. London: Royal Exchange, 1964.

1/4:55. Fleeman, J. D. "The Johnsonian Collection of Mr. and Mrs. Donald F. Hyde," *Manuscripts,* XVI (Fall 1964), 39–40.

*1/4:56. [Ives, Sidney.] *Samuel Johnson, 1709–1784. An Exhibit of Books and Manuscripts from the Johnsonian Collection Formed by Mr. and Mrs. Donald F. Hyde at Four Oaks Farm.* Introduction by W. H. Bond. Cambridge, Mass.: Houghton Library, Harvard University, 1966.

2. EDITIONS

Collected Works

2:1. *The Works of Samuel Johnson, LL.D. Together with his Life, and Notes on his Lives of the Poets. By Sir John Hawkins, Knt.* 11 vols. London: J. Buckland, J. Rivington, etc., 1787. Supplementary Vols. XII, XIII (Debates in Parliament), London: Stockdale, 1787. Supplementary Vol. XIV, London: Stockdale and Robinson, 1788. "Supplementary Vol. XV" (so generally termed, though not so designated on the title page; contains *A Voyage to Abyssinia* and some smaller pieces), ed. George Gleig, London: Elliot and Kay, 1789.

All later collections of Johnson's *Works*, before the Yale edition of 1958, derive from 2:1. The more useful later editions, containing some added pieces and a few deletions of non-Johnsonian pieces included in the 1787–89 collection, are listed below.

2:2. *The Works of Samuel Johnson, LL.D. A new edition . . . With an Essay on his Life and Genius, By Arthur Murphy, Esq.* 12 vols. London: T. Longman, etc., 1792. Murphy's *Essay* replaces Hawkins's *Life*.

2:3. *The Works of Samuel Johnson, LL.D. A new edition. . . .* 12 vols. London, 1806.

2:4. *The Works of Samuel Johnson, LL.D. A new edition. . . .* 12 vols. London, 1816.

2:5. *The Works of Samuel Johnson, LL.D. A new edition. . . .* 12 vols. London, 1823.

The London 1806, 1816, and 1823 editions include successive additions by the editor, Alexander Chalmers. The 1806 and 1823 editions were also printed in 12mo as well as 8vo forms (the 12mo version of 1823 being dated 1824). Other editions sometimes encountered—all merely reprints of one or another of the editions listed above—include:

1793. 6 vols. Dublin.

1796. 12 vols. London.

1801. 12 vols. London.

1806. 15 vols. Edinburgh. 12mo.

1809. 12 vols. New York: Durrel; Boston: Hastings, Etheridge, and Bliss.

1810. 12 vols. London.

1816. 12 vols. Alnwick. 12mo.

1818. 10 vols. London. 12mo.

1825. 2 vols. London: Jones.

1825. 6 vols. Philadelphia: Carey and Lee, etc.; New York: Collins and Hannay, etc.

1837. 2 vols. New York: G. Dearborn ("1st complete American edition" —title page).

1850. 2 vols. London: Bohn.

1850. 2 vols. New York: Harper ("3rd complete American edition").

[1903]. 16 vols. Troy, N.Y.: Pafraets Book Co. ("Literary Club Edition"). Also issued in 8 vols., Cambridge, Mass.: Harvard Cooperative Society; New York: Bigelow, Smith, and Co. ("New Cambridge Edition").

2:6. *The Works of Samuel Johnson, LL.D. . . .* 9 vols. London: William Pickering; Oxford: Talboys and Wheeler, 1825 (Oxford English Classics). Supplementary Vols. X and XI contain the Debates in Parliament. Essentially Chalmers's 1823 edition, though with the useful addition of the *Sermons*, only two of which were printed in the 1823 edition. The legend that this is the "best" of the earlier editions was created by W. T.

Lowndes, who in his *Bibliographer's Manual*, 1834, put it at the head
of his list of editions and described it as having been "carefully edited
and re-arranged." In fact, most of its editorial annotation was taken over
from Chalmers; and Lowndes's reviser, Henry Bohn, candidly explains,
"Lowndes has placed this edition first in compliment to his publisher"—
Pickering, also the publisher of Lowndes's *Manual*. Facsimile reprint,
New York: AMS Press, 1968. The edition "was superintended by Francis
Pearson Walesby" (see item 1/1:12).

2:7. *The Works of Samuel Johnson. I, Rasselas.* [No more published?] London: Routledge; New York: Dutton, [1905]. (New Universal Library.)

*2:8. The Yale Edition of the Works of Samuel Johnson. General ed., Allen
T. Hazen; from 1966, John H. Middendorf. New Haven, Conn.: Yale University Press, 1958–.

Vol. I. *Diaries, Prayers, Annals*, ed. E. L. McAdam, Jr., with Donald and
Mary Hyde. 1958. 2nd ed. (rev.), 1960.

Vol. II. *The Idler* and *The Adventurer*, ed. W. J. Bate, J. M. Bullitt, and L.
F. Powell. 1963.

Vols. III, IV, V. *The Rambler*, ed. W. J. Bate. Textual ed., Albrecht
Strauss. 1969.

Vol. VI. *The Poems*, ed. E. L. McAdam, Jr., with George Milne. 1964.

Vols. VII, VIII. *Johnson on Shakespeare*, ed. Arthur Sherbo, with introduction by Bertrand H. Bronson. 1968.

FORTHCOMING VOLUMES INCLUDE:

A Journey to the Western Islands of Scotland, ed. Mary Lascelles.
Political Writings, ed. Donald J. Greene.
Debates in Parliament, ed. Benjamin B. Hoover.
Sermons, ed. Jean H. Hagstrum and James Gray.
Others are in preparation or planned.

SELECTIONS

*2:10. *Miscellaneous and Fugitive Pieces.* 2 vols. London: T. Davies, 1773.
2nd ed., 1774. Vol. III, London: T. Davies . . . and Carnan and Newbery, 1774. This unauthorized collection of early pieces by Johnson (and
others)—undoubtedly inspired by Johnson's introduction to the *Harleian
Miscellany*, "An Essay on the Origin and Importance of Small Tracts and
Fugitive Pieces"—was of great importance in preserving and establishing
the canon of Johnson's journalistic work. An analysis of the authorship of
the individual pieces in the collection was published in *GM*, November
1774 (item 1/1:1). Thomas Tyers's copy of the collection, annotated with
his own attributions of their authorship—not substantially different from
those of *GM*—is in the British Museum (shelf mark 12270. aaaa. 17).

2:11. [Cooke, William, supposed ed.] *The Beauties of Johnson, consisting of maxims and observations, moral, critical, and miscellaneous, by Dr. Samuel Johnson (accurately extracted from his works and arranged in alphabetical order after the manner of the Duke de la Roche-Foucault's Maxims)*. London: G. Kearsley, 1781. Many later, enlarged editions. See Allen T. Hazen, "The *Beauties of Johnson*," *MP*, XXXV (February 1938), 289–95. The 5th ed. (1782) contains "Memoirs of the Life and Writings of Dr. Samuel Johnson," probably by Cooke. See item 3:17.

2:12. Callender, James Thomson. *Deformities of Dr. Samuel Johnson. Selected from His Works*. Edinburgh: Creech; London: Longman and Stockdale, 1782. 2nd ed., 1782 (with preface dated "Edinburgh, Nov. 21, 1782"). Formerly attributed to John Callender (see item 5:370). Attacks chiefly the *Dictionary*, though it begins with a general attack on Johnson.

2:13. *The Life of Johnson: with Maxims and Observations, Critical and Miscellaneous, Accurately Selected from the Works of Dr. Samuel Johnson and Arranged in Alphabetical Order*. Boston: Marsh, Capel, and Lynn, and H. C. Greene, 1834. "Life" is an abridgment of Murphy's *Essay* (item 3:31); selections correspond to *The Beauties of Johnson*.

2:14. *The Life and Writings of Samuel Johnson, LL.D.*, selected and arranged by the Rev. William P. Page. 2 vols. (Harper's Family Library, Nos. CIX, CX.) New York: Harper and Brothers, 1840 (and later editions). The "life" is Murphy's *Essay* (erroneously attributed in 1st ed. to "Gifford"). The selections are chiefly from the periodical essays, chosen for their concern with "the moral amendment of the heart."

2:15. *Wisdom and Genius of Samuel Johnson*, selected from his prose writings by W. A. Clouston. (Library of Thoughtful Books.) London: Blackwood, [1875].

2:16. Hay, James. *Johnson: His Characteristics and Aphorisms*. Paisley and London: Alexander Gardner, 1884. The "Aphorisms" (pp. 9–173) are chosen from both Johnson's works and conversation, and classified by topic.

2:17. *Wit and Wisdom of Samuel Johnson*, selected by G. B. Hill. Oxford: Clarendon Press, 1888. Discussed by Walter Besant in *Spectator*, LXI (March 10, 1888), 357–58.

2:18. *Samuel Johnson*. (Little Masterpieces Series, ed. William Stead, Jr.) London: Masterpiece Press, 1905.

2:19. *Selections from Samuel Johnson*. (Arnold Prose Books, No. 7.) London: Edward Arnold & Co., [1905].

2:20. *Wit and Wisdom of Dr. Johnson and His Friends: A Calendar for 1909* [Christmas present of A. Edward Newton]. Philadelphia: Stern, 1908.

2:21. *Wit and Sagacity of Dr. Johnson*, selected by Norman J. Davidson. London: Seeley, 1909.

2:22. *Selections from the Works of Samuel Johnson*, ed. Charles G. Osgood. New York: Henry Holt & Co., 1909; London: George Bell & Sons, 1910.

2:23. *Samuel Johnson: Extracts from His Writings*, ed. Alice Meynell and G. K. Chesterton. (Regent Library.) London: Herbert and Daniel, 1911. Chesterton's preface reprinted in *G. K. C. as M. C.*, pp. 63–75, London: Methuen & Co., 1929.

2:24. *The Johnson Calendar: Or Samuel Johnson for Every Day in the Year*, ed. Alexander M. Bell. Oxford: Clarendon Press, 1916. Reviewed by J. C. Squire, *New Statesman*, January 20, 1917, p. 375.

2:25. *Johnson, Prose and Poetry*, ed. R. W. Chapman. (Clarendon Series of English Literature.) Oxford: Clarendon Press, 1922, and frequently reissued.

2:26. *Samuel Johnson: Writer*, ed. S. C. Roberts. New York: Dial Press; London: Herbert Jenkins, 1926.

2:27. *Selections from Johnson*, ed. W. Vaughan Reynolds. (Selected English Classics Series.) London: Ginn and Co., [1936].

2:28. *The Reader's Johnson*, ed. C. H. Conley. New York: American Book Co., 1940.

2:29. *The Portable Johnson and Boswell*, ed. Louis Kronenberger. New York: Viking Press, 1947.

2:30. *Dr. Johnson: Some Observations and Judgements upon Life and Letters*, chosen by John Hayward. London: Zodiac Books, 1948.

2:31. *The Wisdom of Dr. Johnson*, comp. Constantia Maxwell. London: George G. Harrap & Co., 1948.

2:32. *Selected Writings of Samuel Johnson*, ed. Julian Symons. London: Falcon Press, 1949.

2:33. *Johnson* [a full selection of 961 pages], selected by Mona Wilson. (The Reynard Library.) London: Rupert Hart-Davis, 1950. Textual editor, John Crow (text usually that of 1st ed.). Reviewed by Gwin J. Kolb, *MP*, XLIX (August 1951), 70–72.

2:34. *Selected Prose and Poetry*, ed. with introduction and notes by Bertrand H. Bronson. (Rinehart Editions.) New York: Rinehart and Co., 1952. Enl. ed., *Rasselas, Poems, and Selected Prose*, 1958.

2:35. *Selections from Samuel Johnson, 1709–1784*, ed. R. W. Chapman. London: Oxford University Press, 1955. Reprinted in World's Classics, 1962.

2:36. *A Johnson Sampler: Selections from Samuel Johnson*, ed. Henry Darcy Curwen. Cambridge, Mass.: Harvard University Press, 1963.

2:37. *A Johnson Reader*, ed. E. L. McAdam, Jr., and George Milne. New York: Pantheon Books, 1964.

2:38. *A Johnson Selection*, ed. F. R. Miles. London: Macmillan; New York: St. Martin's Press, 1965.

2:39. *Samuel Johnson: Selected Writings*, ed. with introduction and notes by R. T. Davies. London: Faber and Faber; Evanston, Ill.: Northwestern University Press, 1965.

2:40. *Rasselas and Essays*, ed. Charles Peake. (Routledge English Texts series.) London: Routledge and Kegan Paul, 1967.

2:41. *Samuel Johnson: Selected Writings*, ed. Patrick Cruttwell. (Penguin English Library.) London: Penguin Books, 1968.

ANTHOLOGIES OF EIGHTEENTH-CENTURY WRITING CONTAINING
SECTIONS BY JOHNSON (A SELECTION)

2:70. *English Prose*, ed. Henry Craik, IV, 135–85. London: Macmillan, 1894.

2:71. *Readings in English Prose of the Eighteenth Century*, ed. Raymond M. Alden, pp. 341–409. Boston: Houghton Mifflin Co., 1911.

2:72. *The Oxford Book of Eighteenth Century Verse*, chosen by D. Nichol Smith, pp. 320–30. Oxford: Clarendon Press, 1926.

2:73. *An Anthology of English Poetry: Dryden to Blake*, ed. Kathleen Campbell. London: Gerald Duckworth & Co., 1930.

2:74. *A Collection of English Poems, 1660–1800*, ed. Ronald S. Crane, pp. 667–77. New York: Harper and Brothers, 1932.

2:75. *Eighteenth Century Prose*, ed. Louis I. Bredvold, R. K. Root, and George Sherburn, pp. 439–564. New York: Thomas Nelson & Sons, 1933.

2:76. *English Poems from Dryden to Blake*, ed. James W. Tupper, pp. 595–618. New York: Prentice-Hall, 1933.

2:77. *English Prose of the Eighteenth Century*, ed. Cecil A. Moore, pp. 505–83. New York: Henry Holt & Co., 1933.

2:78. *English Prose and Poetry, 1660–1800*, ed. Odell Shepard and Paul Spencer Wood, pp. 606–44. Boston: Houghton Mifflin Co., 1934.

2:79. *English Poetry of the Eighteenth Century*, ed. Cecil A. Moore, pp. 558–74. New York: Henry Holt & Co., 1935.

2:80. *Eighteenth Century Poetry and Prose*, ed. Louis I. Bredvold, A. D. McKillop, and Lois Whitney, pp. 678–752. New York: Thomas Nelson & Sons, 1939. 2nd ed., 1956.

2:81. *English Literature, 1650–1800*, ed. John C. Mendenhall, pp. 714–86. Philadelphia: J. B. Lippincott Co., 1940.

2:82. *A Varied Company: An Eighteenth Century Anthology*, ed. M. M. Cowling. Melbourne: Melbourne University Press, 1946.

2:83. *Enlightened England*, ed. Wylie Sypher, pp. 700–757. New York: W. W. Norton & Co., 1947.

2:84. *The Pelican Book of English Prose*, Vol. III: *Eighteenth-Century*

Prose, 1700–1780, ed. D. W. Jefferson [numerous short excerpts]. Harmondsworth, Middlesex: Penguin Books, 1956.

2:85. *A Collection of English Prose, 1660–1800,* ed. Henry Pettit, pp. 295–368. New York: Harper, 1962.

2:86. *Eighteenth-Century English Literature,* ed. Geoffrey Tillotson, Paul Fussell, Jr., Marshall Waingrow, pp. 967–1130. New York: Harcourt, Brace and World, 1969.

2:87. *Major English Writers of the Eighteenth Century,* ed. Harold E. Pagliaro, pp. 717–833. New York: Free Press; London: Collier-Macmillan, 1969.

3. BIOGRAPHY

Separate Biographies and Miscellaneous Biographical Information

3:1. R., W. [William Rider.] "Mr. Johnson," *An Historical and Critical Account of the Lives and Writings of the Living Authors of Great Britain,* pp. 7–10. London, 1762.

3:2. Baker, David Erskine. "Mr. Samuel Johnson, M.A.," *The Companion to the Play-House,* II, S6ᵛ–T1ᵛ. London: Becket and Dehondt, 1764. New ed. [Isaac Reed, ed.], *Biographia Dramatica,* I, 256–58. London: Rivington, etc., 1782. New ed. [Stephen Jones, ed.], II, 406–10. London, 1812.

3:3. "A Short Character of Dr. Johnson," *London Magazine,* XLII (March 1773), 109–10. Reprinted in *Scots Magazine,* XXXV (March 1773), 133–34.

3:4. [Tytler, James?] "An Account of the Life, and Writings of Dr. Samuel Johnson," *Gentleman and Lady's Weekly Magazine* (Edinburgh), January 28, 1774.

3:5. "Character of Dr. Johnson, and His Writings; from Original Letters by a Young American in London to His Friend in America," *Weekly Magazine* (Edinburgh), XXV (July 7, 1774), 43–45.

3:6. "An Impartial Account of the Life, Character, Genius, and Writings of Dr. Samuel Johnson," *Westminster Magazine,* II (September 1774), 443–46.

3:7. L. "Memoirs of the Life and Writings of Dr. Samuel Johnson," *Universal Magazine,* LXXV (August 1784), 89–97. Reprinted in *Boston Magazine,* May 1785, pp. 172–76; June, pp. 209–12; July, pp. 249–51.

3:8. "Sketch of the Life and Writings of the Late Dr. Johnson," *London Chronicle,* December 14–16, 1784, pp. 577–78; December 16–18, pp. 585–86. Reprinted in *The Craftsman; or Say's Weekly Journal,* December 18, 25; *Town and Country Magazine,* XVI (December 1784), 619–23; (Supplement), 707–10, and other periodicals. Largely derivative from item 3:7.

3:9. [Obituary of Johnson], *GM*, LIV (December 1784), 957–58. Includes report of autopsy.

3:10. T., T. [Thomas Tyers.] "A Biographical Sketch of Dr. Samuel Johnson," *GM*, LIV (December 1784), 899–911; (Supplement), 982; "Additions," LV (February 1785), 85–87. Issued with revisions as a pamphlet, *A Biographical Sketch of Dr. Samuel Johnson*, London, 1785. Reprint of copy of pamphlet with marginal annotations by Tyers and introduction by Gerald D. Meyer, Los Angeles: Augustan Reprint Society, 1952 (Publication No. 34).

3:11. "Johnsoniana," *European Magazine*, VII (January 1785), 51–55. "Of various anecdotes of Dr. Johnson which have been in the public papers, we select the present Collection, as we have every reason to rely on their authenticity." Earlier published in *St. James's Chronicle*, January 13–15, 1785. Often attributed to George Steevens.

3:12. Nichols, John. [Letter transmitting anecdotes (by Anna Seward) about Johnson's early life and about Michael Johnson], *GM*, LV (February 1785), 99–101.

3:13. [Sharp, John.] [Extract from a letter describing Johnson's visit to Cambridge in March, 1765], *GM*, LV (March 1785), 173–74. Reprinted in Boswell, *Life*, ed. G. B. Hill (1887), I, 487–88 (Appendix C); ed. Hill-Powell (1934), I, 517–18.

3:14. [Miscellaneous anecdotes of Johnson], *GM*, LV (April 1785), 288.

3:15. Greene, Richard. Letter to "Mr. Urban," *GM*, LV (July 1785), 495–97. Biographical information on Johnson at Lichfield.

3:16. Boswell, James. *A Journal of a Tour to the Hebrides, with Samuel Johnson, LL.D.* London, 1785. See item 4:12.

3:17. [Cooke, William.] *The Life of Samuel Johnson, with occasional remarks on his writings. . . . To which are added, some papers written by Dr. Johnson, in behalf of a late unfortunate character* [Rev. William Dodd], *never before published.* London: Kearsley, 1785. (But advertised for sale in December 1784.) See item 2:11.

3:18. [Shaw, William.] *Memoirs of the Life and Writings of . . . Samuel Johnson, containing . . . original letters and . . . anecdotes both of his literary and social connections. The whole authenticated by living evidence.* London: J. Walker, 1785. The "living evidence" is said in the preface to include "his servants, Mrs. Du Maulin . . . several others of most intimate acquaintance . . . Mr. Thomas Davies . . . the most valuable communications are from Mr. Elphinston."

3:19. J., S. Letter to "Mr. Urban," *GM*, LVI (September 1786), 729. Contains anecdote of Johnson's charity to a poverty-stricken boy.

3:20. D.I., I. [Isaac D'Israeli.] "Remarks on the Biographical Accounts of the Late Samuel Johnson, LL.D., with an Attempt to Vindicate His Character from Late Misrepresentation," *GM*, LVI (Supplement 1786), 1123–27.

3:21. Harrison, James. "The Life of Dr. Samuel Johnson. By Mr. Harrison," in Johnson, *A Dictionary of the English Language*, [ed. James Harrison], pp. [1–18] at beginning of volume. London: Harrison and Co., 1786. Little more than an abridgement of Hawkins's *Life* (item 3:27), notwithstanding date on title page.

3:22. Piozzi, Hester Lynch (Mrs. Thrale). *Anecdotes of the Late Samuel Johnson, LL.D., during the last twenty years of his life.* London: Cadell, 1786. Reviewed in *English Review*, VII (April 1786), 254–59; by Charles Burney in *Monthly Review*, LXXIV (May 1786), 373–83. Other editions 1822; 1826; 1831; 1835; 1856; 1884 (in *Johnsoniana*, item 3:108); 1887 (ed. Henry Morley); 1897 (in item 3:116); 1925 (ed. S. C. Roberts, Cambridge University Press; reviewed by R. W. Chapman, *RES*, I [July 1925], 372–73); 1932.

3:23. Towers, Joseph. *An Essay on the Life, Character, and Writings of Dr. Samuel Johnson.* London: Dilly, 1786.

3:24. "Johnsoniana," ["collected from Mrs. Piozzi, Mr. Boswell and from oral testimony"], *European Magazine*, XI (March 1787), 197–99; (April), 260–63.

3:25. Occasional Correspondent. Letter to "Mr. Urban," *GM*, LVII (June 1787), 475–76. Suggests "a dissertation on the influence of poverty and distress on the conduct of the Christian and the philosopher," as illustrated by Johnson's life. Defends him against charges of brutality.

3:26. C., D. "Anecdotes," *GM*, LVII (December 1787), 1165. Johnson on Mallet; infection contracted by a surgeon at Johnson's autopsy.

3:27. Hawkins, Sir John. *The Life of Samuel Johnson, LL.D.* London: Buckland, etc., 1787. Vol. I of *The Works of Samuel Johnson*, 1787. 2nd ed., corrected, 1787. Ed. Bertram H. Davis (slightly abr.), New York: Macmillan, 1961. Extracts in item 3:116. Reviewed (savagely) by Arthur Murphy, *Monthly Review*, LXXVI (April 1787), 273–92; (May), 369–84; LXXVII (July 1787), 56–70; (August), 131; (sarcastically) by Richard Porson ("Sundry Whereof"), *GM*, LVII (August 1787), 652–53; (September), 751–53; (October), 847–52. For other attacks see item 3:207.

3:28. Mawbey, Sir Joseph. "Anecdotes of Mr. Thomas Cooke, the Poet" ["Hesiod" Cooke], *GM*, LXI (Supplement 1791), 1183–85. Anecdotes of Johnson.

3:29. Boswell, James. *The Life of Samuel Johnson, LL.D.* London, 1791. See item 4:14.

3:30. Grose, Francis. "Doctor Johnson," *The Olio*, pp. 161–62. London: S. Hooper, 1792. Anecdotes: Johnson in Gough Square; Johnson and Strahan. See also item 17:17.

3:31. Murphy, Arthur. *An Essay on the Life and Genius of Samuel Johnson.* London: Longman, etc., 1792. Also printed in Vol. I of Johnson's *Works*, 1792, and most subsequent editions of the *Works*. Reprinted in *Johnsoniana*, 1884 (item 3:108) and *Johnsonian Miscellanies*, 1897 (item 3: 116).

3:32. Henn, J. [Johnson and Appleby School], *GM*, LXIII (May 1793), 408.

3:33. Anderson, Robert. *The Life of Samuel Johnson, with critical observations on his works.* London: J. and A. Arch, 1795. Also issued as "The Life of Johnson," in Robert Anderson, ed., *The Works of the British Poets, with Prefaces, Biographical and Critical*, XI, 779–836, London: J. and A. Arch, 1795. "Third edition" (rev. and enl.), Edinburgh: Doig and Stirling, etc., 1815.

3:34. "Johnson, Samuel, LL.D.," *A New and General Biographical Dictionary*, VI, 365–66. London: Robinson, etc., 1795. New ed., 1798, VIII, 442–51. By Alexander Chalmers? See also item 3:51.

*3:35. [Gleig, George.] "Samuel Johnson," in *Encyclopaedia Britannica*, 3rd ed., [1788–]97, IX, 296–300. A long, intelligent, and appreciative account—13 columns to Ben Jonson's half column. Repeated with little change in subsequent editions until replaced in the 8th by Macaulay's prejudiced one (item 3:92).

3:36. Anecdotist. [Small notes on Boswell's *Life*], *GM*, LXVII (Supplement 1797), 1110–11.

3:37. "Life of Johnson . . . compiled principally from the voluminous details of Boswell, Piozzi, and Murphy, with the addition of some few particulars unnoticed by any of his biographers," in item 7:1 (1798), I, 323–29.

3:38. B., H. [Account of a journey with Johnson on the Salisbury stage in 1783], *Monthly Magazine*, V (February 1798), 81. Reprinted in item 3:75, pp. 441–42.

3:39. Gee, James. [Anecdotes of Johnson in Lichfield], *GM*, LXIX (January 1799), 7.

3:40. "Narrative of What Passed at the Visits Paid by J. Hoole to Dr. Johnson in His Last Illness, Three Weeks before His Death," *European Magazine*, XXXV (September 1799), 153–58. MS now in Hyde collection.

3:41. H., R. [Anecdote of Walter Harte—Johnson's dining behind screen], *GM*, LXIX (December 1799), 1018–19.

3:42. Warner, Richard. *A Tour through the Northern Counties of England, and the Borders of Scotland*, I, 105. Bath: R. Cruttwell, 1802. The story of the penance in Uttoxeter market.

3:43. "Extracts from the Port-Folio of a Man of Letters," *Monthly Magazine*, XV, no. 2 (March 1803), 151. Anecdote of Johnson's meeting with Count de Holcke, 1768. Reprinted in item 3:75, p. 437.

3:44. Aikin, John. "Johnson, Samuel, LL.D.," *General Biography or, Lives, Critical and Historical*, V, 540–47. London: J. Johnson, etc., 1804. Acknowledges derivation from Hawkins, Boswell, and Murphy. Reprinted with Johnson, *A Dictionary of the English Language . . . 9th ed. corrected and revised*, London: Longman, etc., 1805.

3:45. *An Account of the Life of Dr. Samuel Johnson from his birth to his eleventh year, written by himself. To which are added, original letters to Dr. Samuel Johnson by Miss Hill Boothby: from the mss. preserved by the doctor; and now in the possession of Richard Wright*. London: Phillips, Nichols, 1805. Reviewed (severely) in *Edinburgh Review*, VII (January 1806), 436–41—for doubtful ascription of review to either Henry Brougham or Francis Jeffrey, see Walter E. Houghton, ed., *The Wellesley Index of Victorian Periodicals*, I, 438. "Account" ("Annals") reprinted in items 2:8, Vol. I, and 3:116.

3:46. Blagdon, F. W. "Life of Dr. Johnson," in item 14:2, pp. 1–16.

3:47. Cumberland, Richard. *Memoirs* [references to Johnson, pp. 173–78 and *passim*]. London: Lackington, Allen, & Co., 1806. Also New York and Boston editions.

3:48. Harwood, Thomas. [A short sketch of Johnson in item 7:2, 1806]. Apparently Harwood's projected *Observations on the Writings and Genius of Dr. Johnson*, mentioned in a letter to Boswell of March 12, 1787 (see item 4:20, No. 426), was not published.

3:49. Le Noir, Elizabeth. *Village Anecdotes; or The Journal of a Year from Sophia to Edward*, 2nd ed., I, 238–40 and *passim*. Reading: Printed for the author, 1806. These anecdotes about Johnson were not included in the 1st ed., London, 1804. See also items 3:154 and 3:216.

3:50. Stockdale, Percival. *Memoirs of the Life and Writings of Percival Stockdale, Containing Many Interesting Anecdotes of the Illustrious Men with Whom He Was Connected. Written by Himself.* 2 vols. London: Longman, Hurst, 1809. Much about Johnson.

3:51. Chalmers, Alexander. "The Life of Samuel Johnson," *The Works of the English Poets, from Chaucer to Cowper*, XVI, 549–70. London: J. Johnson, etc., 1810. An adaptation is in *General Biographical Dictionary*, XIX, 47–77, London: Robinson, 1815. See item 3:34.

3:52. [Anecdotes], *European Magazine*, LVII (January 1810), 22–23. Johnson at dinner at the Royal Academy with Savoi, the opera singer; his huge consumption of lemonade.

3:53. Seward, Anna. *Letters of Anna Seward Written Between the Years 1784 and 1807*, [ed. Archibald Constable]. 6 vols. Edinburgh: Constable, 1811. Many anecdotes of Johnson's youth, not always reliable. The letters were heavily rewritten before publication; see item 5:266.

3:54. *Instructive Conversation Cards Consisting of Thirty-Two Biographi-*

cal Sketches of Eminent British Characters. London, 1815. No. 26 is Johnson.

3:55. "Doctor Johnson," *Buds of Genius; or, Some Account of the Early Lives of Celebrated Characters Who Were Remarkable in Their Childhood. Intended as Introduction to Biography,* pp. 45–49. London: Darton, Harvey, and Darton, 1816. In dialogue form; intended for the instruction of children.

3:56. Wrangham, Francis. "Samuel Johnson," *The British Plutarch,* VI, 301–45. London: J. Mawman, etc., 1816. Pp. 345–63 contain a few short extracts from Johnson's writings.

3:57. Bingley, William. "Twenty-Fifth Evening" [Samuel Johnson], *Biographical Conversations, on the Most Eminent and Instructive British Characters . . . ,* pp. 187–201. London: John Sharpe, 1818.

3:58. W——R [Charles-Athanase, baron Walckenaer]. "Johnson (Samuel)," *Biographie Universelle, Ancienne et Moderne,* XXI, 588–97. Paris: L. G. Michaud, 1818.

3:59. S., F. I. "Two Anecdotes," *European Magazine,* LXXIII (April 1818), 324–25. Incidents at Dr. McQueen's and Mrs. Thrale's.

3:60. W. "Original Anecdote of Dr. Samuel Johnson," *European Magazine,* LXXIV (September 1818), 231–32. While visiting Colonel Myddleton of Gwaynynog.

3:61. Ferguson, James. "Historical and Biographical Preface to the Rambler," *The British Essayists,* XIX, [ix]–lxviii. London: G. Offer, etc., 1819.

3:62. "Silva. No. II," *European Magazine,* LXXV (April 1819), 294. Anecdote—Johnson on labor.

3:63. "Life of Dr. Johnson, with Portrait," *Port Folio* (Philadelphia), 4th ser., X (September 1820), 148–63. Largely compiled from Chalmers's and Anderson's *Lives.*

3:64. Singer, Samuel Weller. "The Life of Samuel Johnson, LL.D.," *The British Poets,* Vol. LXVII. Chiswick: Whittingham, 1822.

3:65. Cary, Henry Francis. "Life and Writings of Dr. Johnson," *London Magazine,* VII (July 1823), 57–69; (August), 169–85. Reprinted in his *Lives of English Poets from Johnson to Kirke White, designed as a continuation of Johnson's Lives,* pp. 1–93. London: H. G. Bohn, 1846.

3:66. Hawkins, Laetitia Matilda. *Anecdotes, Biographical Sketches, and Memoirs.* London: Rivington, 1823. *Memoirs, Anecdotes, Facts, and Opinions,* London: Longmans, 1824. Selections from both works reprinted as *Gossip about Dr. Johnson and Others,* ed. Francis H. Skrine, London: Nash and Grayson, 1926. Extracts reprinted in items 3:75 and 3:116.

3:67. Scott, Sir Walter. "Prefatory Memoir to Johnson" [prefaced to *Ras-*

selas], *Ballantyne's Novelist's Library*, V, xl–xlvi. London: Hurst, Robinson, 1823. Reprinted in Scott, *The Lives of the Novelists*, 2 vols., Paris: A. and W. Galignani, 1825. Often reprinted, e.g., in World's Classics, London: Oxford University Press, [1906]; and in Everyman's Library, London: Dent; New York: Dutton, [1910].

3:68. Servois, Jean Pierre. *Notice sur la Vie et les Ouvrages du Docteur Samuel Johnson*. Cambrai: A. F. Hurez, 1823. Appreciative.

3:69. Lynam, Robert. "Biographical, Historical, and Critical Preface [to *The Rambler*]," *The British Essayists*, XII, [vi]–lxxix. London: J. Dove, 1827.

3:70. Cradock, Joseph. *Literary and Miscellaneous Memoirs*. 4 vols. London: Printed for the author by J. Nichols and Son, 1828. Many Johnsonian anecdotes, especially in Vols. I and IV.

3:71. Smith, John Thomas. *Nollekens and His Times*. London: H. Colburn, 1829. Reprinted, ed. Wilfred Whitten, 2 vols., London: John Lane, 1917; Oxford University Press, 1929 (World's Classics); Turnstile Press, 1949. Many anecdotes of Johnson.

3:72. Broughton, James. [Anecdotes of Dr. Johnson's father], *GM*, XCIX (October 1829), 312–14. Abbreviated biography of Johnson's father included.

3:73. Taylor, John [grandson of "Chevalier Taylor" the oculist]. *Records of My Life*. 2 vols. London: L. Bull, 1832. Johnson, I, 231–35, and *passim*; Boswell, I, 214–16. Much amusing gossip about them and their contemporaries.

3:74. Cunningham, George Godfrey, ed. "Samuel Johnson," *Lives of Eminent and Illustrious Englishmen from Alfred the Great to the Latest Times*, VI, 120–32. Glasgow: A. Fullarton, 1836. New ed., *A History of England . . . in the Lives of Englishmen*, London and Edinburgh: A. Fullarton, 1853.

*3:75. *Johnsoniana; or Supplement to Boswell; Being Anecdotes and Sayings of Dr. Johnson*. London: Murray, 1836. A very comprehensive and useful collection of contemporary accounts, including some sources not found in item 3:116. Most of them occur in Croker's ed. of Boswell's *Life*, 1831 (item 4:14), and were segregated as Vols. IX and X of Wright's revision of this, 1835. The illustrations are those of item 8:21. New ed., "revised and enlarged by John Wright," London: H. G. Bohn, 1859.

3:76. Malden, H. "Johnson," *Distinguished Men of Modern Times*, III, 352–63. (Library of Entertaining Knowledge. Under the Superintendence of the Society for the Diffusion of Useful Knowledge.) London: Charles Knight, 1838.

3:77. "The Life of Samuel Johnson," *Englishman's Magazine*, II (May 1842), 97–107.

3:78. Smith, John Thomas. *A Book for a Rainy Day*. London: R. Bentley, 1845. Reprinted, ed. Wilfred Whitten, London: Methuen, [1905].

*3:79. Brougham and Vaux, Henry Brougham, 1st Baron. "Johnson," *Lives of Men of Letters and Science Who Flourished in the Time of George III*, II, 1–85. London: C. Knight and Co., 1846. Intelligent criticism and psychological analysis.

3:80. Russell, John Francis. *The Life of Dr. Samuel Johnson*. London: James Burns, 1847. Derivative.

3:81. [Roche, James.] "Johnson, His Contemporaries and Biographers," *Dublin Review*, XXIII (September 1847), 203–28. Reprinted in *Critical and Miscellaneous Essays. By an Octogenarian*, II, 312–48, Cork: Privately printed by G. Nashe, 1851. A review of items 3:79 and 3:80.

3:82. "Samuel Johnson," *Biographical Sketches of Eminent British Poets, Intended for Teachers and the Higher Classes in Schools*, pp. 326–49. Dublin: Commissioners on National Education in Ireland, 1849.

3:83. Frost, John. "Samuel Johnson," *Lives of Eminent Christians*, pp. 323–31. Hartford: Case, Tiffany, and Co., 1850. Reprinted in *Cyclopedia of Eminent Christians*, New York: World, 1875.

3:84. Barker, Edmund Henry. *Literary Anecdotes and Contemporary Reminiscences, of Professor Porson and Others*, I, 1–2, 46–49; II, 8. London: J. R. Smith, 1852. Johnson and Robert Potter; criticism of Croker's Boswell; Johnson on Milton.

3:85. "Life and Times of Johnson," *National Magazine* (New York), I (November 1852), 393–401; (December), 488–95; II (January 1853), 9–15; (February), 107–12; (March), 206–12; (April), 320–31; (May), 454–63; (June), 488–98; III (July), 18–28; (August), 120–27; (September), 202–11; (October), 295–307.

3:86. Edgar, John George. "Dr. Johnson," in *The Boyhood of Great Men: Intended as an Example to Youth*, pp. 46–58. London: David Bogue, 1853; New York: Harper, 1855.

3:87. "Samuel Johnson," *Biographical Magazine*, IV (1853), 1–12. Reprinted as *Lives of the Illustrious*, London: Partridge and Co., 1856.

*3:88. Campbell, Thomas. *Diary of a Visit to England in 1775, by an Irishman*, ed. Samuel Raymond. Sydney: Waugh and Cox, 1854. Reviewed by Henry Reeve in *Edinburgh Review*, CX (October 1859), 322–42. Ed. from MS as *Dr. Campbell's Diary of a Visit to England in 1775* by James L. Clifford, with introduction by S. C. Roberts, Cambridge: Cambridge University Press, 1947. Reviewed by R. W. Chapman, *RES*, XXIV (July 1948), 256–58. See also David Woolley, "Dr. Campbell's 'Diary,' 1775" [a physical description of the MS], *N&Q*, CXCII (November 27, 1948), 517–19. Extracts in item 3:116.

3:89. Cooper, Thomas. "Johnson," *The Triumphs of Perseverance and Enterprise*, pp. 35–44. New York: Evans and Dickerson, 1854.

3:90. Gilfillan, George. "Memoir" [of Johnson], in item 14:3 (1855), pp. [3]–16. Reprinted in his *Galleries of Literary Portraits*, II, 217–26, Edinburgh: J. Hogg, 1857.

3:91. Hazlitt, William, [Jr.]. "Samuel Johnson," *Johnson's Lives of the British Poets. Completed by William Hazlitt*, IV, 70–93. London: Nathaniel Cooke, 1854.

3:92. Macaulay, Thomas Babington. "Samuel Johnson," *Encyclopaedia Britannica*, 8th ed. (1856), XII, 793–804. Revised for 11th ed. (1910) by Thomas Seccombe. Bibliography supplied by S. C. Roberts for 14th ed. (1929). Separately printed, ed. D. Nichol Smith, Edinburgh: William Blackwood and Sons, 1900. Many other editions. See items 3:35 and 3:213.

3:93. *Answers to Mr. Macaulay's Criticism in the Edinburgh Review on Mr. Croker's Edition of Boswell's Life of Johnson.* London, 1856. Not seen; listed in item 1/4:8, p. 13.

3:94. Reynald, Hermile. *Samuel Johnson: Étude sur sa vie et sur ses principaux ouvrages.* Thesis in Lettres, University of Paris. Paris: Durand, 1856.

3:95. Rogers, Samuel. *Recollections of the Table-Talk of Samuel Rogers. To Which Is Added Porsoniana*, [ed. Alexander Dyce], pp. 9–10, 326–27. London: Edward Moxon, 1856. Miscellaneous anecdotes.

3:96. Elwin, Whitwell. "Boswell—Early Life of Johnson," *Quarterly Review*, CII (April 1858), 279–328. Reprinted (rev.) as "Boswell" in his *Some XVIII Century Men of Letters*, II, 237–266, London: John Murray, 1902. "Review" of Boswell's *Letters to Temple*; Croker's ed. of Boswell's *Life* (1847); *Boswelliana* (1856).

3:97. Elwin, Whitwell. "Life and Writings of Johnson," *Quarterly Review*, CV (January 1859), 176–233. Reprinted (rev.) as "Dr. Johnson" in his *Some XVIII Century Men of Letters*, II, 267–445, London: John Murray, 1902.

3:98. Knight, [Ellis] Cornelia. *Autobiography of Miss Cornelia Knight, Lady Companion to the Princess Charlotte of Wales*, [ed. J. W. Kaye]. London: W. H. Allen, 1861. Chap. I has many anecdotes of Johnson and his circle.

3:99. Winsor, Henry. "Samuel Johnson," *Montrose and Other Biographical Sketches*, pp. 91–114. Boston: Soule and Williams, 1861.

3:100. Horton, W. I. S. "Dr. Johnson," *N&Q*, 3rd ser., II (November 15, 1862), 384. Parish register entry of Michael and Sarah Johnson's marriage.

3:101. Bates, William. "Michael Johnson of Lichfield: The First Book Printed at Birmingham: Wollaston, Author of *The Religion of Nature De-lineated*," *N&Q*, 3rd ser., IV (November 14, 1863), 388–89. Books printed by Michael Johnson; see also *ibid*, IV, 459, and V, 33.

3:102. [Hayman, Henry.] "The *MS* Journal of Captain E[dward] Thompson, R.N., 1783 to 1785," *Cornhill Magazine*, XVII (May 1868), 610–40. Reminiscences of Johnson in 1784; his death and funeral.

3:103. Jewitt, Llewellynn. "Marriage of Dr. Johnson," *N&Q*, 4th ser., VI (July 16, 1870), 44. Parish register entry at St. Werburgh's Derby.

3:104. Stephen, Leslie. *Samuel Johnson*. (English Men of Letters Series.) London: Macmillan, 1878, and later reprintings.

3:105. Twining, Thomas. *Recreations and Studies of a Country Clergyman of the Eighteenth Century*, ed. Richard Twining. London: Murray, 1882. Frequent references to Johnson, especially (pp. 128–29) a detailed account of his funeral.

3:106. Drake, Samuel Adams. "Samuel Johnson," *Our Great Benefactors: Short Biographies of the Men and Women Most Eminent in Literature, Science . . .* , pp. 43–46. Boston: Roberts Bros., 1884.

3:107. Macaulay, James. *Doctor Johnson: His Life, Works and Table Talk*. London: Fisher Unwin, 1884.

3:108. Napier, Robina (Mrs. Alexander), ed. *Johnsoniana*. London: George Bell, 1884. Vol. V of her husband's edition of Boswell's *Life*. Not so large a collection of non-Boswellian material as can be found in items 3:75 and 3:116.

3:109. M[azzinghi], T. J. "Dr. Johnson's Early Life," *N&Q*, 6th ser., X (November 29, 1884), 421–22. Letter from Dean Addenbrooke, commending Johnson as tutor to Thomas Whitby.

3:110. Bolton, Sarah K. "Dr. Samuel Johnson," *Lives of Poor Boys Who Became Famous*, pp. 83–89. New York: Thomas Y. Crowell Co., 1885, 1913, etc.

3:111. Dawson, George. "Dr. Samuel Johnson," *Biographical Lectures*, pp. 159–71. London: Kegan Paul, Trench, 1886.

3:112. Grant, Francis R. C. *Life of Samuel Johnson*. (Great Writers Series.) London: Walter Scott, 1887. Bibliography listed in item 1/1:13.

3:113. Udal, J. S. "Dr. Johnson's Funeral," *N&Q*, 7th ser., X (September 6, 1890), 186–87. See also Henry G. Hope, *ibid.*, October 4, 1890, p. 274.

3:114. Spofford, Harriet Prescott. "Sam Johnson's Boyhood," *Harper's Young People*, XII (November 4, 1890), 18–19.

3:115. Stephen, Leslie. "Samuel Johnson," in *Dictionary of National Biography*, ed. Sidney Lee, XXX, 31–47. London: Smith Elder, 1892.

*3:116. *Johnsonian Miscellanies* [includes numerous non-Boswellian accounts of Johnson], ed. G. B. Hill. 2 vols. Oxford: Clarendon Press, 1897. Reviewed by Leslie Stephen, *National Review*, XXX (September 1897),

61–76. Reprinted, London: Constable; New York: Barnes and Noble, 1966. See comment by J. D. Fleeman, *TLS*, August 24, 1967, p. 768.

3:117. Stephen, Leslie. "Johnsoniana" [largely a review of item 3:116], *Studies of a Biographer*, I, 105–46. London: Gerald Duckworth & Co., 1898.

3:118. "Dr. Johnson and His Century" [largely a review of item 10/6:106], *Spectator*, LXXXIII (July 22, 1899), 118. See also *Book Lover*, I (Winter 1900), 221–22.

3:119. Bouchier, Jonathan. "Samuel Johnson's Father and Elizabeth Blaney," *N&Q*, 9th ser., VI (July 7, 1900), 6–7. See also John T. Page, *ibid.*, August 4, 1900, p. 93.

3:120. Marston, Edward. "Michael Johnson," *Publisher's Circular*, August 3, 1901, p. 103. See also *ibid.*, July 13.

3:121. Luckock, H. M. *A Popular Sketch of Dr. Johnson's Life and Works.* Lichfield: Mercury Press; London: Simpkin, Marshall, 1902. Reprinted, 1923.

3:122. Cox, W. A. "Johnson: An Anecdote" [from recollections of Mrs. Stuart], *N&Q*, 9th ser., XI (May 2, 1903), 345–46.

3:123. Mortimer, Franklin C. "A Brief Account of the Early Life of Doctor Samuel Johnson" [talk before the Oliver Wendell Holmes Society, San Francisco], *The Autocrat: A Chronicle of the Oliver Wendell Holmes Society, San Francisco*, I (June 1903).

3:124. Rowbotham, Francis J. "Samuel Johnson," *Story-Lives of Great Authors*, pp. 11–87. London: Gardner Darton, 1904.

3:125. Reade, Aleyn Lyell. "Mary Shakespere" [Johnson's maternal ancestry], *N&Q*, 10th ser., II (July 30, 1904), 94.

3:126. Dennis, John. *Dr. Johnson.* (Bell's Miniature Series.) London: George Bell & Sons, 1905.

*3:127. Reade, Aleyn Lyell. *The Reades of Blackwood Hill . . . with a Full Account of Dr. Johnson's Ancestry.* London: Spottiswoode, 1906.

3:128. Shorter, Clement. "Dr. Johnson's Ancestry," *Immortal Memories*, pp. 157–82. London: Hodder & Stoughton, 1907.

3:129. Lloyd, C. A. "Dr. Johnson as a Potter," *N&Q*, 10th ser., VII (June 15, 1907), 468–69. See also items 3:174, 3:202.

3:130. Reade, Aleyn Lyell. "Dr. Johnson's Ancestors and Connections," *N&Q*, 10th ser., VIII (October 12–December 14, 1907), 281–83, 382–84, 462–64; IX (January 18–May 30, 1908), 43–46, 144–45, 302–4, 423–25; X (July 18–December 12, 1908), 44–46, 203–5, 343–44, 465–66; XI (February 6–June 12, 1909), 103–5, 223–24, 363–65, 463–65.

*3:131. Reade, Aleyn Lyell. *Johnsonian Gleanings* (privately printed for the author): Pt. I, *Notes on Dr. Johnson's Ancestors and Connexions, and Illustrative of His Early Life*, 1909; Pt. II, *Francis Barber, the Doctor's*

Negro Servant, 1912; Pt. III, *The Doctor's Boyhood*, 1922; Pt. IV, *The Doctor's Boyhood: Appendices*, 1923; Pt. V, *The Doctor's Life 1728–1735*, 1928; Pt. VI, *The Doctor's Life 1735–1740*, 1933; Pt. VII, *The Jervis, Porter and Other Allied Families*, 1935; Pt. VIII, *A Miscellany*, 1937; Pt. IX, *A Further Miscellany*, 1939; Pt. X, *Johnson's Early Life: The Final Narrative*, 1946; Pt. XI, *Consolidated Index of Persons, Parts I to X*, 1952. Reprinted, New York: Octagon Books, 1967. For an important estimate of the value of Reade's researches, see D. Nichol Smith, *Scottish Historical Review*, XX (January 1923), 142–44; XXI (July 1924), 312.

3:132. H., F. "Johnsonian Anecdotes and Relics" [not in Boswell], *N&Q*, 10th ser., XI (April 10, 1909), 281–82.

3:133. Axon, William E. A. "Dr. Johnson and Strahan's 'Virgil,' " *N&Q*, 10th ser., XII (July 31, 1909), 85–86. An account of Lord Buchan's meeting Johnson at Alexander Strahan's.

3:134. Sargisson, C. S. "Dr. Johnson's Ancestry: His Inheritance through His Mother," *Bookman* (London), XXXVI (September 1909), 261–66.

*3:135. Raleigh, Walter. "Johnson without Boswell" [the pre-Boswellian biographies], in item 10/6:146 (1910), pp. 40–74.

3:136. Roberts, S. C. *The Story of Doctor Johnson, Being an Introduction to Boswell's Life.* Cambridge: Cambridge University Press, 1919.

3:137. Reade, Aleyn Lyell. "Dr. Johnson and Stourbridge," in item 7:66 (1920), pp. 7–22.

3:138. Heiron, Arthur. "Was Dr. Sam¹ Johnson a Freemason?" *Ancient Freemasonry and the Old Dundee Lodge, No. 18*, pp. 208–19. London: Kenning, 1921.

3:139. Reade, Aleyn Lyell. "Dr. Johnson's Origins," *TLS*, January 6, 1921, p. 11.

3:140. Reade, Aleyn Lyell. "Dr. Johnson, His Fellow-Collegian, and the Shoes," *TLS*, February 10, 1921, p. 92.

3:141. Heiron, Arthur. "Was Dr. Johnson a Freemason?" *Masonic Record*, XII (1922), 887–90, (1923), 918–21; XIII (1923), 553–55, 982–83, 1009–13.

3:142. Gissing, Algernon. "Samuel Johnson's Academy" [at Edial], *Cornhill Magazine*, n.s., LIV (January 1923), 50–60.

3:143. Whitley, William T. "Farington's Diary" [an anecdote of Johnson], *TLS*, January 11, 1923, p. 29. See item 5:162.

3:144. Reade, Aleyn Lyell. "Dr. Johnson's Schemes of Study," *TLS*, September 18, 1924, p. 577.

3:145. Laithwaite, Percy. *A Short History of Lichfield Grammar School.* Lichfield: The Johnson's Head, 1925.

3:146. Biron, Sir Chartres. "Dr. Johnson's Romance," *National Review*,

LXXXV (May 1925), 416–20. Johnson fell in love with Lucy Porter before marrying her mother.

3:147. Letts, Malcolm. "Dr. Johnson Dines Out. The Record of a Strenuous Month" [April 1778], *Cornhill Magazine*, n.s., LIX (September 1925), 319–23.

*3:148. Gissing, Algernon. "Appleby School: An Extra-Illustration to Boswell" [important new evidence from old records], *Cornhill Magazine*, n.s., LX (April 1926), 404–14.

3:149. Reade, Aleyn Lyell. "Johnson's Ushership at Market Bosworth," *TLS*, June 10, 1926, p. 394.

3:150. Reade, Aleyn Lyell. "The Duration of Johnson's Residence at Oxford," *TLS*, September 16, 1926, pp. 615–16; September 15, 1927, p. 624.

3:151. MacKinnon, Frank D. "Samuel Johnson, Undergraduate," *Cornhill Magazine*, n.s., LXI (October 1926), 444–58. Reprinted in *The Murder in the Temple*, pp. 146–65, London: Sweet & Maxwell, 1935.

3:152. Bensly, Edward. "Riding Weddings" [Johnson's marriage], *N&Q*, CLII (May 28, 1927), 391–92. See also pp. 296, 337, 375.

3:153. Hollis, Christopher. *Dr. Johnson*. London: Gollancz, 1928; New York: Henry Holt & Co., 1929. Reviewed by R. W. Chapman, *TLS*, September 20, 1928, p. 663; F. A. Pottle, *SRL*, V (June 15, 1929), 1112.

3:154. Blunden, Edmund. "A Boswellian Error," *Times* (London), May 20, 1929, pp. 11–12. Reprinted as "New Light on Samuel Johnson," *Living Age*, CCCXXXVI (August 1929), 438–40. Anecdotes of Johnson by Elizabeth Le Noir, daughter of Christopher Smart. See items 3:49 and 3:216.

3:155. Reade, Aleyn Lyell. "Dr. Johnson's Lichfield Origins," *TLS*, June 27, 1929, p. 514.

3:156. Whibley, Leonard. "Dr. Johnson and the Universities," *Blackwood's Magazine*, CCXXVI (September 1929), 369–83.

*3:157. Laithwaite, Percy. "Dr. Johnson's Lichfield Forbears and Dr. Johnson's Academy" (Lynam Memorial Prize Essay), *Transactions of the North Staffs. Field Club*, LXVI (1932), 63–90.

3:158. Ward, J. L. "Dr. Johnson, the Jacobite" [was Johnson involved in the '45 rebellion?], *Chambers's Journal*, 8th ser., I (May 1932), 372–74.

3:159. Talbot, William. "Birmingham's First Bookseller" [Michael Johnson], *Publisher's Circular and Bookseller's Record*, CXXXVII (December 17, 1932), 719.

3:160. Ishida, Kenji. *Dr. Johnson and His Circle* [in Japanese]. Tokyo: Kenkyusha, 1933. A biographical and critical study.

3:161. Kingsmill, Hugh [H. K. Lunn]. *Samuel Johnson*. London: Barker, 1933. Reviewed by R. W. Chapman, *TLS*, January 18, 1934, p. 41; C. B. Tinker, *SRL*, X (March 17, 1934), 555.

3:162. Ishida, Kenji, and Jirô Suzuki. *Johnson* [in Japanese]. Kenkyusha Series of English and American Authors. Tokyo: Kenkyusha, 1934.

3:163. Powell, L. F. [Additional biographical notes on Johnson's will], item 4:14, ed. Hill-Powell (1934), IV, 440–45.

3:164. Roberts, Sydney Castle. *Doctor Johnson.* (Great Lives.) London: Gerald Duckworth & Co., 1935.

3:165. Brunskill, F. R. "The Ancestry of Dr. Johnson's Wife" [largely a review of item 3:131, Pt. VII], *London Quarterly and Holborn Review,* CLXI (April 1936), 228–30.

3:166. Brunskill, F. R. "More Johnsonian Gleanings," *London Quarterly and Holborn Review,* CLXIII (January 1938), 92–95.

3:167. Reade, Aleyn Lyell. " 'Johnsonian Gleanings': Some Unsolved Problems," *N&Q,* CLXXIV (June 4, 1938), 403–4. See also J. Seton-Anderson, *ibid.,* June 18, p. 447.

3:168. Lewis, Frank R. "New Facts about Samuel Johnson" [from records, Royal Society of Arts], *TLS,* June 25, 1938, p. 433.

3:169. Wecter, Dixon. "A Johnson Problem" [date of altercation with Dr. Barnard, *Life,* IV, 115], *TLS,* January 21, 1939, pp. 41–42.

3:170. Phillips, Lawrence. "Johnson's Penance at Uttoxeter," *N&Q,* CLXXVI (February 4, 1939), 84–85.

3:171. Reade, Aleyn Lyell. "Michael Johnson and Lord Derby's Library," *TLS,* July 27, 1940, pp. 363, 365.

3:172. Pottle, Frederick A. "The Dark Hints of Sir John Hawkins and Boswell" [possibility of some sexual irregularity in Johnson's youth], *MLN,* LVI (May 1941), 325–29. Reprinted in item 10/6:306.

3:173. Chapman, Robert William. "Johnson's Literary Earnings: A Problem," *RES,* XIX (October 1943), 403–4.

3:174. "Dr. Johnson and Holland House" [Johnson working in a china factory, etc.], *N&Q,* CLXXXVI (April 8, May 6, 1944), 183, 234; CLXXXVII (August 26, 1944), 108. See item 3:202.

*3:175. Krutch, Joseph Wood. *Samuel Johnson.* New York: Henry Holt & Co., 1944; London: Cassell & Co., 1948 (with footnotes at the bottom of the page, and completely different pagination); tr. into Spanish by Mariano de Alarcón, Buenos Aires: Editorial Sudamericana, [1948]. Reviewed by J. L. Clifford, *New York Times Book Review,* November 19, 1944, pp. 1, 32; C. H. Bennett, *SRL,* December 2, 1944, pp. 31–32; F. A. Pottle, *Yale Review,* XXXIV (Spring 1945), 546–49; E. L. McAdam, *PQ,* XXIV (April 1945), 146–47; W. B. C. Watkins, *Sewanee Review,* LIII (Spring 1945), 311–14; Edmund Wilson, *New Yorker,* November 18, 1944, pp. 84–90 (see item 10/6:280); F. R. Leavis, *Kenyon Review,* VIII (Autumn 1946), 637–57 (see item 10/6:259).

3:176. Thomas, Henry and Dana Lee [Henry Schnittkind]. "Samuel Johnson," *Living Biographies of Famous Men*, pp. 93–102. New York: Garden City Publishing Co., 1944.

3:177. Vulliamy, C. E. *Ursa Major: A Study of Dr. Johnson and His Friends*. London: Michael Joseph, 1946. See also item 10/6:272.

3:178. Brown, John J. "Samuel Johnson and the First Roller-Spinning Machine" [hypothesis that Johnson helped Wyatt and Paul with first roller-spinning machine], *MLR*, XLI (January 1946), 16–23. See also *TLS*, March 30, 1946, p. 151, and rebuttal in letter of J. de L. Mann, *TLS*, May 18, 1946, p. 235 (see also item 3:180).

3:179. Chapman, R. W. " 'Doctor' Johnson" [use of title before 1775], *N&Q*, CXC (February 23, 1946), 74–75.

3:180. Mann, J. de L. "Dr. Johnson's Connection with Mechanical Spinning," *MLR*, XLI (October 1946), 410–11. See also item 3:178.

3:181. Marshall, Charles. *Doctor Johnson*. (The Teaching of English Series.) London: Thomas Nelson & Sons, 1947.

*3:182. Balderston, Katharine C. "Johnson's Vile Melancholy," in item 10/6:273, pp. 3–14.

3:183. Reade, Aleyn Lyell. "Early Career of Dr. Johnson's Father," *TLS*, June 17, 1949, p. 404. See also Ellic Howe, *ibid.*, June 24.

3:184. Petrie, Sir Charles. "Dr. Johnson and the Forty-five," *English Review Magazine*, IV (February 1950), 96–100.

3:185. Norman, Charles. *Mr. Oddity: Samuel Johnson, LL.D.* Drexel Hill, Penn.: Bell Publishing Co., 1951; London: John Murray, 1952.

3:186. Norman, Charles. *The Pundit and the Player: Dr. Johnson and Mr. Garrick: A Biography for Young People*, illustrated by Bruno Frost. New York: David McKay Co., 1951.

3:187. Atkinson, A. D. "A Johnson Conversation," *N&Q*, February 17, 1951, p. 79. Identification of an undated remark in Cooke's *Life* with conversation of April 9, 1778, in Boswell.

3:188. Scarlett, E. P. "The Historic Shudder," *New Trail* (University of Alberta Alumni Association), IX (Spring 1951), 29–30. Reprints an anecdote of Johnson from the *Monthly Magazine*, February 1798 (item 3:38).

3:189. Clifford, James L. "The Mystery of Dr. Johnson's Brother," *Listener*, November 22, 1951, pp. 869–70.

3:190. Hilles, Frederick W. *Dr. Johnson Rebuked: A Hitherto Unrecorded Incident in His Life as Revealed in a Letter from Dr. Samuel Glasse*. New Haven: Privately printed for The Johnsonians [Yale University Press], 1952. With facsimile of letter.

3:191. "A Johnson Anecdote" [in *The Weekly Entertainer*, 1786], *JNL*, XII, No. 1 (February 1952), 11.

*3:192. Taylor, Frank. "Johnsoniana from the Bagshawe Muniments in the

John Rylands Library: Sir James Caldwell, Dr. Hawkesworth, Dr. Johnson, and Boswell's Use of the 'Caldwell Minute,' " *Bulletin of the John Rylands Library*, XXXV (September 1952), 211–47. See also XXXIV (March 1952), 249–50.

3:193. "Johnson and Stourbridge," *JNL*, XII, No. 3 (September 1952), 1–2.

*3:194. Hyde, Donald and Mary. *Dr. Johnson's Second Wife*. Somerville, N.J.: Privately printed [Princeton University Press], 1953. With facsimile of four pages of Boswell's transcript of Johnson's diary. Reprinted in *Manuscripts*, VI (Spring 1954), 144–54. Rev. and reprinted in item 10/6:306, pp. 133–51, with facsimile of one page of Boswell's transcript.

3:195. Cochrane, Peter. "Tetty's Tombstone," *Manchester Guardian*, January 5, 1953, p. 3.

3:196. "Some Little Known Remarks of Johnson" [from Henry Francis Cary's *Lives of English Poets*, 1846], *JNL*, XIII, No. 3 (September 1953), 11–12. See item 3:65.

3:197. "Some New Anecdotes of Johnson" [from Bodleian MS Eng. Misc. e 8, formerly MS collection of Philip Bliss], *JNL*, XIII, No. 4 (December 1953), 11. See also Bertram H. Davis, in *JNL*, XIV, No. 1 (March 1954), 11–12.

3:198. [Beard, G. W.] "Some Johnsonian Addenda" [entries in Johnson's diaries omitted by Boswell; letters from Sir William Boothby to Michael Johnson], *Times* (London), December 14, 1953, p. 10.

3:199. Bronson, Bertrand H. "Samuel Johnson and James Boswell" [introduction to a selection from their works], in *Major British Writers*, ed. G. B. Harrison, I, 843–59. New York: Harcourt, Brace, 1954. Reprinted in his *Facets of the Enlightenment*, pp. 210–40, Berkeley and Los Angeles: University of California Press, 1968.

3:200. Roberts, S. C. *Samuel Johnson*. (Writers and Their Work.) London: Longmans, Green, for the British Council and the National Book League, 1954.

*3:201. Clifford, James L. *Young Sam Johnson*. New York: McGraw-Hill, 1955. *Young Samuel Johnson*, London: Heinemann, 1955 (contains small variations from American edition). Reviewed by Carlos Baker, *New York Times Book Review*, April 17, 1955, pp. 1, 22; John Raymond, *New Statesman and Nation*, December 24, 1955, pp. 860–61; Arthur Sherbo, *JEGP*, LV (January 1956), 162–64; J. H. Hagstrum, *MLN*, LXXI (February 1956), 131–33; John Beer, *Cambridge Review*, LXXVII (April 21, 1956), 497–99; R. P. McCutcheon, *MP*, LIII (May 1956), 282–84; W. R. Keast, *MLQ*, XVIII (December 1957), 342–44. Reprinted (paperbound), New York: Oxford University Press, 1961.

3:202. Wills, Geoffrey. "Ceramic Causerie: Dr. Samuel Johnson and Chelsea," *Apollo*, LXI (January 1955), 14. Rebuts a story in Thomas Faulkner's *History of Chelsea*, 1829 (I, 273), that Johnson experimented in manufacturing china and "afterwards gave a dissertation on this very subject in his works." See item 3:174.

3:203. Clifford, James L. "Samuel Johnson," in *Masterplots: Cyclopedia of World Authors*, ed. Frank N. Magill and Dayton Kohler, Vol. I, pp. 577–80. New York: Salem Press, 1958.

3:204. Pearson, Hesketh. *Johnson and Boswell: The Story of Their Lives.* London: Heinemann; New York: Harper and Brothers, 1958.

3:205. Clifford, James L. "The Complex Art of Biography, or All the Dr. Johnsons," *Columbia University Forum*, I (Spring 1958), 32–37. Revised and reprinted as "A Biographer Looks at Dr. Johnson," in item 10/6:306, pp. 121–31, and in *The Columbia University Forum Anthology*, ed. Peter Spackman and Lee Ambrose, pp. 12–21, New York: Atheneum, 1968.

3:206. Saunders, Beatrice. "Samuel Johnson," *Portraits of Genius*, pp. 58–66. London: Murray, 1959.

*3:207. Davis, Bertram Hylton. *Johnson Before Boswell: A Study of Sir John Hawkins' Life of Samuel Johnson.* New Haven, Conn.: Yale University Press, 1960. (A revision of "Sir John Hawkins' *Life of Johnson*: A Reappraisal" [dissertation, Columbia University, 1956], Ann Arbor, Mich.: University Microfilms, 1956.) Reviewed in *Times* (London), July 28, 1960, p. 13; *Economist*, September 24, 1960, pp. 1190, 1195; by John Rycenga, *Modern Age*, V (Winter 1960–61), 95–98; Gwin J. Kolb, *PQ*, XL (July 1961), 399–400; S. C. Roberts, *MLR*, LVI (April 1961), 254.

3:208. Hodgart, M. J. C. *Samuel Johnson and His Times.* London: Batsford, 1962. Reviewed by Henry Gifford, *MLR*, LVII (July 1962), 423; *TLS*, March 23, 1962, p. 199.

3:209. Land, Myrick. "The Cantankerous Dr. Johnson Battles a Lord—and Some Commoners," *The Fine Art of Literary Mayhem*, pp. 12–32. New York: Holt, Rinehart and Winston, 1962.

3:210. Quinlan, Maurice J. "Samuel Whyte's Anecdotes About Dr. Johnson," *Dartmouth College Library Bulletin*, n.s., V (January 1963), 56–65. In a MS at Dartmouth.

3:211. Greene, Donald. "Johnson, Mrs. Trimmer, and *Paradise Lost*," *JNL*, XXIII, No. 1 (March 1963), 11–12. Anecdote of Johnson and little Sarah Kirby (later Mrs. Trimmer).

3:212. Irwin, M. G. "Johnson's First Visit to Langton in Lincolnshire" [possibly in 1758], *JNL*, XXIII, no. 2 (June 1963), 6–8.

3:213. Roberts, S. C. "Samuel Johnson," *Encyclopaedia Britannica*, 14th ed., XIII, 108–16. Replaces item 3:92.

3:214. De Beer, Esmond S. "Johnson's Italian Tour," in item 10/6:329 (1965), pp. 159–69. Plans for the proposed trip with the Thrales and Baretti in 1776.

3:215. Clifford, James L. "Some Problems of Johnson's Obscure Middle Years" [period 1749–1763], in item 10/6:329 (1965), pp. 99–110.

3:216. Sherbo, Arthur. "Anecdotes by Mrs. Le Noir" [anecdotes from Christopher Smart's daughter], *Durham University Journal*, LVII (June 1965), 166–69. See items 3:49 and 3:154.

3:217. Meyers, Jeffrey. "Swift, Johnson and the Dublin M. A." *American Notes and Queries*, IV (September 1965), 5–6. Although Johnson was not convinced, Swift was powerless to help.

*3:218. Abbott, John L. "Dr. Johnson and the Society," *Journal of the Royal Society for the Encouragement of Arts, Manufactures, and Commerce*, CXV (April 1967), 395–400; (May), 486–91.

3:219. Drescher, Horst W. "Johnson in Scotland: from an Unpublished Notebook," *Anglia*, LXXXVI, no. 1/2 (1968), 113–23. Excerpts from a MS notebook of Henry Mackenzie, now in National Library of Scotland.

3:220. Kelley, Robert Emmett. "The Early Biographies of Samuel Johnson, 1784–1791" (dissertation, Indiana University, 1968), *Dissertation Abstracts*, XXIX, no. 2 (August 1968), 569–70A.

3:221. Wilding, Michael. "Michael Johnson: An Auction Sale," *N&Q*, May 1969, pp. 181–82. Sales in Worcestershire, 1717–18.

*3:222. Chambers, R. L. "Samuel Johnson at Stourbridge," in item 6:23 (1969), pp. 30–38. Important new information.

BIOGRAPHY—MEDICAL AND PSYCHOLOGICAL WORKS

3:701. P., F. [Johnson's use for orange peel], *GM*, LXXV (September 1805), 821.

3:702. "Professional Anecdote," *European Magazine*, LXI (March 1812), 183–84. Johnson consulted Dr. Nankivel some months before death; diagnosis of hypochondriasis.

*3:703. Madden, Richard Robert. "Johnson," *The Infirmities of Genius, illustrated by referring the anomalies in the literary character to the habits and constitutional peculiarities of men of genius*, pp. 113–32. Philadelphia: A. Waldie, 1833.

*3:704. Squibb, George James. "Last Illness and Post-Mortem Examination of Samuel Johnson," *London Journal of Medicine*, I (1849), 615–23.

3:705. Dumont, Dr. Pierre-Louis-Charles (of Monteux). "Lettre à Mons. A. Latour sur l'état pathologique de Samuel Johnson," *L'Union Médicale* (Paris), XI (June 18, 1857), 297–98; (July 2), 321–23.

3:706. Ogle, John W. "Parts of a Clinical Lecture on Aphasia" [the case of Dr. Johnson], *British Medical Journal*, August 8, 1874, pp. 163–64.

3:707. Morrill, Justin S. "Samuel Johnson," *Self-Consciousness of Noted Persons* [pp. 104–7 of 2nd ed.]. Cambridge, Mass.: John Wilson and

Son, 1882. 2nd ed., Boston: Ticknor and Fields, 1886. A study of the "image" of Johnson presented in his writings.

3:708. Gordon, W. J. "The Doctors of Bolt Court," *Leisure Hour,* XLII (October 1893), 814.

3:709. Cahall, W. C. "The Medical History of Dr. Samuel Johnson," *American Medicine,* II (August 31, 1901), 338–39.

3:710. Packard, Francis R. "The Medical History of Dr. Samuel Johnson," *New York Medical Journal,* LXXV (March 15, 1902), 441–45.

3:711. Warbasse, James P. "Doctors of Samuel Johnson and His Court," *Medical Library and Historical Journal,* V (1907), 65–87, 194–210. Reprinted, Brooklyn, N.Y.: Huntington, 1908.

3:712. Rogers, B. M. H. "The Medical Aspects of Boswell's 'Life of Johnson' with Some Account of the Medical Men Mentioned in That Book," *Bristol Medical-Chirurgical Journal,* XXVIII (1910), 289–310; XXIX (1911), 125–48. Abr. in *Alienist and Neurologist,* XXXII (1911), 277–96.

3:713. Wynne, J. D. "Dr. Johnson and the Medical Profession," *Practitioner,* LXXXVI (1911), 447–56.

3:714. Rogers, James F. "Doctor Johnson in the Flesh" [his physical ills, etc.], *Sewanee Review,* XXII (July 1914), 276–82.

3:715. "Samuel Johnson and Dr. Thomas Lawrence" [editorial], *Boston Medical and Surgical Journal,* CLXXIII (September 1915), 479–81.

3:716. Chaplin, Arnold. *Medicine in England during the Reign of George III,* pp. 120–25. London: Privately printed, 1919. Includes postmortem examination of Johnson.

3:717. Moore, Sir Norman. *Johnson and the Physicians.* [See item 6:22.] Lichfield: The Johnson's Head, 1920.

3:718. Treves, Sir Frederick. "Samuel Johnson," *Cassell's Magazine of Fiction,* February 1924, pp. 38–44.

*3:719. Rolleston, Sir Humphry. "Medical Aspects of Samuel Johnson," *Glasgow Medical Journal,* CI (April 1924), 173–91.

3:720. MacLaurin, Charles. "Dr. Johnson," *Mere Mortals: Medico-Historical Essays,* pp. 13–35. London: Jonathan Cape, 1925.

3:721. Bloxsome, H. E. "Dr. Johnson and the Medical Profession," *Cornhill Magazine,* n.s., LVIII (April 1925), 455–71.

3:722. Hutchison, Robert. "Dr. Samuel Johnson and Medicine," *Edinburgh Medical Journal,* August 1925, pp. 389–406. For commentary on original address see *Lancet* (London), May 9, 1925, pp. 988–89; *British Medical Journal,* May 9, 1925, p. 895.

3:723. "The Case of Samuel Johnson," *Canadian Journal of Medicine and Surgery,* LXII (September 1927), 57–61.

3:724. Ladell, R. Macdonald. "The Neurosis of Dr. Samuel Johnson," *British Journal of Medical Psychology,* IX (1929), 314–23.

*3:725. Rolleston, Sir Humphry. "Samuel Johnson's Medical Experiences," *Annals of Medical History*, n.s., I (September 1929), 540–52.

3:726. Brain, W. Russell. "A Post-Mortem on Dr. Johnson," *London Hospital Gazette*, XXXVII (May, June 1934), 225–30, 288–89. Reprinted, London: Metropolis Press, 1934. Abstracted as "The Medical and Mental History of Dr. Samuel Johnson," *British Medical Journal*, September 8, 1934, p. 480.

3:727. Critchen-Browne, Sir James. "What Was the Matter with Samuel Johnson," *From the Doctor's Notebook*, p. 64. London: Duckworth, 1937.

*3:728. Hanes, Frederic M. "The Particularities of Dr. Johnson" [deformities the result of a neurosis called a "tic"], *South Atlantic Quarterly*, XXXIX (April 1940), 203–12.

3:729. East, Terence. "Dr. Samuel Johnson: His Medical History as Recorded by James Boswell," *British Heart Journal*, IV (1942), 43–48.

3:730. Melvin, R. G. "Dr. Johnson's Asthma," *British Medical Journal*, I (May 8, 1943), 584.

3:731. Wieder, Robert. *Le docteur Johnson, critique littéraire (1709–1784) essai de biographie psychologique*. Paris: G. Legrand, 1944.

3:732. Mayerson, H. S. "Samuel Johnson and the Common Cold," *Bulletin of the History of Medicine*, XV (March 1944), 276–83.

3:733. Hitschmann, Edward. "Samuel Johnson's Character: A Psychoanalytic Interpretation," *Psychoanalytic Review*, XXXII (April 1945), 207–18. Reprinted in *Great Men: Psychoanalytic Studies*, pp. 175–85, New York: International Universities Press, 1956.

3:734. Bloxsome, H. E. "Some Apothecaries and Others" [Holder, etc.], *St. Bartholomew's Hospital Journal*, XLIX (September 1945), 105–8.

3:735. Simpson, F. W. "The Death of Dr. Samuel Johnson," *Medical Journal of Australia*, II (September 1948), 286.

3:736. Vincent, Esther H. "The Case of the Eccentric Lexicographer," *Surgery, Gynecology, and Obstetrics*, LXXXVIII (May 1949), 681–85.

3:737. Brain, W. Russell. "Authors and Psychopaths," *British Medical Journal*, II (December 24, 1949), 1433–39.

3:738. Chase, Peter Pineo. "The Ailments and Physicians of Dr. Johnson," *Yale Journal of Biology and Medicine*, XXIII (April 1951), 370–79.

*3:739. Beattie, P. H. "The Ocular Troubles of Dr. Johnson and Mr. Pepys," *Proceedings of the Royal Society of Medicine*, XLVI (August 1953), 591–96.

3:740. Critchley, MacDonald. "The Study of Language-Disorder: Past, Present, and Future" [Johnson's aphasia in 1783], in *The Centennial Lectures, Commemorating the One Hundredth Anniversary of E. R. Squibb and Sons*. New York: G. P. Putnam's Sons, 1959. For a full-length study see item 3:749.

3:741. MacKeith, Ronald. "Samuel Johnson, My Patient," *New Rambler*, June 1958, pp. 13–28. Reprinted in *Oxford Medical School Gazette*, XI March 23, 1959), 4–12.

3:742. "Dr. Johnson's Doctors," *New England Journal of Medicine*, CCLXI (September 17, 1959), 618.

3:743. Bishop, P. James. "Samuel Johnson's Lung" [an illustration of it found in Matthew Baillie, *A Series of Engravings . . . to Illustrate . . . Morbid Anatomy*, 1803], *Tubercle*, XL (December 1959), 478–81. See item 8:16.

3:744. Brain, Russell. *Some Reflections on Genius and Other Essays*, with drawings by Norman Smith. London: Pitman Medical Publishing Co., 1960. Reprints items 3:726 and 11/6:6 and adds two other essays on Johnson.

3:745. Kenney, William. "Dr. Johnson and the Psychiatrists" [review of psychiatric studies of Johnson], *American Imago*, XVII (Spring 1960), 75–82.

3:746. Benton, Arthur L., and Robert J. Joynt. "Early Descriptions of Aphasia" [deals with Johnson's aphasia], *Archives of Neurology*, III (August 1960), 119–20.

3:747. Sagebiel, Richard W. "Medicine in the Life and Letters of Samuel Johnson," *Ohio State Medical Journal*, LVII (April 1961), 382–84; (May), 520–22.

3:748. Brain, Russell. "Dr. Johnson and His Doctors," *New Rambler*, January 1962, pp. 4–12.

*3:749. Critchley, MacDonald. "Dr. Samuel Johnson's Aphasia," *Medical History*, VI (January 1962), 27–44. An important study of his 1783 attack, with illustrations showing handwriting, etc.

3:750. McHenry, Lawrence C., Jr. "Mark Akenside, M.D., and a Note on Dr. Johnson's 'Asthma,'" *New England Journal of Medicine*, CCLXVI (April 5, 1962), 716–18.

3:751. Davies, G. L. "Dr. Johnson as a 'Dabbler in Physic,'" *Guy's Hospital Gazette*, LXXVII (July 1962), 321–24.

*3:752. Irwin, M. G. "Doctor Johnson's Troubled Mind" [his relations with his mother], *Literature and Psychology*, XIII (Winter 1963), 6–11. Reprinted in item 10/6:330, pp. 22–29.

3:753. Brain, Russell. *Doctors Past and Present*. London: Pitman, 1964. Reprints items 3:748, 5:344, and 13:53.

3:754. Abeshouse, Benjamin S. *A Medical History of Dr. Samuel Johnson*. Norwich, N.Y.: Eaton Laboratories [division of Norwich Pharmacal Co.], 1965. Short pamphlet; slight, but with amusing illustrations.

3:755. McHenry, Lawrence C., Jr. "Medical Case Notes on Samuel Johnson in the Heberden Manuscripts," *New Rambler*, June 1964, pp. 11–15. Reprinted in *Journal of the American Medical Association*, CXCV (January 1966), 89–90.

3:756. Larson, Roger K. "Historical Note on Emphysema" [evidence from Johnson's lung], *American Review of Respiratory Diseases*, XCI (February 1965), 277–78. See also *New York State Journal of Medicine*, LXV (May 15, 1965), 1238.

*3:757. McHenry, Lawrence C., Jr., and Ronald MacKeith. "Samuel Johnson's Childhood Illnesses and the King's Evil," *Medical History*, X (October 1966), 386–99. Includes a photograph of Johnson's death mask.

*3:758. McHenry, Lawrence C., Jr. "Dr. Samuel Johnson's Emphysema," *Archives of Internal Medicine*, CXIX (January 1967), 98–105.

*3:759. McHenry, Lawrence C., Jr. "Samuel Johnson's Tics and Gesticulations," *Journal of the History of Medicine and Allied Sciences*, XXII (April 1967), 152–68.

3:760. Madden, J. S. "Samuel Johnson's Alcohol Problem" [a prodromal alcoholic, he had a tendency to heavy drinking, but curbed his desires for long periods], *Medical History*, XI (April 1967), 141–49. Summarized as "The Temptation of Dr. Johnson," *Scientific American*, CCXVII (August 1967), 44.

3:761. MacKeith, R. "The Death Mask of Samuel Johnson," *New Rambler*, June 1968, pp. 41–47.

3:762. McHenry, Lawrence C., Jr. "Art and Medicine: Dr. Johnson's Dropsy," *Journal of the American Medical Association*, CCVI (December 9, 1968), 2507–9. A wax tavern scene by Samuel Percy shows Johnson's dropsical symptoms.

3:763. McHenry, Lawrence C., Jr. "Samuel Johnson: A Medical Portrait," *Jefferson Medical College Alumni Bulletin*, Winter 1969, pp. 2–9.

4. BOSWELL (Works and Events Connected with Johnson)

BIBLIOGRAPHY

*4:1. Pottle, Frederick A. *The Literary Career of James Boswell, Esq., Being the Bibliographical Materials for a Life of Boswell*. Oxford: Clarendon Press, 1929. Reviewed by E. N. S. Thompson, *PQ*, IX (January 1930), 87–88; R. S. Crane, *Yale Review*, XIX (Spring 1930), 616–19; L. F. Powell, *MP*, XXX (August 1932), 116–18. Reprinted, 1965 (Oxford Reprint Series).

4:2. Brown, Anthony E. "Boswellian Studies: A Bibliography," in *Cairo Studies in English, 1964*, ed. Magdi Wahba, pp. 1–75. Cairo, U.A.R., 1966. ("Issued privately by members of the Department of English at the University of Cairo.")

4:10. Boswell, James. *An Account of Corsica. The Journal of a Tour to That Island; and Memoirs of Pascal Paoli.* London: Edward and Charles Dilly, 1768 (2 eds.); 3rd ed., 1769.

Ed. S. C. Roberts. Cambridge: Cambridge University Press, 1923. Reviewed in *TLS*, July 5, 1923, p. 453; by Augustine Birrell, *New Statesman*, July 14, 1923, pp. 417–19.

Ed. Morchard Bishop. London: Williams and Norgate, 1951. With *Memoirs of Pascal Paoli.*

4:11. Boswell, James. "The Hypochondriack," *London Magazine*, XLVI (October 1777) [No. I] to n.s., I (August 1783) [No. LXX].

Ed. Margery Bailey. 2 vols. Palo Alto, Cal.: Stanford University Press, 1928. Reviewed by R. W. Chapman, *TLS*, September 6, 1928, p. 629; F. A. Pottle, *SRL*, V (September 1, 1928), 88. Reprinted (full text, but with less annotation) as *Boswell's Column*, London: William Kimber, 1951.

4:12. Boswell, James. *The Journal of a Tour to the Hebrides, with Samuel Johnson, LL.D.* London: Charles Dilly, 1785 (2 eds.); 3rd ed., 1786; 6th ed., 1813. Reviewed by Samuel Badcock, *Monthly Review*, LXXIV (April 1786), 277–82.

Ed. Robert Carruthers. London: National Illustrated Library, [1852].

Ed. (with item 21:1) R. W. Chapman, London: Oxford University Press, 1924 (reviewed by Augustine Birrell, *Nation-Athenaeum*, August 9, 1924, pp. 591–92); ed. Allan Wendt, Boston: Houghton Mifflin, 1965 (Riverside Editions).

Ed. (with item 4:14) J. W. Croker, 1831, 1835, 1848; Percy Fitzgerald, 1874; Alexander Napier, 1884; Henry Morley, 1885; George Birkbeck Hill, 1887; Clement Shorter, 1922; L. F. Powell (revision of Hill's ed.), 1950, 1964.

Ed. with introduction and notes by Jack Werner, with 20 illustrations by Rowlandson. London: MacDonald and Co.; New York: Coward-McCann, 1956.

Ed. with introduction by L. F. Powell. (Everyman's Library.) London: J. M. Dent; New York: E. P. Dutton, 1958.

With introduction by T. C. Livingstone. (New Collins Classics.) London: Collins, 1958.

Tr. into German (abr.) by Fritz Güttinger, 1951. See item 4:15 (1951).

4:13. Boswell, James. *Boswell's Journal of a Tour to the Hebrides* [original MS], ed. F. A. Pottle and C. H. Bennett. New York: Viking Press, 1936. Reviewed by J. W. Krutch, *Nation*, November 7, 1936, p. 549; *TLS*, November 7, 1936, p. 903; Dixon Wecter, *Yale Review*, XXVI (December 1936), 401–4; F. T. Wood, *Englische Studien*, LXXII (October 1937),

120–22; Margery Bailey, *MLN*, LIII (May 1938), 387–89. See also item 4:125. 2nd ed. (with important additions), New York: McGraw-Hill, 1961. (Vol. 8 of the trade edition of the Yale Editions of the Private Papers of James Boswell.)

4:14. Boswell, James. *The Life of Samuel Johnson, LL.D.* London: Charles Dilly, 1791. Reviewed by Ralph Griffiths, *Monthly Review*, n.s., VII (January 1792), 1–9; *Critical Review*, February 1792, pp. 189–98. Dublin ed., 1792. 2nd ed., 1793; 3rd ed., 1799 (additions by Edmond Malone); 4th ed., 1804, to 6th ed., 1811, supervised by Malone; 9th ed., 1822, supervised by Alexander Chalmers.

＊Ed. John Wilson Croker. 5 vols. London: John Murray, 1831. Rev. by John Wright, 10 vols., 1835, 1848 (contains much material not readily accessible elsewhere). Reviewed in *Monthly Review*, 4th ser., II (June 1831), 452–64; *Westminster Review*, XV (October 1831), 374–99; by J. G. Lockhart in *Quarterly Review*, XLVI (November 1831), 1–46; by W. B. O. Peabody in *North American Review*, XXXIV (January 1832), 91–119; by J. P. Dabney in *Christian Examiner*, XIV (May 1833), 154–63; by John Mitford, *GM*, n.s., IV (November 1835), 451–58. For Macaulay's review, see item 10/6:28, and for Carlyle's, item 10/6:31.

Ed. Percy Fitzgerald. 3 vols. London: Bickers and Son, 1874.

Ed. Alexander Napier. 4 vols. (and an additional volume, item 3:108). London: George Bell, 1884.

Ed. Henry Morley. 5 vols. London: Routledge, 1885.

Ed. George Birkbeck Hill. 6 vols. Oxford: Clarendon Press, 1887. Reprinted, with different pagination, New York: Harper and Brothers, 1889. Reviewed in *Athenaeum*, No. 3113 (June 25, 1887), pp. 825–26.

Ed. Augustine Birrell. 6 vols. Westminster: Constable & Co., 1901.

Ed. Arnold Glover, with introduction by Austin Dobson. 3 vols. London: J. M. Dent & Sons, 1901.

Ed. Roger Ingpen. Profusely illustrated. 2 vols. London: Sir Isaac Pitman & Sons, 1907. New ed., Bath: George Bayntun; Boston: Lauriat, 1925.

Ed. Clement Shorter. (Temple Bar Edition.) New York: Gabriel Wells by Doubleday, Page, 1922. Separate introductions to each volume: I, by A. L. Reade; II, by Augustine Birrell; III, by W. P. Trent; IV, by G. K. Chesterton; V, by A. Edward Newton; VI, by John Drinkwater; VII, by R. B. Adam; VIII, by Walter De la Mare; IX, by C. B. Tinker (portions reprinted in item 4:94); X, by Richard Ashe King. Reviewed by R. W. Chapman, *TLS*, July 20, 1922, p. 471.

First edition, 1791, reprinted verbatim with preface by Clement K. Shorter. 3 vols. London: Navarre Society, 1924.

With introduction by Herbert Askwith. Text of "Malone's sixth edition." 1 vol. (Modern Library "Giant.") New York: Random House [1931] and frequently reissued.

With introduction by Chauncey B. Tinker. 2 vols., often bound together. (Oxford Standard Edition.) New York: Oxford University Press, 1933. Reissued with new index, 1953; with further corrections, 1957; and paperbound, 1960.

*Ed. George Birkbeck Hill, rev. and enl. by Lawrence F. Powell. Oxford: Clarendon Press; Vols. I–IV, 1934; Vols. V–VI, 1950. Reviewed in *TLS*, June 28, 1934, pp. 449–50; by C. B. Tinker, *SRL*, XI (January 26, 1935), 446–47 (see also item 4:123); C. H. Bennett, *JEGP*, XXXIV (April 1935), 256–59; Harold Williams, *MLR*, XXX (July 1935), 375–77; George Sherburn, *PQ*, XIV (October 1935), 374–75; James Sutherland, *RES*, XII (January 1936), 78–80; R. Kilbourne, *MLN*, LI (December 1936), 552–54; Edith J. Morley, *Year's Work in English Studies*, XV (1934), 264–66. 2nd ed., Vols. V, VI, 1964; Vols. I–IV in preparation.

Ed. Edward G. Fletcher, with marginal annotations by H. L. Piozzi. 3 vols. London: Limited Editions Club, 1938. Discussed by Christopher Morley, *SRL*, XIX (December 3, 1938), 13, 26 (reprinted in *Letters of Askance*, pp. 11–12, Philadelphia: J. B. Lippincott Co. 1939).

With introduction by S. C. Roberts and index by Alan Dent. 2 vols. (Everyman's Library.) London: J. M. Dent & Sons, 1949. Original edition, 1906.

4:15. Boswell, James. *The Life of Samuel Johnson, LL.D.* Selected abridgements and translations:

A Collection of Interesting Biography. Containing I. The Life of Samuel Johnson, LL.D. Abridged, principally, from Boswell's celebrated memoirs. . . . The whole revised and abridged by Sir Andrew Anecdote. 2 vols. London: Printed for the editor, 1791.

Donne, M. A. *The Life of Dr. Samuel Johnson. Chiefly compiled from "Boswell's Johnson."* London: S.P.C.K., [1863].

Main, Alexander. *Life and Conversations of Dr. Samuel Johnson (founded chiefly upon Boswell)*, with a preface by George Henry Lewes. London: Chapman and Hall, 1874. Severely criticized in item 4:1, p. 203. See also item 4:61.

Life of Dr. Samuel Johnson: Compiled Chiefly from Boswell's Biography. Madras: Christian Literature Society for India, 1900.

Abr. and ed. with introduction by Charles Grosvenor Osgood. (Modern Student's Library.) New York: Scribner's, 1917.

Everybody's Boswell. Being the Life of Samuel Johnson abridged from James Boswell's complete text and from the Tour to the Hebrides. London: G. Bell, 1930. Profusely illustrated by Ernest H. Shephard. Often reprinted. See also what seems to be an abridgement of this abridgement,

The Great Cham, ed. John Graves, with 10 illustrations by Shephard, London: Bell, 1933.

Tr. into Swedish by Harald Heyman. 4 vols. (Incomplete; only up to 1778.) Stockholm: Albert Bonniers Förlag, 1930. Vol. I reviewed by F. A. Pottle, *SRL*, III (May 14, 1927), 826.

The Conversations of Dr. Johnson [extracted by R. W. Postgate from the *Life*]. London: A. A. Knopf, 1930; Lehmann, 1949; Allison and Busby, 1969.

Johnson, Samuel. *Esperienza e Vita Morale: Conversazioni con Boswell*, tr. with introduction by A. Prospero. Bari: Gius. Laterza & Figli, 1939.

Abr. and with introduction by Bergen Evans. (Modern Library.) New York: Random House, 1952.

Tr. into German (abr. and with introduction) by Fritz Güttinger (with *The Journal of a Tour to the Hebrides*) [*Dr. Samuel Johnson: Leben und Meinungen; mit dem Tagebuch einer Reise nach den Hebriden*]. (Manesse Bibliothek der Weltliteratur.) Zürich: Manesse-Verlag, 1951.

Tr. into Norwegian (abr.) by Solveig Tunold. Oslo: H. Aschehoug and Co., 1951.

Tr. into French by J. P. Le Hoc [*La Vie de Samuel Johnson*]. (Les Classiques Anglais.) Paris: Gallimard, 1954.

Tr. into Serbo-Croat (abr. and with introduction) by Stjepan Krešić. Zagreb: Kultura Publishing Co., 1958.

Abr. by O. B. Davis, *Four English Biographies*, ed. J. B. Priestley and O. B. Davis, pp. 245–435. New York: Harcourt, Brace, 1961. "Afterword" by J. B. Priestley, pp. 436–40.

Ed. and abr. with introduction by Anne and Irvin Ehrenpreis. New York: Washington Square Press, 1965.

Ed. and abr. with introduction by Frank Brady. (Signet Classics.) New York: New American Library, 1968.

Ed. and abr. with introduction by Robert Hunting. (Bantam Critical Editions.) New York: Bantam Books, 1969. Reprints critical material about *Life*.

4:16. *Letters of James Boswell, Addressed to the Rev. W. J. Temple*, [ed. Sir Philip Francis]. London: Bentley, 1857. With introduction by Thomas Seccombe, London: Sidgwick and Jackson, 1908. For reviews, see items 3:96 and 24:67.

*4:17. *Letters of James Boswell*, ed. C. B. Tinker. 2 vols. Oxford: Clarendon Press, 1924. Reviewed in *TLS*, January 15, 1925, pp. 29–30; by Lytton Strachey, *Nation and Athenaeum*, XXXVI (January 31, 1925), pp. 609–10; Leonard Bacon, *SRL*, I (February 28, 1925), 553–54; Sir Chartres

Biron, *London Mercury*, XII (October 1925), 664–66; R. H. Griffith, *Yale Review*, XV (October 1925), 170–72.

4:18. *Boswell's Notebook* [facsimile]. With introduction by A. Edward Newton, Buffalo, N.Y.: Privately printed for R. B. Adam, 1919. With introduction by R. W. Chapman, London: Oxford University Press, 1925. Reviewed by F. A. Pottle, *Yale Review*, XV (July 1926), 817–18.

*4:19. *The Private Papers of James Boswell from Malahide Castle in the Collection of Lt.-Colonel Ralph Heyward Isham*, ed. Geoffrey Scott (Vols. I–VI) and Frederick A. Pottle (Vols. VII–XVIII). Mt. Vernon, N.Y.: Privately printed, 1928–34. A subscription advertisement and summary of first 6 vols., New York: Rudge, 1928. Catalogue by F. A. and Marion S. Pottle, London and New York: Oxford University Press, 1931. For index see item 4:20. Vols. I–VI reviewed by R. W. Chapman, *TLS*, February 6, 1930, pp. 85–86.

4:20. Pottle, Frederick A., J. Foladare, and J. P. Kirby. *Index to the Private Papers of James Boswell* [see item 4:19]. London: Oxford University Press, 1937. Sometimes thought of as Vol. XIX of item 4:19. Reviewed by R. L. Greene in *MLN*, LIII (May 1938), 384–87.

*4:21. The Yale Editions of the Private Papers of James Boswell. Original editorial committee, Edward Aswell, F. W. Hilles, Herman W. Liebert, F. A. Pottle.

Trade Edition

Vol. 1. *Boswell's London Journal, 1762–63*, ed. F. A. Pottle, with preface by Christopher Morley. New York: McGraw-Hill, 1950. Without Morley's preface, but with unsigned publisher's note, London: Heinemann, 1950. Reviewed by Leonard Bacon, *SRL*, XXXIII (November 4, 1950), 11–12; J. W. Krutch, *New York Herald Tribune Book Review*, November 5, 1950, pp. 1, 22; J. L. Clifford, *New York Times Book Review*, November 5, 1950, pp. 1, 26; Rintaro Fukuhara, *The Rising Generation* (Tokyo), XCVIII (1952), 98–99. Limited edition, with essay by F. A. Pottle, "The History of the Boswell Papers," pp. xi–xlii, London: Heinemann, 1951. Reprinted (paperbound), New York: New American Library, 1956 (Signet Books). Tr. into French by Mme. [Émile-Robert] Blanchet, with preface by André Maurois [*Les Papiers de Boswell: Amours à Londres, 1762–1763*], Paris: Hachette, 1952. Tr. into German by Fritz Güttinger [*Boswells Londoner Tagebuch*], Zürich: Diana Verlag, 1953.

Vol. 2. *Boswell in Holland, 1763–1764*, ed. F. A. Pottle. New York: McGraw-Hill; London: Heinemann, 1952.

Vol. 3. See item 5:317.

Vol. 4. *Boswell on the Grand Tour: Germany and Switzerland, 1764,* ed. F. A. Pottle. New York: McGraw-Hill; London: Heinemann, 1953. Tr. into German by Fritz Güttinger [*Boswells Grosse Reise: Deutschland und die Schweiz, 1764*], Zürich: Diana Verlag, 1955. Tr. into French by Celia Bertin, with preface by André Maurois [*Les Papiers de Boswell (2): Boswell Chez les Princes: Les cours allemandes, Voltaire, J. J. Rousseau, 1764*], Paris: Hachette, 1955.

Vol. 5. *Boswell on the Grand Tour: Italy, Corsica, and France, 1765–1766*, ed. Frank Brady and F. A. Pottle. New York: McGraw-Hill; London: Heinemann, 1955.

Vol. 6. *Boswell in Search of a Wife, 1766–1769*, ed. Frank Brady and F. A. Pottle. New York: McGraw-Hill, 1956; London: Heinemann, 1957.

Vol. 7. *Boswell for the Defence, 1769–1774*, ed. W. K. Wimsatt, Jr., and F. A. Pottle. New York: McGraw-Hill, 1959; London: Heinemann, 1960.

Vol. 8. See item 4:13.

Vol. 9. *The Ominous Years, 1774–1776*, ed. Charles Ryskamp and F. A. Pottle. New York: McGraw-Hill; London: Heinemann, 1963.

Research Edition

Vol. 1. *The Correspondence of James Boswell and John Johnston of Grange*, ed. Ralph S. Walker. London: Heinemann; New York: McGraw-Hill, 1966.

*Vol. 2. *The Correspondence and Other Papers of James Boswell Relating to the Making of the Life of Johnson*, ed. Marshall Waingrow. New York: McGraw-Hill; London: Heinemann, 1969.

COMMENTARY

4:50. K., W. [William Kenrick.] *An Epistle to James Boswell, Esq., occasioned by his having transmitted the moral writings of Dr. S. Johnson to Pascal Paoli.* London: Fletcher, 1768.

4:51. Verax. *Remarks on the Journal of a Tour to the Hebrides in a Letter to J. Boswell, Esqr.* London, [1785].

4:52. [James, Sir Walter James.] *A Defence of Mr. Boswell's Journal of a Tour, in a Letter to the Author of the Remarks, signed Verax.* London: W. T. Swift, 1785. For identification of author, see *Life*, VI (2nd ed., 1964), 188 (*s.v.* "James, W.").

4:53. *The Remarker Remarked, or A Parody on the Letter to Mr. Boswell, on His Tour.* London, 1786. Not seen. Entry from item 1/4:8 (1909), p. 6.

4:54. *Epistle to James Boswell, Esq.; occasioned by his long-expected, and now speedily-to-be-published, Life of Dr. Johnson.* London: J. Hookham, 1790. In verse.

4:55. N[ichols], J[ohn]. [Additions and corrections to Boswell], *GM*, LXI (June 1791), 499–500.

4:56. Whyte, Edward Athenry. *Remarks on Boswell's Johnson*. Dublin: Printed for the author, 1797. Reprinted in Samuel and Edward Athenry Whyte, *A Miscellany containing . . . Remarks on Boswell's Johnson*, Dublin: E. A. Whyte, 1799. Later eds., *Miscellanea Nova . . . containing . . . Remarks*, 1800, 1802.

4:57. M[itford], J[ohn]. "Notes on Boswell's Life of Samuel Johnson, LL.D." *GM*, n.s., IV (December 1835), 563–69; V (April 1836), 339–50; VI (July 1836), 15–21; (September), 235–40; VII (February 1837), 132–39; VIII (October 1837), 341–46; (December), 563–69; IX (April 1838), 348–54; X (October 1838), 361–65. Also "Johnsoniana," n.s., VII (May 1837), 462–67; (June) 578–83. Additions to Croker's ed. of the *Life* (item 4:14) and his *Johnsoniana* (item 3:75).

4:58. "Bozzies" [Boswell's method in the *Life*], *Eliza Cook's Journal*, VIII (February 26, 1853), 275–76. Reprinted in *Eclectic Magazine*, XXIX (July 1853), 382–85.

4:59. *Boswelliana*. Oxford: Privately printed for the Philobiblon Society, 1855–56. Miscellaneous anecdotes—a small selection of those in item 4:60. Includes a section "Folium Reservatum," a collection of mildly off-color anecdotes. Preface by R.M.M. [Richard Monckton Milnes, Lord Houghton].

4:60. *Boswelliana. The Commonplace Book of James Boswell. With a memoir and annotations, by Charles Rogers, and introductory remarks by Lord Houghton.* London: Grampian Club, 1874. Includes "Memoir of James Boswell," pp. 1–200, and "Boswelliana," miscellaneous anecdotes (only a few of them about Johnson), pp. 203–329. An earlier selection of these is found in item 4:59.

4:61. [Dennett, J. R.] "The Condensed Boswell," *Nation*, XVIII (April 16, 1874), 253–54. Review of item 4:15, ed. A. Main.

4:62. Philalethes. *Boswell Again*. London: Reeves and Turner, 1878. A defense of Croker's ed. of Boswell's *Life* against Macaulay's attack (item 10/6:28).

4:63. Fitzgerald, Percy. *Croker's Boswell and Boswell. Studies in the Life of Johnson*. London: Chapman and Hall, 1880.

4:64. Shepherd, Richard Herne. "Notes on John Wilkes and Boswell's Life of Johnson," *Walford's Antiquarian*, XI (January 1887), 34–37.

4:65. "Boswell and His Editors" [Napier, Fitzgerald, Grant, G. B. Hill], *Church Quarterly Review*, XXVII (October 1888), 121–38.

4:66. Layard, G. S. "Johnson's Boswell," *Universal Review*, VII (August 1890), 535.

4:67. Fitzgerald, Percy H. "Editing à la Mode: An Examination of Dr.

Birkbeck Hill's New Edition of Boswell's 'Life of Johnson,'" *Time*, n.s., II (September 1890), 944–54. Enl. and separately printed, London: Ward and Downey, [1891].

4:68. Fitzgerald, Percy H. *Further Examination of Dr. Birkbeck Hill's Edition of Boswell's Life of Johnson.* London, 1891.

4:69. Fitzgerald, Percy H. *Life of James Boswell.* London: Chatto & Windus, 1891.

4:70. Hill, George Birkbeck. "The Centenary of Boswell," *Macmillan's Magazine*, LXIV (May 1891), 37–43. Reprinted in item 6:16, pp. 83–91.

4:71. Fitzgerald, Percy H. *More Editing à la Mode: Being a Further Examination of Dr. Birkbeck Hill's Edition of Boswell's Life of Johnson.* London: Sweeting, 1892. A different work from item 4:68.

4:72. " 'Boswell's Johnson,'" *Temple Bar*, XCV (June 1892), 251–58.

4:73. Saintsbury, George. "Some Great Biographies," *Macmillan's Magazine*, LXVI (June 1892), 97–107. Reprinted in his *Collected Essays and Papers*, I, 409–33; (in part) in item 10/2:19.

4:74. Hill, George Birkbeck. "Boswell's Proof-Sheets" [of *Life*], *Atlantic Monthly*, LXXIV (November 1894), 657–68. Reprinted in item 6:16, pp. 51–80.

4:75. Hill, George Birkbeck. *The Boswell Centenary, May 19, 1895.* Privately printed, 1895. From *Illustrated London News*, May 25, 1895, pp. 646–47.

4:76. Leask, William Keith. *James Boswell.* Edinburgh and London: Oliphant, Anderson and Ferrier, 1897.

4:77. Johnson, Lionel P. "Bustling, Breathless, Bragging Boswell" [begins as review of item 4:76], *Academy*, LII (September 18, 1897), 213–14. Reprinted in *Post Liminium*, ed. T. Whittemore, London: Elkin Mathews, 1911.

4:78. Fitzgerald, Percy H. *A Critical Examination of Dr. G. Birkbeck Hill's "Johnsonian" Editions.* London: Bliss, Sands, 1898. Contains material from item 4:67 and later strictures. Reviewed in *Bookman* (London), XIV (May 1898), 52.

4:79. Dobson, Austin. "Boswell's Predecessors and Editors," *A Paladin of Philanthropy*, pp. 137–72. London: Chatto & Windus, 1899.

4:80. *The Life of Samuel Johnson by James Boswell in Fifteen Volumes, Containing Fifteen Hundred and Fifty Illustrations* [a prospectus]. London, 1900.

4:81. Sillard, P. A. "The Prince of Biographers," *Atlantic Monthly*, LXXXVIII (August 1901), 213–21.

4:82. Chesterton, G. K. "Boswell's 'Johnson,'" *Good Words*, XLIV (November 1903), 774–77.

4:83. Caldwell, Joshua W. "A Brief for Boswell," *Sewanee Review*, XIII, no. 3 (July 1905), 336–51.

4:84. Baumann, Arthur A. "The Tardy Bust" [statue of Boswell at Lichfield], *Saturday Review*, CVI (September 19, 1908), 357–59.

4:85. Mallory, George [Leigh]. *Boswell the Biographer*. London: Smith Elder, 1912.

4:86. "Whoever Will Write a Life," *Public Opinion*, May 10, 1912, p. 452.

4:87. Newmark, Leo. [A German translation of the *Life*], *Nation*, XCVII (September 11, 1913), 232.

4:88. Cosulich, Gilbert. "Johnson's Affection for Boswell," *Sewanee Review*, XXII (April 1914), 151–55.

4:89. Nicoll, W. Robertson. "The Six Best Biographies," *A Bookman's Letters*, pp. 17–25. London: Hodder & Stoughton, 1915.

4:90. Barker, F. W. E. "Boswell's Record of Johnson's Table-Talk," *Papers of the Manchester Literary Club*, XLIII (1917), 93–114.

4:91. Newton, A. Edward. "James Boswell—His Book," *The Amenities of Book-Collecting and Kindred Affections*, pp. 145–85. Boston: Atlantic Monthly Press, 1918.

4:92. Russell, A. J. "An Unpardonable Interruption" [*Life*, May 26, 1783], *Bellman*, XXIV (June 15, 1918), 664–65.

4:93. "When Boswell Dared to Differ" [disagreements between Boswell and Johnson], *TLS*, January 9, 1919, pp. 13–14.

*4:94. Tinker, Chauncey B. *Young Boswell*. Boston: Atlantic Monthly Press, 1922. Reviewed by Edward D. Snyder, *MLN*, XXXVII (December 1922), 498–502.

4:95. Smith, Minna Steele. "Manuscript Notes by Madame Piozzi in a Copy of Boswell's 'Life of Johnson,'" *London Mercury*, V (January 1922), 286–93. Reprinted in *Living Age*, CCCXII (March 4, 1922), 536–42.

4:96. Tinker, Chauncey B. "The Magnum Opus" [Boswell's *Life*], *Atlantic Monthly*, CXXIX (March 1922), 356–61. Included in item 4:94.

4:97. *Reproduction of Some of the Original Proof Sheets of Boswell's Life of Johnson*, with introduction by A. Edward Newton. Buffalo, N.Y.: Privately printed for R. B. Adam, 1923. See also *TLS*, January 17, 1924, p. 44.

4:98. Whibley, Leonard. "Boswell's Journals" [the Adam notebook, item 4:18], *Blackwood's Magazine*, CCXIII (March 1923), 395–406.

4:99. Chapman, Robert William. "Birkbeck Hill's Johnson" [plans for reediting], *TLS*, July 26, 1923, p. 504.

4:100. Drinkwater, John. "Johnson and Boswell" [aspects of Johnson not shown by Boswell], *The Muse in Council*, pp. 218–24. London: Sidgwick and Jackson, 1925.

*4:101. Chapman, R. W. "Boswell's Proof-Sheets" [revisions for the *Life*], *London Mercury*, XV (November 1926), 50–58; (December), 171–80.

Reprinted in *Johnson & Boswell Revised by Themselves and Others*, pp. 21–50, Oxford: Clarendon Press, 1928.

4:102. *A Trifle* [page of Mrs. Piozzi's *Anecdotes* with version of Boswell's reply]. Buffalo, N.Y.: Privately printed for R. B. Adam, 1927.

4:103. Windle, B. C. A. "Bozzy," *Catholic World*, CXXV (July 1927), 433–42.

4:104. "How Many Issues Are There of the First Edition of Boswell's Life of Johnson?" *Bulletin of the New York Public Library*, XXXI (October 1927), 826–27.

4:105. *A Letter from James Boswell to Dr. Johnson, March 3, 1772*. Buffalo, N.Y.: Privately printed for R. B. Adam, 1928.

*4:106. Powell, Lawrence F. "The Revision of Dr. Birkbeck Hill's Boswell," *Johnson & Boswell Revised by Themselves and Others*, pp. 53–66. Oxford: Clarendon Press, 1928.

4:107. Buxton, Charles Roden. "Boswell's Life of Johnson," *A Politician Plays Truant*, pp. 83–99. London: Christopher, 1929.

4:108. *Conjugal Fidelity: A Suppressed Dialogue between Boswell and Johnson* [from cancelled page in *Life*]. Stanford Dingley: Mill House Press, 1929. Reprinted in *Life and Letters*, V (September 1930), 164–66. Privately printed, with introduction by A. Edward Newton, Berwyn, Pa., 1929. Cancelled passage also printed in *Life*, III, 406.

*4:109. Scott, Geoffrey, ed. *The Making of the Life of Johnson as Shown in Boswell's First Notes* [Vol. VI of item 4:19, an important analysis of Boswell's technique]. Mt. Vernon, N.Y.: Privately printed, 1929.

4:110. Ward, H. Gordon. "A Spanish Quotation in Boswell's 'Johnson'" [April 9, 1778], *N&Q*, CLVI (February 16, 1929), 111–12. See also L. R. M. Strachan, *ibid.* (March 2), 157.

4:111. Macphail, Andrew. "Johnson's Life of Boswell" [based on new Boswell papers], *Quarterly Review*, CCLIII (July 1929), 42–73.

4:112. Roberts, Sydney Castle. "James Boswell," in *Encyclopaedia Britannica* (14th ed.), III, 940–42. Ca. 1930's. Replaces article by Thomas Seccombe; replaced ca. 1950's by one by F. A. Pottle.

*4:113. Birrell, Augustine. "Boswell Disrobed" [new Boswell papers], *Et Cetera*, pp. 13–48. London: Chatto & Windus, 1930.

4:114. [Chapman, R. W.] "The Making of Boswell's 'Johnson'" [Malahide Castle papers; a review of item 4:19, Vols. I–VI], *TLS*, February 6, 1930, pp. 85–86. See also L. Bettany, *ibid.*, February 13, p. 122, and Rupert T. Gould, *ibid.*, February 27, p. 166.

4:115. Fortescue-Brickdale, Charles. "Dr. Johnson and Mrs. Macaulay: The Credibility of Boswell" [a defense of Mrs. Macaulay], *N&Q*, CLIX (August 16, 1930), 111–12.

4:116. Longaker, John Mark. "Boswell's *Life of Johnson*," *English Biogra-*

phy in the Eighteenth Century, pp. 407–76. Philadelphia: University of Pennsylvania Press, 1931.

4:117. Cox, James E. "The Independent Boswell and the Capricious Dr. Johnson" [in specific criticism Boswell a better literary critic than Johnson], *Quarterly Journal of the University of North Dakota*, XXII (Fall 1931), 51–59.

4:118. Reilly, J. J. "Bozzy: The Man Who Made Johnson," *Dear Prue's Husband*, pp. 68–78. New York: Macmillan, 1932.

4:119. Kanki, S. "Boswell's Art as a Biographer," *Studies in English Literature* (Tokyo), XIII (1933), 154–60.

4:120. Kirwan, H. N. "The Boswell Supplement" [Malahide Castle papers, etc.], *London Mercury*, XXVII (February 1933), 331–40.

4:121. Powell, Lawrence F. "The New Birkbeck Hill" [various problems], *TLS*, August 3, 1933, p. 525.

4:122. Chapman, R. W. "The Johnson Canon: Boswell after 150 Years," *Times* (London), June 22, 1934, pp. 15–16. Essentially a review of item 4.14, ed. Hill-Powell (1034).

4:123. Chapman, R. W. "Hill's Boswell" [a reply to Tinker's review; see item 4:14 (1934)], *SRL*, March 23, 1935, p. 564.

4:124. Radecki, Sigismund von. "Englische Lieblingsbücher," *Hochland*, CCCXXXI (December 1935), 250–56.

*4:125. Powell, Lawrence F. "Boswell's Original Journal of His Tour to the Hebrides and the Printed Version," *Essays and Studies by Members of the English Association*, XXIII (1938), 58–69.

4:126. Roubiček, K. "Strukturální povaha Boswellova Životopisv doktora Johnsona" [structural character of the *Life*], *Casopis pro Moderní filologii*, XXV (1938), 43–56.

4:127. Haraszti, Zoltán. "The Life of Johnson" [composition of *Life*, and other details], *More Books* (Boston Public Library), XIII (March 1938), 99–112.

4:128. Hazen, Allen T. "Boswell's Cancels in the 'Tour to the Hebrides,'" *Bibliographical Notes and Queries*, II, no. 11 (November 1938), 7.

4:129. Togawa, Shûkotsu. "Boswell's *Life of Johnson* as the Theme of Biographical Study" [in Japanese], *Studies in English Literature* (Tokyo), XIX, no. 1 (1939), 1–11.

4:130. Pottle, Frederick A. "Boswell's 'Life of Johnson': Translations," *N&Q*, CLXXVII (January 20, 1940), 50–51.

4:131. Wilson, F. P. "Table Talk" [Boswell's reports of Johnson's conversation considered as in the "ana" genre], *Huntington Library Quarterly*, IV (October 1940), 27–46.

4:132. "James Boswell, *The Life of Samuel Johnson*" [discussion by Ralph Isham, J. W. Krutch, and Mark Van Doren, originally for radio], in *The*

New Invitation to Learning, ed. Mark Van Doren, pp. 283–96. New York: Random House, 1942.

4:133. Powell, Lawrence F. "Boswell's 'Life of Johnson'" [requests for information about various persons], *N&Q*, CLXXXII (March 7, 1942) to CLXXXIV (May 22, 1943), *passim*.

4:134. Osgood, Charles G. "Lady Phillipina Knight and Her Boswell" [marginal annotations by Lady Knight in her copy of the *Life*], *Princeton University Library Chronicle*, IV (February–April 1943), 37–49.

*4:135. Pottle, Frederick A. "The Power of Memory in Boswell and Scott," in *Essays on the Eighteenth Century Presented to David Nichol Smith*, pp. 168–89. Oxford: Clarendon Press, 1945.

4:136. Quennell, Peter. "James Boswell," *Four Portraits* [in the U.S. entitled *The Profane Virtues*], pp. 11–75. London: William Collins Sons & Co., 1945.

4:137. Lewis, D. B. Wyndham. *The Hooded Hawk or the Case of Mr. Boswell*. London: Eyre and Spottiswoode, 1946; New York: Longmans, Green & Company, 1947. Reviewed by H. W. Liebert, *PQ*, XXVII (April 1948), 139–40.

*4:138. Powell, Lawrence F. "The Anonymous Designations in Boswell's 'Journal of a Tour to the Hebrides' and Their Identification," *Edinburgh Bibliographical Society Transactions*, II (1946), 355–71.

*4:139. Pottle, Frederick A. "The Life of Boswell," *Yale Review*, XXXV (Spring 1946), 445–60.

4:140. Gordon, George. "Boswell's Life of Johnson," *More Companionable Books*, pp. 31–36. London: Chatto & Windus, 1947.

*4:141. Liebert, Herman W. [Significance of the Boswell papers], *New York Times*, November 8, 1948, p. 18.

4:142. Pottle, Frederick A. "James Boswell, Journalist," in item 10/6:273, pp. 15–25.

4:143. "The Boswell Papers," *TLS*, August 12, 1949, p. 528.

4:144. Liebert, Herman W. "The Boswell Papers" [their acquisition by Yale], *Yale Alumni Magazine*, XIII (October 1949), 14–16.

4:145. Altick, Richard D. "The Secret of the Ebony Cabinet" [history of the Boswell papers], *The Scholar Adventurers*, pp. 16–36. New York: Macmillan, 1950. Reissued in Macmillan Paperbacks, 1960.

4:146. Butt, John. "Boswell, Johnson, and Garrick" [earlier publication of an anecdote recorded in the *Life*], *JNL*, X, no. 4 (August 1950), 12.

4:147. Horne, Colin J. "Boswell, Burke, and the *Life of Johnson*" [sale comparable to that of Burke's *Reflections on the French Revolution*], *N&Q*, November 11, 1950, pp. 498–99.

4:148. Powell, Lawrence F. "A Task Ended." In item 6:23 (1950).

4:149. Waingrow, Marshall. "Five Correspondences of James Boswell Relating to the Composition of the Life of Johnson." Dissertation, Yale University, 1951. See item 4:21 (Research Edition, Vol. 2).

4:150. Hart, Edward. "The Contributions of John Nichols to Boswell's *Life of Johnson*," *PMLA*, LXVII (June 1952), 391–410. See also Arthur Sherbo, *PQ*, XXXII (July 1953), 260–61.

4:151. Martin, Samuel. *An Epistle in Verse Occasioned by the Death of James Boswell, Esquire, of Auchinleck* [1795], introduction by Robert Metzdorf. Hamden, Conn.: Shoe String Press, 1952.

4:152. Audiat, Pierre. "Héros Inattendus" [includes discussion of *London Journal*], *Revue de Paris*, Année 59 (September 1952), 163–66.

4:153. Baldwin, Louis. "The Conversation in Boswell's *Life of Johnson*," *JEGP*, LI (October 1952), 492–500.

4:154. [Liebert, Herman W.] *To Honor the Two Hundred and Seventeenth Anniversary of the Departure of Samuel Johnson and David Garrick to Try Their Fortunes in the Great Metropolis, 2 March 1737* [with facsimile of page of MS of the *Life*]. New Haven, Conn.: Privately printed for Halsted B. Vander Poel [Yale University Press], 1954. For similar title [1955] see item 23:104.

4:155. Roberts, S. C. "More Boswell Letters," *TLS*, January 1, 1954, p. 16.

4:156. Adams, Sarah F. "Boswell's *Life of Samuel Johnson*" [cancels in copy of 1st edition], *Yale Library Gazette*, XXIX (July 1954), 35–36.

4:157. McKillop, Alan D. "Johnson and Ogilvie" [Ogilvie challenged Boswell's account of the conversation of July 6, 1763], *JNL*, XV, no. 4 (December 1955), 3–4.

4:158. Collins, P. A. W. *James Boswell*. (Writers and Their Work.) London: Longmans, Green, for the British Council and the National Book League, 1956.

4:159. Sherbo, Arthur. "Gleanings from Boswell's *Notebook*," *N&Q*, March 1956, pp. 108–112.

4:160. Collins, P. A. W. "Boswell's Contact with Johnson" [the two were in each other's company on a total of about 425 days], *N&Q*, April 1956, pp. 163–66.

4:161. Reid, B. L. "Johnson's Life of Boswell," *Kenyon Review*, XVIII (Autumn 1956), 546–75. Reprinted in his *The Long Boy and Others*, pp. 1–30. Athens: University of Georgia Press, 1969.

4:162. Sheldon, Esther K. "Boswell's English in the *London Journal*," *PMLA*, LXII (December 1956), 1067–93.

4:163. Edel, Leon. *Literary Biography* [Alexander Lectures, 1955–56], pp. 13–20. London: Rupert Hart-Davis, 1957. On Boswell's *Life of Johnson*.

4:164. Todd, William B. "Cowper's Commentary on the *Life of Johnson*," *TLS*, March 15, 1957, p. 168.

4:165. Monk, Samuel H. "Samuel Johnson Quotes Addison" [unrecognized quotation in the *Life*], *N&Q*, April 1957, p. 154.

4:166. Brooks, Alfred Russell. "The Literary and Intellectual Foundations of James Boswell" (dissertation, University of Wisconsin, 1959), *Dissertation Abstracts*, XIX (1959), 1752–53.

4:167. Wimsatt, William K., Jr. "James Boswell: The Man and the Journal," *Yale Review*, XLIX (Autumn 1959), 80–92. Reprinted (rev.) as "The Fact Imagined: James Boswell," in *Hateful Contraries*, pp. 165–83, Lexington: University of Kentucky Press, 1965.

*4:168. Lonsdale, Roger. "Dr. Burney and the Integrity of Boswell's Quotations," *PBSA*, LIII (4th quarter, 1959), 327–31.

4:169. Butt, John. *James Boswell* [inaugural lecture as Professor of Rhetoric and English Literature, December 1959]. Edinburgh: University of Edinburgh, 1960.

4:170. Stewart, Mary Margaret. "The Search for Felicity: A Study of the Religious Thought of James Boswell in the Light of the Religious Developments of Eighteenth Century England and Scotland" [mentions influence of Johnson] (dissertation, Indiana University, 1959), *Dissertation Abstracts*, XX (1960), 4392–93.

4:171. Hart, Francis R. "Boswell and the Romantics: A Chapter in the History of Biographical Theory," *ELH*, XXVII (March 1960), 44–65.

4:172. Morgan, Lee. "Boswell's Portrait of Goldsmith" [in *Life*], in *Studies in Honor of John C. Hodges and Alwin Thaler*, ed. R. B. Davis and J. L. Lievsay, pp. 67–76. Knoxville: University of Tennessee Press, 1961.

4:173. Stewart, Mary Margaret. "Boswell's Denominational Dilemma," *PMLA*, LXXVI (December 1961), 503–11.

4:174. Kiley, Frederick S. "Boswell's Literary Art in the *London Journal*," *College English*, XXIII (May 1962), 629–32.

4:175. McElderry, B. R., Jr. "Boswell in 1790–91: Two Unpublished Comments," *N&Q*, CCVII (July 1962), 266–68. On his work as biographer; from the Montagu Papers, Huntington Library.

4:176. Fussell, Paul, Jr. "The Force of Literary Memory in Boswell's *London Journal*," *Studies in English Literature* (Rice University), II (Summer 1962), 351–57.

4:177. Liebert, Herman W. "Boswell's *Life of Johnson*, 1791" [lists variants], *American Notes and Queries*, I (September 1962), 6–7.

4:178. Howes, Victor. "Boswell and Pseudo-Events," *Christian Science Monitor*, February 5, 1963, p. 8.

4:179. Werkmeister, Lucyle. "Jemmie Boswell and the London Daily Press, 1785–1795," *Bulletin of the New York Public Library*, LXVII (February 1963), 82–114; (March), 169–85.

4:180. Gray, James. "Johnson as Boswell's Moral Tutor," *Burke Newsletter*, IV (Spring–Summer, 1963), 202–10.

4:181. Greene, Donald J. "Reflections on a Literary Anniversary," *Queen's Quarterly*, LXX (Summer 1963), 198–208. The meeting of Johnson and Boswell.

4:182. Molin, Sven. "Boswell's Account of the Johnson-Wilkes Meeting," *Studies in English Literature* (Rice University), III (Summer 1963), 307–22.

4:183. Lustig, Irma S. "Boswell's Portrait of Himself in *The Life of Johnson*" (dissertation, University of Pennsylvania, 1963), *Dissertation Abstracts*, XXIV (October 1963), 2015–16.

4:184. "The Relationship Between Johnson and Boswell," *NRTA Journal* (National Retired Teachers Association), XIV (3rd quarter, 1963), 9–11.

4:185. Pottle, Frederick A. "The Yale Editions of the Private Papers of James Boswell," *Ventures* (Yale Graduate School), II (Winter 1963), 11–15.

4:186. Pottle, Frederick A. "Boswell Revalued," in *Literary Views*, ed. Carroll Camden, pp. 79–91. Chicago: University of Chicago Press, 1964.

4:187. Ross, Ian. "Boswell in Search of a Father? or a Subject?" *Review of English Literature*, V (January 1964), 19–34.

4:188. Day, D. "Boswell, Corsica and Paoli," *English Studies*, XLV (February 1964), 1–20.

4:189. Stewart, Mary Margaret. "Boswell and the Infidels," *Studies in English Literature* (Rice University), IV (Summer 1964), 475–83.

4:190. Osborn, James M. *"By Appointment to His Majesty Biographer of Samuel Johnson, LL.D."* Privately printed for the annual dinner of The Johnsonians, 1964. Facsimile of letter from Malone to Boswell, May 13, 1793, and Boswell's reply.

4:191. Brady, Frank. *Boswell's Political Career*. New Haven, Conn.: Yale University Press, 1965.

4:192. Jack, Ian. "Two Biographers: Lockhart and Boswell," in item 10/6:329 (1965), pp. 268–85.

4:193. Kendall, Paul Murray. *The Art of Biography*. New York: Norton, 1965. Boswell, pp. 98–99 and *passim*.

4:194. Pottle, Frederick A. "Boswell's University Education," in item 10/6:329 (1965), pp. 230–53.

4:195. Rae, Thomas I. and William Beattie. "Boswell and the Advocates Library," in item 10/6:329 (1965), pp. 254–67.

4:196. Brauer, George C., Jr. "Johnson and Boswell," *CEA Critic*, XXVII (January 1965), 1, 10, 12.

4:197. McCollum, J. I., Jr. "The Indebtedness of James Boswell to Edmond Malone," *New Rambler*, June 1966, pp. 29–45.

4:198. Lustig, Irma S. "Boswell's Literary Criticism in *The Life of Johnson*," *Studies in English Literature* (Rice University), VI (Summer 1966), 529–42.

4:199. Morris, John N. "James Boswell," *Versions of the Self: Studies in English Autobiography from John Bunyan to John Stuart Mill*, pp. 171–210. New York: Basic Books, 1966.

*4:200. Pottle, Frederick A. *James Boswell, the Earlier Years, 1740–1769.* New York: McGraw-Hill, 1966. Reviewed by Roger Lonsdale, *Yale Review*, LV (Autumn 1966), 117–19; John Carroll, *University of Toronto Quarterly*, XXXVI (January 1967), 198–203. A second volume (with Frank Brady) is in preparation.

4:201. Reed, Joseph W., Jr. "Boswell and After," *English Biography in the Early Nineteenth Century*, pp. 3–26. New Haven, Conn.: Yale University Press, 1966.

4:202. Ryskamp, Charles. "James Boswell," in *Four Oaks Library*, ed. Gabriel Austin, pp. 11–18. Somerville, N.J.: Privately printed, 1967.

4:203. Fussell, Paul. "The Memorable Scenes of Mr. Boswell," *Encounter*, XXVIII (May 1967), 70–77.

4:204. De Beer, Esmond S. "Dr. Powell's Index to Boswell's *Life of Johnson*," *Indexer*, V (Spring 1967), 135–39.

4:205. Kerslake, John. *Mr. Boswell.* London, 1967. Catalogue of exhibition at National Portrait Gallery of Scotland, August 18–September 16, and at National Portrait Gallery, October 13–November 30, 1967.

4:206. Palmer, Joyce Arline Cornette. "Boswell's *Life of Johnson* as Literary History" (dissertation, University of Tennessee, 1967), *Dissertation Abstracts*, XXVIII, no. 10 (April 1968), 4139A.

4:207. Rader, Ralph W. "Literary Form in Factual Narrative: The Example of Boswell's *Johnson*," in *Essays in Eighteenth-Century Biography*, ed. Philip B. Daghlian, pp. 3–42. Bloomington: Indiana University Press, 1968.

4:208. Alkon, Paul K. "Boswell's Control of Aesthetic Distance," *University of Toronto Quarterly*, XXXVIII (January 1969), 174–91.

4:209. Amory, Hugh. "Boswell in Search of the Intentional Fallacy," *Bulletin of the New York Public Library*, LXXIII (January 1969), 24–39.

5. JOHNSON'S PERSONAL RELATIONSHIPS

5:1. Hervey, Thomas. *Mr. Hervey's Answer to a Letter He Received from Dr. Samuel Johnson, wherein he* [Johnson] *had endeavoured to dissuade him from parting with his supposed wife. To which are subjoined his letters to Lord Shelburne and Colonel Burgoyne.* [London], 1772. Written in 1763.

5:2. [Account of Burke's defending Johnson from charge of having written *The False Alarm* in payment for his pension], *London Chronicle*, XXVII (March 24, 1770), 288.

5:3. "An Anecdote of Pomposo," *Whitehall Evening Post*, August 15–18, 1772. Johnson's reaction to a takeoff by Foote.

5:4. "The Life of Philip Dormer Stanhope, late Earl of Chesterfield," *Universal Magazine*, LIV (June 1774), 337–42. Contains anecdotes of Johnson and Chesterfield, including the (erroneous) identification of Johnson as Chesterfield's "respectable Hottentot."

5:5. A Lover of Impartial Justice. [Praise of Johnson's conduct in the Dodd affair], *Morning Post*, July 3, 1777.

5:6. Sturz, Helfrich Peter. "Briefe, in Jahre 1768 auf einer Reise in Gefolge des Königs von Dänemark" [account of meeting with Johnson], *Schrifte von Helfrich Peter Sturz*, I, 113–14. Leipzig: Erste Sammlung, 1779; rev. ed., Leipzig, 1786. "First published in incomplete form in the *Deutsches Museum* for March and May 1777 and February 1779": W. D. Robson-Scott, *German Travellers in England, 1400–1800*, p. 140, n.2. Tr. in *Monthly Magazine*, March 1800; reprinted in item 3:75 and in Sturz, *Kleine Schriften*, ed. Franz Blei, pp. 97–99, Leipzig: Insel-Verlag, 1904. See also items 5:136 and 5:262.

5:7. Davies, Thomas. *Memoirs of the Life of David Garrick*. London: Printed for the author, 1780. Contains much about Johnson (who contributed the opening paragraph and much material about Garrick's early life). Reviewed (with hostility toward Johnson) in *Westminster Magazine*, VIII (May 1780), 277–78.

5:8. B. "Memoirs of Mrs. Anne Williams," *London Magazine*, n.s., I (December 1783), 517–21.

5:9. "Memoirs of Mr. Levet, with Dr. Johnson's Elegy on Him," *European Magazine*, VII (January 1785), 55–56. Reprinted in *GM*, LV (February 1785), 101–2.

5:10. Baretti, Joseph. *Tolondron: Speeches to John Bowle about His Edition of Don Quixote*. London: R. Faulder, 1786. Extract reprinted as "Mr. Baretti's Relation of His Rupture with Dr. Johnson," *European Magazine*, XII (August 1787), 111–12.

5:11. Murphy, Arthur. Dedication "To the Malevoli," *The Works of Arthur Murphy*, VII, v–xv. London: Cadell, 1786. Account of Johnson's intervention in a quarrel between Murphy and another writer.

5:12. [Review of John Sidney Hawkins's edition of Ruggle's *Ignoramus*], *GM*, LVIII (January 1788), 49–51. Johnson's assistance to young Hawkins.

5:13. "Anecdotes of Mrs. Frances Brooke," *European Magazine*, XV (February 1789), 99–101. Johnson's tender farewell on her departure for Canada. See also *N&Q*, 5th ser., III (May 15, 1875), 391–92.

5:14. Elphinston, James. *Forty Years' Correspondence Between Geniusses ov Boath Sexes and James Elphinston.* London: Ritchardson, 1791. Includes letters to and from Johnson, in Elphinston's phonetic spelling.

5:15. Priestley, Joseph. *An Appeal to the Public on the Subject of the Riots at Birmingham,* pt. 2, pp. 103–4. Birmingham: J. Thompson; London: J. Johnson, 1791. Johnson's acquaintance with Priestley and Price.

5:16. Lardener. [Johnson and Lauder], *GM*, LXI (May 1791), 432–33.

5:17. Knowles, Mary. "An Interesting Dialogue between the Late Dr. Samuel Johnson and Mrs. Knowles," *GM*, LXI (June 1791), 500–502. See also C. R., *ibid.* (September), 798–99; G. Sael, LXVI (Supplement 1796), 1074. Reprinted separately as *A Dialogue between Dr. Johnson and Mrs. Knowles,* London, 1799; *A Dialogue Between Mrs. Knowles and Dr. Johnson,* London: G. Stower, 1805. See also item 24:52.

5:18. Lackington, James. *Memoirs of the First Forty-Five Years of the Life of James Lackington,* pp. 433–41. "New edition, corrected and much enlarged." London: Printed for the author, 1792 (first published 1791). Various anecdotes; includes a detailed account of a meeting of Johnson and Hume.

5:19. "Account of John Hoole, Esq.," *European Magazine,* XXI (March 1792), 163–65. Much on his relations with Johnson.

5:20. B. [Johnson and Chesterfield], *GM*, LXIV (January 1794), 18.

5:21. Parr, Samuel. [Contradicts Boswell's denial that Johnson met Priestley], *GM*, LXV (March 1795), 179–81. See also Filiolus, *ibid.* (May), 392–93.

5:22. Seward, William. *Supplement to Anecdotes of Some Distinguished Persons, chiefly of the present and two preceding centuries,* pp. 149–51. London: Cadell and W. Davies, 1797. Quotes two letters to Susan Thrale.

5:23. Reynolds, Sir Joshua. *The Works of Sir Joshua Reynolds, Knight,* ed. Edmond Malone, I, xix–xxi. London: Cadell and Davies, 1797. A personal tribute to Johnson's influence on him, quoted by Malone from notes for a possible future "Discourse." Reprinted in item 3:116 (1897).

5:24. [Obituary of John Ryland; much about his relations with Johnson], *GM*, LXVIII (July 1798), 629–30. H. S., *ibid.* (September), 762, and Philologicus, (Supplement), 1109, deny assertion in obituary that Johnson, Ryland, Hawkins, and Payne "lived in the profession of what is now called Calvinistic Christianity."

5:25. [Knight, Phillipina, Lady.] "Mrs. Anna Williams," *European Magazine,* XXXVI (October 1799), 225–27. Reprinted in items 3:75. (1836) and 3:116 (1897).

5:26. Seward, Anna. *Memoirs of the Life of Dr. Darwin, Chiefly During His*

Residence in Lichfield, pp. 48–55. London: J. Johnson; Philadelphia: W. Poyntell, 1804. Erasmus Darwin's acquaintance with Johnson.

5:27. Teignmouth, John Shore, Lord. *Memoirs of the Life, Writings, and Correspondence of Sir William Jones.* London: Hatchard, 1804. A new edition of Jones's correspondence, by Garland Cannon, is in preparation.

5:28. Forbes, Sir William. *An Account of the Life and Writings of James Beattie, LL.D.* 2 vols. London: Longmans, 1806. Many references to Johnson in Beattie's letters. Extracts reprinted in item 3:75.

5:29. Wooll, John. *Biographical Memoirs of the Reverend Joseph Warton.* London: Cadell, 1806.

5:30. Pennington, Montagu. *Memoirs of the Life of Mrs. Elizabeth Carter.* London: Rivington, 1807. 2nd ed., 1818.

5:31. Carter, Elizabeth, and Catherine Talbot. *A Series of Letters between Mrs. Elizabeth Carter and Miss Catherine Talbot, from 1741 to 1770*, ed. Montagu Pennington. 2 vols. London: Rivington, 1808. New ed., 4 vols., London: Rivington, 1809.

5:32. Hardy, Francis. *Memoirs of the Political and Private Life of James Caulfield, Earl of Charlemont.* London: Cadell, 1810. 2nd ed., 1812.

5:33. Seward, Anna. *The Poetical Works of Anna Seward; with Extracts from Her Literary Correspondence*, ed. Walter Scott. 3 vols. Edinburgh: Ballantyne, 1810.

5:34. W., T. S. "Notices of Dr. Johnson and Francis Barber," *European Magazine*, LVIII (October 1810), 275. Chiefly on Mrs. Barber.

5:35. Nichols, John. *Literary Anecdotes of the Eighteenth Century.* 9 vols. London: Printed for the author, 1812–15. Incorporates his *Anecdotes, Biographical and Literary, of the Late William Bowyer, Printer* (London, 1778). Facsimile reprint, New York: AMS Press, 1967. Abr. (1 vol.) by Colin Clair, Fontwell, Sussex: Centaur Press, 1967.

5:36. Northcote, James. *The Memoirs of Sir Joshua Reynolds . . . comprising original anecdotes of many distinguished persons, his contemporaries.* London: Colburn, 1813. 2nd ed., "revised and augmented," *The Life of Sir Joshua Reynolds*, 2 vols., London: Colburn, 1819.

5:37. Wraxall, Sir Nathaniel William. *Historical Memoirs of My Own Time*, I, 139–56. London: Cadell and Davies, 1815. Johnson, Mrs. Montagu, Mrs. Thrale, and others. See also his *Posthumous Memoirs of His Own Time*, I, 232–35, London: Bentley, 1836. Both *Memoirs* ed. H. B. Wheatley, 5 vols., London: Bickers and Son, 1884.

5:38. Carter, Elizabeth. *Letters from Mrs. Elizabeth Carter to Mrs. Montagu between the Years 1755 and 1800*, ed. Montagu Pennington. 3 vols. London: Rivington, 1817.

5:39. Nichols, John. *Illustrations of the Literary History of the Eighteenth Century . . . Intended as a Sequel to the Literary Anecdotes.* 8 vols.

London: Printed for the author, 1817–58. Vols. 6–8 comp. by John Bowyer Nichols. Facsimile reprint, New York: AMS Press, 1967.

5:40. Walpole, Horace, 4th Earl of Orford. *Private Correspondence. Now first collected.* London: Rodwell and Martin; Colburn, 1820. *Letters*, ed. Peter Cunningham, London: Richard Bentley, 1857. *Letters*, ed. Mrs. Paget Toynbee, Oxford: Clarendon Press, 1903–5. *Correspondence*, ed. W. S. Lewis, New Haven, Conn.: Yale University Press, 1937– (Yale Edition). Numerous references to Johnson and Boswell.

5:41. Baverstock, J. H. *Treatises on Brewing* [contains letters of Henry Thrale], pp. xvii–xviii. London: G. and W. B. Whittaker, 1824.

5:42. Prior, Sir James. *Memoir of the Life and Character of Edmund Burke.* London: Baldwin, 1824. 2nd ed., 2 vols., 1826. Later editions.

5:43. "Baron Maseres," *Annual Biography and Obituary*, IX (1825), 393. Brief account of his meeting with Johnson.

5:44. [Gooch, Robert.] "Two Days with Dr. Parr," *Blackwood's*, XVIII (November 1825), 596–601. Contains anecdote of Johnson and Parr.

5:45. Anspach, Elizabeth, Margravine of (née Berkeley; then Lady Craven). *Memoirs of the Margravine of Anspach*, II, 109–15. London: Colburn, 1826. Anecdotes of her acquaintance with Johnson.

5:46. [Marsh, Charles.] "Recollections of Dr. Parr, Between the Years 1818 and 1825," *Monthly Magazine*, n.s., I (January 1826), 21–26; (February), 134–41. Anecdotes and comment on Johnson, Baretti, and others.

5:47. Barker, Edmund Henry. *Parriana: or Notices of the Rev. Samuel Parr, LL.D. collected from various sources, printed and manuscript.* 2 vols. London: J. Bohn, 1828–29.

5:48. Field, William. *Memoirs of the Life, Writings, and Opinions of the Rev. Samuel Parr, LL.D.* 2 vols. London: Colburn, 1828.

5:49. Best, Henry Digby. *Personal and Literary Memorials*, pp. 62–66. London: Colburn, 1829. The Langton family; a visit of Johnson to Langton.

5:50. Piozzi, Hester Lynch. [Letter describing her first meeting with Johnson], *Blackwood's*, XXVI (November 1829), 753–55.

5:51. Northcote, James. *The Conversations of James Northcote, Esq., R.A.*, ed. William Hazlitt. London: Colburn and Bentley, 1830. Ed. Edmund Gosse, London: Bentley, 1894. Anecdotes of Reynolds and Johnson.

5:52. Burney, Frances. *Memoirs of Dr. Burney.* London: Moxon, 1832.

5:53. More, Hannah. *Memoirs of the Life and Correspondence of Mrs. Hannah More*, ed. William Roberts. 4 vols. London: R. B. Seely and W. Burnside, 1834. Frequent references to Johnson. Reviewed (harshly with regard to account of Johnson's religion) by J. G. Lockhart (assisted by J. W. Croker), *Quarterly Review*, LII (November 1834), 416–41. (See Lockhart-Croker correspondence, *N&Q*, June 1946, p. 233.)

*5:54. Burney, Frances. *Diary and Letters of Madame d'Arblay . . .*

edited by her niece [Charlotte Barrett]. 7 vols. London: H. Colburn, 1842–46. Reviewed by T. B. Macaulay, *Edinburgh Review* (item 5:55); in *U.S. Magazine and Democratic Review*, XI (1842), 161–65. See also item 5:109. A full edition of the Burney family papers is in progress (general ed., Joyce Hemlow).

5:55. Macaulay, Thomas Babington. "Madame d'Arblay" [review of items 5:52 and 5:54], *Edinburgh Review*, LXXVI (January 1843), 523–70. Reprinted in his *Critical and Historical Essays*, London: Longmans, 1843, and often reprinted.

5:56. "Dr. Johnson and Miss Hannah More, An Imaginary Dialogue," *Chambers' Journal*, XV (June 14, 1851), 380–82. A discussion of Garrick, after receiving news of his death.

5:57. Crosland, Mrs. Newton (Camilla Dufour Crosland). "Madame d'Arblay and Mrs. Piozzi," *Memorable Women: The Story of Their Lives*, pp. 53–120. London: D. Bogue; Boston: Ticknor and Fields, 1854.

5:58. "Memoirs of Psalmanazar," *Retrospective Review*, 3rd ser., II (August 1854), 379–96.

5:59. Waylen, J. "Dr. Johnson's Visit to Heale House" [home of William Bowles], *N&Q*, XII (August 25, 1855), 149–50.

5:60. [Letter from Carlyle, Dickens, and Forster, printing a memorial signed by themselves, Tennyson, Macaulay, Thackeray, Disraeli, and others asking help for Johnson's goddaughter, Miss Lowe, now destitute], *Times* (London), November 1, 1855, p. 7. Contains paragraphs (probably by Carlyle) praising Johnson's dictionary.

5:61. De Morgan, A. "Dr. Johnson and Dr. Maty," *N&Q*, 2nd ser., V (October 31, 1857), 341.

5:62. Attwood, E. "Memoirs of Samuel Johnson" [1785], *N&Q*, 2nd ser., V (May 8, 1858), 377–78. Johnson's relations with William Shaw, the supposed author.

5:63. Hopper, Cl. "Johnsoniana," *N&Q*, 2nd ser., VI (September 4, 1858), 187. Inquiry for whereabouts of Baretti's commonplace book; also prints Johnson's verses "At sight of sparkling bowls." For recovery of the book, by Alan T. McKenzie, see "An Important Baretti Discovery," *JNL*, XXVIII (September 1968), 7–8.

*5:64. Piozzi, Hester Lynch (Mrs. Thrale). *Autobiography, Letters, and Literary Remains of Mrs. Piozzi (Thrale)*. Ed. with notes and introductory account of her life and writings by Abraham Hayward. 2 vols. London: Longmans, Green; Boston: Ticknor and Fields, 1861. 2nd ed., with added material, 1861.

5:65. "Dr. Johnson and Mrs. Thrale," *St. James's Magazine*, I (April–July 1861), 243–48. Partly a review of item 5:64.

5:66. Taunton, Henry Labouchere, 1st Baron. "From the Windham Papers,"

Miscellanies of the Philobiblon Society, VIII, 3–12. London: Whittingham and Wilkins, 1863–64. Notes of the conversation of Johnson in August 1784 and other scraps. See item 5:71.

5:67. Wylie, Charles. "Dr. Johnson," *N&Q*, 3rd ser., III (May 7, 1863), 187. Johnson corrects George Anne Bellamy's pronunciation.

5:68. Fitzgerald, Percy. *A Famous Forgery; Being the Story of the Unfortunate Doctor Dodd*. London: Chapman and Hall, 1865.

5:69. Leslie, Charles R., and Tom Taylor. *The Life and Times of Sir Joshua Reynolds*. 2 vols. London: Murray, 1865. Frequent references to Johnson.

5:70. [Cadell, Cecilia Mary.] "Sir Joshua Reynolds and Dr. Johnson," *The Month*, III (October 1865), 403–10. ("By the author of *Wild Times*.")

5:71. Windham, William. *The Diary of the Rt. Hon. William Windham*, ed. Mrs. Henry Baring. London: Longmans, 1866. Ed. R. W. Ketton-Cremer, *The Early Life and Diaries of William Windham*, London: Faber and Faber, 1930. Contains (pp. 253–74) "The Friendship of Doctor Johnson and Windham."

5:72. "Two Portraits: A Satirist and an Actor" [Foote and Garrick], *Dublin University Magazine*, LXIX (April 1867), 465–81.

5:73. Reece, R. "An Unpublished Page in The Life of Lauder," *N&Q*, 4th ser., V (January 22, 1870), 83–85. His later life.

5:74. Wylie, Charles. "Dr. Johnson," *N&Q*, 4th ser., VI (October 22, 1870), 342. Criticism of Johnson's eating habits and other manners by Mrs. James ("Hermes") Harris in *Letters of the First Earl of Malmesbury* (1870). Reply by James Crossley, *ibid.*, 418.

5:75. Fitzgerald, Percy. "Dr. Johnson and Mrs. Piozzi," *Belgravia*, XV (2nd ser., V) (August 1871), 183–96.

5:76. Tyerman, Luke. *The Oxford Methodists*, p. 410. New York: Harper, 1873. Johnson's friendship with John Wesley's sister Martha ("Patty") Hall (Mrs. Westley Hall).

5:77. Glazebrook, H. Sydney. "Dr. Johnson and Mrs. Turton, née Hickman," *N&Q*, 5th ser., I (January 10, 1874), 30–31. See also *ibid.*, 112, 249; and V, 13–14. Johnson's Hickman connections.

5:78. Masson, Rosaline Orme. "Mrs. Thrale: The Friend of Dr. Johnson," *Macmillan's Magazine*, XXXIII (April 1876), 524–35; XXXIV (May 1876), 35–45. Reprinted in *Living Age*, CXXIX (1876), 281–90, 609–18.

5:79. Jewett, Llewellynn. "Unpublished Episodes in the Life of Dr. Johnson," *GM*, n.s., XXI (December 1878), 692–712. Johnson and William Davenport; MSS now in Bodleian Library, Oxford.

5:80. Darwin, Charles. "Preliminary Notice," in Ernst Krause, *Erasmus Darwin* (tr. W. S. Dallas), pp. 40–41. London: Murray, 1879. Brief family reminiscences of relations between Johnson and Erasmus Darwin, with text of Darwin's epigram on Johnson and Thomas Seward.

5:81. Hill, George Birkbeck. "Lord Macaulay and Dr. Johnson's Wife," *Cornhill Magazine*, XLII (November 1880), 573–81. Attacks Macaulay's prejudiced treatment of Tetty. Reprinted in *Living Age*, CXLVII (1885), 627–33.

5:82. Waller, J. F. *Boswell and Johnson: Their Companions and Contemporaries*. London: Cassell & Co., [1881].

5:83. Flint, Stamford Raffles. *Mudge Memoirs. Being a record of Zachariah Mudge and some members of his family*. Truro: Netherton and Worth, 1883.

5:84. Welsh, Charles. *A Bookseller of the Last Century: Being Some Account of the Life of John Newbery*. London: Griffith, Farren, Okeden and Welsh, 1885.

5:85. Hughes, T. Cann. "Johnson and Miss Hickman," *N&Q*, 7th ser., IV (November 26, 1887), 431.

5:86. Pike, G. Holden. "Life in the Eighteenth Century—Dr. Johnson and His Friends," *Fireside*, 1888, pp. 792–96, 872–76.

*5:87. Burney, Frances. *The Early Diary of Fanny Burney, 1768–1778, with a selection from her correspondence and from the journals of her sisters Susan and Charlotte Burney*, ed. Annie Raine Ellis. 2 vols. London: Bell, 1889. Reprinted, 1907.

5:88. Guiney, Louise Imogen. "Dr. Johnson's Favorites" [Langton and Beauclerk], *Macmillan's Magazine*, LIX (January 1889), 185–93. Reprinted in *Living Age*, CLXXX (February 2, 1889), 281–88; *Eclectic Magazine*, CXII (February 1889), 270–78; *A Little English Gallery*, pp. 173–227, New York: Harper and Brothers, 1894.

5:89. McCarthy, Justin H. "Mrs. Thrale-Piozzi," *The Queens of Society*, II, 107–46. London: Jarvis, 1890.

5:90. Seeley, L. B. *Mrs. Thrale Afterwards Mrs. Piozzi*. London: Seeley, 1891.

5:91. Hitchcock, Thomas. "Dr. Johnson and Mrs. Thrale," *Unhappy Loves of Men of Genius*, pp. 45–76. London: Osgood, McIlvaine, 1892.

5:92. "George III and Dr. Johnson," *Leisure Hour*, XLII (August 1893), 712.

5:93. Caetani, L. *Baretti e Johnson*. Rome: Tip. Terme Diocleziane, 1894. Not seen; listed in Luigi Piccioni, *Bibliografia Analitica di Guiseppe Baretti*, 1942.

5:94. Dent, Robert K. "Dr. Johnson and Edmund Hector," *The Making of Birmingham*, pp. 159–62; also pp. 67–68, 75–76. Birmingham: J. L. Allday; London: Simpkin, Marshall, 1894.

5:95. Saunders, Bailey. *The Life and Letters of James Macpherson*, pp. 191–97, 241–57, etc. London: Swan Sonnenschein, 1894.

5:96. "Epitaph on Dr. Johnson" [Soame Jenyns, etc.], *N&Q*, 8th ser., VIII (August 17, 1895), 131–32.

5:97. Hale, Susan. "Evelina and Dr. Johnson," *Men and Manners of the Eighteenth Century*, pp. 233–70. Philadelphia: Jacobs, 1898.

5:98. Millar, A. H. "William Lauder, the Literary Forger," *Blackwood's Magazine*, CLXVI (September 1899), 381–96.

5:99. Sargeaunt, John. "The Round Robin to Johnson" [identity of William Vachell], *N&Q*, 7th ser., VIII (October 19, 1889), 308–9. See also *Life*, III, 482–83.

5:100. Knutsford, Viscountess (Margaret J. T. Holland). *Life and Letters of Zachary Macaulay*, pp. 2, 93–97, etc. London: Edward Arnold & Co., 1900.

5:101. Morris, Edward E. "Doctor John Hawkesworth, Friend of Dr. Johnson and Historian of Captain Cook's First Voyage," *GM*, CCLXXXIX (September 1900), 218–38.

5:102. "Dr. Johnson and His Friends at the Society of Arts," *Journal of the Society of Arts*, XLVIII (October 12, 1900), 829–31.

5:103. Marston, Edward. *Sketches of Some Booksellers of the Time of Dr. Samuel Johnson*. London: Sampson Low, Marston & Co., 1902.

5:104. Matthews, P. "Sam Johnson und Lord Chesterfield," *Deutsche Zeitschrift*, XI and XII (1902), 443–46.

5:105. Courtney, William P. "A Sporting-Man of the Eighteenth Century" [Sir John Lade], *Temple Bar*, CXXV (February 1902), 199–215.

5:106. Wilson, Sarah. "In Dr. Johnson's Circle" [Percival Stockdale], *Chambers's Journal*, 6th ser., V (November 1902), 817–19.

5:107. *The Orrery Papers*, ed. Countess of Cork and Orrery, II, 6, 8, 99, 111, etc. 2 vols. London: Gerald Duckworth & Co., 1903.

5:108. Mims, Edwin. "Dr. Johnson and John Wesley," *Methodist Review*, LXXXV (July 1903), 543–54.

5:109. Burney, Frances. *Diary and Letters of Madame d'Arblay*, ed. Austin Dobson. 6 vols. London: Macmillan, 1904–5. See also item 5:54.

5:110. Forbes, Margaret. *Beattie and His Friends*. London: Constable & Co., 1904.

5:111. [Pepys, W. W.] *A Later Pepys. The Correspondence of Sir William Weller Pepys, Bart., Master in Chancery, 1758–1825*, ed. Alice C. C. Gaussen. 2 vols. London: J. Lane, 1904.

5:112. Parsons, Mrs. Clement. *Garrick and His Circle*, pp. 219–27, etc. London: Methuen & Co., 1906.

5:113. "Dr. Johnson and David Garrick," *Chautauquan*, XLV (January 1907), 239–44.

5:114. Farrer, J. A. *Literary Forgeries*, pp. 82–97, 161–74. London: Longmans, Green, 1907. Chap. V, "Psalmanazar: The Famous Formosan"; Chap. IX, "The Shame of Lauder."

*5:115. Hill, Constance. *The House in St. Martin's Street*. London: John Lane, 1907. Contains evidence from hitherto unpublished manuscripts of the Burney family.

5:116. Hill, Joseph. *The Book Makers of Old Birmingham—Authors, Printers and Book Sellers*. Birmingham: Shakespeare Press, 1907. Johnson's connection with Thomas Warren, etc.

5:117. Huchon, René Louis. *Mrs. Montagu and Her Friends*, pp. 255–62. London: John Murray, 1907.

5:118. Lucas, E. V. "A Philosopher That Failed" [Oliver Edwards and Johnson], *Character and Comedy*, pp. 63–69. London: Methuen & Co., 1907.

5:119. Lucas, E. V. *A Swan and Her Friends* [Anna Seward]. London: Methuen & Co., 1907.

5:120. Simms, Rupert. "Dr. Johnson: Dr. John Swan: Dr. Watts" [a letter to Johnson from Swan recommending Watts], *N&Q*, 10th ser., VII (May 4, 1907), 348–49; VIII (August 31), 178. See also John T. Page, *ibid.*, VII (June 15), 475.

5:121. Gaussen, Alice C. C. *Percy: Prelate and Poet*. London: Smith Elder, 1908.

5:122. Reade, Aleyn Lyell. "Samuel Johnson's Schoolmasters," *TLS*, December 17, 1908, p. 478.

5:123. Collison-Morley, Lacy. *Giuseppe Baretti*. London: John Murray, 1909. Reviewed by Virginia Woolf, *TLS*, July 29, 1909 (reprinted in item 5:349).

5:124. Martin, Stapleton. *Anna Seward and Classic Lichfield*. Worcester: Deighton and Co., 1909.

5:125. Percy, Thomas. *Thomas Percy und William Shenstone: Ein Briefwechsel aus der Entstehungszeit der Reliques of Ancient Poetry mit Einleitung und Anmerkungen von Dr. Hans Hecht*. (Quellen und Forschungen, No. 103.) Strasbourg: Trübner, 1909.

5:126. Brown, Agnes H. "Famous Literary Groups," *Bookman* (New York), XXX (October 1909), 159–69.

5:127. Broadley, A. M. "Dr. Johnson's 'Kitty Chambers,'" *Outlook* (London), XXVI (September 3, 1910), 317.

5:128. Broadley, A. M. *Doctor Johnson and Mrs. Thrale* [contains Welsh journals of Johnson and Mrs. Thrale]. With introduction by Thomas Seccombe. London: John Lane, 1910.

5:129. Courtney, William P. "Philip Metcalfe, M.P., Friend of Johnson and Reynolds," *Eight Friends of the Great*, pp. 14–34. London: Constable & Co., 1910.

5:130. Dobson, Austin. "Sir John Hawkins, Knight," *Old Kensington Palace and Other Papers*, pp. 112–39. London: Chatto & Windus, 1910.

5:131. Lobban, J. H. *Dr. Johnson's Mrs. Thrale*. Edinburgh and London: Foulis, 1910. A selection from item 5:64.

5:132. Straus, Ralph. *Robert Dodsley*. London: John Lane, 1910.

5:133. "The Tombs of Catherine Chambers and Lucy Porter," *Staffordshire Advertiser*, September 3, 1910. Separately reprinted; see item 6:22.

*5:134. *Dr. Johnson and Fanny Burney, Being the Johnsonian Passages from the Works of Mme. D'Arblay*, ed. C. B. Tinker. New York: Moffat, Yard, 1911.

5:135. Taylor, Thomas. *A Life of John Taylor*. London: St. Catherine Press, [1911].

5:136. Richards, Alfred E. "Dr. Johnson and H. P. Sturz," *MLN*, XXVI (June 1911), 176–77. See also items 5:6 and 5:262.

5:137. Biron, Sir Chartres. "Dr. Johnson and Dr. Dodd," *National Review*, LVIII (November 1911), 455–63. Reprinted in item 6:28, pp. 13–28.

5:138. Austen-Leigh, Richard A. *The Story of a Printing House: Being a Short Account of the Strahans and Spottiswoodes*. 2nd ed. London: Spottiswoode, 1912.

5:139. Orr, Lyndon. "Dr. Johnson and Mrs. Thrale," *Munsey's Magazine*, XLVII (May 1912), 205–10.

5:140. Axon, William E. A. [Dialogue between Dr. Johnson and Mrs. Knowles], *Nation*, XCV (November 7, 1912), 429–30.

5:141. Jarvis, Chauncey G. "Mrs. Boswell's Johnson" [his relations with Mrs. Boswell], *University Magazine* (Toronto), XI (December 1912), 653–72.

5:142. Copeland, Charles T. "Johnson and His Friendships," in *Anniversary Papers by Colleagues and Pupils of George Lyman Kittredge*, pp. 55–61. Boston: Ginn and Co., 1913.

5:143. H., W. B. "Johnson and Garrick; Epigram," *N&Q*, 11th ser., VII (February 22, 1913), 149.

5:144. Axon, William E. A. [Charlotte Lennox and Johnson], *Nation*, XCVII (December 25, 1913), 614–15.

5:145. Meynell, Alice C. T. "Mrs. Johnson," *Essays*, pp. 213–18. London: Burns and Oates; New York: Charles Scribner's Sons, 1914.

5:146. Hutton, William H. "Dr. Johnson's Friends and the Cotswolds" [papers relating to Samuel Crisp, etc.], *Transactions of the Bristol and Gloucester Archaeological Society*, XXXVII (1915), 195–219.

5:147. Reade, Aleyn Lyell. "Dr. Johnson and Lord Chesterfield," *Sphere*, LXIII (October 30, 1915), 132.

5:148. Isaacs, Lewis M. "A Friend of Dr. Johnson" [Dr. Charles Burney, Sr.], *Musical Quarterly*, I (October 1915), 583–91.

5:149. Roscoe, Edward Stanley. *Lord Stowell*, pp. 8–15. London: Constable & Co., 1916.

5:150. Houston, Percy H. "Some Contemporary Criticism of Doctor Johnson" [*Lexiphanes*, Kenrick, Watson, etc.], *Texas Review*, II (July 1916), 54–65.

5:151. Clodd, Edward. "Dr. Johnson and Lord Monboddo," *Fortnightly Review*, CI (May 1917), 849–62. Reprinted in item 6:28, pp. 31–54.

5:152. Newton, A. Edward. "A Light-Blue Stocking" [Mrs. Thrale-Piozzi], *Atlantic Monthly*, CXXI (June 1918), 783–94. Reprinted in *The Amenities of Book-Collecting*, pp. 186–225, Boston: Atlantic Monthly Press, 1918.

5:153. Rivington, Septimus. *The Publishing Family of Rivington*, p. 67, etc. London: Rivingtons, 1919.

5:154. Beerbohm, Max. "A Clergyman" [cf. *Life*, April 7, 1778], *The Owl: A Miscellany* (London: Martin Secker), No. 1 (May 1919), 18–22. Reprinted in *Living Age*, CCCII (August 30, 1919), 544–47; *Bookman* (New York), LI (March 1920), 1–4; and in numerous anthologies. See item 5:387.

5:155. Thomas, L. C. "Sir Joshua Reynolds," in item 6:28, pp. 181–96.

5:156. Whitford, Robert C. "Lexiphanes: Satire's View of Dr. Johnson," *South Atlantic Quarterly*, XIX (April 1920), 141–56.

5:157. O'Hara, James. "Frank Barber. Dr. Johnson's Black Servant," *N&Q*, 12th ser., VII (July 3, 1920), 13.

5:158. Dobson, Austin. "The Learned Mrs. Carter," *Later Essays 1917–1920*, pp. 97–123. London: Oxford University Press, 1921.

5:159. Reade, Aleyn Lyell. "A New Clerical Cousin of Dr. Johnson" [Samuel Ford], *TLS*, September 15, 1921, p. 596.

5:160. Reade, Aleyn Lyell. "A Cousin of Doctor Johnson" [Phoebe Ford], *TLS*, September 29, 1921, p. 628. See also H. M. Beatty, *ibid.*, October 6, p. 644.

5:161. Markland, Russell. "Dr. Johnson and the Rev. George Butt," *N&Q*, 12th ser., IX (October 29, 1921), 351.

5:162. Farington, Joseph. *The Farington Diary*, ed. James Greig. 8 vols. London: Hutchinson, 1922–28. Frequent references to Johnson, Boswell, Reynolds, the Thrales, and others.

5:163. Merritt, E. Percival. "Piozzi-Johnson Annotations," *Gazette of the Grolier Club*, No. 3 (May 1922), pp. 58–63.

5:164. Asquith, Herbert H., Earl of Oxford and Asquith. *Dr. Johnson and Fanny Burney*. Privately printed, 1923. Reprinted in *Studies and Sketches*, pp. 77–94, London: Hutchinson & Co., 1924.

5:165. Blunt, Reginald. *Mrs. Montagu: "Queen of the Blues."* London: Constable, 1923.

5:166. Ridley, H. M. "Great Friendships: Mrs. Thrale and Samuel Johnson," *Canadian Magazine*, LX (January 1923), 252–56.

5:167. Radcliffe, Susan M. "A Sidelight on Dr. Johnson," *TLS*, April 26, 1923, pp. 287–88. A description of Johnson in a letter from Sir Joshua Reynolds's nephew.

5:168. Austen-Leigh, Richard A. "William Strahan and His Ledgers," *Library*, III (March 1923), 261–87.

5:169. Sparke, Archibald. "Anna Williams," *N&Q*, 13th ser., I (September 8, 1923), 198–99.

5:170. Russell, Sir Charles. "Dr. Johnson and Walpole" [Horace Walpole], *Fortnightly Review*, CXIV (October 1923), 658–66.

5:171. Beatty, Joseph M., Jr. "Doctor Johnson and 'Mur' " [Arthur Murphy], *MLN*, XXXIX (February 1924), 82–88.

5:172. Russell, Constance. "Sizars and the Woolsack," *N&Q*, CXLVI (May 31, 1924), 399–400. Anecdote of Johnson in 1781, contained in notes of Sir Henry Russell—Johnson on Lord Hardwicke.

5:173. Piccioni, Luigi. "Un altro Italiano amico di Samuele Johnson . . ." [Francesco Sastres], *Rivista d'Italia*, XXVII, no. 8 (August 15, 1924), 444–53.

5:174. Markland, Russell. *Links between Dr. Samuel Johnson and Rev. Gilbert White*. Lytham: N. Ling & Co., 1925.

5:175. Merritt, E. Percival. *Piozzi Marginalia*. Cambridge, Mass.: Harvard University Press, 1925.

5:176. Walkley, Arthur B. "Mrs. Emmet" [actress mentioned in *Life*, II, 464], *Still More Prejudice*, pp. 210–14. London: Wm. Heinemann; New York: Alfred A. Knopf, 1925. See also "A. B.," *Times* (London), March 20, 1923.

5:177. P., J. "William Levett" [*sic*; some facts about Dr. Levet], *British Medical Journal*, April 11, 1925, pp. 705–6.

5:178. Roscoe, Edward Stanley. "The Friendship of Dr. Johnson and Windham," *National Review*, LXXXV (July 1925), 767–74. Reprinted in item 10/6:204, pp. 45–64.

5:179. Forman, W. Courthope. "Dr. Johnson and Izaak Walton," *N&Q*, CXLIX (August 1, 1925), 79–80. See also Edward Bensly, *ibid.* (September 5), 170.

5:180. Smith, Frederick M. "A Tallow-Chandler's Wife" [Mrs. Gardiner], *Sewanee Review*, XXXIII (October 1925), 386–95. Reprinted in item 5:208.

5:181. Balderston, Katharine C. *The History and Sources of Percy's Memoir of Goldsmith*. Cambridge: Cambridge University Press, 1926.

5:182. Boyle, Sir Edward. "Johnson and Sir John Hawkins," *National Review*, LXXXVII (March 1926), 77–89. Reprinted in *Biographical Essays*,

1790–1890, pp. 100–114, London: Oxford University Press, 1936. See also *National Review*, LXXXVIII (November 1926), 433–41.

5:183. Constable, Eric A. "Links between Dr. Johnson and Burns," *Scots Magazine*, IV (March 1926), 457–63.

5:184. Merritt, E. Percival. "Piozzi on Boswell and Johnson," *Harvard Library Notes*, No. 17 (April 1926), pp. 104–11.

5:185. Smith, Frederick M. "An Eighteenth-Century Gentleman: The Honorable Topham Beauclerk," *Sewanee Review*, XXXIV (April 1926), 205–19. Reprinted in item 5:208.

5:186. Russell, Sir Charles. "Johnson, Gibbon and Boswell" [Phoebe Ford, Johnson's cousin, servant in Gibbon's house], *Fortnightly Review*, CXIX (May 1926), 629–35. See item 5:160.

5:187. Chapman, Robert William. "Dr. Johnson and Dr. Taylor," *RES*, II (July 1926), 338–39. Taylor's *Letter to Samuel Johnson*, 1787; see item 24:45.

5:188. Murray, Grace A. *Personalities of the Eighteenth Century*. London: Heath Cranton, 1927. Sketches of many minor figures with whom Johnson was acquainted.

5:189. Gow, A. S. F. "Dr. Johnson's Household," *Empire Review*, XLV (January 1927), 23–32.

5:190. Stewart-Brown, R. "Dr. Johnson and Peter Bodvel," *TLS*, December 15, 1927, p. 961.

5:191. Whitley, William T. *Artists and Their Friends in England 1770–1799*, II, 15–18, etc. London: Medici Society, 1928.

5:192. Mathew, Theobald. "Dr. Johnson and the Old Bailey" [efforts in behalf of Baretti and Dr. Dodd], *Cambridge Law Journal*, III, no. 2 (1928), 182–94.

5:193. Dixon, Ronald A. *Dr. Robert Levit* [sic], *1705–1782*, reprinted from the *Hull and Yorkshire Times*, March 10, 1928.

5:194. "Boswell and His Father" [some discussion of Johnson and the elder Boswell], *Blackwood's Magazine*, CCXXIII (March 1928), 325–42.

5:195. Sackville-West, Victoria. "The Wit and the Wanderer" [Johnson and Psalmanazar], *Nation-Athenaeum*, XLIII (June 16, 1928), 358–59.

5:196. Reade, Aleyn Lyell. "Oliver Edwards," *TLS*, April 26, 1928, p. 313. See also *ibid.*, November 29, p. 938.

5:197. Powell, Lawrence F. "Dr. Johnson and Dr. James," *TLS*, January 3, 1929, p. 12.

5:198. Woolf, Virginia. "Dr. Burney's Evening Party," *Life and Letters*, III (September 1929), 243–63. Reprinted in *The Common Reader: Second Series*, pp. 108–25, London: Hogarth Press, 1932.

5:199. Brown, Joseph Epes. "Horses to His Chariot: An Episode in the Life of Doctor Johnson" [Johnson's relations with Jonas Hanway], *Sewanee Review*, XXXVII (October 1929), 407–20.

5:200. Radcliffe, Susan M. *Sir Joshua's Nephew* [Rev. Samuel Johnson, 1754–78], pp. 86–88, etc. London: J. Murray, 1930.

5:201. Crane, Ronald S. "Johnson and Evan Evans," *MLN*, XLV (January 1930), 31–32.

5:202. Reade, Aleyn Lyell. "A New Admirer for Dr. Johnson" [Mrs. Nicholas's letters], *London Mercury*, XXI (January, February 1930), 243–53, 356.

5:203. Baker, H. Arthur. "Chesterfield and Johnson," *Contemporary Review*, CXXXVII (March 1930), 353–60.

5:204. Pottle, Frederick A. "The Character of Dr. Johnson" [anonymous essay, 1792, probably by W. J. Temple; see item 10/6:19], *TLS*, May 22, 1930, p. 434.

5:205. Mabbott, Thomas O. "Dr. Johnson, Mr. Smith, and Lady Hamilton," *N&Q*, CLVIII (May 31, 1930), 383.

5:206. Thomas, P. G. "Fresh Light on the Johnson Circle" [from Percy's correspondence with Farmer], *Welsh Outlook*, July 1930, pp. 186–87.

5:207. Ashmun, Margaret. *The Singing Swan* [Anna Seward]. New Haven, Conn.: Yale University Press, 1931.

5:208. Smith, Frederick M. *Some Friends of Doctor Johnson* [Topham Beauclerk, Mrs Abington, General Oglethorpe, George Psalmanazar, Mrs. Gardiner, Arthur Murphy, Dr. John Taylor, Dr. William Adams, and Lady Craven]. London: Hartley, 1931.

5:209. Gray, W. Forbes. "Dr. Johnson's Publisher" [Andrew Millar], *Fortnightly Review*, CXXIX (February 1931), 245–50.

5:210. *Poetess Friend of Dr. Johnson: The Portrait of Anna Williams*. London: Times Publishing Co., 1931. Reprinted from *Times* (London), April 14, May 1, 1931.

5:211. Ashmun, Margaret. "Johnson's Schoolmaster" [Rev. John Hunter], *TLS*, July 30, 1931, p. 597. See also G. W. Craig, *ibid.*, August 6, p. 609.

5:212. Morley, Christopher. "Star-Dust from Mrs. Thrale" [Rylands Piozziana], *SRL*, VIII (August 8, 1931), 38.

5:213. Devalle, Albertina. *La critica letteraria nel 1700. Giuseppe Baretti, suoi rapporti con Voltaire, Johnson e Parini*. Milan: U. Hoepli, 1932.

5:214. Laithwaite, Percy. "Anna Seward and Dr. Johnson," *TLS*, January 7, 1932, p. 12.

5:215. Bracey, Robert. "Dr. Johnson and Miss Hill Boothby," *Blackfriars*, XIII (April 1932), 223–30.

*5:216. Wright, Herbert G. "The Relations of the Welsh Bard Iolo Morganwg with Dr. Johnson, Cowper and Southey," *RES*, VIII (April 1932), 129–38.

5:217. Powell, Lawrence F. "Petty and Graunt" [Johnson's allusions to Petty explained], *TLS*, October 20, 1932, p. 761. See also Lord Lansdowne, *ibid.*, September 8, p. 624; October 13, p. 734; N. G. Brett-James, *ibid.*, September 15, p. 643.

5:218. Abraham, James J. *Lettsom: His Life, Times, Friends and Descendants*, p. 181 [John Coakley Lettsom's character of Johnson]. London: Wm. Heinemann, 1933.

5:219. Brown, A. T. *One or Two Johnsonians* [Susanna Thrale, Sir John Salusbury]. Liverpool: Privately printed, 1933.

5:220. Sadler, Ernest A. "The Mansion, Ashbourne" [Residence of Rev. John Taylor], *Journal of the Derbyshire Archaeological and Natural History Society*, LIII for 1932 (1933), 39–50.

5:221. Ketton-Cremer, Robert W. "Doctor Messenger Monsey," *London Mercury*, XXVIII (July 1933), 240–48.

5:222. Reade, Aleyn Lyell. "Gilbert Walmesley," *TLS*, July 13, 1933, p. 480.

5:223. Snodgrass, A. E. "Dr. Johnson's Petted Lady" [Hannah More], *Cornhill Magazine*, CXLVIII (September 1933), 336–42.

5:224. Walker, George Gilbert. "Bennet Langton," *Lincolnshire Magazine*, I (November–December 1933), 247–51; January–February, 1934), 296–98.

5:225. Bennett, William. *Doctor Samuel Johnson and the Ladies of the Lichfield Amicable Society, 1775*. Birmingham: City of Birmingham School of Printing, 1934.

5:226. Holstein, Mark. "The Unfortunate Dr. Dodd," *Colophon*, Pt. XVIII, no. 6 (1934), unpaged. Reprinted, New York: Harbor Press, 1934.

5:227. Reade, Aleyn Lyell. "Francis Barber," *TLS*, April 12, 1934, p. 262. See also A. Werner, *ibid.*, April 19, p. 282.

5:228. Swanzy, T. Erskine. "Gibbon and Johnson," *TLS*, July 12, 1934, p. 492.

5:229. Scott, Sir Samuel. "Dr. Johnson and Mrs. Thrale," *Nineteenth Century*, CXVI (September 1934), 308–18.

5:230. Bennett, William. *Richard Greene: The Lichfield Apothecary & His Museum of Curiosities*. Birmingham: City of Birmingham School of Printing, 1935.

5:231. Page, Eugene R. *George Colman the Elder*. New York: Columbia University Press, 1935.

*5:232. Small, Miriam R. *Charlotte Ramsay Lennox*. New Haven, Conn.: Yale University Press, 1935.

5:233. Smith-Dampier, J. L. *Who's Who in Boswell?* Oxford: Blackwell, 1935.

5:234. Baretti, Giuseppe. *Epistolario*, ed. Luigi Piccioni. Bari: Gius. Laterza & Figli, 1936.

5:235. Ettinger, Amos A. *James Edward Oglethorpe: Imperial Idealist*, pp. 291–329. Oxford: Clarendon Press, 1936.

*5:236. Hilles, Frederick W. *The Literary Career of Sir Joshua Reynolds*. Cambridge: Cambridge University Press, 1936.

5:237. Vulliamy, C. E. *Mrs. Thrale of Streatham*. London: Jonathan Cape, 1936.

5:238. Clifford, James L. "The Printing of Mrs. Piozzi's *Anecdotes of Dr. Johnson*," *Bulletin of the John Rylands Library*, XX (January 1936), 157–72.

*5:239. Wright, Herbert G. "Robert Potter as a Critic of Dr. Johnson," *RES*, XII (July 1936), 305–21.

5:240. Babcock, R. W. "Dr. Thomas Birch as Transcriber of Johnson," *PQ*, XVI (April 1937), 220–21.

5:241. Addleshaw, S. "The Swan of Lichfield: Anna Seward and Her Circle," *Church Quarterly Review*, CXXIV (April–June 1937), 1–34.

5:242. Chapman, R. W. "Miss Aston," *TLS*, June 12, 1937, p. 452.

5:243. J., W. H. "Gibbon and Johnson," *N&Q*, CLXXIII (August 7, 1937), 97.

5:244. Clifford, James L. "Lucy Porter to Dr. Johnson: Her Only Known Letter," *TLS*, August 28, 1937, p. 620.

5:245. Chapman, R. W. "Robert Levet," *TLS*, January 1, 1938, p. 12.

5:246. Reade, Aleyn Lyell. "Parson Ford," *TLS*, August 6, 1938, pp. 519–20.

5:247. Kent, Muriel. "A Lichfield Group" [Anna Seward, etc.], *Cornhill Magazine*, CLVIII (September 1938), 347–52.

5:248. Bryant, Donald C. *Edmund Burke and His Literary Friends*. (Washington University Studies in Language and Literature, No. 9.) St. Louis, Mo., 1939.

5:249. Connely, Willard. *The True Chesterfield*. London: Cassell & Co., 1939.

5:250. Davis, Rose Mary. *The Good Lord Lyttelton*. Bethlehem, Pa.: Times Publishing Co., 1939.

5:251. Gallup, Donald. "Baretti in England." Dissertation, Yale University, 1939.

5:252. Magnus, Philip. *Edmund Burke*. London: John Murray, 1939.

5:253. Simmons, Walter Lee. "Sir John Hawkins, Knight," *Abstracts of Dissertations, Ohio State University, 1938–39*, No. 29 (1939), pp. 123–30.

5:254. Kennedy, T. J. "Dr. Johnson and Dr. Dodd," *Central Literary Magazine* (Central Library Association; Denham, Bucks), January 1939, pp. 31–35.

5:255. Lewis, Frank R. "Dr. Samuel Madden, Dr. Johnson and Benjamin Franklin," *Irish Book Lover*, XXVI (May 1939), 98–102.

*5:256. Sadler, Ernest A. *Dr. Johnson's Ashbourne Friends*. Separately printed from *Ashbourne Telegraph*, June 1939. Reprinted in *Derbyshire Archaeological and Natural History Society Journal*, LX (1940), 1–20.

5:257. Bradford, Curtis B. "Arthur Murphy's Meeting with Johnson," *PQ*, XVIII (July 1939), 318–20.

5:258. Charles, B. G. "Peggy Owen and Her Streatham Friends," *Cornhill Magazine*, CLX (September 1939), 334–51.

5:259. Clifford, James L. "Dr. Johnson's Mr. Thrale" [letter from Henry Thrale to Charles Lyttelton], *TLS*, December 30, 1939, p. 755.

5:260. Hutchins, John H. *Jonas Hanway*, pp. 141–44, etc. London: Society for Promoting Christian Knowledge, 1940. Quarrel over *Essay on Tea*.

5:261. Hare, Kenneth. "Lord Chesterfield and Dr. Johnson" [defense of Chesterfield and attack on Johnson], *Quarterly Review*, CCLXXIV (January 1940), 139–57.

5:262. Levy, H. L. "H. P. Sturz and Dr. Johnson," *TLS*, February 10, 1940, p. 80; July 13, p. 339. See also items 5:6 and 5:136.

5:263. Altick, Richard D. *Richard Owen Cambridge: Belated Augustan*, pp. 75–85, etc. Dissertation, University of Pennsylvania. Philadelphia, 1941.

*5:264. Clifford, James L. *Hester Lynch Piozzi (Mrs. Thrale)*. Oxford: Clarendon Press, 1941. For commentary see F. A. Pottle and C. H. Bennett, *MP*, XXXIX (May 1942), 421–30. Reviewed in *TLS*, February 1, 1941, p. 51; by Virginia Woolf, *New Statesman and Nation*, March 8, 1941, p. 250 (reprinted in item 5:293); John Butt, *RES*, XVII (July 1941), 359–61; A. T. Hazen, *MLQ*, II (December 1941), 652–53; R. L. Greene, *MLN*, LVII (May 1942), 391–92. 2nd ed., 1952. Reprinted with rev. bibliography, 1968.

5:265. Clifford, James L. "Thomas Coxeter the Younger to Dr. Johnson" [letter of April 23, 1771], *N&Q*, CLXXX (April 12, 1941), 257–58.

5:266. Clifford, James L. "The Authenticity of Anna Seward's Published Correspondence" [later revisions of Johnsonian passages], *MP*, XXXIX (November 1941), 113–22. Reprinted in *Studies in the Literature of the Augustan Age: Essays Collected in Honor of Arthur Ellicott Case*, ed. R. C. Boys, pp. 50–60, Ann Arbor, Mich.: George Wahr Publishing Co., 1952.

5:267. R[endall], V[ernon]. "Johnson, Boswell and Grattan," *N&Q*, CLXXXI (November 15, 1941), 273.

5:268. *Reminiscences of Sarah Kemble Siddons, 1773–1785*, ed. William Van Lennep, pp. 13–15. Cambridge, Mass.: Harvard University Library, 1942.

5:269. Shepperson, Archibald B. *John Paradise and Lucy Ludwell of London and Williamsburg*, pp. 100–119. Richmond, Va.: Dietz, 1942. Reviewed by J. L. Clifford, *MLQ*, VI (March 1945), 99–100.

5:270. *Sketch of the Life of Bennet Langton, LL.D.* Manchester: Sherrat and Hughes, 1942.

*5:271. *Thraliana: The Diary of Mrs. Hester Lynch Thrale (Later Mrs. Piozzi) 1776–1809*, ed. Katharine C. Balderston. 2 vols. Oxford: Clarendon Press, 1942. Selections previously published as *Mrs. Piozzi's Thraliana*, ed. Charles Hughes, London: Simpkin, Marshall, 1913. Reviewed in *TLS*, May 30, 1942, p. 270; by John Butt, *RES*, XIX (January 1943), 93–95; Gwyn Jones, *MLR*, XXXVIII (January 1943), 55–57; J. L. Clifford, *PQ*, XXII (April 1943), 167–69; R. L. Greene, *MLN*, LIX (January 1944), 67–69. 2nd ed., 1951.

5:272. S., H. G. "Yet Johnson Would Not Meet Him" [Sir John Pringle], *Clinical Excerpts*, XVII (July–September 1942), 29–31.

5:273. Chapman, R. W. "Johnson, Brocklesby and Juvenal," *N&Q*, CLXXXV (October 23, 1943), 256.

5:274. Brown, John J. "The Great Twalmley" [*re Life*, IV, 193], *N&Q*, CLXXXV (December 4, 1943), 349.

*5:275. Percy, Thomas. *The Percy Letters*, general eds. D. Nichol Smith and Cleanth Brooks. Baton Rouge: Louisiana State University Press, Vol. I, 1944; Vol. II, 1946; Vol. III, 1951; Vol. IV, 1954; Vol. V, 1957; Vol. VI, 1961.

5:276. "Dr. Johnson's Apothecary" [Mr. Holder (possibly Robert)], *N&Q*, CLXXXVI (March 25, 1944), 162.

5:277. Osgood, Charles G. "An American Boswell" [Dr. Benjamin Rush's recollections of Johnson, Goldsmith, etc.], *Princeton University Library Chronicle*, V (April 1944), 85–91.

5:278. De Quincey, Thomas. *Dr. Johnson and Lord Chesterfield* [newly discovered essay, printed with facsimile]. New York: Ben Abramson, 1945.

5:279. Butterfield, Lyman H. *Benjamin Rush's Reminiscences of Boswell and Johnson*. Princeton, N.J.: Privately printed for Mr. and Mrs. Donald Hyde, Princeton University Press, 1946.

5:280. Dunbar, Howard H. *The Dramatic Career of Arthur Murphy*. New York: Modern Language Association, 1946.

5:281. Emery, John Pike. *Arthur Murphy*. Philadelphia: University of Pennsylvania Press (for Temple University), 1946.

5:282. *Isaac Reed Diaries, 1762–1804*, ed. Claude E. Jones, pp. 148, etc. Berkeley: University of California Press, 1946.

5:283. Powell, Lawrence F. "Sir William Jones and The Club," *Bulletin of the School of Oriental and African Studies*, XI, no. 4 (1946), 818–22.

5:284. Esdaile, Arundell. "Hester Thrale," *Quarterly Review*, CCLXXXIV (April 1946), 179–94.

5:285. Warner, James H. "The Macaroni Parson" [Dr. Dodd], *Queen's Quarterly*, LIII (Spring 1946), 41–53.

5:286. Jones, Claude E. "Johnson and Mrs. Montagu: Two Letters" [addressed to Herbert Croft], *N&Q*, CXCI (September 7, 1946), 102–3.

5:287. Adams, Martin Ray. "Samuel Parr, 'The Whig Johnson,'" *Studies in the Literary Backgrounds of English Radicalism*, pp. 267–311. Lancaster, Pa.: Franklin and Marshall College, 1947.

5:288. Hopkins, Mary Alden. *Hannah More and Her Circle*, pp. 52–61, 106–7, etc. New York: Longmans, Green & Co., 1947.

5:289. *Autobiography of Benjamin Rush*, ed. George W. Corner, pp. 58–60, etc. Princeton, N.J.: Princeton University Press, 1948.

5:290. Barton, Margaret. *Garrick*. London: Faber & Faber, 1948.

5:291. Emden, Cecil S. "Oriel Friends of Dr. Johnson" [William Seward and Sir Richard Musgrave], *Oriel Papers*, pp. 133–46. Oxford: Clarendon Press, 1948. See also item 5:329.

5:292. Scholes, Percy A. *The Great Dr. Burney*. 2 vols. London: Oxford University Press, 1948. Reviewed by John Butt, *PQ*, XXVIII (July 1949), 385.

5:293. Woolf, Virginia. "Mrs. Thrale" [review of item 5:264], *The Moment and Other Essays*, pp. 45–49. London: Hogarth Press, 1947; New York: Harcourt, Brace, 1948.

5:294. Quinlan, Maurice. "An Intermediary between Cowper and Johnson" [Benjamin Latrobe], *RES*, XXIV (April 1948), 141–47.

5:295. Copeland, Thomas W. *Our Eminent Friend Edmund Burke*. New Haven, Conn.: Yale University Press, 1949.

5:296. Liebert, Herman W. *Dr. Johnson and the Misses Collier*. New Haven, Conn.: Privately printed for The Johnsonians, 1949.

5:297. Emery, Clark. "Dr. Johnson on Dr. Hill" [John Hill], *MLN*, LXIV (January 1949), 15–18.

5:298. Gulick, Sidney L., Jr. "Johnson, Chesterfield, and Boswell," in item 10/6:273, pp. 329–40. See also item 5:323.

5:299. Lewis, Wilmarth S. "The Young Waterman," *Virginia Quarterly Review*, XXV (January 1949), 66–73. Reprinted in item 10/6:306 (1959), pp. 1–7.

5:300. Quinlan, Maurice. "Dr. Franklin Meets Dr. Johnson," *Pennsylvania Magazine of History and Biography*, LXXIII (January 1949), 34–44. Reprinted in item 10/6:306, pp. 107–20.

5:301. Donnelly, Lucy M. "The Celebrated Mrs. Macaulay," *William and Mary Quarterly*, VI (April 1949), 173–207.

5:302. Krishnamurti, S. "Sir Robert Chambers: A Johnsonian in India," *Journal of the University of Bombay*, XVIII (September 1949), 1–5.

5:303. Stevenson, Robert. " 'The Rivals'—Hawkins, Burney, and Boswell," *Musical Quarterly*, XXXVI (January 1950), 67–82.

5:304. Lane, Margaret. "Dr. Johnson at Home," *Listener*, XLIV (August 17, 1950), 240–41.

5:305. Scudder, Harold H. "Dr. Johnson at Chatsworth" [comments by Duchess of Devonshire], *N&Q*, CXCV (October 28, 1950), 474–75.

5:306. Lubbers-Van der Brugge, Catharina J. M. *Johnson and Baretti: Some Aspects of Eighteenth-Century Literary Life in England and Italy.* Groningen: J. B. Wolters, 1951. Reviewed by E. A. Bloom, *JEGP*, LI (July 1952), 450–52; G. A. Bonnard, *English Studies*, XXXIII (October 1952), 224–26.

5:307. Miller, Clarence A. *Sir John Hawkins: Dr. Johnson's Friend-Attorney-Executor-Biographer: A Reorientation of The Knight, The Lady, and Boswell.* Washington, D.C.: Privately printed for the author, 1951.

5:308. Reynolds, Frances. *An Enquiry Concerning the Principles of Taste* [materially helped by Johnson], introduction by James L. Clifford. Los Angeles: Augustan Reprint Society, 1951 (Publication No. 27).

5:309. *Three Centuries* [history of the Barclay-Perkins brewery]. London: Barclay, Perkins Co., 1951.

5:310. Foster, W. E. "Samuel Johnson and the Dodd Affair," in item 6:23 (1951–52), pp. 36–49.

*5:311. Hemlow, Joyce. "Dr. Johnson and Fanny Burney—Some Additions to the Record" [passages cut out of the diary], *Bulletin of the New York Public Library*, LV (February 1951), 55–65. Revised version in item 10/6:316, pp. 319–39.

5:312. Carter, H. S. "Samuel Johnson and Some Eighteenth-Century Doctors," *Glasgow Medical Journal*, XXXII (July 1951), 218–27.

5:313. Greene, Donald J. "Johnson, Jenkinson, and the Peace of Paris," *JNL*, XI, no. 4 (September 1951), 8–11.

5:314. Reynolds, Frances. "Some Unpublished Recollections of Dr. Johnson," *Tablet*, CXCVIII (December 22, 1951), 464–66; (December 29), 484–85. "Copied by her niece, Theophila Gwatkin, in whose family they have been preserved"—contains variants of the version published in item 3:116.

5:315. Gray, James. "Beattie and the Johnson Circle," *Queen's Quarterly*, LVIII (Winter 1951–52), 519–32.

5:316. Quennell, Peter. "Mrs. Thrale," *The Singular Preference*, pp. 51–61. London: Collins, 1952.

*5:317. Reynolds, Sir Joshua. *Portraits by Sir Joshua Reynolds*, ed. with introduction and notes by Frederick W. Hilles. New York: McGraw-Hill; London: Heinemann, 1952. Vol. 3 of the Yale Editions of the Private Papers of James Boswell (item 4:21).

5:318. Doubleday, F. N. "Some Medical Associations of Samuel Johnson," *Guy's Hospital Reports*, CI, no. 1 (1952), 45–51.

5:319. Haden, D. J. "Dr. Johnson's Headmaster at Stourbridge" [John Wentworth], *Birmingham Post*, September 16, 1952.

5:320. Hilles, Frederick W. "David Garrick and Sir Joshua" [based on item 5:317], *SR*, October 11, 1952, pp. 20–21, 30.

5:321. Metzdorf, Robert F. "Isaac Reed and the Unfortunate Dr. Dodd," *Harvard Library Bulletin*, VI (Autumn 1952), 393–96.

5:322. Scholes, Percy A. *The Life and Activities of Sir John Hawkins.* London: Oxford University Press, 1953. Reviewed by B. H. Bronson, *MLN*, LXIX (November 1954), 521–24.

5:323. Boyce, Benjamin. "Johnson and Chesterfield Once More" [comment on item 5:298], *PQ*, XXXII (January 1953), 93–96.

5:324. Sarason, Bertram D. "George Croft and Dr. Johnson," *N&Q*, March 1953, pp. 106–7.

*5:325. Mild, Warren. "Johnson and Lauder: A Re-examination," *MLQ*, XIV (June 1953), 149–53.

5:326. Cooke, Arthur. "Anecdotes of Johnson and Garrick" [by Sir Richard Kaye], *JNL*, XIII, no. 3 (September 1953), 10.

5:327. [Isham, Ralph.] "Dr. Johnson's Barber" [identified as "Mr. Collett"], *JNL*, XIII, no. 3 (September 1953), 1–2, 9.

*5:328. Osborn, James M. "Dr. Johnson's Intimate Friend" [Stephen Barrett], *TLS*, October 9, 1953, p. 652.

5:329. E[mden], C[ecil] S. "More Oriel Friends of Dr. Johnson" [John Myddelton and Thomas Apperley; see item 5:291], *Oriel Record* (Oxford), 1954, pp. 12–16.

5:330. Gray, James. "Dr. Johnson and the King of Ashbourne" [John Taylor], *University of Toronto Quarterly*, XXIII (April 1954), 242–52.

5:331. Bloom, Edward A. "The Paradox of Samuel Boyse," *N&Q*, April 1954, pp. 163–65.

5:332. Bloom, Edward A. "Dr. Johnson's Landlord" [Richard Russell—Bolt Court, 1765–76], *N&Q*, August 1954, pp. 350–51.

*5:333. Osborn, James M. *Dr. Johnson and the Contrary Converts* [James Compton and John Walker]. New Haven, Conn.: Privately printed for The Johnsonians [Yale University Press], 1954. Revised and reprinted in item 10/6:306, pp. 297–317.

5:334. Ruhe, Edward. "Hume and Johnson" [dinner guests together in 1763], *N&Q*, November 1954, pp. 477–78.

5:335. Sledd, James H., and Gwin J. Kolb. "Lord Chesterfield and Dr. Johnson," Chap. III in item 17:136 (1955).

5:336. Gillis, William. "Johnson and Macpherson" [letter from Sir William

Forbes on the Johnson-Macpherson controversy], *JNL*, XV, no. 1 (March 1955), 7–8.

5:337. Derrick, Michael. "Dr. Johnson's Monastic Cell Where He Thought of Ending His Days" [see item 5:333], *Tablet*, CCV (March 19, 1955), 274.

5:338. Fifer, C. N. "Dr. Johnson and Bennet Langton," *JEGP*, LIV (October 1955), 504–6. Reprinted in *Studies by Members of the English Department, University of Illinois, in Memory of John Jay Parry*, pp. 44–46, Urbana: University of Illinois Press, 1957.

5:339. Allison, James. "Mrs. Thrale's Marginalia in Joseph Warton's *Essay*," *Huntington Library Quarterly*, XIX (February 1956), 155–64.

5:340. Scholes, Percy A. "Johnson's Two Musical Friends—Burney and Hawkins," *Canadian Music Journal*, I (Autumn 1956), 7–19.

5:341. Ketton-Cremer, R. W. "Johnson's Last Gifts to Windham," *Book Collector*, V (Winter 1956), 354–56.

5:342. Gallagher, Robert E. "John Hawkesworth: A Study toward a Literary Biography" (dissertation, Northwestern University, 1957), *Dissertation Abstracts*, XVII (1957), 3002.

5:343. Wardle, Ralph M. *Oliver Goldsmith*. Lawrence: University of Kansas Press, 1957. Reviewed by Morris Golden, *MLN*, LXXIII (June 1958), 442–44; K. C. Balderston, *PQ*, XXXVIII (July 1959), 327–28.

5:344. Brain, Sir Russell. "Thomas Lawrence, M.D., P.R.C.P. (1711–83)" [relationship with Johnson], *Medical History*, I (October 1957), 293–306. Reprinted in item 3:753.

5:345. Hyde, Mrs. Donald F. (Mary C.) "Tetty and Johnson," in item 6:23 (December 1957), pp. 34–46.

*5:346. Hemlow, Joyce. *The History of Fanny Burney*. Oxford: Clarendon Press, 1958. Reviewed in *TLS*, March 21, 1958, p. 152; by V. S. Pritchett, *New Statesman and Nation*, March 22, 1958, pp. 380–81; A. D. McKillop, *MLR*, LIV (January 1959), 98–99; J. L. Clifford, *MLN*, LXXIV (November 1959), 644–46.

*5:347. [Liebert, Herman W.] *A Constellation of Genius* [account of Baretti's trial for murder and Johnson's evidence, with facsimiles of original documents]. New Haven, Conn.: Privately printed for The Johnsonians [Yale University Press], 1958.

5:348. Willoughby, Edwin E. "The Unfortunate Dr. Dodd: The Tragedy of an Incurable Optimist," *Essays by Divers Hands* (Royal Society of Literature), XXIX (1958), 124–43.

5:349. Woolf, Virginia. "A Friend of Johnson" [Baretti], *Granite and Rainbow*, pp. 187–91. London: Hogarth Press; New York: Harcourt, Brace, 1958. Reprint of a review of item 5:123.

5:350. Sherwin, Oscar. "A Man with a Tail—Lord Monboddo," *Journal of the History of Medicine and Allied Sciences*, XIII (October 1958), 435–65.

*5:351. Ruhe, Edward. "Birch, Johnson, and Elizabeth Carter: An Episode of 1738–1739," *PMLA*, LXXIII (December 1958), 491–500.

5:352. Lubbers-Van Der Brugge, Catharina J. M. "A Lost Pamphlet of Giuseppe Baretti" [*The Voice of Discord*, and Johnson's help], *English Miscellany* (Rome), X (1959), 157–88.

*5:353. Hemlow, Joyce. "Dr. Johnson and the Young Burneys," in item 10/6:306, pp. 319–39.

5:354. Mathias, Peter. "Henry Thrale and John Perkins," *The Brewing Industry in England, 1700–1830*, pp. 265–76, etc. Cambridge: Cambridge University Press, 1959.

5:355. Taylor, E. G. R. "A Reward for the Longitude" [work of Zachariah Williams], *Mariner's Mirror*, XLV (February 1959), 59–66; (November), 339–41.

*5:356. Jones, W. Powell. "Johnson and Gray, a Study in Literary Antagonism," *MP*, LVI (May 1959), 243–53.

5:357. McHenry, Lawrence C., Jr. "Doctors Afield: Robert Anderson, M.D., and His Life of Samuel Johnson," *New England Journal of Medicine*, CCLXI (September 17, 1959), 605–7.

5:358. Wedgwood, Sir John. "Wedgwood and Johnson" [the first Josiah Wedgwood], in item 6:23, December 1959, pp. 51–54.

5:359. Tucci, Gerald Alfred. "Baretti and the Shakespearean Influence in Italy: A Study in Eighteenth Century Polemics in Italy" (dissertation, New York University, 1960), *Dissertation Abstracts*, XX (1960), 4664. Discusses influence of Johnson.

5:360. Wimsatt, William K., Jr. "A Philadelphian Meets Johnson" [John Ewing], *TLS*, January 1, 1960, p. 7.

5:361. Leicester, J. H. "Dr. Johnson and William Shenstone," *New Rambler*, June 1960, pp. 29–42.

5:362. Low, D. M. "Edward Gibbon and the Johnsonian Circle," *New Rambler*, June 1960, pp. 2–14.

5:363. "Johnsoniana from Thomas Cooper," *JNL*, XX (September 1960), 9–10. See item 20:58.

5:364. Powell, L. F. "Edmund Southwell, His Sisters, and Dr. Johnson," *TLS*, December 30, 1960, p. 845.

5:365. Childs, J. Rives. *Casanova*, p. 184. London: Allen and Unwin, 1961. Johnson presumably met Casanova in the autumn of 1763. Interview later described in Casanova's *À Leonard Snetlage*, p. 53.

*5:366. Middendorf, John H. "Dr. Johnson and Adam Smith," *PQ*, XL (April 1961), 281–96.

5:367. Verosky, Sister M. Victorine. "John Walker's One Clergyman" [John Milner; *Life*, IV, 206], *N&Q*, April 1961, pp. 126–28.

5:368. Hyde, Mary C. "Two Distinguished Dr. Johnsons," *Columbia Library Columns*, X (May 1961), 3–11. Samuel Johnson, D.D., 1696–1772.

5:369. Deelman, Christian. "Garrick at Edial," *JNL*, XXI, no. 3 (September 1961), 12. Garrick's inspiration for *Lethe* possibly Johnson's instruction in Lucian.

5:370. Congleton, J. E. "James Thomson Callender, Johnson and Jefferson" in item 10/6:316 (1962), pp. 161–72. The career of Callender from the *Deformities* in 1782 to death in America in 1803.

5:371. Torbarina, J. "The Meeting of Boškovíc with Dr. Johnson," *Studia Romanica et Anglica Zagrabiensia* (Zagreb, Yugoslavia), Nos. 13–14 (July–December 1962), pp. 3–11. Evidence contained in unpublished correspondence of Boškovíc. First meeting, June 29, 1760.

5:372. Dankert, Clyde E. "Two Eighteenth-Century Celebrities" [Johnson and Adam Smith], *Dalhousie Review*, XLII (Autumn 1962), 364–75.

5:373. Draper, F. W. M. "Topham Beauclerk at the Grove, Muswell Hill," *New Rambler*, June 1963, pp. 5–8.

5:374. Weston, John C., Jr. "Edmund Burke's Wit," *Review of English Literature*, IV (July 1963), 95–107. On Johnson's "He is . . . continually attempting wit, but he fails."

5:375. Sambrook, A. J. "Fanny Burney's First Letter to Dr. Johnson" [in National Library of Wales, Aberystwyth], *RES*, n.s., XIV (August 1963), 273–75.

5:376. Hemlow, Joyce. *Morning at Streatham: From the Journal of Susannah Elizabeth Burney* [with facsimile]. Privately printed for the annual dinner of The Johnsonians, 1963.

5:377. Thomas, D. S. "The Publication of Henry Fielding's *Amelia*," *Library*, 5th ser., XVIII (December 1963), 303–7. Discusses Johnson's account given to Mrs. Thrale.

5:378. Cochrane, James A. *Dr. Johnson's Printer: The Life of William Strahan*. Cambridge, Mass.: Harvard University Press, 1964. Reviewed by William B. Todd, *MP*, LXIV (May 1967), 350–51; *TLS*, December 31, 1964, p. 1179; J. D. Fleeman, *RES*, n.s., XVI (November 1965), 432–34; P. B. Daghlian, *JEGP*, LXV (January 1966), 199–201.

5:379. Osborn, James M. "Edmond Malone: Scholar-Collector," *Library*, 5th ser., XIX (1964), 11–17.

5:380. Stollery, C. W. "Casanova's Meeting with Samuel Johnson," *Casanova Gleanings*, ed. J. Rives Childs, VII (1964), 1–4.

5:381. Rowell, Phyllis. "The Women in Johnson's Life," *New Rambler*, January 1964, pp. 22–28.

*5:382. Lonsdale, Roger. *Dr. Charles Burney: A Literary Biography.* Oxford: Clarendon Press, 1965.

5:383. Lonsdale, Roger. "Johnson and Dr. Burney," in item 10/6:329, pp. 21–40. See also *New Rambler*, June 1964, pp. 16–18.

5:384. Draper, F. W. M. "Johnson's Friend Baretti," *New Rambler*, January 1965, pp. 5–11.

*5:385. Cannon, Garland. "Sir William Jones and Dr. Johnson's Literary Club," *MP*, LXIII (August 1965), 20–37.

*5:386. Fleeman, J. D. "Dr. Johnson and Henry Thrale, M.P.," in item 10/6:329, pp. 170–89. Help with election addresses.

5:387. Liebert, Herman W. " 'A Clergyman': II" [Edward Embry], in item 10/6:329, pp. 41–46. See item 5:154.

*5:388. Osborn, James M. "Edmond Malone and Dr. Johnson," in item 10/6:329, pp. 1–20.

5:389. Quinlan, Maurice J. "Johnson's American Acquaintances" [Benjamin Rush, William White, William Johnson, Thomas Cooper, and others], in item 10/6:329, pp. 190–207.

5:390. Ryskamp, Charles. *Johnson and Cowper.* Privately printed for annual dinner of The Johnsonians, 1965.

5:391. Winnett, A. R. "Johnson and Hume," *New Rambler*, June 1966, pp. 2–14.

5:392. Emden, Cecil S. "Dr. Johnson's Ménage" [Miss Williams, Dr. Levet, Francis Barber, etc.], *Quarterly Review*, No. 649 (July 1966), pp. 281–87.

5:393. Derry, Warren. "The Johnsonian," *Dr. Parr: A Portrait of the Whig Dr. Johnson*, pp. 169–90. Oxford: Clarendon Press, 1966.

5:394. Parish, Charles. "Priestley and Dr. Johnson," *History of the Birmingham Library*, pp. 103–4. London: Library Association, 1966.

5:395. Swinnerton, Frank. *A Galaxy of Fathers* [Charles Burney, Thomas Seward—Anna's father—and others]. London: Hutchinson, 1966. Lively and entertaining, if somewhat inaccurate, picture of the Johnson circle.

5:396. Hardy, John. "Stockdale's Defence of Pope" [includes discussion of Johnson's relations with Stockdale], *RES*, n.s., XVIII (February 1967), 49–54.

5:397. Isles, Duncan E. "Johnson and Charlotte Lennox," *New Rambler*, June 1967, pp. 34–48.

5:398. Lipking, Lawrence. "The Curiosity of William Oldys: An Approach to the Development of English Literary History," *PQ*, XLVI (July 1967), 385–407. Much on the relationship of Oldys and Johnson.

5:399. Brown, Peter. *The Chathamites*, pp. 36–37, 150–53, 241–43, 326–28, 385–88, 399–40, etc. London: Macmillan, 1967. Johnson's relations with

Shelburne, Wesley, John Dunning, Sir William Jones, and Bishop Shipley.

5:400. Clifford, James L. "Hester Lynch Salusbury Thrale Piozzi," in *Four Oaks Library*, ed. Gabriel Austin, pp. 19–28. Somerville, N.J.: Privately printed, 1967. Includes some of her unprinted jottings about Johnson.

5:401. Sherbo, Arthur. *Christopher Smart: Scholar of the University.* East Lansing: Michigan State University Press, 1967.

5:402. Abbott, John L. "John Hawkesworth and 'The Treatise on The Arts of Peace'" [MS not by Hawkesworth; cf. item 3:218], *Journal of The Royal Society for the Encouragement of Arts, Manufactures and Commerce*, CXV (July 1967), 645–49. A biography of Hawkesworth by Abbott is in progress.

5:403. "The Burneys' Circle" [plans for the Burney edition, with cover showing family relationships], *Bulletin of the New York Public Library*, LXXI (September 1967), 414.

5:404. Whiteley, D. Pepys. "A Later Pepys Encounters Dr. Johnson" [William Weller Pepys], *History Today*, XVII (November 1967), 765–71.

5:405. Blunden, Edmund. "Friends of Samuel Johnson," presidential address, Johnson Society, Lichfield, in item 6:23, December 1967, pp. 25–36.

5:406. Knapp, Lewis M. "Smollett and Johnson, Never Cater-Cousins?" *MP*, LXVI (November 1968), 152–54. A survey of their personal relations.

5:407. Gibbs, Denis. "Sir John Floyer (1649–1734)," in item 6:23, December 1968, pp. 19–30. Johnson's childhood physician.

5:408. Isham, Gyles. "Thomas Percy and Samuel Johnson," *Easton Mauduit and the Parish Church of SS. Peter and Paul*, pp. 25–28. Northampton (England): Privately printed, 1969.

5:409. Woodruff, Douglas. "Doctor Johnson's Catholic Contemporaries," *New Rambler*, January 1969, pp. 17–23.

5:410. Gold, Joel J. "In Defense of Single-Speech Hamilton," *Studies in Burke and His Time*, X (Winter 1968–69), 1138–53. Discusses suggestion that W. G. Hamilton's famous speech may have been composed by Johnson.

6. CLUBS AND ASSOCIATIONS

6:1. N. "An Essay on Men of Genius," *Westminster Magazine*, I (May 1773), 301–2. Contains attack on the Literary Club.

6:2. [Letter listing membership to date of the Literary Club], *GM*, LV (February 1785), 98–99.

6:3. Aldebaran [John Nichols]. "Rules of Dr. Johnson's Club in Essex-street," *GM*, LV (February 1785), 99.

6:4. Cooke, William. *Conversation: A Didactic Poem. The 4th edition, revised and enlarged, with Poetical Portraits of the Principal Characters of Dr. Johnson's Club.* London: Underwood, 1815. Earlier title, *The Pleasures of Conversation*. Verse "portraits" of Johnson, Burney, Windham, Garrick, Boswell, Brocklesby, Nichols, and others.

6:5. Hatchett, Charles. "The Club," Appendix I to Vol. II of *Life*, ed. J. W. Croker, rev. John Wright. London: Murray, 1835 ("Croker's second edition," very frequently reprinted). A full listing of the membership from its beginning to 1835.

6:6. Curry, Daniel. "The Literary Club," *Ladies Repository*, XXII (February 1862), 73–76.

6:7 Thornbury, Walter. "The Johnson Club," *Belgravia*, VI (October 1868), 513–17. Reprinted in *Living Age*, No. 1278 (November 28, 1868), pp. 553–56.

6:8. "The Johnson Club," *N&Q*, 4th ser., IV (October 30, 1869), 379. Notice of its organization.

6:9. The Johnson Club [London]. Founded in its present form 1884, but see item 6:8. Not to be confused with "The Club" (or "The Literary Club") founded by Johnson and Reynolds in 1764 (still in existence in 1969) or with the Johnson Society of London, founded 1928 (item 6:31).

6:10. N., H. [H. Norman.] "The Doctor Johnson Club," *Nation*, XLI (September 10, 1885), 214. The contemporary Club (T. Fisher Unwin, president).

6:11. *Johnson Club* [list of members up to June 1889]. Privately printed, n.d.

6:12. Neff, Elizabeth Clifford. "The London Johnson Club" [a query about London *Rasselas* society of 1810], *Critic*, n.s., XXIII (March 2, 1895), 170–71.

6:13. Hill, George Birkbeck. "The Johnson Club" [chiefly an account of a pilgrimage to Lichfield, etc.], *Atlantic Monthly*, LXXVII (January 1896), 18–30.

6:14. Birrell, Augustine. "The Johnson Club," *Great Thoughts*, VIII (November 1896), 101.

6:15. Gennadius, Joannes. *The Johnson Club at Bath*. Bath: J. B. Keene, 1899. Reprinted from *Bladud*, June 21, 1899.

6:16. *Johnson Club Papers*, ed. George Whale and John Sargeaunt. London: Fisher Unwin, 1899. See also item 10/6:108.

6:17. "The Johnson Club" [stems from item 6:16], *Unwin's Chap Book*, 1899–1900, pp. 14–16. London: T. Fisher Unwin, 1900.

6:18. "A Reminiscence of the Johnson Club at Lichfield," *Tatler*, No. 5 (July 31, 1901), pp. 211.

6:19. *The Club, 1764–1905*, ed. M. E. G. Duff. London: Privately printed, Ballantyne Press, 1905.

6:20. Abrahams, Aleck. "Dr. Johnson's Club and the Literary Club," *N&Q*, 10th ser., VI (October 13, 1906), 294.

6:21. *Bi-Centenary of the Birth of Dr. Samuel Johnson* [official guide to celebrations at Lichfield, September 15–19, 1909], ed. J. T. Raby. Stafford: J. and C. Mort, 1909. Reprinted from the *Staffordshire Advertiser*. Beginning of the Johnson Society of Lichfield.

6:22. The Johnson Society of Lichfield, England. Founded 1909. Separate accounts of birthday celebrations in September, from 1910 through 1938 and in 1945, 1947, 1948, and 1949. Usually reprinted from the *Lichfield Mercury* by The Mercury Head or The Johnson's Head printers. (The 1914–18 reports are merely descriptions of informal gatherings.) These are now published in an annual booklet as the Society's *Transactions* (see next entry).

6:23. [Annual] *Transactions of the Johnson Society* [Lichfield]. From 1947.

6:24. *Rules of the Johnson Society, Lichfield, and List of Members for 1910–11*. Lichfield: The Johnson's Head, 1911.

6:25. *Annals of The Club: 1764–1914*, eds. Sir Frederic G. Kenyon, G. W. Prothero, Wilfrid Ward, and Lord Welby. Limited ed. London: Oxford University Press, 1914. An enlarged revision of item 6:19.

6:26. Escott, T. H. S. *Club Makers and Club Members*, pp. 37–38, 136–39, etc. London: T. Fisher Unwin, 1914.

6:27. "The Johnson Society: Spring Meeting in Derby," *Lichfield Mercury*, May 22, 1914.

6:28. *Johnson Club Papers*, Second Series, ed. George Whale and John Sargeaunt. London: Fisher Unwin, 1920. Reviewed by James H. Pitman, *MLN*, XXXVI (November 1921), 436–38.

6:29. Whale, George. *The Forty Years of the Johnson Club, 1884–1924*. Cambridge: Cambridge University Press, 1925.

6:30. *Objects and Rules of the Johnson Society of London*. London: Johnson Society, 1928.

6:31. The Johnson Society of London. Reports, etc. Society founded June 1928. First annual dinner report, 1932; others printed for 1935 through 1939. Annual reports, with financial accounts, issued from the start. For more details see *JNL*, May 1950, pp. 4–5. Publishes irregularly—usually twice a year—*The New Rambler*. See item 1/2:7.

6:32. The Johnson Society of London. A series of addresses at St. Clement Danes commemorating Johnson's death, separately printed.

6:33. Chapman, Robert William. *The Johnson Club 1884–1934* [account of the club with a list of members, etc.]. Oxford: Printed for the members, Clarendon Press, 1938.

6:34. Weiss, C. "Dr. Johnson's Rotary Club," *Rotarian*, LV (September 1939), 2.

6:35. The Johnson Society of the River Plate, Buenos Aires, Argentina. Founded by A. S. Hall Johnson. Miscellaneous items connected with September birthday dinners.

6:36. Societas Johnsoniana of Oslo, Norway. Rolv Laache, first president. Only publication a report of speeches at the first meeting held after the occupation, on December 2, 1945. For a full account of the society see *JNL*, X (August 1950), 1–4. President is now (1970) Leiv Amundsen of Jar, near Oslo.

6:37. *Boswell in Chicago* [records of Boswell Club of Chicago], ed. Frank L. Beals. Chicago: Issued privately, 1946.

6:38. Miller, Clarence A. *An Evening with the Literary Club*. Washington, D.C.: Issued privately, 1947.

6:39. The Johnsonians (eastern United States). Founded in 1948 (see also item 6:47). At annual "Johnson's birthday" dinners in September issues privately printed pamphlets.

6:40. Miller, Clarence A. *Anecdotes of the Literary Club*. New York: Exposition Press, 1948.

6:41. Fifer, C. N. "The Founding of Dr. Johnson's Literary Club," *N&Q*, July 1956, pp. 302–3.

6:42. The Johnson Society of the Central Region (incorporating the Johnson Society of the Great Lakes Region, 1959 to 1966, and the Johnson Society of the Midwest, 1961 to 1966). Publishes occasional *Transactions* and a *Newsletter*.

6:43. The Johnson Society of Kansas. Founded 1961.

6:44. "Johnsonian Societies," *JNL*, XXI, no. 3 (September 1961), 1–3. Account of those in existence at that date.

6:45. Curtis, Lewis P., and Herman W. Liebert. *Esto Perpetua: The Club of Dr. Johnson and His Friends, 1764–1784*. Hamden, Conn.: Archon Books, 1963.

6:46. The Johnson Society of the North West (western Canadian provinces and northwestern United States). Founded 1966.

6:47. Kay, Elizabeth. "The First American Birthday Party for Dr. Johnson" [account of a Johnsonian dinner at Four Oaks Farm, Somerville, N.J., in 1946]. Privately printed for the annual dinner of The Johnsonians, 1967.

7. HOMES AND PLACES

7:1. Shaw, Stebbing. *The History and Antiquities of Staffordshire*, I, 231–

376, and *passim*. London: J. Nichols, 1798–1801. Lichfield and other Staffordshire localities associated with Johnson.

7:2. Harwood, Thomas. *The History and Antiquities of the Church and City of Lichfield*. Gloucester: Printed for Cadell and Davies, London, 1806.

7:3. "The House of the Late Samuel Johnson, LL.D. (With a view)," *European Magazine*, LVII (May 1810), 353–54. In Bolt Court; with a plate.

7:4. "A Tribute to the Memory of Dr. Johnson," *Living Age*, XXX (July–September, 1851), 66. Placing of tablet at his seat in St. Clement Danes.

7:5. A., M. "Johnson's House, Bolt Court," *N&Q*, V (March 6, 1852), 232. See also Tee Bee and B. B., *ibid.*, pp. 232–33.

7:6. Hawthorne, Nathaniel. "Uttoxeter," *Harper's Magazine*, XIV (April 1857), 639–41. Describes Hawthorne's visit to Lichfield and Uttoxeter. Also appeared in *The Keepsake* (London), 1857. Expanded version, "Lichfield and Uttoxeter," in *Our Old Home: A Series of English Sketches*, Boston: Ticknor and Fields, 1863.

7:7. "Haunted London: The Ghost of Samuel Johnson," *All the Year Round*, I (May 21, 1859), 92–96.

7:8. "Dr. Johnson's House in Bolt Court," *All the Year Round*, I (July 9, 1859), 251–52. Chiefly on the fire which destroyed it in 1819.

7:9. Thornbury, Walter. "Boswell's Life of Johnson," *N&Q*, 4th ser., VII (June 24, 1871), 532. Dates of Johnson's residence in Staple Inn.

7:10. Cooke, Chr. "Edial Hall," *N&Q*, 5th ser., IV (September 4, 1875), 186. Said not to be destroyed. See also *JNL*, September 1968, p. 6.

7:11. Timmins, Samuel. "Dr. Johnson in Birmingham," *Transactions, Excursions, and Reports of the Archaeological Section of the Birmingham and Midland Institute*, VII (1876), 39–46. Published 1880.

7:12. Fitzgerald, Percy. "Dr. Johnson and the Fleet Street Taverns," *GM*, n.s., XXVI (March 1881), 305–17. Mainly on connection of Johnson and the Cheshire Cheese.

7:13. Wheatley, Henry B. "Samuel Johnson at Lichfield," *Antiquary*, X (December 1884), 233–39.

7:14. "Dr. Johnson's Homes in London," *Builder* (December 13, 1884), 786–87.

*7:15. Hutton, Lawrence. "Samuel Johnson," *Literary Landmarks of London*, pp. 155–71. London: T. Fisher Unwin, 1885. A careful tabulation of Johnson's residences and other haunts.

7:16. Arthur, W. "Dr. Samuel Johnson in Wales," *Red Dragon*, VII (January–June 1885), 51–60. Includes (p. 60) a set of verses by Gerald Thompson, "Dr. Johnson's Centenary (December 13th, 1884)."

7:17. Noble, T. C. "Dr. Johnson and Lichfield," *N&Q*, 7th ser., IV (November 19, 1887), 402–4.

7:18. Ward, C. A. "Johnson's Tavern Resorts and Conversation," *Bookworm*, I (1888), 224–28, 249–53, 276–80, 315–17, 383–87.

7:19. Ward, C. A. "London Homes of Dr. Johnson," *Antiquary*, XVII (January, February 1888), 12–15, 53–55.

7:20. Wheatley, Henry B. *London Past and Present*. 3 vols. London: John Murray, 1891.

7:21. Winter, William. "The Home of Dr. Johnson" [birthplace], *Gray Days and Gold*, pp. 207–21. Edinburgh: D. Douglas, 1891.

7:22. Dobson, Austin. "A Garret in Gough Square," *Christian Union*, December 5, 1891, pp. 1082–83. Reprinted in his *Eighteenth Century Vignettes*, First Series, pp. 93–103, London: Chatto & Windus, 1892.

7:23. Whale, George. "Round the Town with Dr. Johnson" [relics of Johnson's London], *GM*, CCLXXIV (February 1893), 120–29. Reprinted in item 6:16, pp. 239–56.

7:24. Fitzgerald, Percy H. "Rambles in Johnson-Land" [trips to Lichfield, Ashbourne, etc.], *GM*, CCLXXIV (August 1893), 145–57. Reprinted in *Eclectic Magazine*, n.s., LIII (September 1893), 356–63.

7:25. Dobson, Austin. "Johnson's Houses," *Illustrated London News*, March 10, 1894, p. 295. A plea for the preservation of the Gough Square house.

7:26. "Dr. Johnson in Lichfield," *Critic*, n.s., XXIV (November 23, 1895), 353–54.

7:27. Dent, Robert K., and Joseph Hill. "Samuel Johnson and His Home," *Historic Staffordshire*, pp. 294–303. Birmingham: Midland Educational Co., 1896.

7:28. Parry, Evelyn B. "Glimpses of Johnson in Eighteenth Century Oxford," *Leisure Hour*, XLV (August, September 1896), 651–56, 713–19.

*7:29. Dent, Robert K., and Joseph Hill. *Memorials of the Old Square*. Birmingham: Achilles Taylor, 1897.

7:30. Macleane, Douglas. *A History of Pembroke College Oxford*. (Oxford Historical Society Publications, Vol. 33.) Oxford: Clarendon Press, 1897.

7:31. "Dr. Johnson's Pew" [in St. Clement Danes], *Academy*, LIV (August 6, 1898), 132–33.

7:32. Page, John T. "Dr. Johnson's Residence in Bolt Court, Fleet St.," *N&Q*, 9th ser., I (June 25, 1898), 506. See also G. Pearson, *ibid.*, II (July 23, 1898), 71–72; W. C. B., *ibid.* (August 13), 132.

7:33. Radford, George H. "Dr. Johnson and Lichfield," in item 6:16, pp. 155–70.

7:34. Lynn, W. T. "Johnson's House at Frognall," *N&Q*, 9th ser., III (March 25, 1899), 228. See also John T. Page, *ibid.* (April 29), p. 334; also *ibid.* (May 27), p. 415.

7:35. Hubbard, Elbert. "Samuel Johnson," *Little Journeys to the Homes of*

English Authors, VI (June 1900), 119–44. Reprinted (same title), New York, 1916, V, 144–70.

7:36. Overton, F. J. "Johnson's Birthplace," *N&Q*, 9th ser., V (June 9, 1900), 452. See also John T. Page, *ibid.* (June 23), p. 505.

7:37. Beeching, H. C. "Provincial Letters" [Johnson and Lichfield], *Cornhill Magazine*, n.s., X (May 1901), 688–97. Reprinted in *Provincial Letters and Other Papers*, pp. 17–36, London: Smith, Elder and Co., 1906.

7:38. Sidebotham, W. "Dr. Johnson and St. Clement Danes," *Leisure Hour*, XLIX (June 1901), 619–24.

7:39. Grey, Rowland. "Fleet Street Memories," *Great Thoughts*, IX (October 1901), 37.

7:40. Dobson, Austin. "Dr. Johnson's Haunts and Habitations," in item 4:14, ed. Arnold Glover, 1901. Reprinted in *Side-walk Studies*, pp. 148–86, London: Chatto & Windus, 1902.

*7:41. *Dr. Samuel Johnson and His Birthplace*. Lichfield: The Johnson's Head, 1902. Guidebook compiled by the Johnson House committee; many later editions.

7:42. Hutton, Lawrence. "Pembroke College," *Literary Landmarks of Oxford*, pp. 196–202. London: G. Richards; New York: Scribner's, 1903.

7:43. Worsfold, T. Cato. *Staple Inn*. London: Bumpus, 1903.

7:44. Mortimer, John. "Ashbourne and Dr. Johnson," *Manchester Quarterly*, XXIII (1904), 54–61.

7:45. Freeman, H. B. "Dr. Johnson and Lichfield," *Evening Standard* (London), October 7, 1904.

7:46. Lee, Sidney. "The Johnson Club: A Literary Pilgrimage to Rochester," *Pall Mall Magazine*, n.s., II (October 1905), 513–21.

7:47. Reid, W. Lewis. "Sterne and Johnson at 'The Cheshire Cheese,'" *N&Q*, 10th ser., V (February 10, 1906), 108.

7:48. "Dr. Johnson and Oxford," *GM*, CCCI (July 1906), 46–58.

7:49. Coleridge-Roberts, W. R. "The Johnson Memorial at Lichfield," *Nation* (New York), LXXXVI (March 12, 1908), 233–34.

7:50. Mabie, Hamilton W. "Dr. Johnson at Lichfield," *Outlook*, XC (September 26, 1908), 193–201.

7:51. Pennington, John J. H. S. *Interesting Reminiscences of St. Clement Danes Church, Strand*, pp. 12, 37–38, etc. London: Diprose, Bateman Co., 1909.

7:52. Raby, J. T. "Lichfield and Dr. Johnson," in W. Beresford, *Memorials of Old Staffordshire*, pp. 206–35. London: George Allen, 1909.

7:53. Kirke, Henry. "Dr. Johnson in Derbyshire," *Journal of the Derbyshire Archaeological and Natural History Society*, XXXII (1910), 113–22.

7:54. White-Thomson, Sir Robert. [Certain Johnsonian connections in Lichfield.] Lichfield address, 1910; see item 6:22.

7:55. Boynton, P. H. "Johnson's London," *Chautauquan*, LXI (January 1911), 175–99.

7:56. Geyer, G. C. "Ye Olde Cheshire Cheese," *Chautauquan*, LXII (May 1911), 379–85.

7:57. Broadley, A. M. "Literary Patriotism" [Johnsonian shrines in London], *Outlook* (London), XXVII (May 6, 1911), 567–68.

7:58. Adcock, A. St. J. "Homes and Haunts of Johnson and Boswell," *Famous Houses and Literary Shrines of London*, pp. 68–88. London: J. M. Dent, 1912.

7:59. "Visits to Uttoxeter, Ashbourne, and Cubley," *Staffordshire Advertiser*, May 11, 1912. Reprinted; see item 6:22.

7:60. Grant, Arthur. "The Ladies of the Vale" [spires of Lichfield cathedral], *In the Old Paths*, pp. 159–72. London: Constable, 1913.

7:61. Tearle, Christian. "Johnson's House in Gough Square" and "At Lichfield," *The Pilgrim from Chicago*, pp. 286–95, 296–316. London: Longmans, Green & Co., 1913.

7:62. "Visit to Oxford," *Staffordshire Advertiser*, May 31, 1913. Reprinted; see item 6:22.

7:63. Dobson, Austin. "Streatham Place," *National Review*, LXII (October 1913), 270–85. Reprinted in *Rosalba's Journal*, pp. 32–62, London: Chatto & Windus, 1915.

7:64. Eliot, George E. *Ye Olde Chesshire Cheese*. New Haven, Conn.: Privately printed, Yale University Press, 1918.

*7:65. Arnot, L., and W. Godfrey Allen. "Dr. Johnson's House in Gough Square," *Architectural Review*, XLIV (December 1918), 111–14.

7:66. *Visit to Stourbridge, June 23, 1920, by the Johnson Society of Lichfield* [see item 6:22]. Lichfield: Mercury Press, 1920. First printed in *Stourbridge County Express*, June 26, July 10, 1920.

7:67. "Visit to Chatsworth, Okeover, etc." *Lichfield Mercury*, May 19, 1922. Reprinted; see item 6:22.

7:68. "Visit to Cudworth, Packwood, and Stratford-on-Avon, May 30, 1923," *Lichfield Mercury*, June 1, 1923. Reprinted; see item 6:22.

7:69. Wellstood, F. C. "Johnson, Boswell, Garrick and Stratford-upon-Avon," *Lichfield Mercury*, June 1, 1923. Reprinted as part of item 7:68.

7:70. Grundy-Newman, S. A. "Appleby Magna School," *Lichfield Mercury*, May 23, 1924. Reprinted in item 7:68.

7:71. "Visit to Appleby Magna, Market Bosworth, and Ashby-de-la-zouch," *Lichfield Mercury*, May 23, 1924. Reprinted; see item 6:22.

7:22. Gissing, Algernon. "On Foot to Market Bosworth: A Johnson Pilgrimage," *Cornhill Magazine*, n.s., LVII (July 1924), 7–16.

7:73. Bamford, A. Bennett. "Dr. Samuel Johnson at Warley Camp," *Essex Review*, XXXIII (July, October 1924), 145–48, 213–17.

*7:74. MacKinnon, Frank D. "Dr. Johnson and the Temple," *Cornhill Magazine*, n.s., LVII (October 1924), 465–77. Reprinted in *The Murder in the Temple*, pp. 69–85, London: Sweet & Maxwell, 1935.

7:75. Harmsworth, Cecil. *Dr. Johnson's House Gough Square* [pamphlet on sale at the house]. 1924. Rev. ed., London: Spottiswoode, Ballantyne & Co., 1947. See also *N&Q*, CLXXII (May 8, 1937), 326.

7:76. Foord, Edward. *St. Clement Danes, Strand, London* [guidebook]. London, 1925.

7:77. Parker, Alfred D. *A Sentimental Journey in and about Lichfield*. Lichfield: Lomax, 1925.

7:78. Newton, A. Edward. "The Ghosts of Gough Square" [Johnson's house, etc.], *Atlantic Monthly*, CXXXV (June 1925), 818–25. Reprinted in *The Greatest Book in the World*, pp. 54–74, Boston: Little, Brown & Co., 1925.

7:79. Phelps, Sydney K. "Two of Our Invisible Hosts" [houses of John Wesley and Johnson], *Nineteenth Century*, XCVIII (July 1925), 128–36.

7:80. Harper, Charles George. "Dr. Johnson's London," *A Literary Man's London*, pp. 138–77. London: Cecil Palmer, 1926.

7:81. Sadler, Ernest A. *A Famous Pew in Ashbourne Church*. Reprinted from the *Derbyshire Archaeological and Natural History Society Journal*, Ashbourne, 1926.

7:82. Norwood, F. W. *Samuel Johnson and His London: An Appeal to Young People to Come and Conquer His City: A Lecture*. London: City Temple Literary Society, 1927.

7:83. "Here Dr. Johnson Lived," *Mentor*, XV (May 1927), 15.

7:84. Charnwood, Dorothea, Lady. "A Habitation's Memories: Johnsoniana" [Stowe House, Lichfield), *Cornhill Magazine*, n.s., LXIII (November, December 1927), 535–47, 664–77.

7:85. *Dr. Johnson's House, Gough Square, London. Souvenir of Dedication Dinner, Wednesday, 11th December, 1929*. London: George W. Jones.

7:86. Reid, Thomas W. *The Book of the Cheese*. Rev., 10th ed. London: The Cheshire Cheese, 1929. First published in 1886 under the title *Traits and Stories of ye Olde Cheshire Cheese*; later revised by William Hussey Graham, R. R. D. Adams, and Frank Banfield.

7:87. *Sir J. M. Barrie and Mr. Johnson: A Message from J. M. Barrie* [concerns Gough Square House]. Privately printed, [1929].

7:88. Hollis, Christopher. "Johnson in London," *Catholic World*, CXXIX (June 1929), 346–47.

7:89. Berry, Marion. "Intimate Museums" [Gough Square House], *Living Age*, CCCXXXVI (July 1929), 364.

7:90. Jones, George W. *Doctor Samuel Johnson and the Sign of the Dolphin in Gough Square London*. London: George W. Jones, n.d. [ca. 1920s?].

7:91. Newton, A. Edward. *Men and Ghosts of Gough Square* [pamphlet for sale at Gough Square Johnson House]. London, 1930. Rev. ed., with foreword by Lord Harmsworth, London: Spottiswoode, Ballantyne & Co., 1947. Entitled "Adventures in Gough Square," reprinted in *Derby Day*, pp. 120–38, Boston: Little, Brown & Co., 1934.

7:92. *The Story of an Ancient Brewery* [Thrale's brewery, etc.]. London: Barclay Perkins and Co., [1930].

7:93. Dane, M. "Where Dr. Johnson Lived" [Gough Square House], *Homes and Gardens*, XII (October 1930), 181–83.

7:94. Bell, Walter G. "Dr. Johnson's Surviving Home," *Blue Peter*, XI (December 1931), 602.

*7:95. Bromhead, Harold W. *The Heritage of St. Leonard's Parish Church Streatham*, pp. 22–45. London: Hatchards, 1932. Johnson's connection with Streatham.

7:96. Sitwell, Edith. *Bath*, pp. 224–28, etc. London: Faber & Faber, 1932.

7:97. Chancellor, E. Beresford. "The Age of Johnson," *Literary Ghosts of London*, pp. 202–28. London: Richards, 1933.

7:98. "Dr. Johnson's House," *Cabinet Maker and Complete Furnisher*, December 15, 1934, pp. 417–18.

7:99. Sitwell, Osbert, and Margaret Barton. "At Mrs. Thrale's," *Brighton*, pp. 68–93. London: Faber & Faber, 1935.

7:100. "London's Smaller Museums: V. Dr. Johnson's House," *Sunday at Home*, February 1939, pp. 303–5.

7:101. Craigie, C. "To Think of Tea, and Doctor Johnson! Visit to 17 Gough Square," *America*, LX (April 8, 1939), 642–43.

7:102. Alnwick, Arthur B. "In Dr. Johnson's Footsteps," *London Quarterly and Holborn Review*, CLXV (April 1940), 218–24. Description of two trips to Uttoxeter, Lichfield, etc., by modern admirers.

7:103. Wright, John. "Dr. Johnson in Sussex," *Sussex County Magazine*, XVII (July 1943), 188–89.

7:104. Harmsworth, Cecil. "Dr. Johnson's House in Gough Square," *Old London Magazine*, I (Christmas 1948), 8–10.

7:105. Hopewell, S. "Johnson and His Times," *The Book of Bosworth School*. Leicester: W. Thornley and Son, 1950. Many errors; does not use Reade.

7:106. [Liebert, Herman W.] *Dr. Johnson and Oxford*. Privately printed for The Johnsonians, 1950. In honor of R. W. Chapman.

7:107. Clifford-Smith, H. "Dr. Johnson's House" [Gough Square], *Apollo*, LII (November 1950), 136–40; (December), 165–68.

7:108. Laithwaite, Percy. "The Beginnings of Lichfield," in item 6:23, 1950.

7:109. Hopkins, Mary Alden. *Dr. Johnson's Lichfield*. New York: Hastings House, 1952; London: Peter Owen, 1956.

7:110. Meynell, Rosemary. "Johnsonian Mysteries in Derbyshire," *Derbyshire Countryside*, July–September 1952, pp. 64–65.

7:111. Christian, Roy. "Johnson's Lichfield," *Coming Events in Britain* (British Travel Association), September 1952, p. 25.

7:112. Thompson, L. V. *Blue Plaque Guide to the Historic London Houses.* London: Newman Neame, 1953.

7:113. Lockspeiser, Sir Ben. "City of Philosophers" [Lichfield], in item 6:23, December 1953, pp. 18–30.

*7:114. Laithwaite, Percy. *Dr. Samuel Johnson and His Birthplace.* Rev. ed. Lichfield: Johnson Birthplace Committee, 1955.

7:115. Meynell, Laurence. "Samuel Johnson," *Great Men of Staffordshire*, pp. 7–47. London: The Bodley Head, 1955.

7:116. Ogden, C. R. B. "Dr. Johnson in Bedfordshire," *Bedfordshire Magazine*, V (Winter 1955–56), 93–97.

7:117. Bartel, Roland, ed. *Johnson's London: Selected Source Materials for Freshman Research Papers.* New York: D. C. Heath and Co., 1956.

7:118. *Dr. Johnson's House, Gough Square, London, E.C., 1748–1958: A Brief History.* London: George W. Jones, [1958].

7:119. Bevan, Bryan. "Dr. Johnson's Year," *Coming Events in Britain* (British Travel Association), July 1959, pp. 12–15.

7:120. *Dr. Johnson and Birmingham: An Account of the Birmingham Celebrations of the 250th Anniversary of the Birth of Dr. Samuel Johnson,* ed. Eric Knight. Birmingham: Birmingham and Midland Institute, 1960.

7:121. "Dr. Johnson's Summer House Returns" [the Thrales' Streatham summer house], *Times* (London), September 15, 1964, p. 12. See also *JNL*, XXVI (December 1966), 14–15.

7:122. Brittain, Robert. [Johnson and his environment], *Letters from England*, No. 5 (December 1964), pp. 1–4, and "Teacher's Supplement," pp. 1–4. This is designed for high school students and supplies much interesting material and illustrations.

7:123. Ehrlich, Blake. "The London of Dr. Samuel Johnson," *London on the Thames*, pp. 140–202. Boston: Little, Brown, 1966.

7:124. Kahrl, George M. "Garrick, Johnson, and Lichfield," *New Rambler*, June 1966, pp. 15–28.

7:125. *Johnson's House, Gough Square.* London, 1967. A guide to the house and furnishings.

7:126. Yung, K. K. "Some Notes on Johnson's Birthplace," in item 6:23, December 1967, pp. 17–22.

8. PICTURES, RELICS, ASSOCIATION ITEMS

8:1. "The Irish Stubble alias Bubble Goose" [caricature]. London, 1763. No.

4068 in *British Museum Catalogue of . . . Political and Personal Satires*. Johnson as lexicographer and pensioner.

8:2. Stockdale, Percival. "An Elegy on the Death of Dr. Johnson's Favourite Cat," *Poetical Works*, II, 255–57. London: Longman, Hurst, 1810. Dated "1764." Reprinted in item 8:62.

8:3. Townshend, George Townshend, 1st Marquess. "The Secret Council of the Heads" [caricature]. London, 1768. Nos. 4217, 4218 in *British Museum Catalogue of . . . Political and Personal Satires*. Johnson as member (with others) of secession from Society of Artists which founded the Royal Academy.

8:4. Bunbury, Henry William. "A Chop-House" [satiric print]. London: W. Dickinson, 1781. No. 5922 in *British Museum Catalogue of . . . Political and Personal Satires*. Johnson and Boswell dining. Reproduced in item 8:72.

8:5. Gillray, James. "Old Wisdom Blinking at the Stars" [satiric print]. London: W. Rennie, 1782. No. 6103 in *British Museum Catalogue of . . . Political and Personal Satires*. Johnson as an owl, blinking at busts of Pope and Milton. Reproduced in item 8:72.

8:6. Gillray, James. "Apollo and the Muses Inflicting Penance on Dr. Pomposo Round Parnassus" [satiric print]. London: Holland, 1783. No. 6325 in *British Museum Catalogue of . . . Political and Personal Satires*. Johnson, in his underwear and with a dunce's cap, is whipped for "defaming . . . the Beauties of British Poetry." Reproduced in item 8:72.

8:7. Stringer, E. "View near Lichfield, including a most remarkably large Willow Tree ["Johnson's Willow"]," *GM*, LV (April 1785), facing p. 411. Engraved by T. Cook.

*8:8. Rowlandson, Thomas [etched from designs by Samuel Collings]. *Picturesque Beauties of Boswell*. London: E. Jackson, 1786. Reprinted as *The Beauties of Boswell*, San Francisco: Book Club of California, 1942. Twenty caricatures of Johnson and Boswell on the journey to the Hebrides.

8:9. Sayers, James. "The Biographers" [satiric print]. London: T. Cornell, 1786. No. 7052 in *British Museum Catalogue of . . . Political and Personal Satires*. Mrs. Piozzi, Boswell, and Courtenay. Contains satiric poem, item 9:38.

8:10. Trotter, Thomas. "Dr. Johnson in His Travelling Dress as Described in Boswell's Tour" [satiric print]. London: G. Kearsley, 1786. No. 7028 in *British Museum Catalogue of . . . Political and Personal Satires*.

8:11. Sayers, James. "Frontispiece for the 2nd Edition of Dr. J——n's Letters" [engraving]. London: T. Cornell, 1788. No. 7417 in *British Museum Catalogue of . . . Political and Personal Satires*. Johnson's ghost returning to haunt Mrs. Piozzi and other biographers. Contains satiric poem, item 9:45.

8:12. Newton, Richard. "A Lesson for Spendthrifts." London: William Holland, 1794. Eight engravings based on Johnson's verses to Sir John Lade, "A Short Song of Congratulation."

8:13. "Urn to the Memory of the Late Dr. Johnson," *European Magazine*, XXV (March 1794), 211. Plate of urn at Gwaynynog.

8:14. "Monument of Dr. Johnson" [Bacon's in St. Paul's], *European Magazine*, XXIX (March 1796), 160.

8:15. B. [Has seen plaster death mask of Johnson], *GM*, LXVI (April 1796), 298.

8:16. Baillie, Matthew. *A Series of Engravings, Accompanied with Explanations, Which Are Intended To Illustrate the Morbid Anatomy of Some of the Most Important Parts of the Human Body.* London: J. Johnson and G. Nicol, 1799. Fasciculus II, Plate 6, Figure 1 is said (item 3:743) to be a drawing of Johnson's lung. Its description (in Baillie's *Morbid Anatomy*, 1793, which this work is intended to accompany) is said to be the first clinical description of emphysema.

8:17. [Boswell and the Ghost of Johnson—satiric print.] Hampstead: C. Bestland, 1803. No. 8281 in *British Museum Catalogue of . . . Political and Personal Satires*; "probably a reissue or copy of a print published on the appearance of Boswell's *Life of Johnson.*" Ghost of Johnson standing on a cloud and gesturing ominously at Boswell, who is writing at a table.

8:18. D., C. "Strictures on Dr. Johnson's Monument in St. Paul's Cathedral," *European Magazine*, XLV (February 1804), 98.

8:19. "Dr. Johnson's Room. Left Wing," *Streatham Park, Surrey. A Catalogue of . . . Household Furniture . . . Library, etc. . . . property of Mrs. Piozzi* [Squibb sale catalogue], May 10, 1816, p. 34. Describes furnishings of the room.

8:20. Simpson, Thomas. [Miniature of Johnson painted in 1736], *GM*, LXXXVIII (February 1818), 194.

*8:21. *Graphic Illustrations of the Life and Times of Samuel Johnson, LL.D.* London: Murray, 1836. The illustrations of Croker's ed. of Boswell's *Life*, 1835, and of *Johnsoniana* (item 3:75) published separately.

8:22. Paternoster, Rich. "Dr. Johnson's Chair," *N&Q*, 2nd ser., VIII (July 23, 1859), 68; also (October 29, 1859), 363.

8:23. Paul, George. "Portraits of Dr. Johnson," *N&Q*, 3rd ser., IV (October 17, 1863), 316. Portrait by Reynolds for John Taylor in writer's possession.

8:24. Thackeray, William Makepeace. Drawing of Johnson and Goldsmith passing Goldsmith's tailor's; captioned "To a new plum-coloured coat,

Dr. Goldsmith . . . To S. Filby, Dr.," *North British Review*, XL (February 1864), 256.

8:25. Pycroft, James. "Dr. Johnson's Watch," *N&Q*, 4th ser., VII (March 18, 1871), 243. In the possession of the writer, a descendant of George Steevens, who obtained it after Johnson's death.

8:26. Thoms, William J. "Portraits of Dr. Johnson," *N&Q*, 5th ser., I (January 17, 1874), 2. See also *ibid.*, 55; III, 117, 156; and 6th ser., VII, 213.

8:27. Q., E. "Boswell's *Johnson*" [on his watch and punchbowl], *N&Q*, V (January 14, 1882), 26–27. Formerly owned by Rev. Hugh P[B?]ailye.

8:28. Walford, E. "Dr. Johnson Painted by Reynolds," *Antiquarian Magazine and Bibliographer*, IV (July 1883), 1–8.

8:29. "Johnson's Monument in St. Paul's," *Saturday Review*, LVIII (October 4, 1884), 436–37. Chiefly on Parr's epitaph.

8:30. Hutton, Laurence. *Portraits in Plaster*, pp. 110–11 [death mask]. New York: Harper and Brothers, 1894.

8:31. "Portraits of Samuel Johnson" [from the Adam collection], *Bookman* (London), XI (March 1897), 168—73.

8:32. Clayton, E. G. "Dr. Johnson's Teapot," *N&Q*, 8th ser., XI (April 3, 1897), 270.

8:33. Roberts, W. "Dr. Johnson's Portrait by Zoffany," *N&Q*, 9th ser., I (March 5, 1898), 186.

8:34. Maxwell, Patrick. [Johnson's monument in St. Paul's], *N&Q*, 9th ser., I (May 14, June 4, 1898), 385–86, 452. See also John Murray, *ibid.* (May 21, 1898), p. 409.

8:35. *Portraits: Dr. Samuel Johnson, His Friends, Acquaintances and Others*, Catalogue 8 of Engravings. London: Daniel, n.d. [19th century].

8:36. Morris, Edward E. "Johnson's Monument" [letters from Windham and Banks about monument in St. Paul's], *Longman's Magazine*, XXXVI (May 1900), 32–39.

8:37. Newton, A. Edward. *A Johnson Bookplate*. Daylesford, Pa.: Privately printed, 1909. Newton's own bookplate with quotation from Johnson, etc.

8:38. H., F. "Dr. Johnson's Watch," *N&Q*, 10th ser., XI (June 19, 1909), 494–95.

8:39. "Dr. Johnson's Teapot" [at Pembroke College], *Graphic*, LXXX (September 18, 1909), 378.

8:40. Beerbohm, Max. "In the Shades, 1915." Caricature of Johnson and Boswell, drawn for the Johnson house, Gough Square, and exhibited there. Contains a piece of mock dialogue between Johnson and Boswell, reproduced in brochure for dedication dinner, Johnson House, December 11, 1929.

8:41. Abrahams, Aleck. "Dr. Johnson's Knocker," *N&Q*, 12th ser., I (March 25, 1916), 246.

8:42. Wheatley, Henry B. "Johnson's Monument and Parr's Epitaph on Johnson," in item 6:28, pp. 221–38.

8:43. Bensly, Edward. "Dr. Johnson: Portrait in Hill's Edition of Boswell," N&Q, 12th ser., VIII (April 2, 1921), 274. See also A. Sparke, ibid. (April 9), pp. 298–99.

8:44. *Dr. Samuel Johnson: From an Original Portrait in the Johnson Collection of A. Edward Newton* [Christmas issue, 1922]. Daylesford, Pa., 1922.

8:45. Tinker, Chauncey B. *The Wedgwood Medallion of Samuel Johnson: A Study in Iconography*. Cambridge, Mass.: Harvard University Press, 1926. Reviewed in SRL, January 8, 1927, p. 507. See also Life, IV, 462, for important additional evidence.

8:46. Tinker, Chauncey B. "Flaxman's Medallion of Dr. Johnson," TLS, March 10, 1927, p. 160. See item 8:45.

8:47. Birrell, Augustine. "A New Portrait of Dr. Johnson" [by James Roberts, made in 1784 for Miss Adams], *Burlington Magazine*, LI (December 1927), 266–68.

8:48. Bulliet, C. J. "Relic of Dr. Johnson" [teapot], *Chicago Evening Post Magazine*, December 27, 1927.

8:49. Scott, Lindley. "Early Portrait of Dr. Johnson," *Country Life*, April 14, 1928, pp. 524–25.

8:50. Jackson, E. Nevill. "The Shade of Dr. Johnson" [profile painted on convex glass], *Connoisseur*, LXXXIII (January 1929), 103.

8:51. Long, Basil S. [A caricature of Johnson and Boswell by Samuel Collings], *Connoisseur*, LXXXV (January 1930), 29.

8:52. Waters, A. W. "Johnson Copper Tokens," N&Q, CLIX (December 6, 1930), 403–4.

8:53. Esdaile, Mrs. Arundell. "Johnson and St. Paul's" [his monument there], *Times* (London), December 13, 1930, pp. 13–14.

8:54. Powell, Lawrence F. "The Portraits of Johnson," N&Q, CLXIV (January 28, 1933), 64–65; SRL, April 22, 1933, p. 553.

*8:55. Powell, Lawrence F. "The Portraits of Johnson," in Life, Appendix H, IV, 447–64.

*8:56. Powell, Lawrence F. "The Monuments of Johnson," in Life, Appendix I, IV, 464–72.

8:57. Powell, Lawrence F. "Johnson's D.C.L. Diploma," *Bodleian Quarterly Record*, VIII (Winter 1937–38), 458. See also item 8:63.

8:58. Gardner, Bellamy. "Souvenirs of Doctor Samuel Johnson" [teapot, mug, etc.], *Connoisseur*, CIII (April 1939), 203–6, 230.

8:59. S., A. "Johnson's Teapots," *Interchange Fortnightly*, I (June 14, 1940), 30.

8:60. Loane, George G. "Johnson and Tunbridge Wells" [Johnson not in

Loggan's drawing], *N&Q*, CLXXXIV (March 27, 1943), 198; CLXXXV (July 3, 1943), 24.

8:61. Dawson, S. W. "The Johnson Monument in St. Paul's Cathedral," *House of Dawson*, I (January 7, 1948), 2, 8.

8:62. *An Elegy on the Death of Dr. Johnson's Favourite Cat by Percival Stockdale, with a Note on Dr. Johnson's Cats*, ed. Herman W. Liebert. New Haven, Conn.: Privately printed, 1949.

8:63. [Waingrow, Marshall.] "Johnson's Degree Diplomas" [Boswell received them from Hawkins, not from Frank Barber; see item 8:57], *Bodleian Library Record*, III (December 1951), 238–39.

8:64. "Dr. Johnson: An Imaginary Portrait" ["The Infant Johnson" by Reynolds, now in the Hyde collection], *Book Collector*, I (Summer 1952), 94–95. See comment by E. Rosenbaum, *TLS*, July 11, 1952, p. 453, and C. Roy Huddleston, *Book Collector*, I (Autumn 1952), 192. See also Edgar Wind, "Humanitätsidee und heroisiertes Porträt in der englischen Kultur des 18. Jahrhunderts," *Vorträge der Bibliothek Warburg* (1931–32), pp. 156–229.

8:65. Letts, Malcolm. "Dr. Johnson's Cat," *TLS*, November 7, 1952, p. 732.

8:66. *Garrick, Johnson, and the Lichfield Circle: An Exhibition of Paintings* [Lichfield Coronation Festival]. Lichfield, 1953. Introduction by K. J. Garlick.

8:67. Nuttall, Geoffrey F. "Johnson's Fighting Septuagint" [with which he knocked down Osborne; it still survives], *TLS*, March 27, 1959, p. 177. See item 9:96.

8:68. L[iebert], H[erman] W. *Johnson's Head: The Story of the Bust of Dr. Samuel Johnson Taken from the Life by Joseph Nollekens, R.A., in 1777*. With plates. New Haven: Privately printed for The Johnsonians [Yale University Press], 1960.

8:69. Levine, David. [Caricature of Edmund Wilson as Johnson], *New York Review of Books*, November 25, 1965, p. 5.

8:70. Simmons, J. S. G. "Samuel Johnson 'On the Banks of the Neva': A Note on a Picture by Reynolds in the Hermitage," in item 10/6:329, pp. 208–14. Figure of Tiresias in painting "The Infant Hercules Slaying Serpents" has Johnson's features.

8:71. "Johnson in Miniature" [a woodcarving by R. Carpenter, 1784, possibly of Johnson], *New Rambler*, June 1967, p. 32.

8:72. George, M. Dorothy. *Hogarth to Cruikshank: Social Change in Graphic Satire*, pp. 126–30. New York: Walker and Co., 1967. Johnson in satiric prints.

9. FICTION, PARODY, *JEUX D'ESPRIT*, VERSE ABOUT JOHNSON

(General; parody and verse relating to individual works are normally listed in the sections dealing with those works)

9:1. [Derrick, Samuel.] *Fortune: A Rhapsody. Inscribed to Mr. Garrick.* London: R. Manby and H. S. Cox, 1751. Contains a reference to Johnson's lack of "fortune."

9:2. Murphy, Arthur. *A Poetical Epistle to Mr. Samuel Johnson, A.M.* London: Vaillant, 1760. Reprinted in Murphy's *Works*, VII, 3–12, London: Cadell, 1786. About Murphy's quarrels with other authors, rather than about Johnson.

9:3. Churchill, Charles. *The Ghost.* Books I–III, London: W. Flexney, 1762. Book IV, London: Coote, Flexney, etc., 1763. A fantasy on the Cock Lane Ghost incident. Johnson is attacked as "Pomposo," especially in Book II, lines 653–98, and Book III, lines 793–832. Johnson is also alluded to in Churchill's *Rosciad* (1761), lines 61–62, and *The Author* (1763), line 254.

9:4. Mellifont. "Classicus, a Literary Character," *St. James's Chronicle,* January 25–27, 1763. Verse; mixed blame and praise.

9:5. Greene, Edward Burnaby. *The Laureat, a Poem. Inscribed to the memory of C. Churchill.* London: J. Ridley, 1765. Hostile allusion to Johnson. See *Life*, I, 517, n. 1.

9:6. [Shaw, Cuthbert.] *The Race, by Mercurius Spur, Esq.* London: Printed for the author, 1765. 2nd ed., 1766. Passage referring to Johnson quoted *Life*, II, 31.

9:7. "A Rhapsody on the Many Illiberal Invectives Thrown Out against Mr. Samuel Johnson," *St. James's Chronicle,* No. 746 [printed "747"] (December 12–14, 1765). Verse; compares Johnson to a lion, "the prince of beasts," beset by "a troop of monkies." Answered by "One of the Monkies," *St. James's Chronicle,* No. 747 (December 14–17) in an epigram asserting that Johnson is indeed "the Prince of Beasts."

9:8. D., C. "On Certain Scribblers, who are dayly cavilling at Mr. S. Johnson," *St. James's Chronicle,* No. 752 (December 26–28, 1765). Verse; "On parent dunghill, where begot,/ There let the toad-stool mushrooms rot,/ Unnoticed and unknown."

9:9. Hayes, Daniel. *The Authors.* London: W. Griffin, 1766. Verse; contains eulogy of Johnson. See D. J. Greene, *N&Q*, June 1953, pp. 243–44; Walter Armytage, *ibid.*, September 1953, p. 506.

9:10. [Lloyd, Evan.] *The Powers of the Pen, a Poem, Addressed to John Curre, Esq.*, pp. 21–24. London: Printed for the author, 1766. A hostile characterization of Johnson's works.

9:11. "A Session of the Poets," *Whitehall,* April 2–4, 1771. Verse; headed "The Helicon Bag."

9:12. "Nipclose, Sir Nicholas, Baronet." *The Theatres*, pp. 30–31. London: John Bell, 1772. A verse characterization of Johnson.

9:13. Barbauld, Anna Letitia (née Aikin). "On Romances, an Imitation," in J. and A. L. Aikin, *Miscellaneous Pieces in Prose*, pp. 39–46. London: J. Johnson, 1773. A reasonably good imitation of Johnson's *Rambler* style. See Courtney (item 1/1:19), p. 139.

9:14. Fergusson, Robert. "To the Principal and Professors of the University of St. Andrews, on Their Superb Treat to Dr. Samuel Johnson," *Weekly Magazine* (Edinburgh), XXI (September 2, 1773), 305–6. Reprinted in his *Poems on Various Subjects*, Pt. II, pp. 49–53, Edinburgh: 1779.

9:15. [Man, Henry.] *Cloacina: A Comi-Tragedy*. London: Kearsley, 1775. Verse; "Johnsonoddle" is a character (Burke and Chesterfield also appear).

9:16. Mimos. "A Pedestrious Ramble from Hyde-Park Corner, to Farnham. Written for the Encouragement of Johnson's Dictionary," *Monthly Miscellany*, III (March 1775), 93–95. Parody of "Johnsonese."

9:17. "London; or, Part of the Third Satire of Juvenal Imitated," *Lloyd's Evening Post*, XXXVIII (September 4–6, 1775). *Jeu d'esprit*; an omnibus attack on Johnson.

9:18. *The Asses Ears, a Fable*. London: G. Riley, 1777. Verse; Johnson, as "Bruin," is a candidate for the poet laureateship of the animals.

9:19. [Mason, William.] *An Epistle to Dr. Shebbeare*. London: Almon, 1777. Verse; includes attack on Johnson's diction and politics. Johnson is also glanced at in Mason's *An Heroic Epistle to Sir William Chambers*, London: Almon, 1773.

9:20. [Mason, William.] "The Bustle among the Busts; or, the Poets-Corner in an Uproar. A Poem occasioned by the appearance of Dr. Goldsmith's monument in Westminster-Abbey. By M. Macgreggor, Esq.," *London Review*, VII (February 1778), 156–60; (March), 233–40. Johnson appears as "a huge Greenland bear."

9:21. Parsons, Philip. "Dialogue VII. Mr. Addison and Dr. Johnson," *Dialogues of the Dead with the Living*, pp. 161–67. London: N. Conant and H. Payne, 1779. Mild strictures on Johnson's polysyllabic style, rough controversial manner, and partisanship.

9:22. *The Abbey of Kilkhampton*, p. 122. London: Kearsley, 1780. A rather insulting "epitaph" on Johnson. British Museum catalogue attributes "some satiric epitaphs" to Sir Herbert Croft.

9:23. "On Reading an Advertisement of a Publication Intitled The Deformities of Johnson," *London Courant*, September 24, 1782. Verse; hostile. See item 2:12.

9:24. [Boswell, James.] *Ode by Dr. Samuel Johnson to Mrs. Thrale upon Their Supposed Approaching Nuptials.* London: R. Faulder, 1784.

9:25. E., H. "On the Much Lamented Death of Dr. Samuel Johnson," *GM*, LIV (December 1784), 934. An epitaph.

9:26. P., S. T. "Lines on the Death of Dr. Samuel Johnson," *GM*, LIV (December 1784), 934. An epitaph. Innumerable other short verse epitaphs on Johnson appeared in the London journals about this time; no attempt is made here to list them all.

9:27. *An Ode on the Much Lamented Death of Dr. Samuel Johnson. Written the 18th December, 1784.* London: Printed by J. Rozea and sold by J. Bew, 1785. Preface dated December 29, 1784; "the Author is descended from a Welch family."

9:28. [Butt, George.] *A Dialogue between the Earl of C——d and Mr. Garrick, in the Elysian Shades.* London: Printed by J. Nichols, 1785. In verse; contains a tribute by Garrick to Johnson.

9:29. Hobhouse, Thomas. *Elegy to the Memory of Dr. Samuel Johnson.* London: Stockdale, 1785.

9:30. *Johnson's Laurel: or, Contest of the Poets: A Poem.* London: S. Hooper, 1785. His laurel is eventually bestowed on Anna Seward!

9:31. *One Glass of Helicon; or, A Short Flight to Parnassus,* pp. 9, 37. Norwich: William Chase and Co., 1785. Contains short poems in English about Johnson, with Latin titles.

9:32. S., I., Damnoniensis. "A Small Tribute to the Memory of the Late Excellent Dr. Johnson," *GM*, LV (April 1785), 305. Elegiac verse.

9:33. [Percy, Thomas, the younger.] *Verses on the Death of Dr. Samuel Johnson.* London: C. Dilly, 1785.

9:34. Simpson, Joseph. *The Patriot. A Tragedy from a Manuscript of the late Dr. Samuel Johnson, corrected by himself.* London: G. Goulding, 1785. Simpson sent the MS to Johnson for his inspection; it was found after Johnson's death among his papers and was printed as his, perhaps with an intent to defraud (see *Life*, III, 28). A MS of the work in the Houghton Library, Harvard University, has the title page "Leonidas, a Tragedy. 1750." It seems, however, to have no corrections, but to be a fair copy.

9:35. *Anecdotes of the Learned Pig, with Notes, Critical and Explanatory; and Illustrations from Bozzy, Piozzi, &c., &c.* London: T. Hookman, 1786. Burlesque biographical account.

9:36. Courtenay, John. *A Poetical Review of the Literary and Moral Character of the late Samuel Johnson. With Notes.* London: Charles Dilly, 1786. Reprinted with introduction by Robert E. Kelley, Los Angeles: William Andrews Clark Memorial Library, 1969. Augustan Reprint Society Pub. No. 133.

9:37. *A Poetical Epistle from the Ghost of Dr. Johnson, to His Four Friends: The Rev. Mr. Strahan. James Boswell, Esq. Mrs. Piozzi. J. Courtney, Esq. M.P.* London: Harrison and Co., 1786.

9:38. [Satiric poem on Johnson's biographers; begins "Three Authors in three sister kingdoms born"], inscribed on Sayers's print "The Biographers," 1786 (item 8:9).

9:39. Wolcot, John ["Peter Pindar"]. *A Poetical and Congratulatory Epistle to James Boswell, on his Journal of a Tour to the Hebrides, with the celebrated Dr. Johnson.* London: Kearsley, 1786.

9:40. Wolcot, John ["Peter Pindar"]. *Bozzy and Piozzi; or, The British Biographers; A Town Eclogue.* London: Kearsley, 1786. With a plate by Rowlandson.

9:41. [Moody, Elizabeth.] "Dr. Johnson's Ghost" [a "ballad"], *GM*, LVI (June 1786), 475–76 ("by a Lady"). Reprinted in her *Poetic Trifles*, pp. 59–62, London: Baldwin, 1798; and in item 3:75.

9:42. Colman, George [the elder]. "A Posthumous Work of S. Johnson. An Ode," *Prose on Several Occasions, accompanied with some pieces in verse.* London: T. Cadell, 1787. The "Ode" (in which Johnson, "in the shades," chastises his biographers) is dated "April 15, 1786." Reprinted in item 3:75.

9:43. "Francis, Barber." *More Last Words of Dr. Johnson, consisting of important and valuable anecdotes . . . to which are added, several . . . facts relative to his Biographical Executor* [Hawkins]. *By Francis, Barber.* London: Rich, 1787. A satire.

9:44. Blake, William. "Lo the Bat with Leathern Wing" [verse lampoon on Johnson], in his *An Island in the Moon* (ca. 1787), *The Writings of William Blake,* ed. Geoffrey Keynes. London: Nonesuch Press, 1925. 1 vol. ed., 1927, pp. 682–83.

9:45. [Satiric poem on Johnson's biographers; Johnson speaks, "Madam (my debt to nature paid),/ I thought the grave with hallow'd shade/ Would now protect my name"], inscribed on Sayers's print "Frontispiece for the 2nd edition of Dr. J——n's Letters," 1788 (item 8:11). Reprinted in item 3:75.

9:46. Potter, Robert. "A Dream," *The Art of Criticism* (1789; item 22:49), pp. 195–250. Imaginary conversation between Joseph Warton and Johnson, chiefly on the subject of literary criticism.

9:47. Beattie, James Hay. "Dialogues of the Dead. I. Addison, Johnson. II. Socrates, Johnson, and a Fine Gentleman," *Essays and Fragments in Prose and Verse,* [edited by his father, James Beattie]. Edinburgh: J. Moir, 1794. Reprinted as *Miscellanies* in James Beattie, *The Minstrel,* 1799, and in his *Works* (Vol. X), Philadelphia, 1809. The second dialogue is dated "August, 1787."

9:48. Mathias, Thomas James. *The Pursuits of Literature, or What You Will. A Satiric Poem in Dialogue.* Part I. London: J. Owen, 1794. Frequently reprinted and expanded. Numerous references, on the whole favorable, to Johnson.

9:49. Stevenson, John Hall. "A Fragment of an Epic Poem. Book IV," *Works*, II, 147–70. London: Debrett and Becket, 1795. L. H. Butterfield, *Harvard Studies and Notes in Philology and Literature*, XV (1933), attributes to Charles Churchill; Douglas Grant, ed., *The Poetical Works of Charles Churchill* (Oxford: Clarendon, 1956), pp. 564–65, controverts this. Satire of Johnson.

9:50. Chalmers, Alexander. *A Lesson in Biography; or How to Write the Life of One's Friend, Being an Extract from the Life of Dr. Pozz, in Ten Volumes Folio, Written by James Bozz, Esq.* London: J. Debrett, 1798. Reprinted in item 3:75 (1836), pp. 469–74. Reprinted, Edinburgh: Aungervyle Society Reprints, series 4, 1887. A clever burlesque of Boswell's *Life*. Probably appeared in newspapers earlier than 1798.

9:51. "A Dialogue between Johnson and Boswell in the Shades" [half-title, "Dialogues of the Dead. Boz and Poz in the Shades"], in "Attalus" [William Mudford], *A Critical Enquiry into the Moral Writings of Dr. Samuel Johnson . . . to which is added . . . A Dialogue . . .* London: Cobbett and Morgan, 1802 (item 10/6:21). Reprinted in *Two New Dialogues of the Dead, the first between Handel and Braham, the second between Johnson and Boswell. By J. B.*, London: J. Johnson, 1804. Boswell meets his death from "excessive *mahogany*"—a mixture of gin and treacle.

9:52. A. [Imaginary conversation between Johnson and William Godwin], *Companion*, I, no. 17 (February 23, 1805), 129–32.

9:53. Poole, John. *Hamlet Travestie, in Three Acts, with* [burlesque] *Annotations by Dr. Johnson and G. Steevens, Esq., and Other Commentators*. London: J. M. Richardson, 1810; often reprinted.

9:54. Wolcot, John ["Peter Pindar"]. "Unpublished Lines on Dr. Johnson. By the Late Dr. Wolcot," *New Monthly Magazine*, n.s., XXVI (1829), 390. Dated "Nov. 6, 1814." A dozen caustic lines on "Johnson's turgid style."

9:55. Reynolds, Sir Joshua. *Johnson and Garrick* [two imaginary dialogues: I. Johnson and Reynolds; II. Johnson and Gibbon]. London: Nichols and Bentley, 1816 [printed, but not published]. Reprinted by "Biographicus," *New Monthly Magazine*, VI (August 1816); in *North American Review*, IV (November 1816), 38–47; in item 3:66 (1824); item 3:75 (1836); item 3:116 (1897); ed. with introduction by R. Brimley Johnson, London: Cayme Press, 1927; ed. from MS by F. W. Hilles in item 5:317 (1952). See also item 5:320.

9:56. "Johnson's Midnight Walk," *Blackwood's*, III (June 1818), 274–77. Fictional dialogue among Johnson, Savage, and Derrick; makes Savage contemporary with the Cock Lane Ghost!

9:57. Landor, Walter Savage. "Conversation IX: Samuel Johnson and Horne Tooke," *Imaginary Conversations of Literary Men and Statesmen*, II, 153–73. London: Taylor and Hessey, 1824. Often reprinted. On the *Dictionary*.

9:58. *Rasselas; Or, The Happy Valley.* Described on a playbill of the St. James's Theatre, London, as "the new and original Burletta." 1835.

*9:59. Hawthorne, Nathaniel. "Samuel Johnson," *Biographical Stories for Children*, pp. 61–82. Boston: Tappan and Dennet, 1842. Often reprinted in collections of Hawthorne's tales. A charming imaginative account of the penance at Uttoxeter.

9:60. "Dr. Johnson and Miss Hannah More. An Imaginary Dialogue," *Chambers' Journal*, XV (June 14, 1851), 380–82. Chiefly about Garrick.

9:62. Brough, Robert Barnabas. *Dr. Johnson: A Fairy Tale, Told to My Daughter on New Year's Night.* Reprinted from *Welcome Guest*, January 14, 1860, by the Urban Club.

9:63. H. "Satirical Allusion to Johnson," *N&Q*, 2nd ser., XI (January 12, 1861), 30; (January 19), 52–53; (February 2), 91–92; (March 9), 197–98. In *The Last Masquerade at Mrs. C——y's, with a Plate of the Characters*, 1772.

9:64. "Johnson and Blondin. Extracted, by permission, from the latest edition of Boswell's Life of Dr. Johnson," *Punch*, XL (June 15, 1861), 246–47. Johnson and Boswell go to his acrobatic performance at the Crystal Palace.

9:65. Brough, William. *Rasselas, Prince of Abyssinia; or, The Happy Valley. An extravaganza founded on Dr. Johnson's well-known tale, but at times getting very wide of the mark.* (Lacy's Acting Editions of Plays, Vol. 57.) London: T. H. Lacy, 1863. What later came to be called in England a "pantomime"; in verse; first produced at the Theatre Royal, Haymarket, December 26, 1862. "Dr. Johnson" appears in it as "Chorus." Includes some characters and details from Cornelia Knight's *Dinarbas* (item 18:20).

9:66. *Memoirs of Mrs. Laetitia Boothby, Written by Herself.* Ed. [or rather written] by Clark Russell. London: Henry S. King, 1872. Fiction; contains delightful descriptions of Johnson and Mrs. Thrale.

9:67. Grand, Georges. *Nouvelles anglaises: Une aventure de Samuel Johnson* . . . Paris: Delagrave, 1883.

9:68. Buckley, W. E. "Satirical Epitaph on Dr. Johnson," *N&Q*, 6th ser., X (August 23, 1884), 145. Quoted in George Mason's edition of Hoccleve's *Poems*, 1796.

9:69. Watson, William. "Dr. Johnson on Modern Poetry," *Excursions in Criticism*, pp. 140–66. London: Elkin Mathews, 1893.

9:70. Dobson, Austin. *A Postscript to Dr. Goldsmith's Retaliation, Being an Epitaph on Samuel Johnson, LL.D.* Oxford: Privately printed, Horace Hart, 1896.

9:71. Bangs, John Kendrick. *A House-Boat on the Styx.* New York: Harper and Brothers, 1895.

9:72. Traill, Henry D. "The Revolution in Grub Street" [imaginary Boswellian fragment], *Fortnightly Review*, LVIII (July 1895), 78–88. Reprinted in *The New Fiction*, pp. 226–48, London: Hurst and Blackett, 1897.

9:73. Bangs, John Kendrick. *The Pursuit of the House-Boat.* New York: Harper and Brothers, 1897.

9:74. Lang, Andrew. "Dr. Johnson on the Links" [at St. Andrews], in *A Batch of Golfing Papers*, ed. R. Barclay, pp. 66–73. New York: M. F. Mansfield, 1897.

9:75. Moore, F. Frankfort. *The Jessamy Bride.* Chicago: H. S. Stone, 1897. Johnson a character.

9:76. Colville, Harriet E. *Life's Anchor: A Tale of the Days of Dr. Johnson and Hannah More.* London: Religious Tract Society, [1900].

9:77. Traill, Henry D. "Johnson and Coleridge" [imaginary dialogue], *The New Lucian* (new ed.), pp. 223–42. London: Chapman & Hall, 1900.

9:78. "A Supper at the 'Cheshire Cheese'" [fictitious dialogue], *Temple Bar*, CXX (June 1900), 238–45.

9:79. Vivian, Herbert. *The [Restored] Rambler*, June 29, 1901, to March 22, 1902. 3 vols. London: Ballantyne Press, 1901–2.

9:80. Everett, William. "A Possible Glimpse of Samuel Johnson," *Atlantic Monthly*, XC (November 1902), 622–26. Johnson with the Pretender's forces in 1745, using references in Drummond Papers.

9:81. Norman, William. "Dr. Johnson and 'The New London Spy,'" *N&Q*, 10th ser., VI (August 4, 1906), 89. On a character possibly representing Johnson in the 1772 work.

9:82. Minchin, Harry C. "Shenstone and Dr. Johnson" [fictitious dialogue], *Cornhill Magazine*, n.s., XXXVII (November 1914), 671–76.

9:83. Markland, Russell. "Dr. Johnson" [a sonnet], in item 5:161.

9:84. Roberts, Sydney Castle. *Doctor Johnson in Cambridge.* London: G. P. Putnam's Sons, 1922; Cambridge: Cambridge University Press, 1926. Essays in Boswellian imitation which appeared originally in *Cambridge Review*.

9:85. Freeman, R. M. *The New Boswell.* London: John Lane, 1923. Portions originally published in periodicals.

9:86. Newton, A. Edward. *Doctor Johnson: A Play*. Boston: Atlantic Monthly Press, 1923.

9:87. Wister, Owen. *Watch Your Thirst: A Dry Opera in Three Acts, with a Preface by Samuel Johnson*. New York: Macmillan, 1923. The preface, in "Johnsonese" and dated "Eternity Place, April 1, 1923," twits Americans about Prohibition.

9:88. Williams, Iolo A. "Dr. Johnson in Poetry" [contemporary verse satires on Johnson], *Cornhill Magazine*, n.s., LIV (May 1923), 530–42.

9:89. Murdock, Harold. *Earl Percy Dines Abroad: A Boswellian Episode*. Boston: Houghton Mifflin Co., 1924.

9:90. Buchan, John. *Midwinter*. London: Thomas Nelson & Sons, 1925. Johnson goes north to join the Pretender.

9:91. Wilson, Edmund. "A Letter to Elinor Wylie," *New Republic*, October 7, 1925. Reprinted in his *The Shores of Light*, pp. 259–63, New York: Farrar, Straus, and Giroux, 1952 (reissued in paperback, New York: Noonday Press, 1967). Signed "Sam. Johnson" and composed in "Johnsonian" prose; criticism of her novels.

9:92. Povey, Kenneth. "A Caricature of Johnson" [in Hayley's comedy *The Mausoleum*], *TLS*, June 17, 1926, p. 414.

9:93. Chesterton, G. K. *The Judgement of Dr. Johnson: A Comedy in Three Acts*. London: Sheed & Ward, 1927. See also *Radio Times* (London), May 16, 1952, pp. 6, 18.

9:94. Knox, Ronald A. "Materials for a Boswellian Problem" [*Life, Journals*, etc., are apocryphal], *Essays in Satire*, pp. 239–61. London: Sheed and Ward, 1928.

9:95. Porter, Agnes. "The Man with the Book" [play in six scenes, Johnson the chief character], *Copy: 1928*, pp. 1–102. New York: Appleton, 1928.

9:96. Marquand, J. P. "Do Tell Me, Doctor Johnson," *Saturday Evening Post*, July 14, 1928, pp. 8–9, 83–88. Reprinted by the Rowfant Club, Cleveland, Ohio, 1928. Johnson and Thomas Osborne.

9:97. Lucas, F. L. "Literary Trifling" [imaginary conversation between Johnson and Bernard Shaw], *Nation-Athenaeum*, XLVI (November 16, 1929), 249–51.

9:98. Newton, A. Edward. [Comedy in one act about an imaginary meeting of Franklin and Johnson.] *Lichfield Mercury*, September 26, 1930. Reprinted; see item 6:22. Reprinted as *Mr. Strahan's Dinner Party*, with note by Edward F. O'Day, for the Book Club of California, San Francisco: J. H. Nash, 1930. Reprinted in *Derby Day*, pp. 139–67, Boston: Little, Brown, 1934.

9:99. O'Day, Edward F. "An Inquiry into Mr. Addison's Drinking," *An Essay by Joseph Addison: The Trial of the Winebrewers*. San Francisco:

J. H. Nash, 1930. Contains a fictitious dialogue between Johnson and modern questioner.

9:100. Lawrence, Charles E. "The Great Cham: An Episode, Hitherto Unrecorded, in the Life of Dr. Johnson," *Cornhill Magazine*, n.s., LXXI (September 1931), 271–83.

9:101. Kingsmill, Hugh [H. K. Lunn]. "Parodies: Remarks by Dr. Johnson on Certain Writers of the Present Age," *English Review*, LIII (November 1931), 734–42.

9:102. Zamick, M., ed. "Three Dialogues by Hester Lynch Thrale" [Johnson a character], *Bulletin of the John Rylands Library*, XVI (January 1932), 77–114.

9:103. Hilles, Frederick W. "Dr. Johnson Visits Trumbull [College, Yale University]," *Trumbullian*, II (Autumn 1934), 11–16.

9:104. John, Evan. *Strangers' Gold: An Historical Comedy in One Act* [Johnson and Boswell in the Hebrides]. Glasgow: Brown and Ferguson, 1936.

9:105. Howell, William Boyman. "A Meeting Which Never Took Place: A Play in Half an Act" [Johnson and John Hunter], *Annals of Medical History*, n.s., VIII (November 1936), 541–46.

9:106. Gray, Ernest. *The Diary of a Surgeon in the Year 1751–1752* [fictitious conversations of Johnson, etc.], pp. 47–55. New York: Appleton-Century, 1937.

9:107. Carter, Winifred. *Doctor Johnson's Mrs. Thrale* [play]. Kingston-on-Thames: King's Stone Press, 1938.

9:108. Rubinstein, H. F. *Johnson Was No Gentleman* [comedy laid in anteroom of Chesterfield's library]. London: Victor Gollancz, 1938.

9:109. Goudge, Elizabeth. "Fanny Burney," *Three Plays*, pp. 221–318. London: Gerald Duckworth & Co., 1939.

9:110. Knox, Ronald A. "Lost Causes: 1738" [Chap. V stems from the *Life*], *Let Dons Delight*, pp. 111–44. London: Sheed and Ward, 1939.

9:111. Linklater, Eric. *The Raft and Socrates Asks Why: Two Conversations* [Johnson a character in the latter], pp. 54–121. London: Macmillan, 1942.

9:112. Goldman, L. "Creative Attitude toward the Classics: Dramatization of Macaulay's Essay on Boswell's Life of Johnson," *Education*, LXII (May 1942), 559–65.

9:113. Gleason, Harold W. "Sam'l Johnson" [sonnet attacking his writing], *Commonweal*, XXXVI (September 11, 1942), 488. See also item 10/6:250.

9:114. [Morley, Christopher.] *Another Letter to Lord Chesterfield from Samuel Johnson and Christopher Morley*. New York: Ben Abramson, 1945.

9:115. Ó Néill, Séamus. *"Ní chuireann siad síol"*: *nó*, *"Poll bocht"* [transliteration of Irish title; translated as *"They sow no seed,"* or *"Poor Poll"*]. Baile Átha Cliath [Dublin]: Oifig an tSoláthair, [1945]. One-act play, with Goldsmith and Johnson as characters.

9:116. Bevington, Helen. *Dr. Johnson's Waterfall* [contains some poems on Johnson]. Boston: Houghton Mifflin Co., 1946.

9:117. De la Torre, Lillian (Mrs. George McCue). *Dr. Sam: Johnson, Detector.* New York: Alfred A. Knopf, 1946. Portions originally published in *Ellery Queen's Mystery Magazine.*

9:118. George, Daniel. "The Lost Diary of Dr. Johnson," *Saturday Book*, VI (1946), 260–63.

9:119. Rose, Kenneth. "Portrait the Second: Boswell Meets Johnson," *Georgiana: Seven Portraits*, pp. 10–15. London: Frederick Muller, 1947.

9:120. Trease, Geoffrey. *"A Dish of Tea"*: *A Derbyshire Play in One Act.* Published by the Derbyshire Rural Community Council, Derby, n.d. [before 1950].

9:121. Carter, Winifred. *Dr. Johnson's "Dear Mistress"* [a novel]. London: Selwyn and Blount, 1950.

9:122. Krutch, Joseph Wood. "The Last Boswell Paper," *SR*, July 21, 1951, pp. 13–15. Reprinted, New York: P. and F. Duschnes, 1951.

9:123. Watt, T. S. "A Pension for Johnson," *Punch*, June 17, 1953, pp. 712–14.

9:124. "Still Raise for Good the Supplicating Voice." Buenos Aires, 1954. Johnson's lines from *The Vanity of Human Wishes* set to music by Mrs. Ruby K. de Rodger, for the Johnson Society of the River Plate.

9:125. Gillis, William. "Johnson, Boswell, and Fergusson," *JNL*, XIV, no. 2 (June 1954), 6–7. Poems on Johnson and Boswell attributed to the Scottish poet. See items 9:14 and 17:8.

9:126. Blunden, Edmund. "Lives of the Poets: If Dr. Johnson Had Lived Rather Longer" [imaginary lives of Coleridge and Wordsworth], *TLS*, May 20, 27, 1955, pp. 276, 292.

9:127. Hart, Charles R. *Samuel Johnson: A Portrait* [play in 11 scenes]. Eton, Windsor: Shakespeare Head Press, 1959.

9:128. Roberts, S. C. "Johnson in Parody," in item 10/6:306, pp. 285–96.

9:129. De la Torre, Lillian (Mrs. George McCue). *The Detections of Dr. Sam: Johnson.* Garden City, N.Y.: Doubleday, 1960. Fictional stories with Johnson as hero.

9:130. Carr, H. Wildon. "Berkeley and Dr. Johnson: An Imaginary Dialogue" [on Johnson's "refutation" of Berkeley], *Personalist*, XLI (Winter 1960), 13–14.

9:131. Beatty, John and Patricia. *At the Seven Stars.* New York: Macmillan, 1963. Novel for young readers with Johnson as a character.

9:132. Wain, John. *Wildtrack*, pp. 25–27 and *passim*. London: Macmillan, 1965. A poem, with several passages about Johnson.

9:133. " 'Boswell's Original Preface, Enlisting the Aid of Dr. Johnson,' Edited by Robert D. Spector" [fiction], *Satire Newsletter*, II (Spring 1965), 122–23.

9:134. *Johnson Preserv'd*. Opera with libretto by Jill Watt and music by Richard Stoker. First produced in London, July 4, 1967. Characters include Johnson, Boswell, Mrs. Thrale, Piozzi. Described by E. Brophy, "Dr. Johnson Operatically 'Preserv'd,' " *Opera*, XVIII (July 1967), 543–46.

9:135. Manzalaoui, Mahmoud. "Soame Jenyns's 'Epitaph on Dr. Samuel Johnson,' " *N&Q*, May 1967, pp. 181–82.

9:136. Burgess, Anthony. "Johnson (?) on Johnson," *Horizon*, X (Summer 1968), 60–64. An imaginary addition to the *Lives of the Poets*, with Johnson describing his own life.

10. GENERAL COMMENT ON JOHNSON

10/1. JOHNSON AS CRITIC: GENERAL STUDIES

(See also Section 19, Shakespeare, and Section 22, *Lives of the Poets*)

10/1:1. Wordsworth, William. "Preface," *Lyrical Ballads and Other Poems*, 2nd ed. London: Longman, 1800. On Johnson's ballad-parody, "I put my hat upon my head,/And walked into the Strand."

10/1:2. Wordsworth, William. "Essay Supplementary to the Preface," *Poems* . . . London: Longman, 1815. A longer and harsher treatment of Johnson than in the 1800 Preface.

10/1:3. Hettner, Hermann. "Die Kritik Samuel Johnsons," *Geschichte der englischen Literatur, 1660–1770*, Book III, Chap. III, Sec. 2. Braunschweig: F. Vieweg, 1856, and often reprinted. Hostile.

10/1:4. Boucher, Léon. "Un dictateur littéraire: Samuel Johnson et ses critiques," *Revue des Deux Mondes*, 3rd ser., XXXVII (February 1, 1880), 674–97. A review article based on items 3:104, 10/6:61, and 22:2, ed. Arnold.

10/1:5. P., S. L. "A Barren Rascal," *N&Q*, 6th ser., VIII (August 25, 1883), 144. Johnson's "loose talk," such as his phrase about Fielding, not to be taken seriously; his real (and higher) opinion to be found in his writings.

*10/1:6. Saintsbury, George. "Johnson," *A History of Criticism*, II, 477–97. Edinburgh and London: William Blackwood & Sons, 1902.

10/1:7. Kleuker, Robert. *Dr. Samuel Johnsons Verhältnis zur französischen Literatur*. Dissertation. Strasbourg: Du Mont Schauberg, 1907.

10/1:8. Omond, T. S. *English Metrists in the Eighteenth and Nineteenth*

Centuries, pp. 17–19 and *passim*. London: Oxford University Press, 1907.

10/1:9. Houston, Percy H. "Dr. Johnson as a Literary Critic." Thesis, Harvard University, 1910.

10/1:10. Saintsbury, George. "Johnson," *A History of English Criticism*, pp. 210–30. Edinburgh and London: William Blackwood & Sons; New York: Dodd, Mead & Co., 1911.

10/1:11. Houston, Percy H. "Dr. Johnson, Sentimentalism and Romanticism?" *University of California Chronicle*, XV (January 1913), 1–24.

10/1:12. Teggart, Stuart. "Dr. Johnson as a Literary Critic," *Westminster Review*, CLXXX (September 1913), 291–98.

10/1:13. Meier, Hans. *Dr. Samuel Johnsons Stellung zu den literarischen Fragen seiner Zeit*. Dissertation, University of Basel. Zürich: Leemann, 1916.

*10/1:14. Brown, Joseph Epes. *Critical Opinions of Samuel Johnson*. Princeton, N.J.: Princeton University Press, 1926. Reviewed by R. S. Crane, *MP*, XXIII (May 1926), 497–98; R. D. Havens, *MLN*, XLI (June 1926), 420–21; F. A. Pottle, *Yale Review*, XV (July 1926), 817–19; R. W. Chapman, *RES*, II (July 1926), 354–56; C. B. Tinker, *SRL*, III (February 5, 1927), 560. Reprinted, New York: Russell and Russell, 1961.

10/1:15. "The Authority of Johnson" [his criticism], *TLS*, September 2, 1926, pp. 569–70. Comment on item 10/1:14.

*10/1:16. Babbitt, Irving. "Dr. Johnson and Imagination," *Southwest Review*, XIII (October 1927), 25–35. Reprinted in *On Being Creative*, pp. 80–96, Boston: Houghton Mifflin Co., 1932. See also F. B. Kaye, *PQ*, VII (April 1928), 178.

10/1:17. Cazamian, Louis. "Doctrinal Classicism: Johnson," *A History of English Literature* (with Émile Legouis), rev. ed., pp. 824–41. New York: Macmillan, 1929.

10/1:18. Bosker, Aisso. *Literary Criticism in the Age of Johnson*, pp. 92–106. Dissertation. Groningen: J. B. Wolters, 1930. 2nd ed., 1953. See also R. S. Crane, *PQ*, X (April 1931), 177–78.

10/1:19. Christiani, Ellen Sigyn. *Samuel Johnson als Kritiker im Lichte von Pseudo-Klassizismus und Romantik*. Dissertation, University of Munich. (Beiträge zur englischen Philologie, no. 18.) Leipzig: Tauchnitz, 1931. Reviewed by R. S. Crane, *PQ*, XI (April 1932), 196.

*10/1:20. Powell, Lawrence F. "Thomas Tyrwhitt and the Rowley Poems" [Johnson and Chatterton], *RES*, VII (July 1931), 314–26.

10/1:21. Stephen, A. M. "Dr. Samuel Johnson Views Our Poets" [Johnson's theories applied to modern writers], *Dalhousie Review*, XI (January 1932), 493–506.

10/1:22. Martyn, Howe. "Samuel Johnson, Critic of Poetry," *Queen's Quarterly*, XXXIX (August 1932), 425–50.

10/1:23. Housman, Alfred E. *The Name and Nature of Poetry*. Cambridge: Cambridge University Press, 1933. Leslie Stephen Lecture, 1933.

10/1:24. Hooker, Edward N. "Johnson's Understanding of Chaucer's Metrics," *MLN*, XLVIII (March 1933), 150–51.

10/1:25. Reynolds, W. Vaughan. "Johnson's Opinions on Prose Style," *RES*, IX (October 1933), 433–46.

10/1:26. Sarma, D. S. *Johnson's Theory of Poetry*. Madras: Gita Publishing House, 1934.

10/1:27. Schinz, Albert. "Samuel Johnson, le Boileau anglais," *Revue des Deux Mondes*, 8th ser., XXV (February 1, 1935), 684–91.

10/1:28. Osborn, James M. "Johnson on the Sanctity of an Author's Text" [evidence from Bodley MS Malone 30, folio 64–65], *PMLA*, L (September 1935), 928–29.

*10/1:29. Watkins, Walter B. C. *Johnson and English Poetry before 1660*. Princeton, N.J.: Princeton University Press, 1936. Reprinted, New York: Gordian Press, 1965. Reviewed by R. Stamm, *English Studies*, XVIII (April 1936), 87–88; P. Meissner, *Beiblatt zur Anglia*, XLVII (November 1936), 333–34; Doris B. Saunders, *MP*, XXXIV (February 1937), 326–29; F. A. Pottle, *MLN*, LII (June 1937), 450–51.

*10/1:30. Brown, Stuart Gerry. "Dr. Johnson, Poetry, and Imagination," *Neophilologus*, XXIII (April 1938), 203–7.

10/1:31. Sato, Kiyoshi. "Samuel Johnson on Milton and Shakespeare" [in Japanese], *Studies in English Literature* (Tokyo), XIX, no. 3 (1939), 339–50. Johnson owes much to Dryden and Addison in his criticism of Milton and Shakespeare.

10/1:32. Wellek, René. *The Rise of English Literary History*, pp. 96–98, 107–13, 137–42, etc. Chapel Hill: University of North Carolina Press, 1941.

10/1:33. Sato, Kiyoshi. "Critical Principles of Samuel Johnson" [in Japanese], *Studies in English Literature* (Tokyo), XXI, no. 1 (1941), 11–22.

10/1:34. Mays, Morley J. "Johnson and Blair on Addison's Prose Style," *SP*, XXXIX (October 1942), 638–49.

*10/1:35. Abrams, Meyer H. "Unconscious Expectations in the Reading of Poetry" [largely concerned with Johnson's criticism], *ELH*, IX (December 1942), 235–44. Reprinted as "Dr. Johnson's Spectacles" in item 10/6:306 (1959), pp. 177–87.

10/1:36. Watts, Helena B. "Johnson's Theory and Practice in Regard to the Didactic Theory of Poetry." Dissertation, Duke University, 1943.

10/1:37. Havens, Raymond D. "Johnson's Distrust of the Imagination," *ELH*, X (September 1943), 243–55.

10/1:38. H., R. "Johnson on a Metaphor of Dryden's," N&Q, CLXXXV (October 23, 1943), 256.

*10/1:39. Krutch, Joseph Wood. "Samuel Johnson as Critic," Nation, CLVIII (February 19, 1944), 218–22.

10/1:40. Moore, Wilbur E. "Samuel Johnson on Rhetoric," Quarterly Journal of Speech, XXX (April 1944), 165–68.

*10/1:41. Leavis, Frank Raymond. "Johnson as Critic," Scrutiny, XII (Summer 1944), 187–204. Reprinted in The Importance of Scrutiny, ed. Eric Bentley, New York: George W. Stewart, 1948; New York University Press, 1964; in item 10/6:330; in A Selection from Scrutiny, ed. F. R. Leavis, Cambridge: Cambridge University Press, 1968.

10/1:42. Schmitz, Robert M. "Dr. Johnson and Blair's Sermons," MLN, LX (April 1945), 268–70. See also his Hugh Blair, New York: King's Crown Press, 1948.

*10/1:43. Bate, Walter J. "Johnson and Reynolds: The Premise of General Nature," From Classic to Romantic, pp. 59–79. Cambridge, Mass.: Harvard University Press, 1946.

10/1:44. Watkins, Walter B. C. "Dr. Johnson on the Imagination: A Note," RES, XXII (April 1946), 131–34.

10/1:45. Keast, William Rea. "The Foundations of Samuel Johnson's Literary Criticism." Dissertation, University of Chicago, 1947.

*10/1:46. Elledge, Scott. "The Background and Development in English Criticism of the Theories of Generality and Particularity," PMLA, LXII (March 1947), 147–82. See also W. R. Keast, PQ, XXVII (April 1948), 130–32.

10/1:47. Wimsatt, William K., Jr. "The Structure of the 'Concrete Universal' in Literature," PMLA, LXII (March 1947), 262–80. Reprinted in The Verbal Icon, pp. 69–83, Lexington: University of Kentucky Press, 1954.

*10/1:48. McNulty, John B. "The Critic Who Knew What He Wanted," College English, IX (March 1948), 299–303.

*10/1:49. Hagstrum, J. H. "Johnson's Conception of the Beautiful, the Pathetic, and the Sublime," PMLA, LXIV (March 1949), 134–57.

10/1:50. Diaz, Alberto Franco. "Johnson, un dictador literario," Aquí Está (Argentina), XIV (November 14, 1949), 12–13.

10/1:51. Atkins, J. W. H. "The Great Cham of Literature: Johnson," English Literary Criticism: 17th and 18th Centuries, pp. 268–313. London: Methuen and Co., 1951.

10/1:52. Moore, Robert E. "Dr. Johnson on Fielding and Richardson," PMLA, LXVI (March 1951), 162–81.

*10/1:53. Bloom, Edward A. "The Allegorical Principle" [Johnson's ideas of allegory], ELH, XVIII (September 1951), 163–90.

10/1:54. Emley, Edward. "Dr. Johnson and Modern Criticism," Philological

Papers: University of West Virginia, Series 52, no. 4-1 (October 1951), 66–82.

*10/1:55. Hagstrum, Jean H. *Samuel Johnson's Literary Criticism.* Minneapolis: University of Minnesota Press, 1952. Reprinted, with new preface, Chicago: University of Chicago Press, 1967. Reviewed by Ian Jack, *PQ,* XXXII (July 1953), 274–76; W. K. Wimsatt, Jr., *MLN,* LXIX (February 1954), 128–30; D. J. Greene, *RES,* n.s., V (April 1954), 200–3; M. H. Abrams, *Kenyon Review,* XVI (Spring 1954), 307–13.

*10/1:56. Keast, W. R. "The Theoretical Foundations of Johnson's Criticism," in *Critics and Criticism, Ancient and Modern,* ed. R. S. Crane, pp. 389–407. Chicago: University of Chicago Press, 1952. See also Jean H. Hagstrum, *PQ,* XXXII (July 1953), 276–78.

10/1:57. Sutherland, James R. *The English Critic,* pp. 9–12 and *passim.* Inaugural lecture as Lord Northcliffe Professor of Modern English Literature, University College, London. London: University College [H. and K. Lewis Co.], 1952. See also *TLS,* December 12, 1952, p. 819.

10/1:58. Atkinson, A. D. "Dr. Johnson's English Prose Reading," *N&Q,* February 1953, pp. 60–63; March, 107–10; May, 206–10; July, 288–93; August, 344–46.

10/1:59. Baldeshwiler, Sister Joselyn. "Johnson's Doctrine of Figurative Language." Dissertation, Fordham University, 1954.

*10/1:60. Donner, H. W. "Dr. Johnson as a Literary Critic," *Edda* (Oslo), LIV (1954), 325–37. Inaugural lecture as Professor of English Language and Literature in the University of Uppsala. Reprinted in item 10/6:330.

10/1:61. Fussell, Paul, Jr. *Theory of Prosody in Eighteenth-Century England,* pp. 24–26, 41–44, and *passim.* New London, Conn.: Connecticut College, 1954.

10/1:62. McBride, Edwin M. "The Ethical Implications in Samuel Johnson's Critical Theory." Dissertation, St. Louis University, 1954.

10/1:63. Kallich, Martin. "The Association of Ideas in Samuel Johnson's Criticism," *MLN,* LXIX (March 1954), 170–76.

10/1:64. Havens, Raymond D. "Solitude and the Neoclassicists," *ELH,* XXI (December 1954), 251–73.

10/1:65. Wellek, René. "Dr. Johnson," *A History of Modern Criticism,* I, 79–104. New Haven, Conn.: Yale University Press, 1955. See item 10/1:69.

10/1:66. Daiches, David. *Critical Approaches to Literature,* particularly pp. 241–60, "Possibilities and Limitations of a Method." New York: Prentice-Hall, 1956.

*10/1:67. Eliot, T. S. "Johnson as Critic and Poet," *On Poetry and Poets,* pp. 162–92. London: Faber and Faber; New York: Harcourt, Brace, 1957.

10/1:68. Wimsatt, William K., Jr. "The Neo-Classic Universal: Samuel

Johnson," in W. K. Wimsatt, Jr., and Cleanth Brooks, *Literary Criticism: A Short History*, Chap. 15. New York: Alfred A. Knopf; London: Routledge, 1957.

10/1:69. Molin, Sven E. "Criticism in Vacuo" [an attack on item 10/1:65], *University of Kansas City Review*, XXIV (December 1957), 156–60. Reply by Wellek and comment by Molin, *ibid.* (June 1958), 283–86.

10/1:70. Emley, Edward. "Dr. Johnson and the Writers of Tudor England" (dissertation, New York University, 1958), *Dissertation Abstracts*, XXIII (July 1962), 224.

10/1:71. Akiyama, Hajime. "Dr. Johnson's Critical Ideas" [in Japanese], *Bulletin of Kansai University* (English Language and Literature), No. 2 (1960).

10/1:72. Gray, James. "Dr. Johnson and the 'Intellectual Gladiators'" [on Restoration comedy], *Dalhousie Review*, XL (Autumn 1960), 350–59.

10/1:73. Daniel, Robert W. "Johnson on Literary Texture," in *Studies in Honor of John C. Hodges and Alwin Thaler*, ed. R. B. Davis and J. L. Lievsay, pp. 57–65. Knoxville: University of Tennessee Press, 1961.

10/1:74. Delaune, Henry Malcolm. "An Examination of the Literary Prejudices of Dr. Samuel Johnson" (dissertation, Tulane University, 1961), *Dissertation Abstracts*, XXII (April 1962), 3643–44. Johnson, in a period of change, had an open mind.

10/1:75. Kaul, R. K. "Johnson on Imagery and Description," *Literary Criterion, Mysore*, V, no. 2 (Summer 1962), 9–13.

10/1:76. Weitz, Morris. "Reasons in Criticism" [Johnson one of the critics discussed], *Journal of Aesthetics and Art Criticism*, XX (Summer 1962), 429–37.

10/1:77. Hardy, John. "Two Notes on Johnson" [an approach to his criticism, and Locke as source of *metaphysical*], in item 10/6:316 (1962), pp. 223–33.

10/1:78. Tillotson, Geoffrey. "Our Solemn Young Critics" [uses Johnson as principal example of a critic], *Sewanee Review*, LXXI (Spring 1963), 283–86.

10/1:79. Lascelles, Mary. "Samuel Johnson" [as a critic], *Times* (London), July 25, 1963, p. 13.

10/1:80. Delaune, Henry Malcolm. "Johnson and the Matter of Imitation," *Xavier University Studies*, III (1964), 103–22.

10/1:81. Hardy, John P. "Dr. Johnson as Critic of the English Poets including Shakespeare." D. Phil. thesis, Oxford University, 1964.

10/1:82. McKenzie, Donald B. "Parnassus Rejected: Dr. Samuel Johnson and the Eighteenth-Century Pastoral" (dissertation, University of Pennsylvania, 1965), *Dissertation Abstracts*, XXVII (November 1966), 1342–43A.

10/1:83. Rai, Vikramaditya. "Dr. Samuel Johnson," in Ramawadh Dwivedi and Vikramaditya Rai, *Literary Criticism*, pp. 191–216. Delhi: Motilal Banarsidass, 1965.

*10/1:84. Sen, Sailendra Kumar. *English Literary Criticism in the Second Half of the Eighteenth Century: A Reconsideration.* Calcutta: Calcutta University Press, 1965. Contains much in praise of the "modernity" of Johnson's criticism, particularly his dramatic criticism.

10/1:85. Terry, Charles Laymen, III. "Samuel Johnson and the Idea of Originality" (dissertation, University of Michigan, 1965), *Dissertation Abstracts*, XXVII (August 1966), 462–63A.

10/1:86. Wesling, Donald. "An Ideal of Greatness: Ethical Implications in Johnson's Critical Vocabulary," *University of Toronto Quarterly*, XXXIV (January 1965), 133–45.

10/1:87. Misenheimer, James B., Jr. "Samuel Johnson and the Didactic Aesthetic" (dissertation, University of Colorado, 1964), *Dissertation Abstracts*, XXV (April 1965), 5934.

10/1:88. Drumm, Sister Robert Mary. "Johnson, Arnold, and Eliot as Literary Humanists" (dissertation, Western Reserve University, 1965), *Dissertation Abstracts*, XXVII (September 1966), 745A.

10/1:89. Kaul, R. K. "Dr. Johnson on the Emotional Effect of Tragedy," in *Cairo Studies in English*, ed. Magdi Wahba, pp. 203–11. Cairo: Privately printed, 1966.

10/1:90. *Literary Criticism in England, 1660–1800*, ed. Gerald W. Chapman [selections from Johnson included], pp. 397–527. New York: Knopf, 1966.

10/1:91. Wright, John Williams. "Johnson and Method in Criticising" (dissertation, University of Rochester, 1967), *Dissertation Abstracts*, XXVIII, no. 5 (November 1967), 1801A.

10/1:92. Tutt, Ralph. "Samuel Johnson on Pastoral Poetry," *Serif* (Kent State University), IV (September 1967), 12–16.

10/1:93. Misenheimer, James B., Jr. "Dr. Johnson's Concept of Literary Fiction," *MLR*, LXII (October 1967), 598–605.

10/1:94. Hamilton, Harlan W. "Samuel Johnson's Appeal to Nature," *Western Humanities Review*, XXI (Autumn 1967), 339–45.

10/1:95. Johnston, Shirley White. "Samuel Johnson's Critical Principles: A Chronological Study." Dissertation, University of New Mexico, 1968.

10/1:96. Marks, Emerson R. "Samuel Johnson," *The Poetics of Reason: English Neoclassical Criticism*, pp. 110–45. New York: Random House, 1968.

10/1:97. Misenheimer, James B. "Dr. Johnson on Prose Fiction," *New Rambler*, January 1968, pp. 12–18.

10/1:98. Kelly, Richard. "Johnson among the Sheep," *Studies in English*

Literature, VIII (Summer 1968), 475–85. Johnson's criticism of the pastoral mode consistent with his view of *Lycidas.*

10/1:99. Ingham, Patricia. "Dr. Johnson's 'Elegance' " [Johnson's use of the term], *RES,* n.s., XIX (August 1968), 271–78.

10/1:100. Alkon, Paul K. "Johnson's Conception of Admiration," *PQ,* XLVIII (January 1969), 59–81.

10/1:101. Page, Alex. "Faculty Psychology and Metaphor in Eighteenth-Century Criticism," *MP,* LXVI (February 1969), 237–47.

10/2. JOHNSON AS BIOGRAPHER: GENERAL STUDIES

(See also Section 13, *Life of Savage,* and Section 22, *Lives of the Poets*)

10/2:1. Knox, Vicesimus. "No. XCIV. Cursory Thoughts on Biography," *Essays Moral and Literary,* II, 48–52. London: Dilly, 1782.

10/2:2. "Anecdote of Literature," *European Magazine,* I (January 1782), 24. Johnson said to be planning a biography of Spenser.

10/2:3. "Reflections upon the Moral and Biographical Writings of Dr. Johnson," *European Magazine,* LXXXVII (April 1825), 320–26. Chiefly on *Life of Savage.* See also *ibid.* (May), 422–25, 426–33; (June), 518–22.

10/2:4. Dunn, Waldo H. *English Biography,* pp. 102–29. London: J. M. Dent & Sons; New York: E. P. Dutton & Co., 1916.

10/2:5. Thayer, William Roscoe. *The Art of Biography,* pp. 84–100. New York: Charles Scribner's Sons, 1920.

10/2:6. Nicolson, Harold. *The Development of English Biography,* pp. 79–86. London: Hogarth Press, 1927.

10/2:7. Brown, Joseph Epes. "Goldsmith and Johnson on Biography," *MLN,* XLII (March 1927), 168–71.

10/2:8. Maurois, André. *Aspects de la Biographie,* pp. 81–85. Based on his Clark Lectures, 1928. Paris: Au Sans Pareil, 1928 (La Conciliabule des Trente). Translated by S. C. Roberts as *Aspects of Biography,* Cambridge: Cambridge University Press; New York: Appleton, 1929. *Rambler* 60; Johnson as precursor of Lytton Strachey.

10/2:9. Evans, Bergen B. "Dr. Johnson as a Biographer," *Harvard University Summaries of Theses 1932,* pp. 248–51.

10/2:10. Tillotson, Arthur. "Dr. Johnson and the 'Life of Goldsmith' " [projected but not written], *MLR,* XXVIII (October 1933), 439–43.

*10/2:11. Evans, Bergen B. "Dr. Johnson's Theory of Biography," *RES,* X (July 1934), 301–10.

10/2:12. Clark, Arthur Melville. *Autobiography: Its Genesis and Phases,* pp. 10–15. Edinburgh: Oliver and Boyd, 1935. On *Idler* 84.

10/2:13. Britt, Albert. "Johnson and Boswell," *The Great Biographers,* pp. 67–76. New York: Whittlesey House, [1936].

*10/2:14. Warburg, Frede. *Samuel Johnson als Biograph.* Dissertation. Hamburg: [Preilipper], 1937.

*10/2:15. Stauffer, Donald A. "Samuel Johnson," *The Art of Biography in Eighteenth Century England,* I, 386–402. Princeton, N.J.: Princeton University Press, 1941.

*10/2:16. Tracy, Clarence R. "Johnson and the Art of Anecdote" [his theory and practice as a biographer], *University of Toronto Quarterly,* XV (October 1945), 86–93.

10/2:17. Garraty, John A. *The Nature of Biography.* New York: Knopf, 1957. Johnson, pp. 25–28, 79–91, and *passim;* Boswell, pp. 93–96, and *passim.*

*10/2:18. Butt, John. *Biography in the Hands of Walton, Johnson, and Boswell.* Ewing Lectures, 1962. Los Angeles: University of California, 1966.

10/2:19. Clifford, James L., ed. *Biography as an Art: Selected Criticism, 1560–1960,* pp. 40–53. London: Oxford University Press, 1962.

10/2:20. Tillinghast, Anthony J. "The Moral and Philosophical Basis of Johnson's and Boswell's Idea of Biography," in item 10/6:316 (1962), pp. 115–31.

10/2:21. Howes, Victor. "Dr. Johnson as Biographer," *Christian Science Monitor,* August 29, 1964, p. 8.

10/2:22. Altick, Richard D. "Johnson and Boswell," *Lives and Letters: A History of Literary Biography in England and America,* pp. 46–74. New York: Knopf, 1965.

10/2:23. Clifford, James L. "How Much Should a Biographer Tell? Some Eighteenth-Century Views," in *Essays in Eighteenth-Century Biography,* ed. Philip B. Daghlian, pp. 67–95. Bloomington: Indiana University Press, 1968.

10/2:24. Greene, Donald J. "The Uses of Autobiography in the Eighteenth Century," in *Essays in Eighteenth-Century Biography,* ed. Philip B. Daghlian, pp. 43–66, 115. Bloomington: Indiana University Press, 1968. On Johnson's *Diaries; Idler* 84.

10/2:25. Kelley, Robert E. "Studies in Eighteenth-Century Autobiography and Biography: A Selected Bibliography," in *Essays in Eighteenth-Century Biography,* ed. Philip B. Daghlian, pp. 102–4 (Boswell), 106–8 (Johnson). Bloomington: Indiana University Press, 1968.

10/2:26. Folkenflik, Robert. "Samuel Johnson as Biographer" (dissertation, Cornell University, 1968), *Dissertation Abstracts,* XXIX, no. 6 (December 1968), 1894A.

10/2:27. Sullivan, Victoria D. "The Biographies of Samuel Johnson: A Study of the Relationship of the Biographer to His Subject." Dissertation, Columbia University, 1969.

10/3:1. "Anecdotes and Bon Mots," *Westminster Magazine,* I (January 1773), 66; (February), 180. Three Johnsonian ones.

10/3:2. *Johnsoniana: or, A Collection of Bon Mots, etc. By Dr. Johnson, and others. Together with the choice sentences of Publius Syrus, now first translated into English.* London: J. Ridley, etc., 1776. New enl. ed., 1777. "Most of these Bon Mots were collected by a person of fashion and sense, lately deceased, at his leisure hours. As he was, in the limited sense, a *bon vivant,* they were for the most part, the produce of his own circle, which was composed of men of the first wit and conversation. Being a great admirer of doctor Johnson . . . he was particularly anxious in collecting all his *Bon Mots*": Preface. Reviewed (by William Kenrick?) in *London Review,* III (April 1776), 329–30 ("most of the smart sayings are forged or invented"; adds some satiric ones).

10/3:3. *Dr. Johnson's Table Talk, or Conversations of the late Samuel Johnson, LL.D., on a Variety of Useful and Entertaining Subjects.* London: G. G. J. and J. Robinson, 1785. "Partly collected by a person who had the honour of enjoying many conversations with Dr. Johnson and partly extracted from the anecdotes in Mr. Boswell's late journal": Preface. Often reprinted.

10/3:4. S., Q. R. [Echoes of Shakespeare, Fielding, Milton in some of Johnson's quips], *European Magazine,* XIV (July 1788), 17–18.

10/3:5. Boswell, James, ed. *A Conversation between His Most Sacred Majesty George III and Samuel Johnson, LL.D.* London: C. Dilly, 1790.

10/3:6. Merry, J. [pseud.] *The Witticisms, Anecdotes, Jests, and Sayings of Dr. Samuel Johnson . . . collected from Boswell . . . and other gentlemen . . . and a full account of Dr. Johnson's conversation with the King. To which is added, a . . . number of jests. By J. Merry, esq. of Pembroke College.* London: D. Brewman, etc., 1791.

10/3:7. Jones, Stephen, comp. *Dr. Johnson's Table Talk, containing aphorisms on literature, life, and manners. . . . Selected and arranged from Mr. Boswell's Life of Johnson.* London: C. Dilly, 1798. "Undertaken in the lifetime of Mr. Boswell, and with his cordial approbation": Preface.

10/3:8. Opie, John. [Johnson's conversation not "harsh"], *Lectures on Painting,* p. 40. London: Longmans, 1809.

10/3:9. *The Table Talk of Samuel Johnson, LL.D., Comprising His Most Interesting Remarks and Observations. Collected by James Boswell, Esq. F.R.S. With a Sketch of the Life of Samuel Johnson, LL.D.* 2 vols. London: J. Coxhead, 1818.

10/3:10. Uneda. "Anecdote," *N&Q,* 2nd ser., X (December 8, 1860), 448. Improbable—Johnson objecting to "baby-talk."

10/3:11. Russell, William Clark. "Johnson's Table-Talk," *The Book of Table-Talk*, pp. 95–123. London: Routledge, 1874. A collection of unidentified samples.

10/3:12. *Johnsoniana: Life, Opinions, and Table Talk of Dr. Johnson*, arranged and collected by R. W. Montagu. (Handy Aldine Series.) London: A. Boot and Son, [1884?].

10/3:13. *Johnson's Table Talk*, arranged by W. A. Lewis Bettany. Boston: H. M. Caldwell, 1904.

10/3:14. *Dr. Johnson's Table-Talk*, ed. J. Potter Briscoe. (Bibelot's Series.) London: Gay and Bird, 1900. Another ed., London: George Routledge & Sons, [1907].

10/3:15. *The Sayings of Dr. Johnson*. (Watergate Booklets.) London and Edinburgh, 1908.

10/3:16. *Sir, Said Dr. Johnson*, comp. Sir Chartres Biron. London: Gerald Duckworth & Co., 1911; London: Jonathan Cape, 1932.

10/3:17. Edge, J. H. *Horace Walpole, the Great Letter-Writer: Samuel Johnson, the Great Talker*. Dublin: Privately printed, Ponsonby and Gibbs, 1913.

10/3:18. Tinker, Chauncey B. "Johnson and the Art of Conversation," *The Salon and English Letters*, pp. 217–35. New York: Macmillan, 1915.

10/3:19. Hughes, Spencer L. "Dr. Johnson's Expletives," in item 6:28, pp. 67–83. His retorts and invective.

10/3:20. Biron, Sir Chartres. "Immortal Talk," *Pious Opinions*, pp. 59–77. London: Gerald Duckworth & Co., 1923.

10/3:21. Whibley, Leonard. "Dr. Johnson's Conversation," *Blackwood's Magazine*, CCXIV (July 1923), 103–21.

10/3:22. Murray, Michael. "He Talked Himself into Fame," *Radio Times*, March 14, 1930, p. 634.

10/3:23. Teall, Gardner. "Dr. Johnson and the Art of Conversation," *Catholic World*, CXXXI (August 1930), 513–21.

10/3:24. Hawkins, Sir Anthony Hope. [Johnson's talk], *Lichfield Mercury*, September 25, 1931. Reprinted; see item 6:22.

10/3:25. R[endall], V[ernon]. "Johnson: Two Sayings," *N&Q*, CLXXII (February 13, 1937), 116–17. Remarks, possibly apocryphal, attributed by "Peter Pindar" and Hazlitt.

10/3:26. Kevin, Neil. "Johnson Talking," *Irish Ecclesiastical Record*, 5th ser., LVIII (December 1941), 481–92. Kevin had discussed Boswell *ibid.* (November 1941), 401–13.

10/3:27. "Quintus Quiz" [Edward Shillito]. "Talking of Conversation," *Christian Century*, LIX (November 4, 1942), 1345.

10/3:28. Krutch, Joseph Wood. "On the Talk of Samuel Johnson and His Friends," *American Scholar*, XIII (Summer 1944), 363–72.

10/3:29. Coleman, William H. "The Johnsonian Conversational Formula," *Quarterly Review*, CCLXXXII (October 1944), 432–45.

10/3:30. Aguiar, A. "Great Talkers," *Irish Monthly*, LXXIV (May 1946), 205–10.

10/3:31. H., W. J. "Haydon on Johnson's Talk," *N&Q*, CXCII (February 8, 1947), 59.

10/3:32. Todd, William B. "A Johnsonian Anecdote," *JNL*, XV, no. 3 (September 1955), 12. On version in *London Evening Post*, 1773, of a quip to Robertson about the "kirk."

10/3:33. Davis, Bertram H. "Another Johnsonian Anecdote," *JNL*, XV, no. 1 (December 1955), 12. About a toast to Miss Williams; from *Liber Facetiarium*, 1811.

10/3:34. Krutch, Joseph Wood. "The Great Talker," *New York Times Magazine*, September 12, 1959.

10/3:35. McAdam, E. L., Jr. "A Johnsonian Retort" [counterblast to the waterman], *TLS*, July 21, 1961, p. 449.

10/3:36. Greene, Donald J. "A Johnsonian Retort" [made to Walmesley about *Irene*], *TLS*, October 13, 1961, p. 683.

10/3:37. McDonald, Daniel. "The Ribaldry of Dr. Johnson," *American Notes and Queries*, II (May 1964), 136–37.

10/3:38. Brookes, E. H. " 'Sir,' Said Dr. Johnson," *Theoria* (University of Natal), No. 24 (June 1965), pp. 39–48. Assembles a variety of quotations from Johnson's works and Boswell's *Life* and renders them as conversation.

10/3:39. Chamberlin, William Henry. "The Withering Wit of Samuel Johnson," *SR*, September 4, 1965, pp. 14–15, 45.

10/3:40. Weidhorn, Manfred. "The Conversation of Common Sense," *University Review* (Kansas City), XXXIV (Autumn 1967), 3–7.

10/4. Comparisons of Johnson with Other Individuals

10/4:1. Hayley, William. *Two Dialogues: containing a comparative view of the lives, characters, and writings of Philip, the late Earl of Chesterfield, and Dr. Samuel Johnson.* London: T. Cadell, 1787. Later ed., *Anecdotes of Philip, late Earl of Chesterfield, and Dr. Johnson: a comparative view of their lives, characters, and merit, and extracts from their writings. By a Student of Cambridge*, London: A. Cleugh, 1800.

10/4:2. Gale, Gustavus. "A Comparative View of the Writings of Addison and Johnson," *Miscellanies in Prose and Verse*, pp. 12–17. London: Printed for the author, 1794.

10/4:3. [Howison, William.] "Samuel Johnson and David Hume," *Blackwood's*, III (August 1818), 511–13.

10/4:4. R., C. [James Crossley.] "On the Literary Characters of Bishop Warburton and Dr. Johnson," *Blackwood's*, VIII (December 1820), 243–52.

10/4:5. Alciphron. "Speculations on Literary Pleasure, No. XIV," *GM*, XCIX (May 1829), 402–4. Comparison of Goldsmith and Johnson.

10/4:6. "Speculations on Literary Pleasure, No. XIV," *GM*, XCIX (June 1829), 498–502. Comparison of Franklin and Johnson.

10/4:7. "Oliver Goldsmith and Dr. Johnson," *De Bow's Review*, XXVIII (n.s., III) (May 1860), 504–13.

10/4:8. Friswell, Hain. "Dr. Johnson and Charles Dickens," *N&Q*, 4th ser., VIII (October 21, 1871), 323. Story in *Pickwick* of man eating crumpets before committing suicide taken from Boswell's *Life*; also *ibid.*, pp. 425–26.

10/4:9. Burroughs, John. "Dr. Samuel Johnson and Thomas Carlyle," *Critic*, V (January 2, 1886), 1–2. Reprinted as "Dr. Johnson and Carlyle," *Indoor Studies*, pp. 195–203, Boston and New York: Houghton, Mifflin, 1889. A (moderate) reply to Augustine Birrell's assertion that Johnson was greater than Carlyle.

10/4:10. Roose, P. W. "Dr. Johnson and Charles Lamb" [a parallel], *Temple Bar*, LXXXVI (June 1889), 237–57.

10/4:11. Tate, W. R. "Fénélon and Johnson: A Parallel Expression," *N&Q*, 7th ser., XII (September 26, 1891), 244.

10/4:12. Phelps, William Lyon. "King Samuel and King Ben—with a Eulogy of Boswell," *Booklover's Magazine*, I (April 1903), 384–88.

10/4:13. "Johnson and Holmes" [Oliver Wendell Holmes, Sr.], *Academy*, LXXVII (August 28, 1909), 464–65.

10/4:14. "Two Centenaries" [comparison of Johnson and Tennyson], *Spectator*, CIII (September 18, 1909), 409–10.

10/4:15. Chubb, Edwin W. "Dr. Johnson and Charles Lamb," *Stories of Authors*, pp. 28–32. New York: Sturgis and Walton, 1910.

10/4:16. Waterton, T. M. "The Dean and the Doctor" [comparison of Swift and Johnson], *The Month*, CXVIII (July 1911), 27–32.

10/4:17. Thompson, Edward Raymond. "Dr. Johnson as the Original of Pickwick" [comparison of two men, and influence of Boswell on Dickens], *Nineteenth Century*, LXXXV (March 1919), 512–22.

10/4:18. Waterton, T. M. "Johnson and Swift—A Study in Comparisons," *The Month*, CXXXIV (October 1919), 315–20.

10/4:19. Clodd, Edward. "Dr. Johnson and Cicero on Friendship," *Fortnightly Review*, CXIV (July 1923), 134–43.

10/4:20. Elovson, Harald. "Samuel Johnson, Goethe och Patriotismen under Sjuttonhundratalet," *Årsbok 1926* (Vetenskaps-Societeten i Lund, 1926), pp. 31–49.

10/4:21. Roscoe, Edward Stanley. "Dr. Johnson and Anatole France," *Cornhill Magazine*, n.s., LXIII (September 1927), 319–24. Reprinted in item 10/6:204, pp. 82–96.

10/4:22. Roscoe, Edward Stanley. "Johnson and Selden" [a comparison], in item 10/6:204, pp. 65–81.

10/4:23. Lovat-Fraser, J. A. "Samuel Johnson and Walter Scott" [comparison], *Lichfield Mercury*, September 23, 1932. Reprinted; see item 6:22. Reprinted also in *Inverness Courier*, September 27–October 11, 1932.

10/4:24. Alexander, Henry. "Jonson and Johnson" [comparison of the two men], *Queen's Quarterly*, XLIV (Spring 1937), 13–21.

10/4:25. Altick, Richard D. "Mr. Sherlock Holmes and Dr. Samuel Johnson" [comparison, etc.], in *221 B: Studies in Sherlock Holmes*, ed. Vincent Starrett, pp. 109–28. New York: Macmillan, 1940.

10/4:26. Schinz, Albert. "Les dangers du cliché littéraire: Le Dr. Johnson et Jean-Jacques Rousseau" [some resemblances between the two men], *MLN*, LVII (November 1942), 573–80.

*10/4:27. Mossner, Ernest C. "Hume and Johnson," *The Forgotten Hume*, pp. 189–209. New York: Columbia University Press, 1943. See also *N&Q*, CLXXXV (July 31, August 28, 1943), 77–78, 147.

*10/4:28. Sewall, Richard B. "Dr. Johnson, Rousseau, and Reform," in item 10/6:273, pp. 307–17.

10/4:29. Savage, Oliver D. "Johnson and Dickens: A Comparison," *Dickensian*, LXVIII (December 1951), 42–44.

10/4:30. Metzdorf, Robert F. "Thackeray and Johnson," *New Rambler*, July 1952, pp. 6–8. References to Johnson by Thackeray.

10/4:31. Manchester, William. "H. L. Mencken at Seventy-Five: America's Sam Johnson," *SR*, September 10, 1955, pp. 11–13, 64–65. See also D. J. Greene, *JNL*, XVIII, no. 2 (June 1958), 5–6.

10/4:32. Bradbrook, Frank W. "Dr. Johnson and Jane Austen," *N&Q*, CCV (March 1960), 108–12. Johnson's influence. See also *ibid.*, July 1960, p. 271.

10/4:33. Chapin, Chester F. "Johnson, Rousseau, and Religion," *Texas Studies in Literature and Language*, II (Spring 1960), 95–102.

10/4:34. Coffey, Warren. "Johnson and Wittgenstein," *JNL*, XXI, no. 4 (December 1961), 11–12. The philosopher's acquaintance with Johnson's writings.

10/4:35. Stasny, John F. "Doctor Johnson and Walter Pater on Stoicism: A Comparison of Views," *West Virginia University Bulletin: Philological Papers*, XIV (October 1963), 18–25.

10/4:36. Mowat, John. "Samuel Johnson and the Critical Heritage of T. S. Eliot" [many resemblances as critics], *Studia Germanica Gandensia* (Ghent, Belgium), VI (1964), 231–47.

10/4:37. Lewis, Wilmarth S. *The Accords and Resemblances of Johnson and Walpole*. Privately printed for The Johnsonians, 1967. Reprinted in *Bulletin of the Rocky Mountain Modern Language Association*, XXII (June 1968), 7–12. Johnson and Horace Walpole.

10/4:38. Hagstrum, Jean H. "The Rhetoric of Fear and the Rhetoric of Hope," *Tri-Quarterly*, No. 11 (Winter 1968), pp. 109–21. Contrast between Johnson's and Blake's view of life.

10/4:39. Wain, John. "Orwell and the Intelligentsia," *Encounter*, XXXI (December 1968), 72–80. Contains comparison of George Orwell and Johnson.

10/5. JOHNSON'S REPUTATION

*10/5:1. Chapman, R. W. "Johnson's Reputation," *TLS*, September 1, 1921, pp. 553–54. (See also R. S. Garnett, *ibid.*, September 8, p. 580.) Reprinted in *Living Age*, CCCXI (October 8, 1921), 84–90.

*10/5:2. *Contemporary Criticisms of Dr. Samuel Johnson, His Works, and His Biographers* [from *Monthly Review*], ed. John Ker Spittal. London: John Murray, 1923. Reviewed by R. W. Chapman, *TLS*, October 18, 1923, p. 686.

10/5:3. Ellis, Havelock. "The Problem of Dr. Johnson's Fame," *Questions of Our Day*, pp. 245–47. London: John Lane, 1936.

10/5:4. Addington, Marion H. "A Contemporary Comment on Dr. Johnson" [in *Royal Chronicle* . . . January 18–20, 1762], *N&Q*, CLXXI (December 12, 1936), 418–19.

10/5:5. Lang, Daniel R. *Dr. Samuel Johnson in America* [his reputation, 1750–1812]. Abstract of thesis, University of Illinois, 1939.

10/5:6. Lass, Robert N. "A Brief History of the Criticism of Dr. Johnson." Dissertation, University of Iowa, 1942. Summary in [Iowa State University], *Doctoral Dissertations: Abstracts and References*, VI (1953), 428–29.

10/5:7. George, Dorothy. "Samuel Johnson and the Journals of the Romantic Period: His Reputation as a Literary Critic." Dissertation, Louisiana State University, 1950.

10/5:8. Morgan, Ira L. "Contemporary Criticism of the Works of Samuel Johnson" (dissertation, University of Florida, 1954), *Dissertation Abstracts*, XIV (1954), 2071.

10/5:9. Kenney, William. "The Modern Reputation of Samuel Johnson." Dissertation, Boston University, 1956. Abstract (separate pamphlet), Boston: Boston University Graduate School, 1956.

*10/5:10. McGuffie, Helen Louise. "Samuel Johnson and the Hostile Press" (dissertation, Columbia University, 1961), *Dissertation Abstracts*, XXII

(October 1961), 1182–83. Attacks on Johnson in newspapers, periodicals, and pamphlets, 1749–1784.

10/5:11. Rowland, John Carter. "The Reputation of Dr. Samuel Johnson in England, 1779–1835." Dissertation, Western Reserve University, 1962.

10/5:12. Greene, Donald J. "How Popular is Johnson?" *JNL*, December 1964, pp. 11–12. More scholarly articles and books published on Johnson between 1950 and 1963 than on any other English author of 16th to 18th centuries except Shakespeare and Milton.

10/5:13. Walker, Isaac Newton. "Johnson's Criticism Criticized: The Contemporary View of Johnson's Later Reputation" (dissertation, University of Texas, 1965), *Dissertation Abstracts*, XXVII (July 1966), 216–17A. Study of contemporary reactions to the *Lives of the Poets*, etc.

10/5:14. Fitzpatrick, Edward Timothy. "The Anti-Johnsonians. A Study of the Contemporary Detractors of Samuel Johnson" (dissertation, Fordham University, 1967), *Dissertation Abstracts*, XXVIII, no. 10 (April 1968), 4125–26A.

10/5:15. Walker, Ian C. "Dr. Johnson and *The Weekly Magazine*" [attacks on Johnson, 1769–75], *RES*, n.s., XIX (February 1968), 14–24.

10/6. General Assessments of Johnson and Miscellaneous Comment

10/6:1. [Thicknesse, Philip.] "Of Dr. J—n—n," *Sketches and Characters of the Most Eminent and Most Singular Persons Now Living*, I, 59. London: John Wheble, 1770 (printed at Bristol). A brief paragraph defending his pension.

10/6:2. A Free Enquirer. [Open letter to Johnson], *London Museum*, I (April 1770), 220; II (July), 17–20. A general attack on Johnson.

10/6:3. "A Parallel between Diogenes the Cynic and Doctor J——n, by a Very Eminent Hand," *Town and Country*, VII (March 1775), 115–18.

10/6:4. Chiaro Oscuro [George Colman the elder]. "Literary Portrait of Dr. Johnson," *London Packet*, No. 962 (December 20–22, 1775). Reprinted in his *Prose on Several Occasions*, II, 97–100. London: T. Cadell, 1787.

10/6:5. [Callender, James Thomson.] *A Critical Review of the Works of Dr. Samuel Johnson, Containing a Particular Vindication of Several Eminent Characters*. London: Cadell and Stockdale, 1783. (Also Edinburgh.) London: R. Rusted, 1787.

10/6:6. "The Man in the Moon, or Travels into the Lunar Regions by the Man of the People," *Weekly Magazine* (Edinburgh), LVII (September 25, 1783), 405–8; LVIII (October 23), 117–18. Includes a general attack on Johnson.

10/6:7. Fordyce, James. [Long prose epitaph on Johnson], *GM*, LV (April 1785), 411–12.

10/6:8. "Impartial Character of Dr. Samuel Johnson Said to be Written by Miss Seward," *European Magazine*, VII (May 1785), 331–32.

10/6:9. "Of Great Men; and of Dr. Samuel Johnson," *Sylva; or The Wood*, pp. 290ff. London, 1786. Reprinted in *European Magazine*, IX (May 1786), 319–20. Hostile; has been attributed to Ralph Heathcote.

10/6:10. Anti-Stiletto. [Defense of Johnson's *Prayers and Meditations* and Boswell's *Journal of a Tour to the Hebrides*], *GM*, LVI (January 1786), 17–23. An important footnote by the editor, John Nichols, p. 22, asserts that Johnson was closely involved in the supervision of the collection of the works of the English poets for which he wrote the *Lives*.

10/6:11. Benvolio [Anna Seward]. [General attack on Johnson], *GM*, LVI (February 1786), 125–26; (April), 302–4.

10/6:12. Pro Me, Si Merear, In Me. Letter to "Mr. Urban," *GM*, LVI (May 1786), 386–88. Savage attack on Boswell's *Life* and Johnson.

10/6:13. Erica. "Observations on the Character of Dr. Johnson" [hostile], *European Magazine*, X (August 1786), 128–30.

10/6:14. *A Rational Estimate of the Character of Dr. Johnson* [?London, 1787]. Not seen; extract given in "Review of New Publications," *GM*, LVII (February 1787), 155–56.

10/6:15. Horne, George (later Bishop of Norwich). *Olla Podrida* [a periodical], XIII (June 9, 1787), 132–41. A thoughtful survey of the various biographies of Johnson. Reprinted in *GM*, LXX (January 1800), 9–11, and in item 3:75.

10/6:16. Knox, Vicesimus. *Winter Evenings, or Lucubrations on Life and Letters*. London: 1788. No. 11, "On the Character of Doctor Johnson and the Abuse of Biography"; No. 22, "On Dr. Johnson's Prayers, with a Remark on His Style." Often reprinted.

10/6:17. "Mr. Tyrwhitt vindicated from a Reflection of Dr. Johnson," *GM*, LVIII (March 1788), 187–88. Equally a "vindication" of George Steevens (probably the author) from a suggestion by Johnson that Steevens and Tyrwhitt had believed in the authenticity of Chatterton's Rowley poems.

10/6:18. T., T. "The Character of Dr. Johnson Calmly Investigated," *GM*, LX (June 1790), 511–13.

10/6:19. [Temple, William Johnson.] *The Character of Dr. Johnson. With Illustrations from Mrs. Piozzi, Sir J. Hawkins, and J. Boswell*. London: C. Dilly, 1792. Text headed "Character of Dr. Johnson. Written Soon after the Publication of the Lives of the Poets." "Written in the early 80's": F. A. Pottle, *TLS*, May 22, 1930, p. 434.

10/6:20. "Original Letters on the Character of Dr. Johnson" [by Anna Seward and William Hayley], *GM*, LXIII (March 1793), 197–99.

10/6:21. [Mudford, William.] "A Critical Enquiry into the Moral Writings of Dr. Samuel Johnson," *Porcupine*, No. 291 (October 3, 1801); No. 296

(October 9); No. 314 (November 2); No. 324 (November 13); No. 326 (November 16). Reprinted as *A Critical Enquiry into the Moral Writings of Dr. Samuel Johnson, by Attalus . . . to which is added . . . a Dialogue between Johnson and Boswell in the Shades*, London: Cobbett and Morgan, 1802.

10/6:22. Hayley, William. *The Life and Posthumous Writings of William Cowper.* 3 vols. London: J. Johnson, 1803–4. Many references to Johnson in Cowper's letters, here first published, especially concerning his *Life of Milton* and his religion. Additional letters in T. S. Grimshawe, ed., *The Works of William Cowper*, London: Saunders, Otley, 1835. (The standard modern edition of Cowper's correspondence is that ed. T. Wright, 1904.)

10/6:23. Hunt, Leigh. *Classic Tales, Serious and Lively, with Critical Essays on the Merits and Reputation of the Authors*, III, 1–13. London: J. Hunt and C. Reynell, 1807. Introducing *Rasselas*.

10/6:24. Burdon, Richard. *A Comparative Estimate of the English Literature of the Seventeenth and Eighteenth Centuries.* Oxford: Privately printed, 1814. Oxford English Prize Essay. Various slighting references to Johnson.

10/6:25. *Byroniana: Bozzies and Piozzies*, pp. 2–6. London: Sherwood, Jones and Co., 1825. Contradictions in Johnson's criticism.

10/6:26. Chedworth, John Howe, 4th Baron. *Letters from the Late Lord Chedworth to the Rev. Thomas Crompton; Written in the Period from January 1780 to May 1798.* London: Hurst, Chance, and Co., 1828. Numerous references to Johnson, chiefly about his criticism.

10/6:27. Wilson, John ("Christopher North"). "Noctes Ambrosianae No. XLII" [general appreciation of Johnson], *Blackwood's*, XXV (April 1829). Reprinted in *The Works of Professor Wilson*, ed. Ferrier, Edinburgh and London: Blackwood, 1855–58; also in R. Brimley Johnson, ed., *Famous Reviews*, pp. 298–99, London: Sir I. Pitman and Sons, 1914. See also "Noctes Ambrosianae No. LIX" [defense of Croker's *Boswell* against Macaulay's attack], *Blackwood's*, XXX (November 1831), 829–38. Reprinted in Wilson's *Works*, ed. Ferrier.

10/6:28. Macaulay, Thomas Babington. "Boswell's Life of Johnson" [review of Croker's ed., 1831], *Edinburgh Review*, LIV (September 1831), 1–38. Reprinted in his *Critical, Historical, and Miscellaneous Essays*, London: Longmans, 1843; ed. D. Nichol Smith, Oxford: Clarendon Press, [1909]. Many other editions.

10/6:29. Campbell, Sir James. *Memoirs of Sir James Campbell of Ardkinglas. Written by Himself*, I, 254–63. London: Colburn and Bentley, 1832. An unsympathetic sketch of Johnson.

10/6:30. Ladd, Joseph Brown. "Critical Remarks on the Writings of the

Late Dr. Johnson," *The Literary Remains of Joseph Brown Ladd, M.D. Collected by His Sister, Mrs. Elizabeth Haskins of Rhode Island*, p. 181. New York: H. C. Sleight, Clinton Hall, 1832.

10/6:31. Carlyle, Thomas. [Review of Croker's ed. of Boswell's *Life*], *Fraser's Magazine*, V (May 1832), 379–413. Reprinted as "Biography" and "Boswell's *Life of Johnson*" in his *Critical and Miscellaneous Essays*, III, 96–113, 114–94, London: James Fraser, 1839, and many later editions.

10/6:32. Mézières, Louis. "Johnson," *Histoire Critique de la Littérature Anglaise*, II, 28–131. Paris: Baudry, 1834. Includes translation of original *Idler* 22.

10/6:33. Coleridge, Samuel Taylor. *Specimens of the Table Talk of Samuel Taylor Coleridge*, [ed. H. N. Coleridge]. London: Murray, 1835, and often reprinted. Comments on Johnson under dates July 4, November 1, 1833.

10/6:34. Mackintosh, Sir James. *Memoirs of Sir James Mackintosh, edited by his son* [Robert James Mackintosh], II, 166–71. London: Moxon, 1835. Severe strictures on Johnson's style and criticism.

10/6:35. Carlyle, Thomas. "Lecture V: The Hero as Man of Letters" [discusses Johnson pp. 285–98], *On Heroes and Hero-Worship*. London: James Fraser, 1841. Many later eds.

10/6:36. Goodrich, Samuel Griswold ("Peter Parley"). "Samuel Johnson," *Famous Men of Modern Times*, pp. 207–27. Boston: Bradbury, Soden and Co., 1843.

10/6:37. Chasles, Philarète. *Le Dix-Huitième Siècle en Angleterre*, p. 28. Paris: D'Amyot, 1846. Notice of Johnson in "Les Excentriques et les Humoristes."

10/6:38. Anderson, James Stuart Murray. "Samuel Johnson," *Addresses on Miscellaneous Subjects*, Address No. II. London: Rivington, 1849.

10/6:39. B. "Dr. Johnson and Professor de Morgan," *N&Q*, I (December 15, 1849), 107–8. Reply to a criticism by De Morgan.

10/6:40. Mitford, Mary Russell. "Authors Associated with Places. Samuel Johnson," *Recollections of a Literary Life*, I, 218–26. 3 vols. London: R. Bentley, 1852.

10/6:41. "Dr. Johnson as a Christian and a Critic," *Eclectic Review*, CI (February 1855), 153–68.

10/6:42. D., G. "Samuel Johnson," *Literary Gazette*, January 17, 1857, pp. 62–65. Reprinted in *Living Age*, LII (1857), 742–50. A protest against Macaulay's *Encyclopaedia Britannica* article on Johnson (item 3:92).

10/6:43. "Stepping-Stones," *Household Words*, XVI (October 24, 1857), 402–7. Johnson as link between Pope and Disraeli.

10/6:44. "Johnson, Boswell, Goldsmith, etc.," *De Bow's Review*, XVIII (April 1860), 410–23.

10/6:45. Craik, George L. "Johnson," *A Compendious History of English Literature and of the English Language,* II, 306–10. London: Griffin, Bohn, 1861. Frequently reprinted, later as *A Manual of English Literature and the English Language.*

10/6:46. Corney, Bolton. "Johnsonian Quotations" [their inaccuracy], *N&Q,* 2nd ser., XI (June 22, 1861), 482–83.

10/6:47. Whitaker, D. K. "The Literary Character of Dr. Sam'l Johnson," *Southern Literary Messenger,* XXXIII (August 1861), 142–47. Ends with a set of verses in "tribute to his genius from the pen of a South Carolina poetess."

10/6:48. Collier, William Francis. "Samuel Johnson," *A History of English Literature, in a series of biographical sketches.* London: T. Nelson, 1862. Often reprinted. One of the very worst examples of Victorian ignorance and distortion of Johnson.

10/6:49. Taine, Hippolyte Auguste. [Johnson], *Histoire de la Littérature anglaise,* III, 336–45 (Book III, Chap. VI, Sec. 7). Paris: Hachette, 1863. Tr. H. Van Laun, New York: Holt, 1871, and often reprinted.

10/6:50. Allibone, S. A. "Works and Reviewers of Dr. Johnson," *Evangelical Review,* XV (1864), 141–55.

10/6:51. Reynolds, Sir Joshua. [Character sketch of Johnson], in item 5:69 (1865), II, 454–62. Reprinted in item 3:116 (1897). Edited from MS by F. W. Hilles in item 5:317 (1952).

10/6:52. Ross, George. "Dr. Johnson," *Studies, Biographical and Literary,* pp. 63–118. London: Simpkin, Marshall, and Co., [1867].

10/6:53. Russell, William Clark. "Samuel Johnson," *The Book of Authors: A collection of criticisms, ana, môts. . . .* [quotations from various sources], pp. 217–21. (The Chandos Library.) London: F. Warne; New York: Scribner's, [1871].

10/6:54. Minto, William. "Samuel Johnson," *A Manual of English Prose Literature,* pp. 474–92. Edinburgh and London: Blackwood, 1872.

10/6:55. Yonge, Charles Duke. "Johnson," *Three Centuries of English Literature,* pp. 389–406. New York: Appleton, 1872.

10/6:56. "Dr. Johnson," *New Monthly Magazine,* 3rd ser., III (May 1873), 376–84; (June) 432–40.

10/6:57. Duyckinck, Evert A. "Samuel Johnson," *Portrait Gallery of Eminent Men and Women of Europe and America,* I, 5–27. New York: Johnson, Wilson and Co., [ca. 1873].

10/6:58. Stephen, Leslie. "Hours in a Library, No. VIII. Dr. Johnson's Writings," *Cornhill Magazine,* XXIX (March 1874), 280–97. Reprinted in *Hours in a Library,* Second Series, pp. 198–241, London: Smith, Elder, 1876.

10/6:59. Bascom, John. [Discussion of Johnson], *Philosophy of English Lit-*

erature: A course of lectures delivered in the Lowell Institute, pp. 199–208. New York: Putnam, 1874.

10/6:60. Ritchie, J. Ewing. "Samuel Johnson," *Christian World Magazine and Family Visitor*, XIII (November 1877), 824–33. Hostile and ill-informed.

10/6:61. Hill, George Birkbeck. *Dr. Johnson: His Friends and His Critics*. London: Smith, Elder, 1878.

10/6:62. Cyples, William. "Johnson Without Boswell" [his own works], *Contemporary Review*, XXXII (July 1878), 707–27. Reprinted in *Living Age*, CXXXVIII (1878), 541–52. Primarily concerned with the periodical essays.

10/6:63. [Dicey, A. V.] "The Worship of Johnson," *Nation*, XXVII (November 21, 1878), 318–19. Review article based on items 3:104 and 10/6:61.

10/6:64. Ritchie, J. Ewing. "Dr. Johnson in Society," *Christian World Magazine*, XIV (October 1878), 826–36.

10/6:65. Mason, Edward T. *Samuel Johnson, His Words and His Ways: what he said, what he did, and what men thought and spoke concerning him* [extracts from many sources]. New York: Harper, 1879.

10/6:66. "Dr. Johnson: His Biographers and Critics," *Westminster Review*, III (January 1879), 1–39. Review article, hostile to Johnson, based on items 3:104, 10/6:61, 4:15 (Main), etc. Concludes "We cannot refrain from expressing our gratitude that our lot is cast in a time when in society such a man as Samuel Johnson is an impossibility."

10/6:67. White, Lucy Cecil. "Doctor Johnson and His Times," *Wide Awake*, VIII (May 1879), 322–26; (June), 391–95; IX (October), 261–64.

10/6:68. Dennis, John. "Dr. Johnson," *British Quarterly Review*, LXX (October 1879), 347–71. Review article based on items 3:104, 4:15 (Main), etc.

10/6:69. Dulcken, Henry William. "Dr. Samuel Johnson," *Worthies of the World, a series of . . . sketches . . .* pp. 97–112. London: Ward and Lock, 1881.

10/6:70. Richardson, Abby Sage. "Talk XLVI: On Dr. Samuel Johnson," *Familiar Talks on English Literature*, pp. 307–13. Chicago: Jansen, McClurg and Co., 1881. Often reprinted.

10/6:71. Buckland, Anna. "Samuel Johnson and his friends," *The Story of English Literature*, pp. 442–57. London: Cassell, 1882.

10/6:72. Testard, Henri. "Johnson," *Histoire de la Littérature anglaise*, pp. 315–21. Paris: J. Bonhoure, 1882.

10/6:73. Welsh, Alfred H. "Samuel Johnson," *Development of English Literature and Language*, Vol. II, pp. 172–78. Chicago: S. C. Griggs & Co., 1882.

10/6:74. Nicoll, Henry James. "Dr. Johnson and His Contemporaries," *Landmarks of English Literature*, pp. 237–75. New York: Appleton, 1883.

10/6:75. Perry, Thomas Sergeant. "Johnson," *English Literature in the Eighteenth Century*, pp. 403–15. New York: Harper, 1883.

10/6:76. Andrews, Samuel. "Samuel Johnson," *Our Great Writers; or Popular Chapters on Some Leading Authors*, pp. 199–208. London: Elliot Stock, 1884.

10/6:77. Hazlitt, William Carew. "Dr. Johnson," *Offspring of Thoughts in Solitude: Modern Essays*, pp. 47–56. London: Reeves and Turner, 1884.

10/6:78. Hood, E. Paxton. "Samuel Johnson, The King of Fleet Street," *Leisure Hour*, XXXIII (1884), 705–12. A centenary tribute.

10/6:79. Russell, Addison Peale. "Doctor Johnson," *Characteristics: Sketches and Essays*, pp. 52–73. Boston and New York: Houghton, Mifflin, 1884.

10/6:80. [Leading article], *Times* (London), October 10, 1884, p. 7. Doubts probable success of Johnson centenary celebrations in Lichfield; few read Johnson; "The infatuated admiration which he inspired . . . is not wholly comprehensible to this generation."

10/6:81. Hill, George Birkbeck. "The Johnson Centenary and the Times" [a slashing reply to item 10/6:80], *Saturday Review*, LVIII (October 25, 1884), 528–29. See also W. T. Lynn, *N&Q*, 6th ser., X (November 15, 1884), 384.

10/6:82. Gosse, Edmund. "Dr. Samuel Johnson," *Fortnightly Review*, XLII (December 1884), 780–86. A centenary article—one of the worst Victorian depreciations. Reprinted in *Eclectic Magazine*, CIV (1884), 178–84; *Living Age*, CLXIII (1884), 803–7.

10/6:83. Walford, Edward. "Dr. Johnson," *Antiquarian Magazine*, VI (December 1884), 259–63. A centenary tribute from "the last and only surviving Editor of the *Gentleman's Magazine* in its former shape."

10/6:84. "The Johnson Centenary," *Times* (London), December 13, 1884, p. 8 (see item 10/6:80). *Times*, December 15, contains a report of commemorations at the Temple and at Lichfield.

10/6:85. "The Centenary of Dr. Johnson's Death," *Athenaeum*, December 20, 1884, p. 806.

10/6:86. [Craik, Henry.] "Samuel Johnson and His Age" [review of new editions of Boswell, Leslie Stephen's and James Macaulay's books on Johnson, and a facsimile edition of *Rasselas*], *Quarterly Review*, CLIX (January 1885), 147–74. Reprinted in *Living Age*, CLXV (1885), 323–38.

10/6:87. Birrell, Augustine. "Dr. Johnson," *Contemporary Review*, XLVII (January 1885), 25–39. Reprinted in *Obiter Dicta*, Second Series, pp. 107–47, London: Elliot Stock, 1887.

10/6:88. Hale, Edward Everett. "Johnson," *Lights of Two Centuries*, pp. 175–88. New York: Barnes and Co., 1887.

10/6:89. Saunders, Frederick. "Dr. Johnson," *The Story of Some Famous Books*, pp. 90–95. London: Elliot Stock, 1887.

10/6:90. Wotton, Mabel E. "Samuel Johnson," *Word Portraits of Famous Writers*, pp. 150–52. London: Richard Bentley, 1887.

10/6:91. [Apocryphal anecdotes of Johnson], *N&Q*, 7th ser., V (March 3, 1888), 166; 7th ser., X (October 18, 1890), 309; 8th ser., III (June 24, 1893), 488; 8th ser., VII (March 9, 1895), 191; 9th ser., V (January 13, 1900), 24; 10th ser., III (June 10, 1905), 447; 10th ser., XII (July 3, 1909), 12; 11th ser., IV (August 5, 1911), 105; 12th ser., I (January 1, 1916), 18; 12th ser., VII (October 23, 1920), 332; CLXXI (August 1, 1936), 89; CXC (May 4, 1946), 193–94. See also *JNL*, November 1945, p. 7; May 1946, p. 11; July 1946, pp. 9–10; November 1946, p. 11.

10/6:92. Gleeson, Joseph M. *History of Eighteenth Century Literature (1660–1780)*, pp. 283–95. London: Macmillan, 1889.

10/6:93. Massingham, H. W. "Some Johnson Characteristics" [commonsense criticism, etc.], *GM*, CCLXVIII (February 1890), 155–64. Reprinted in item 6:16, pp. 133–51.

10/6:94. Hoste, James William. *Johnson and His Circle* [notices of recent Johnsonian publications]. London: Jarrold, [1891].

10/6:95. Besant, Walter. "Over Johnson's Grave: A Causerie," *Harpers*, LXXXII (May 1891), 927–32. Reprinted in *Essays and Historiettes*, pp. 251–70, London: Chatto & Windus, 1903.

10/6:96. Byers, S. H. M. "Good Things from Dr. Johnson," *Magazine of American History*, XXVI (October 1891), 302–11.

10/6:97. Hill, George Birkbeck. *Writers and Readers*. London: Fisher Unwin, 1892.

10/6:98. "Boswell's Johnson" [adverse criticism of Johnson's writings], *Temple Bar*, XCV (June 1892), 251–58.

10/6:99. Gleeson, Joseph M. *Doctor Johnson: His Life, Works and Table Talk*. New York: Frederick A. Stokes Co., [1893].

10/6:100. Uchida, Mitsugu. *Dr. Johnson* [in Japanese]. Tokyo: Minyusha, 1894. Said to be the first single essay written on Johnson to appear in Japan.

10/6:101. Jebb, Sir Richard. "Samuel Johnson" [lecture at Newnham College, Cambridge, March 3, 1894], *Essays and Addresses*, pp. 479–505. Cambridge: Cambridge University Press, 1907.

10/6:102. Jowett, Benjamin. "Addresses on . . . Boswell and Johnson, and Johnson's own writings and character," in *Essays on Men and Manners*, ed. P. Lyttelton Gell. London: John Murray, 1895. Apparently never published; "It seems to exist only in a proof-state. Balliol has a number of paper-bound, crown 8vo, imperfect copies." Not seen; information from Sir Geoffrey Faber, *Jowett*, 1957, p. 432.

10/6:103. Mitchell, Donald G. *English Lands Letters and Kings*, III, 88–143. New York: Charles Scribner's Sons; London: Sampson Low, Marston & Co., 1895.

10/6:104. Phillips, Maude Gillette. "Dr. Samuel Johnson," *A Popular Manual of English Literature*, II, 3–54. New York: Harper, 1895.

10/6:105. Spurgeon, Caroline F. E. *The Works of Dr. Samuel Johnson.* Quain Essay, University College, London, 1898. London: H. K. Lewis, 1898.

10/6:106. Barker, W. R. *Dr. Johnson as Representative of the Character of the Eighteenth Century.* Chancellor's English Essay Prize, Oxford, 1899. London: Robinson & Co., 1899. Reviewed in *Spectator*, LXXXIII (July 22, 1899), 118.

10/6:107. Dawson, William J. "Johnson's Mission" [making authorship dignified] and "Boswell's Johnson," *The Makers of Modern Prose*, pp. 13–24, 24–38. New York: T. Whittaker, 1899.

10/6:108. Birrell, Augustine. "On Samuel Johnson" [largely a review of item 6:16], *Outlook*, LXIII (November 4, 1899), 542–46.

10/6:109. Seccombe, Thomas. "Samuel Johnson," *The Age of Johnson*, pp. 1–19. London: George Bell & Sons, 1900.

10/6:110. Sharp, Robert F. "Johnson," *Architects of English Literature*, pp. 78–91. New York: E. P. Dutton & Co., 1900.

10/6:111. Birrell, Augustine. "The Transmission of Dr. Johnson's Personality," in item 6:16, pp. 3–16. Extracts in *Critic*, XXXVI (February 1900), 140–47. Also in *Unwin's Chap Book*, 1899–1900, pp. 17–19.

10/6:112. "Memorials of Dr. Johnson" [various recent books], *Church Quarterly Review*, L (July 1900), 355–70.

10/6:113. Wake, Henry T. [The spelling of Johnson's name], *N&Q*, 9th ser., VII (February 2, 1901), 88. See also *ibid.* (March 2), 176; (March 23), 237; (April 13), 295–96.

10/6:114. Birrell, Augustine. "Do We Really Know Dr. Johnson?" [address at Lichfield on opening of Johnson's house as museum], *Outlook*, LXIX (December 7, 1901), 906–15. See also *English Illustrated*, XXVII (April 1902), 47.

10/6:115. Millar, John Hepburn. "Johnson," *The Mid-Eighteenth Century*, pp. 103–8, etc. New York: Charles Scribner's Sons, 1902.

10/6:116. Gosse, Edmund. "Johnson," *English Literature: An Illustrated Record*, III, Pt. II, 328–38. London: Wm. Heinemann, 1903.

10/6:117. Hawthorne, Julian. "The Moral Greatness of Samuel Johnson," *Booklover's Magazine*, I (April 1903), 388–90.

10/6:118. Parrott, Thomas M. "Dr. Johnson's Personality," *Booklover's Magazine*, I (April 1903), 375–84. Reprinted in *Studies of a Booklover*, pp. 132–72, New York: J. Pott, 1904.

10/6:119. Seccombe, Thomas. "Samuel Johnson," *Bookman* (London), XXIV (July 1903), 125–33. The entire number is dedicated to Johnson, and 42 illustrations from the Adam collection are included.

10/6:120. Black, Peter. *Johnson and Boswell: An Appreciation.* Talk before Cavendish Literary Society. Manchester: Sherrat and Hughes, 1904.

10/6:121. Gwynn, Stephen. *The Masters of English Literature,* pp. 231–39. New York: Macmillan, 1904.

10/6:122. Stephen, Leslie. *English Literature and Society in the Eighteenth Century,* Chap. 5. London: Gerald Duckworth & Co., 1904.

10/6:123. Birrell, Augustine. "The Johnsonian Legend," *In the Name of the Bodleian,* pp. 84–90. London: Elliot Stock, 1905.

10/6:124. Seccombe, Thomas, and W. Robertson Nicoll. "Samuel Johnson," *The Bookman Illustrated History of English Literature,* II, 317–22. London: Hodder & Stoughton, 1905–7.

10/6:125. "Samuel Johnson," *Bookman* (London), XXX (May 1906), 55–57.

10/6:126. N., J. A. "Dr. Samuel Johnson. A Birthday Tribute," *Tribune* (London), September 18, 1906, p. 2.

10/6:127. Doyle, A. Conan. [General appreciation of Johnson] in *Through the Magic Door,* pp. 51–68. New York: McClure, 1908, and later reissues. Originally serialized in *Cassell's Magazine,* 1906.

10/6:128. Ramage, Archibald. *An Essay on Dr. Johnson.* Read at the Campden School of Arts and Crafts in February 1906. Campden, Gloucestershire: Essex House Press, 1906.

10/6:129. Shorter, Clement. "To the Immortal Memory of Dr. Samuel Johnson." Lichfield address, 1906. Reprinted in *Immortal Memories,* pp. 3–27, London: Hodder & Stoughton, 1907.

10/6:130. Bailey, John. "Johnson without Boswell" [reviews of Ingpen, White, Raleigh, etc.], *TLS,* August 16, 1907, pp. 249–50. Reprinted in *Poets and Poetry,* pp. 89–98, Oxford: Clarendon Press, 1911.

10/6:131. Raleigh, Walter. *Samuel Johnson.* Leslie Stephen Lecture, Cambridge. Oxford: Clarendon Press, 1907. Reprinted in item 10/6:146.

10/6:132. Hinchman, Walter S., and Francis B. Gummere. "Samuel Johnson," *Lives of Great English Writers,* pp. 210–30. Boston: Houghton Mifflin Co., 1908.

10/6:133. Nicoll, William Robertson. [Address at Lichfield], *British Weekly,* September 24, 1908.

10/6:134. Raleigh, Walter. "Samuel Johnson" [bicentenary first-page article], *TLS,* September 16, 1909, pp. 329–30. Reprinted in item 10/6:146 as "On the Two-Hundredth Anniversary of Johnson's Birth."

10/6:135. Churchill, William. *The Marvellous Year* [men born in 1709]. New York: Huebsch, 1909.

10/6:136. Chesterton, G. K. "The Real Dr. Johnson," *The Common Man*, pp. 118–21. London: Sheed and Ward, 1950. Appeared earlier in *Daily Graphic* (London), 1909; see John Sullivan, *G. K. Chesterton: A Bibliography*, 1958, p. 124.

10/6:137. Rosebery, Archibald Philip Primrose, 5th Earl of. *Dr. Johnson*. Presidential address, Johnson Society, Lichfield. London: Humphreys, 1909. Reviewed in *Saturday Review*, CVIII (September 25, 1909), 375–76; by Lionel A. Tollemache, *Spectator*, CIII (October 9, 1909), 553–54.

10/6:138. Blanchamp, H. [Review of Johnson's work], *Bibliophile*, IV (September 1909), 25–30.

10/6:139. Seccombe, Thomas. "Johnson" [numerous illustrations], *Bookman* (London), XXXVI (September 1909), 249–57.

10/6:140. Scott, H. Spencer. "Dr. Johnson's Literary Work," *Bookman* (London), XXXVI (September 1909), 257–60. See also item 6:28, pp. 159–78.

10/6:141. Trent, William P. "Thoughts Occasioned by the Bi-Centenary of Dr. Johnson," *Nation*, LXXXIX (September 16, 1909), 249–51. Reprinted in *Longfellow and Other Essays*, pp. 109–19, New York: Thomas Y. Crowell Co., 1910.

10/6:142. Seccombe, Thomas. "Dr. Johnson as a Great Englishman," *Graffic*, LXXX, Supplement (September 18, 1909), 1–4.

10/6:143. Warburton, R. "Doctor Samuel Johnson: Essayist, Lexicographer, Clubman," *Journal of Education*, LXX (September 30, 1909), 313–14.

10/6:144. Hodell, Charles W. "Doctor Johnson: The Great Cham of Literature after Two Centuries," *Putnam's Magazine*, VII (October 1909), 33–44.

10/6:145. "The Original Autocrat and His Boswell," *Century Magazine*, LXXVIII (October 1909), 958–59.

*10/6:146. Raleigh, Walter. *Six Essays on Johnson*. Oxford: Clarendon Press, 1910. Reprinted, New York: Russell and Russell, 1965.

10/6:147. Roe, Frederick W. "Boswell and Johnson" [Carlyle's criticism], *Thomas Carlyle as a Critic of Literature*, pp. 121–30. New York: Columbia University Press, 1910.

10/6:148. Matthews, Brander. "The Devil's Advocate" [attack on Johnson the writer and critic], *Century Magazine*, LXXX (July 1910), 339–40. Reprinted in *Gateways to Literature*, pp. 108–12, New York: Charles Scribner's Sons, 1912.

10/6:149. Macdonald, Frederic W. *Recreations of a Book-Lover*. London and New York: Hodder and Stoughton, [1911]. Chap. II, "Dr. Johnson—Personal and Domestic"; Chap. III, "The Religion of Dr. Johnson."

10/6:150. Cross, Alexander. *Dr. Johnson: Lexicographer, Scholar, Man of Letters.* Lecture to Parkhead Literary Club. London: St. Catherine Press, [1911].

10/6:151. Fitch, George Hamlin. "Old Dr. Johnson and His Boswell," *Comfort Found in Good Old Books*, pp. 116–23. San Francisco: Paul Elder, 1911.

10/6:152. "In Memory of Samuel Johnson," *Independent*, LXX (May 4, 1911), 972.

10/6:153. Tyrrell, R. Y. "Samuel Johnson: An Unbiased Appreciation," *Fortnightly Review*, XC (August 1911), 240–46. Reprinted in *Living Age*, CCLXX (September 23, 1911), 783–88.

10/6:154. "Dr. Johnson" [largely a review of items 2:23 and 10/6:150], *Athenaeum*, September 9, 1911, pp. 289–91. Reprinted in *Living Age*, CCLXXI (November 11, 1911), 371–74.

10/6:155. Williamson, A. Wallace. [The basis of Johnson's fame], *South Staffordshire Times*, September 22, 1911, pp. 7–8; also *Lichfield Mercury*. Reprinted; see item 6:22.

10/6:156. Braithwaite, B. *Dr. Johnson and His Times.* Lecture at Epsom Literary and Scientific Society. Epsom: Birch and Whittington, 1912.

10/6:157. Collins, J. Churton. "Samuel Johnson," *Posthumous Essays of John Churton Collins*, ed. L. C. Collins, pp. 26–49. London: J. M. Dent & Sons; New York: E. P. Dutton & Co., 1912.

10/6:158. Lang, Andrew. "Samuel Johnson," *History of English Literature*, pp. 471–74. London: Longmans, Green & Co., 1912.

10/6:159. Adkins, Sir Ryland. [Johnson and the average man], *Lichfield Mercury*, September 20, 1912. Reprinted; see item 6:22.

10/6:160. Bailey, John. *Dr. Johnson and His Circle.* London: Williams & Norgate, 1913. New ed. (Home University Library), with bibliography by L. F. Powell, London: Oxford University Press, 1944. Bailey's deficiencies as an interpreter of Johnson are pointed out by Paul Elmer More in *American Review*, VII (April 1936), 17–19. See also *N&Q*, CLXX (May 2, 1936), 307.

*10/6:161. Smith, D. Nichol. "Johnson and Boswell," *Cambridge History of English Literature*, X, 157–94 (Chap. VIII). Cambridge: Cambridge University Press, 1913. For commentary see *Living Age*, CCLXXX (February 14, 1914), 432–36.

10/6:162. Benson, Arthur C. "Dr. Johnson," *Where No Fear Was*, pp. 106–18. London: Smith, Elder, 1914.

10/6:163. Chubb, Edwin W. "Samuel Johnson," *Masters of English Literature*, pp. 142–62. Chicago: A. C. McClurg & Co., 1914.

10/6:164. Mair, G. H. "Dr. Johnson and His Time," *Modern English Literature*, pp. 172–203. New York: Henry Holt & Co., 1914.

10/6:165. Engel, Eduard. "Samuel Johnson," *Geschichte der englischen Literatur*, pp. 301–3. Leipzig: Brandstetter, 1915.

*10/6:166. Saintsbury, George. "Johnson, Boswell, and Goldsmith," *The Peace of the Augustans*, pp. 177–212. London: George Bell & Sons, 1916. Reprinted in World's Classics, London: Oxford University Press, 1946.

10/6:167. Swinburne, Algernon Charles. *The Character and Opinions of Dr. Johnson* [essay written probably while at Oxford]. Preface by T. J. Wise. London: Eyre and Spottiswoode, 1918.

10/6:168. Chapman, R. W. "Samuel Johnson," *The Portrait of a Scholar and Other Essays*, pp. 65–79. London: Oxford University Press, 1920.

10/6:169. Rogers, Robert William. *Doctor Johnson: His Words and Works: Prospectus of a Lecture*. Madison, N.J.: Privately printed, Omagh Press, [ca. 1920].

10/6:170. Squire, Sir John C. "Dr. Johnson," *Life and Letters*, pp. 90–96. London: Hodder & Stoughton, [1920].

10/6:171. Stewart, H. F. "Samuel Johnson" [in French], *Revue de l'Université de Bruxelles*, XXVI, no. 6 (March 1921), 377–93.

10/6:172. Dobson, Austin. "A Casual Causerie: Johnsoniana," *Later Essays 1917–1920*, pp. 161–62. London: Oxford University Press, 1921.

10/6:173. King, W. H. "Dr. Johnson and His Age," *Bookland*, pp. 147–55. London: George Philip, [1921].

10/6:174. Green, J. Frederick. [The typical Englishman], *Lichfield Mercury*, September 23, 1921. Reprinted; see item 6:22.

10/6:175. Hirn, Yrjö. *Dr. Johnson och James Boswell*. Lund: Gleerup; Helsinki: Holger Schildt, 1922.

10/6:176. Roscoe, Edward Stanley. "Dr. Johnson on the Art of Living," *National Review*, LXXX (December 1922), 598–603. Reprinted in item 10/6:204, pp. 3–15.

10/6:177. Murry, John Middleton. "Dr. Johnson and the Swallows" [some random thoughts about Johnson], *Pencillings*, pp. 168–75. London: William Collins Sons & Co., 1923.

10/6:178. Jones, Edgar De Witt. "How Great Was Dr. Johnson?" *Christian Century*, XL (February 1, 1923), 141–43.

10/6:179. Le Gallienne, Richard. "A Day with Dr. Johnson at the Turk's Head," *Literary Digest International Book Review*, I (July 1923), 25–27, 64.

10/6:180. Harmsworth, Cecil. *Dr. Johnson: A Great Englishman*. Reprinted from *Lichfield Mercury*, September 21, 1923. Again reprinted; see item 6:22.

10/6:181. Tinker, Chauncey B. "King of Letters," *Literary Review of the New York Evening Post*, January 5, 1924, pp. 417–18. Reprinted in *Es-*

says in Retrospect, pp. 23–33, New Haven, Conn.: Yale University Press, 1948.

10/6:182. Gennadius, Joannes. *Dr. Johnson and Homer.* London: Eyre & Spottiswoode, 1924. Johnson Club paper, October 15, 1924; Johnson's indebtedness to and use of Homer in various works.

10/6:183. Pagan, Anna M. *Dr. Johnson and His Circle.* (Rambles in Biography.) London: Blackie & Son, 1925.

10/6:184. Silvester, James. *The Great Cham of Literature* [reproduced from the *Clacton Graphic* of May 9, 1925]. Clacton, 1925.

10/6:185. Lewis, Noël Lawson. *The Second Greatest Man* [next to Shakespeare, Johnson most quoted]. Cleveland: Privately printed for the Cheshire Cheese Club, February 1925.

10/6:186. "Dr. Samuel Johnson," *Anchor Magazine*, V (April 1925), 39–44.

10/6:187. Russell, Sir Charles. "Echoes of Johnson" [his effect on later writers], *Lichfield Mercury*, September 25, 1925. Reprinted; see item 6:22.

10/6:188. Clark, Charles Hopkins. "The Great Doctor Johnson" [unflattering characterization], *North American Review*, CCXXII December 1925–February 1926), 321–30.

10/6:189. McCamic, Charles. "Hours with Doctor Samuel Johnson," *Methodist Review*, CIX (September 1926), 684–701.

10/6:190. Esdaile, Arundell. "Johnson the English Scholar," *Lichfield Mercury*, September 24, 1926. Reprinted; see item 10/6:243; see also item 6:22.

10/6:191. Chapman, Robert William. *Address Delivered at St. Clement Danes on 13 December 1926* [see item 6:32]. London, 1927.

10/6:192. Collins, Arthur Simons. *Authorship in the Days of Johnson.* London: R. Holden, 1927.

10/6:193. Green, Julien. "Samuel Johnson," *Suite anglaise*, pp. 5–40. Paris: Les Cahiers de Paris, 1927.

10/6:194. Hearn, Lafcadio. "Dr. Johnson," *A History of English Literature*, I, 334–46. Tokyo: Hokuseido Press, 1927.

10/6:195. Whibley, Charles. "Samuel Johnson: Man of Letters," *Blackwood's Magazine*, CCXXI (May 1927), 663–72.

10/6:196. Birrell, Augustine. "Links of Empire—Books (IV): 'Dr. Johnson,'" *Empire Review*, XLVI (August 1927), 118–24.

10/6:197. Noyes, Alfred. "Johnson's Literary Dominance," *Lichfield Mercury*, September 23, 1927. Reprinted; see item 6:22.

10/6:198. Lynd, Robert. "Yet Again" [Johnson's good resolutions], *New Statesman*, XXX (December 31, 1927), 376–77.

10/6:199. Elton, Oliver. "Johnson and Boswell," *A Survey of English Literature, 1730–1780*, I, 124–59. London: Edward Arnold & Co., 1928.

10/6:200. Fehr, Bernhard. "Dr. Johnson," *Die englische Literatur von der*

Renaissance bis zur Aufklärung, pp. 269–72. (Akademische Verlagsgesellschaft Athenaion M. B. H., XV.) Wildpark-Potsdam, 1928.

10/6:201. George, Mary Dorothy. *England in Johnson's Day.* London: Methuen & Co., 1928.

10/6:202. Lynd, Robert. *Dr. Johnson and Company.* London: Hodder & Stoughton; New York: Doubleday & Co., 1928; London: Penguin Books, 1946. Reprinted (as separate essays) in *Essays on Life and Literature,* pp. 57–146, London: J. M. Dent; New York: E. P. Dutton, 1951 (Everyman's Library).

10/6:203. Morley, Christopher. "Two Days We Celebrate" [Johnson's birthday and the day he met Boswell], *Essays,* pp. 275–88. New York: Doubleday, Doran & Co., 1928. Reprinted in *Essays Light and Serious,* ed. W. G. Langford, pp. 34–35, Toronto: Longmans (Canada), 1954.

10/6:204. Roscoe, Edward Stanley. *Aspects of Doctor Johnson.* Cambridge: Cambridge University Press, 1928.

10/6:205. Whitman, Walt. [Some general notes on Johnson], *Rivulets of Prose,* ed. Carolyn Wells and Alfred Goldsmith, pp. 224–25. New York: Greenberg, Publisher, 1928.

10/6:206. Gould, Gerald. "A Happy Legend" [attack on Johnson as a writer and as a man], *Saturday Review,* CXLV (January 14, 1928), 32–33. See also his "Seu Jane Libentius Audis" [snobbery], *ibid.* (April 28), 517–18.

10/6:207. Roscoe, Edward Stanley. "Dr. Johnson at Harwich," *Cornhill Magazine,* n.s., LXIV (March 1928), 330–33. Reprinted in item 10/6:204, pp. 115–26.

10/6:208. Buxton, Charles Roden. "Was Dr. Johnson a Great Man?" *Socialist Review,* n.s., XXXV (December 1928), 32–41.

10/6:209. Sampson, George. "Our Johnson," *Bookman* (London), LXXV (December 1928), 162–64.

10/6:210. Groom, Bernard. "Dr. Johnson and His Circle," *A Literary History of England,* pp. 203–19. New York: Longmans, Green & Co., 1929.

10/6:211. Salpeter, Harry. *Dr. Johnson and Mr. Boswell.* New York: Coward-McCann, 1929.

10/6:212. Smith, H. H. "Wit and Wisdom of Dr. Samuel Johnson," *Methodist Quarterly Review,* LXXVIII (January 1929), 87–93.

10/6:213. Jenkins, T. Atkinson. "An Inaccurate Quotation from Dr. Johnson" [by Sir Walter Scott], *PMLA,* XLIV (March 1929), 313.

10/6:214. Roberts, Sydney Castle. "The Focus of the Lichfield Lamps," *Lichfield Mercury,* September 20, 1929. Reprinted; see item 6:22 and 10/6:216.

10/6:215. Heyman, Harald. "Samuel Johnson och James Boswell," in preface to item 4:15 (1930). A 75-page critical essay.

10/6:216. Roberts, Sydney Castle. *An Eighteenth-Century Gentleman and*

Other Essays [four essays concerned with Johnson]. Cambridge: Cambridge University Press, 1930.

10/6:217. Vines, Sherard. *The Course of English Classicism*, pp. 112–16, etc. London: Hogarth Press, 1930.

10/6:218. Noyes, Alfred. "The Originality of Dr. Johnson," *Bookman* (London), LXXVII (March 1930), 323–29.

10/6:219. Gow, A. S. F. "The Unknown Johnson" [little-known aspects of Johnson], *Life and Letters*, VII (September 1931), 200–15.

10/6:220. *Johnson's England*, ed. Arthur Stanley Turberville. Oxford: Clarendon Press, 1933. Reviewed by Harry Hayden Clark, *American Review*, II (February 1934), 504–8; A. Tillotson, *RES*, XI (April 1935), 233–37. See also item 10/6:225.

10/6:221. Struble, Mildred C. *A Johnson Handbook*. New York: Crofts, 1933. Reviewed by A. Tillotson, *RES*, XI (January 1935), 103–4.

10/6:222. Rendall, Vernon. "Johnson and the Unlearned," *London Mercury*, XXVIII (July 1933), 249–55.

10/6:223. MacKinnon, Sir Frank. "Dr. Johnson Once More," *Lichfield Times*, October 7, 1933. Reprinted; see item 6:22. Included also in *The Murder in the Temple*, pp. 178–89, London: Sweet & Maxwell, 1935.

10/6:224. Breyfogle, W. A. "A Note on Johnson," *Canadian Forum*, XIV (July 1934), 394–95. A general appreciation.

10/6:225. Holdsworth, Sir William S. "Johnson's England," *Law Quarterly Review*, L, no. 199 (July 1934), 337–53. Review article based on item 10/6:220.

10/6:226. Osgood, Charles G. *The Voice of England*, pp. 346–54. New York: Harper and Brothers, 1935.

10/6:227. Coleman, William H. "Samuel Johnson after a Century and a Half," *Dalhousie Review*, XIV (January 1935), 479–92.

10/6:228. Smith, Florence A. "The Light Reading of Dr. Johnson" [novels], *University of Toronto Quarterly*, V (October 1935), 118–27.

10/6:229. Thomson, Mark A. "The Age of Johnson" [general review], *History*, XX (December 1935), 221–32.

10/6:230. Williams, Iolo A. *Samuel Johnson*. Address, December 13, 1935; see item 6:32.

10/6:231. Stockley, J. J. G. "Johnson and Life," *Lichfield Mercury*, September 25, 1936. Reprinted; see item 6:22.

10/6:232. Kingsmill, Hugh [H. K. Lunn]. "Samuel Johnson," in *From Anne to Victoria*, ed. Bonamy Dobrée, pp. 216–27. London: Cassell & Co., 1937.

10/6:233. Powys, Llewelyn. "Dr. Johnson—Idler, Rambler, and Straggler," *Dublin Magazine*, XII (April–June 1937), 9–15.

10/6:234. Fox, G. "As Kind as He Was Wise," *St. Nicholas*, LXIV (September 1937), 17–18.

10/6:235. Napier, S. Elliott. "Doctor Johnson: A Literary Anomaly," *Australian National Review*, December 1, 1937, pp. 40–43.

10/6:236. Harmsworth, Cecil. *Dr. Johnson.* Address, December 12, 1937; see item 6:32.

10/6:237. Johnson, Maurice. *Walt Whitman as a Critic of Literature*, pp. 25–26 [Whitman's opinion of Johnson]. University of Nebraska Studies, No. 16 (1938).

10/6:238. Seligo, Irene. "Wunderliche Weisheit: Dr. Johnson," *Zwischen Traum und Tat: Englische Profile*, pp. 164–207. Frankfort on the Main: Societätsverlag, [1938].

10/6:239. Williams, Harold. "Dr. Johnson's Favourite Pursuits" [philosophy and biography], *Nineteenth Century*, CXXIII (May 1938), 616–29.

10/6:240. Chesterton, G. K. "Johnson Is Immortal," *Catholic World*, CXLVII (September 1938), 739–41.

10/6:241. Deane, Anthony. "Johnson in a World of Today," *Lichfield Mercury*, September 23, 1938. Reprinted; see item 6:22.

10/6:242. Watkins, Walter B. C. *Perilous Balance*, pp. 25–98. Princeton, N.J.: Princeton University Press, 1939. Reprinted (paperbound), Cambridge, Mass.: Walker-De Berry, 1960. Reviewed by F. A. Pottle, *MLN*, LVI (May 1941), 394–95.

10/6:243. Esdaile, Arundell. "Aspects of Johnson," *Autolycus' Pack*, pp. 36–73. London: Grafton, 1940.

10/6:244. Kingsmill, Hugh [H. K. Lunn]. *Johnson without Boswell* [a portrait from non-Boswellian sources]. London: Methuen & Co., 1940.

10/6:245. Knox, Ronald A. "Dr. Johnson," in *English Wits*, ed. Leonard Russell, pp. 29–46. London: Hutchinson, 1940. Reprinted in Ronald A. Knox, *Literary Distractions*, pp. 83–96, London: Sheed and Ward, 1958.

10/6:246. Noyes, Alfred. "Johnson," *Pageant of Letters*, pp. 75–99. New York: Sheed & Ward, 1940.

10/6:247. Osgood, Charles G. "Johnson," *Poetry as a Means of Grace*, pp. 106–25. Princeton, N.J.: Princeton University Press, 1941.

10/6:248. Kronenberger, Louis. *Kings and Desperate Men*, pp. 309–13, etc. New York: Alfred A. Knopf, 1942.

10/6:249. MacManus, F. "Dr. Johnson's Elegance," *Irish Monthly*, LXX (March 1942), 100–103.

10/6:250. Maynard, Theodore. "Dr. Johnson as a Writer" [reply to item 9:113], *Commonweal*, XXXVII (October 30, 1942), 34–36.

10/6:251. Bullard, Sir Reader William. *Samuel Johnson: A Public Lecture* (with Persian translation by L. Suratgar). Lecture given at the University of Teheran, November 2, 1943, by the British Ambassador. Teheran: British Council, [1943].

10/6:252. Wood, Paul Spencer. "Introduction to Johnson," *Masters of English Literature*, II, 20–36. New York: Macmillan, 1943.

10/6:253. Tucker, William J. "John Bull as Man of Letters," *Catholic World*, CLVII (June 1943), 264–70.

*10/6:254. Bronson, Bertrand H. "Johnson Agonistes," *Johnson and Boswell: Three Essays*, pp. 363–98. (University of California Publications in English, III, no. 9.) 1944. Reprinted in *Johnson Agonistes & Other Essays*, pp. 1–52, Cambridge: Cambridge University Press, 1946. Reprinted, Cambridge: Cambridge University Press, 1966, with addition of 10/6: 283. Reviewed by C. H. Bennett, *PQ*, XXIV (April 1945), 144–46; R. L. Greene, *MLN*, LX (May 1945), 343–44; *N&Q*, CXC (June 29, 1946), 285; Douglas Hubble, *New Statesman and Nation*, n.s., XXXII (December 28, 1946), 485.

10/6:255. McCutcheon, Roger P. "Johnson and Boswell Today," *Addresses Made before the Friends of the Howard-Tilton Memorial Library of Tulane University*, pp. 16–28. New Orleans, La.: Tulane University, 1944.

10/6:256. Roberts, Sydney Castle. "Samuel Johnson," *Proceedings of the British Academy*, XXX (1944), 51–71. Issued as separate pamphlet, London: Oxford University Press, 1944.

10/6:257. Pyles, Thomas. "The Romantic Side of Dr. Johnson," *ELH*, XI (September 1944), 192–212. See also Arthur Friedman and Louis Landa, *PQ*, XXIV (April 1945), 148–49.

*10/6:258. Chapman, R. W. *Two Centuries of Johnsonian Scholarship*. David Murray Foundation Lecture. Glasgow: Jackson, Son & Co., 1945.

10/6:259. Leavis, Frank Raymond. "Doctor Johnson" [largely a review of item 3:175], *Kenyon Review*, VIII (Autumn 1946), 637–57. Reprinted as "Johnson and Augustanism" in *The Common Pursuit*, pp. 97–115, London: Chatto & Windus; New York: George W. Stewart, 1952.

10/6:260. Starrett, Vincent. "Boswell and Dr. Johnson," *Books and Bipeds*, pp. 200–202. New York: Argus Books, 1947. See also item 6:38, pp. 15–16.

10/6:261. Vulliamy, C. E. "Dr. Johnson," *Penguin Parade*, Second Series, No. 1, ed. J. E. Morpurgo, pp. 53–63. London: Penguin Books, 1947.

10/6:262. "Whale among Fishes," *Scholastic*, XLIX (January 6, 1947), 22.

10/6:263. Gregory, T. S. "Patriarch and Prodigal," *Tablet*, CLXXXIX (January 11, 1947), 23–24.

10/6:264. Haworth, Sir Norman. *The Humanist and the Scientist* [see item 6:23]. Lichfield: The Johnson's Head, 1948.

10/6:265. McKillop, Alan D. "Samuel Johnson," *English Literature from Dryden to Burns*, pp. 323–32. New York: Appleton-Century-Crofts, 1948.

10/6:266. Meynell, Laurence W. *Dr. Johnson the Great Englishman* [see item 6:23]. Lichfield: The Johnson's Head, 1948.

*10/6:267. Radbruch, Gustav. "Dr. Johnson und sein Biograph," *Gestalten* *und Gedanken: Acht Studien*, pp. 50–75. Leipzig: Koehler & Amelang, 1948. Reprinted (with small additions) in *Gestalten und Gedanken: Zehn Studien*, pp. 49–69, 211–12. Stuttgart: K. F. Koehler, 1954.

10/6:268. Roberts, Sydney Castle. "Dr. Johnson and the Fairies," *Tribute to Walter De la Mare on His Seventy-fifth Birthday*, pp. 186–91. London: Faber & Faber, 1948. Johnson and "imagination," fairies, and *The Fountains*.

10/6:269. Sherburn, George. "Dr. Johnson," *A Literary History of England*, ed. A. C. Baugh, pp. 989–1004. New York: Appleton-Century-Crofts, 1948. 2nd ed., rev. by Donald F. Bond, 1967.

10/6:270. Thomson, James Alexander Kerr. *The Classical Background of English Literature*, pp. 207ff. London: George Allen & Unwin, 1948.

10/6:271. Tinker, Chauncey B. "Samuel Johnson: II. The Unaccountable Companion," *Essays in Retrospect*, pp. 33–36. New Haven, Conn.: Yale University Press, 1948.

*10/6:272. Liebert, Herman W. "Reflections on Samuel Johnson: Two Recent Books and Where They Lead" [referring to item 3:131 and 3:177], *JEGP*, XLVII (January 1948), 80–88.

*10/6:273. *The Age of Johnson: Essays Presented to Chauncey Brewster Tinker*, ed. F. W. Hilles. New Haven, Conn.: Yale University Press, 1949. Reprinted, 1964.

10/6:274. Mais, S. P. B. "Dr. Samuel Johnson, 1709–84," *The Best of Their Kind*, pp. 163–78. London: Richards, 1949.

10/6:275. McCutcheon, Roger P. *Eighteenth-Century English Literature*, pp. 73–87. New York: Oxford University Press, 1949.

*10/6:276. Smith, D. Nichol. *Johnsonians and Boswellians* [a plea for reading Johnson's works]. See item 6:23 (1949).

10/6:277. "Clasicos Ingleses: Samuel Johnson," *La Voz de Londres* (Buenos Aires), January 23, 1949, p. 1.

10/6:278. Bredvold, Louis I. "Samuel Johnson," in *A History of English Literature*, ed. Hardin Craig, pp. 418–23. New York: Oxford University Press, 1950.

10/6:279. Butt, John. "Johnson," *The Augustan Age*, pp. 115–34. (Hutchinson's University Library.) London, 1950.

10/6:280. Wilson, Edmund. "Reexamining Dr. Johnson" [review of item 3:175], reprinted in *Classics and Commercials*, pp. 244–49. New York: Farrar, Straus, and Cudahy, 1950; London: Allen, 1951. Reprinted in *A Literary Chronicle, 1920–1950*, pp. 328–30, New York: Doubleday, 1956 (Anchor Books), and in item 10/6:330.

10/6:281. Tracy, Clarence R. "Democritus, Arise! A Study of Johnson's Humour," *Yale Review*, XXXIX (Winter 1950), 294–310.

10/6:282. Lascelles, Mary. "A Physician in a Great City" [Johnson], in item 6:23 (1951–52), pp. 25–35.

*10/6:283. Bronson, Bertrand H. "The Double Tradition of Dr. Johnson," *ELH*, XVIII (June 1951), 90–106. Reprinted in *Eighteenth-Century English Literature: Modern Essays in Criticism*, ed. J. L. Clifford, pp. 285–99, New York: Oxford University Press, 1959 (Galaxy Books). Reprinted with item 10/6:254 in 1966.

10/6:284. S[ieburg], F[riedrich]. "Der Dr. Johnson" [partly a notice of item 4:21, ed. Güttinger], *Die Gegenwart* (Frankfort on the Main), VII, no. 12 (1952), 373–74.

10/6:285. Sherbo, Arthur. "George III, Franklin, and Dr. Johnson" [quotations from Shakespeare used by the King to characterize Franklin and Johnson], *N&Q*, January 19, 1952, pp. 37–38.

10/6:286. De Beer, E. S. "Macaulay on Croker, Boswell, and Johnson," *New Rambler*, July 1952, p. 5.

10/6:287. Chapman, R. W. *Johnsonian and Other Essays and Reviews*. Oxford: Clarendon Press, 1953. Reprints numerous essays listed separately.

10/6:288. De Selincourt, Aubrey. "Dr. Johnson," *Six Great Englishmen*, pp. 43–72. London: Hamish Hamilton, 1953.

10/6:289. Humphreys, Arthur R. *The Augustan World: Life and Letters in Eighteenth-Century England, passim.* London: Methuen, 1954.

10/6:290. Meynell, Laurence. [Johnson and "true civility"] in item 6:23, December 1954, pp. 15–23.

*10/6:291. Bate, Walter Jackson. *The Achievement of Samuel Johnson.* New York: Oxford University Press, 1955. Reviewed by E. R. Marks, *Kenyon Review*, XVIII (Spring 1956), 311–18; Arthur Sherbo, *JEGP*, LV (April 1956), 326–28; Gwin J. Kolb, *PQ*, XXXV (July 1956), 302–4; J. H. Hagstrum, *MP*, LIV (August 1956), 66–69; in *TLS*, March 16, 1957, p. 162; by Ian Watt, *MLN*, LXXII (November 1957), 546–49; J. C. Bryce, *RES*, n.s., IX (May 1958), 217–19.

10/6:292. Joyce, Michael. *Samuel Johnson.* (Men and Books Series.) London: Longmans, Green, 1955.

10/6:293. Kronenberger, Louis. "Johnson and Boswell," *The Republic of Letters*, pp. 89–123. New York: Knopf, 1955. See item 2:29.

10/6:294. *Modern English Literature: Essays Presented to Professor Rintarô Fukuhara on His Sixtieth Birthday* [in Japanese]. Tokyo: Kenkyusha, 1955. Contains eleven essays on various aspects of Johnson.

10/6:295. "Salute to Sam," *Life*, XXXVIII (May 3, 1955), 165–66.

10/6:296. Hubble, Douglas V. "Samuel Johnson in Friendship," in item 6:23, December 1956, pp. 21–31.

10/6:297. Humphreys, A. R. "Johnson," in *The Pelican Guide to English Literature*, ed. Boris Ford, Vol. IV, pp. 399–419. Penguin Books, 1957.

10/6:298. Lascelles, Mary. "Johnson's Last Allusion to Mary, Queen of Scots" [in *Letters* No. 972; other references by Johnson to Mary], *RES*, n.s., VIII (February 1957), 32–37.

10/6:299. Moore, J. R. "An Early Allusion to Samuel Johnson?" [as "the pretty ingenious gentleman at St. John's Gate" in *A Dialogue in the Shades*, 1745], *JNL*, XVII, no. 2 (July 1957), 8–9.

10/6:300. Lucas, F. L. *The Search for Good Sense*, pp. 27–128. London: Cassell; New York: Macmillan, 1958. Reviewed by Paul Fussell, Jr., *PQ*, XXXVIII (July 1959), 292.

10/6:301. Mullik, B. R. *Johnson*. (Studies in Prose Writers, Vol. V.) Delhi: S. Chand & Co., 1958; 2nd ed., 1963.

10/6:302. Roberts, S. C. *Dr. Johnson and Others*. Cambridge: Cambridge University Press, 1958.

10/6:303. Tucker, Susie I. "Dr. Johnson, Mediaevalist," *N&Q*, January 1958, pp. 20–24.

10/6:304. Clifford, James L. "Johnson's Works in Our Day," in item 6:23, December 1958, pp. 37–49.

10/6:305. Jones, Howard. "Doctor Johnson," *Men of Letters*, pp. 1–28. London: G. Bell and Sons, 1959. Written for BBC Children's Hour.

*10/6:306. *New Light on Dr. Johnson: Essays on the Occasion of His 250th Birthday*, ed. Frederick W. Hilles. New Haven, Conn.: Yale University Press, 1959. (Individual items are separately listed.) Reviewed by Sir Harold Nicolson, *Observer*, March 6, 1960; in *TLS*, May 20, 1960, p. 324; by Ian Jack, *PQ*, XXXIX (July 1960), 333–35; Jacques Chauvin, *Études Anglaises*, XIII (July–September 1960), 379–80.

10/6:307. Untermeyer, Louis. "The Decline of Elegance: Samuel Johnson," *The Lives of the Poets*, pp. 258–63. New York: Simon and Schuster, 1959.

10/6:308. Watt, Ian. "Dr. Samuel Johnson after 250 Years," *The Listener*, September 24, 1959, pp. 476–79. Reprinted as "Dr. Johnson and the Literature of Experience" in item 10/6:316, pp. 15–22.

10/6:309. Matthews, Roger G. "Homage to Samuel Johnson," *The Rising Generation* (Tokyo), CV, no. 10 (October 1, 1959), 530–34.

10/6:310. Chamberlin, William Henry. "Immortal Sam," *National Review* (New York), December 5, 1959, pp. 528–30.

10/6:311. Haley, Sir William. "The 250th Anniversary of the Birth of Dr. Johnson," in item 6:23, December 1959, pp. 54–61.

10/6:312. Powell, L. F. "A Friend of Johnson: Dr. Birkbeck Hill," *New Rambler*, January 1960, pp. 4–10.

10/6:313. McCutcheon, Roger P. "Samuel Johnson: 1709–1959," *Tennessee Studies in Literature*, VI (1961), 109–17.

10/6:314. Wright, W. G. "Dr. Samuel Johnson—the Man," in item 6:23, December 1961, pp. 14–29.

10/6:315. Strauss, Albrecht B. "English and American Celebrations of Dr. Samuel Johnson's 250th Birthday," *Books Abroad*, XXXV (Winter 1961), 23–26.

*10/6:316. *Johnsonian Studies*, ed. Magdi Wahba. Cairo, U.A.R.: Privately printed, 1962 (distributed outside U.A.R. by Oxford University Press). Individual items are separately listed.

10/6:317. Hart, Jeffrey. "Some Thoughts on Johnson as Hero," in item 10/6:316 (1962), pp. 23–36.

10/6:318. Pearson, Hesketh. "Samuel Johnson," *Lives of the Wits*, pp. 52–69. London: Heinemann, 1962.

10/6:319. Bredvold, Louis I. "Dr. Johnson for Our Time," *Ball State Teachers College Forum*, III (Spring 1962), 13–19.

10/6:320. Wain, John. "Samuel Johnson," *Essays on Literature and Ideas*, pp. 171–76. London: Macmillan, 1963.

10/6:321. Adams, J. Donald. "Speaking of Books" [revival of interest in Johnson], *New York Times Book Review*, October 6, 1963, p. 2.

10/6:322. Jefferson, D. W. "Speculations on Three Eighteenth-Century Prose Writers" [Smollett, Goldsmith, and Johnson], in *Of Books and Humankind: Essays and Poems Presented to Bonamy Dobrée*, pp. 81–91. London: Routledge and Kegan Paul, 1964.

10/6:323. Keirce, William F. "The Place of Samuel Johnson in the History of the Literary Character" (dissertation, Duke University, 1964), *Dissertation Abstracts*, XXVII (August 1966), 457–58A. Johnson used the older "character" tradition in *The Rambler* and other works.

10/6:324. Tibbetts, Arnold M. "The Satire of Samuel Johnson" [in various works] (dissertation, Vanderbilt University, 1964), *Dissertation Abstracts*, XXV (October 1964), 2523.

10/6:325. Kazin, Alfred. "The Imagination of a Man of Letters" [Johnson as an example], *American Scholar*, XXXIV (Winter 1964–65), 19–27.

10/6:326. Brown, Ivor. *Dr. Johnson and His World*. With numerous illustrations. London: Lutterworth Press, 1965.

10/6:327. Fussell, Paul. *The Rhetorical World of Augustan Humanism*. Oxford: Clarendon Press, 1965. *Passim*.

10/6:328. Greene, Donald J. " 'Pictures to the Mind': Johnson and Imagery" in item 10/6:329 (1965), pp. 137–58.

*10/6:329. *Johnson, Boswell and Their Circle: Essays Presented to Lawrence Fitzroy Powell in Honour of His Eighty-Fourth Birthday*, ed. Mary M. Lascelles, James L. Clifford, J. D. Fleeman, and John P. Hardy. Oxford: Clarendon Press, 1965. Reviewed by Arthur Sherbo, *RES*, n.s., XVIII (February 1967), 80–81; by J. T. Boulton, *N&Q*, May 1967, pp. 196–97.

*10/6:330. *Samuel Johnson: A Collection of Critical Essays*, ed. with introduction by Donald J. Greene. (Twentieth Century Views.) Englewood Cliffs, N.J.: Prentice-Hall, 1965.

10/6:331. Akiyama, Hajime. "The Romantic Elements in Dr. Johnson" [in Japanese], *Studies in English Literature* (Tokyo), XLI (March 1965), 145–64. Synopsis in English, pp. 289–90.

10/6:332. Clifford, James L. "The Eighteenth Century" [new approaches to Johnson], *MLQ*, XXVI (March 1965), 130–34.

*10/6:333. Currie, H. MacL. "Johnson and the Classics," *New Rambler*, June 1965, pp. 13–27.

10/6:334. Birch, Nigel. Presidential address, Johnson Society, Lichfield, in item 6:23 (1966), pp. 30–34.

10/6:335. "Footprints of a Gigantic Cham" [full page review of various recent Johnsonian books], *TLS*, February 24, 1966, p. 141.

10/6:336. Halliday, F. E. *Doctor Johnson and His World*. London: Thames and Hudson, 1967. Written primarily for young people. Profusely illustrated.

10/6:337. Metzdorf, Robert F. "Samuel Johnson," *Four Oaks Library*, ed. Gabriel Austin, pp. 3–10. Somerville, N.J.: Privately printed, 1967.

10/6:338. Wiles, Roy M. "*Felix qui* . . . Standards of Happiness in Eighteenth-Century England," *Studies on Voltaire and the Eighteenth Century*, LVIII (1967), 1857–67. Largely about Johnson—*Rasselas, Theodore, Adventurer*, etc.

10/6:339. Wiltshire, John. "Dr. Johnson's Seriousness," *Critical Review* (Melbourne/Sydney), No. 10 (1967), 63–73.

10/6:340. Brinitzer, Carl. *Dr. Johnson und Boswell*. Mainz: Florian Kupferberg Verlag, 1968. Reviewed in *Der Spiegel*, January 20, 1969, pp. 95–96.

10/6:341. Ketton-Cremer, R. W. "Johnson and the Antiquarian World," *New Rambler*, January 1968, pp. 5–11.

10/6:342. Hartley, Lodwick. "A Late Augustan Circus: Macaulay on Johnson, Boswell, and Walpole," *South Atlantic Quarterly*, LXVII (Summer 1968), 513–26.

10/6:343. Fukuhara, Rintarô. *The Great Dr. Johnson* [in Japanese]. Vol. II of *The Collected Works of Rintarô Fukuhara*. Tokyo: Kenkyusha (expected in 1970). Previously appeared in the journal *Gakutô*, September 1966–September 1968.

10/6:344. Grant, Douglas. "Johnson, the Sage," in item 6:23, December 1968, pp. 33–42.

10/6:345. Jones, J. Clement. "Dr. Johnson—Mass Communicator," in item 6:23 (1969), pp. 19–29.

10/6:346. Greene, Donald. *Samuel Johnson*. (Twayne's English Authors Series.) New York: Twayne (expected 1970).

11. JOHNSON'S VIEWS AND ATTITUDES ON VARIOUS SUBJECTS

11/1. THE ARTS

11/1:1. Martin. "Remarks on Dr. Johnson's Conversation with Boswell, Respecting Players," *Monthly Mirror*, n.s., V (June 1809), 364–65. Answered by "Carlos," *ibid.*, n.s., VI (September 1809), 160–62.

11/1:2. "Dr. Johnson on the Theory of Arches," *Architect*, January 7, 1887, pp. 13ff.

11/1:3. Sargeaunt, John. *Johnson and Music*. Johnson Club paper, March 14, 1892. Privately printed. Reprinted in item 6:16, pp. 173–89.

11/1:4. "Dr. Johnson and Art," *Architect and Contract Reporter*, July 21, 1899, pp. 34–35.

11/1:5. Maslen, B. J. "Celebrities and Music. I. Dr. Johnson," *Musical Opinion*, LIV (July 1931), 862.

11/1:6. White, Eric. "Dr. Johnson and Opera," *TLS*, March 28, 1958, p. 169.

11/2. EDUCATION AND THE YOUNG

11/2:1. [Johnson's "Scheme for the Classes of a Grammar School"], *GM*, LV (March 1785), 266.

11/2:2. Humberstone, T. L. "Dr. Johnson as Educationist," *Journal of Education*, LVI (January 1924), 31–32.

11/2:3. Hornberger, Theodore. "A Note on the Probable Source of Provost Smith's Famous Curriculum for the College of Philadelphia" [*The Preceptor*], *Pennsylvania Magazine of History and Biography*, LVIII (October 1934), 370–77.

11/2:4. Boas, Guy. "Dr. Johnson on Schools and Schoolmasters," *Lichfield Mercury*, September 24, 1937. Reprinted; see item 6:22 and *English* I, no. 6 (Autumn 1937), 537–49.

11/2:5. Esdaile, Arundell. "Dr. Johnson and the Young," *English*, IV (Spring 1943), 110–16.

11/2:6. Bonin, Sister Hélène du Sacré-Coeur. "Samuel Johnson's Theories of Education" (dissertation, Fordham University, 1962), *Dissertation Abstracts*, XXIII (March 1963), 3349–50.

11/2:7. Conrad, Lawrence H., Jr. "Samuel Johnson on Education," *Ball State University Forum*, VIII, no. 2 (1967), 20–26.

11/3. LAW

11/3:1. "Considerations [by the late Dr. Samuel Johnson] on the Case of Dr. T[rapp]'s Sermons," *GM*, LVII (July 1787), 555–57. Written in 1739. MS now in Hyde collection.

11/3:2. "Dr. Johnson on Literary Copyright," *Bookman* (London), XII (May 1897), 31–32. See also *Critic*, XXV (November 10, 1894), 314, and item 11/3:15.

11/3:3. "Samuel Johnson on Law and the Lawyers," *Green Bag*, IX (September 1897), 403–8.

11/3:4. Spokes, Arthur H. "Dr. Johnson's Associations with the Law, the Lawyers, and Legal Haunts," in item 6:16, pp. 203–15.

11/3:5. "Dr. Johnson on Law and Lawyers," *Green Bag*, XII (October 1900), 501–3.

11/3:6. Roscoe, Edward Stanley. "Johnson and the Law," in item 6:28, pp. 125 36. Another version in item 10/6:204, pp. 16–31.

11/3:7. "Dr. Johnson on Copyright," *Living Age*, CCCXXXVII (December 1, 1929), 419.

11/3:8. Roscoe, Edward Stanley. *Dr. Johnson and the Administration of Justice*. London: Privately printed, 1931.

11/3:9. Sinn, Ephraim E. "Johnson, Jurisconsult" [his ideas on the law], *Case and Comment*, XLIV (January 1939), 5–10. Condensed from *Bulletin of the New Haven Bar Association*, May 1934.

*11/3:10. McAdam, Edward L., Jr. "Dr. Johnson's Law Lectures for Chambers: An Addition to the Canon," *RES*, XV (October 1939), 385–91; XVI (April 1940), 159–68. See also items 11/3:17 and 11/3:18.

11/3:11. Gray, W. Forbes. "The Douglas Cause: An Unpublished Correspondence" [Andrew Stuart's, concerning his *Letters to Lord Mansfield*, 1773; see *Life*, April 27, 1773], *Quarterly Review*, CCLXXVI (January 1941), 69–80.

11/3:12. McNair, Sir Arnold D. "Dr. Johnson and the Law," *Law Quarterly Review*, LXIII (July 1947), 302–22.

11/3:13. McNair, Sir Arnold D. *Dr. Johnson and the Law*. Cambridge: Cambridge University Press, 1948. Reviewed by Donald F. Hyde, *PQ*, XXIX (July 1950), 282–83; E. L. McAdam, Jr., *MLN*, LXVI (January 1951), 64–66.

*11/3:14. Radzinowicz, Leon. *A History of English Criminal Law and Its Administration from 1750: The Movement for Reform, 1750–1833*. London: Stevens; New York: Macmillan, 1948. Chap. 10, "The Reformers (1)," Sec. 3, "Some Expressions of Doubt as to the Merits of the Penal System: Dr. Johnson," pp. 336–39 (his *Rambler* and *Idler* essays on the subject). Chap. 14, "Growth of Public Uneasiness: The Case of Dr. Dodd," pp. 450–72 (a careful account of Johnson's part in it).

*11/3:15. Bloom, Edward A. "Samuel Johnson on Copyright," *JEGP*, XLVII (April 1948), 165–72.

11/3:16. McNair, Sir Arnold D. *Dr. Johnson and the Law* [see item 6:23]. Lichfield: The Johnson's Head, 1949.

11/3:17. Krishnamurti, S. "Dr. Johnson and the Law Lectures of Sir Robert Chambers," *MLR*, XLIV (April 1949), 236–38. See also item 11/3: 10.

*11/3:18. McAdam, E. L., Jr. *Dr. Johnson and the English Law*. Syracuse, N.Y.: Syracuse University Press, 1951. Reviewed by Lester E. Denonn, *American Bar Association Journal*, XXXVIII (April 1952), 305; Gwin J. Kolb, *PQ*, XXXI (July 1952), 279–80; George D. Hornstein, *Columbia Law Review*, LIII (January 1953), 136–38.

11/3:19. Michot, Paulette. "Doctor Johnson on Copyright," *Revue des langues vivantes* (Brussels), XXIII (1957), 137–47.

11/3:20. Hanbury, Harold G. *The Vinerian Chair in Legal Education*, pp. 52–56. Oxford: Blackwell, 1958. Johnson and Sir Robert Chambers; does not make use of E. L. McAdam—item 11/3:18.

11/3:21. Addison, William. "Dr. Johnson on Crime and Punishment," *New Rambler*, June 1962, pp. 10–18.

11/3:22. Howard, William J. "Dr. Johnson on Abridgment—a Re-examination," *PBSA*, LX (2nd quarter, 1966), 215–19. Johnson merely argues for the *status quo*.

11/4. THE OCCULT

11/4:1. Pyle, Howard. "The Cock Lane Ghost," *Harper's Magazine*, LXXXVII (August 1893), 327–38.

11/4:2. Lang, Andrew. "Cock Lane and Common-Sense," *Cock Lane and Common-Sense*, pp. 161–79. London: Longmans, Green & Co., 1894.

11/4:3. Barrett, Frederick. "Samuel Johnson and the Occult," *Occult Review*, XXIV (December 1916), 347–53.

11/4:4. Prince, Walter F. "Samuel Johnson as a Psychic Researcher," *Journal of the American Society for Psychical Research*, XI (December 1917), 701–19.

11/4:5. Clodd, Edward. "Dr. Johnson and Second Sight," *Cornhill Magazine*, n.s., XLVIII (June 1920), 758–68.

11/4:6. Beatty, Joseph M., Jr. "Doctor Johnson and the Occult" [his intelligent questioning in the Cock Lane Ghost investigation], *South Atlantic Quarterly*, XXI (April 1922), 144–51.

11/4:7. R., L. A. "Johnson as Superstitious," *N&Q*, CLXVIII (January 12, 1935), 25.

11/4:8. Hall, Trevor H. "The Cock Lane Ghost: A Historical Note," *International Journal of Parapsychology*, IV (Winter 1962), 71–87.

*11/4:9. Grant, Douglas. *The Cock Lane Ghost*, pp. 58–80 and *passim*. London: Macmillan; New York: St. Martin's Press, 1965.

11/5. PLACES

11/5:1. Plain, Henry. [Johnson as enemy of Scotland], *Weekly Magazine* [Edinburgh], XV (January 9, 1772), 40–43.

11/5:2. "Dr. Johnson from a Scottish View," *All the Year Round*, 2nd ser., III (May 14, 1870), 561–65.

11/5:3. "Dr. Johnson on Ireland," *Westminster Review*, CXXIX (January 1888), 12–21.

11/5:4. Kelly, R. J. "Dr. Johnson and Ireland," *Irish Review*, I (July 1911), 234–42.

11/5:5. Griffiths, John L. "Dr. Johnson and America," *Lichfield Mercury*, September 10, 1913. Reprinted; see item 6:22.

11/5:6. O'Connor, John. "Dr. Johnson and Ireland," in item 6:28, pp. 87–99.

11/5:7. McCamic, Charles. *Doctor Samuel Johnson and the American Colonies*. Cleveland: Rowfant Club, 1925.

11/5:8. Harvey, Charles W. "Johnson's Hatred of America," *Cornhill Magazine*, n.s., LXVII (December 1929), 655–68.

11/5:9. Fan Tsen-Chung. *Dr. Johnson and Chinese Culture*. (China Society Occasional Papers, n.s., No. 6.) London: Luzac and Co., 1945. See also *N&Q*, CLXXXIX (August 11, 1945), 45.

11/5:10. Krishnamurti, S. "Dr. Johnson and India," *Journal of the University of Bombay*, XVII (September 1948), 65–71.

11/5:11. Brunner, Karl. "Did Dr. Johnson Hate Scotland and the Scottish?" *English Studies*, XXX (October 1949), 184–90.

11/5:12. Atkinson, A. D. "Dr. Johnson and Sweden," *English*, VIII (Spring 1951), 184–88.

11/5:13. Clifford, James L. "Johnson and the Americans," *New Rambler*, January 1959, pp. 13–18.

11/5:14. Dircks, Richard J. "Johnson's Knowledge of Ireland," *N&Q*, May 1967, pp. 172–76.

11/5:15. Brown, Terence. "America and Americans as Seen in James Boswell's *The Life of Samuel Johnson, LL.D.*, and in the Letters of Johnson and Boswell," *New Rambler*, January 1969, pp. 44–51.

11/6. SCIENCE

11/6:1. Broadley, A. M. "The Soaring Curiosity of Samuel Johnson" [his interest in ballooning], *Living Age*, CCLXV (April 23, 1910), 244–47.

11/6:2. Thorpe, W. H. "Dr. Johnson on Aeronautics," *Scientific American Supplement*, LXXXV (February 16, 1918), 99.

11/6:3. Hodgson, J. E. "Dr. Johnson on Ballooning and Flight," *London Mercury*, X (May 1924), 63–72. Reprinted, London: Elkin Mathews, 1925.

11/6:4. Brown, John J. "Samuel Johnson and Eighteenth-Century Science." Dissertation, Yale University, 1943.

11/6:5. Brown, John J. "Samuel Johnson 'Making Aether,'" *MLN*, LIX (April 1944), 286.

11/6:6. Brain, W. Russell. "Doctor Johnson on Science," *London Hospital Gazette*, February 1947, 14–20.

11/6:7. Swaine, D. J. "Samuel Johnson's Interest in Scientific Affairs," *Journal of Chemical Education*, XXIV (August 1948), 458–59.

11/6:8. Atkinson, A. D. "Dr. Johnson and Science," *N&Q*, CXCV (August 5, 1950), 338–41; (November 25), 516–19; (December 9), 541–44; (December 23), 561–63. Chiefly a list of scientists quoted in the *Dictionary*.

11/6:9. Van Liere, Edward J. "Doctor Johnson and the Weather," *Philological Papers: University of West Virginia*, Series 52, no. 4-1 (October 1951), 40–48.

11/6:10. Spector, Robert D. "Dr. Johnson's Swallows" [who hibernate under water; contemporary theories about them], *N&Q*, December 22, 1951, pp. 564–65.

11/6:11. Atkinson, A. D. "Dr. Johnson and the Royal Society," *Notes and Records of the Royal Society of London*, X (April 1953), 131–38.

11/6:12. Lawrence, R. G. "Dr. Johnson and the Art of Flying," *N&Q*, August 1957, pp. 348–51.

11/6:13. Pettit, Henry. "Dr. Johnson and the Cheerful Robots" [attitude toward science], *Western Humanities Review*, XIV (Autumn 1960), 381–88.

11/6:14. Mitchell, Stephen O. "Dr. Johnson's Philosophy of Science." Dissertation, Indiana University, 1961.

11/6:15. Cooper, Peter. "An Unlikely Chemist: Samuel Johnson," *Pharmacological Journal*, CXC (May 25, 1963), 482.

11/6:16. Schwartz, Richard Brenton. "Samuel Johnson's Attitudes Toward Science" (dissertation, University of Illinois, 1967), *Dissertation Abstracts*, XXVIII, no. 8 (February 1968), 3156A.

11/7. SPORT AND THE OUTDOORS

11/7:1. Pierpoint, Robert. "Dr. Johnson in the Hunting Field," *N&Q*, 11th ser., III (January 21, 1911), 52.

11/7:2. "Dr. Johnson on Fishing," *N&Q*, 12th ser., I (January 1, January 29, February 19, 1916), 18, 98, 157.

11/7:3. Roscoe, Edward Stanley. "Dr. Johnson in the Country," *National Review*, XC (January 1928), 729–35. Reprinted in item 10/6:204, pp. 127–43.

11/7:4. Rendall, Vernon. "Dr. Johnson on Flowers," *New Statesman*, XXXIII (July 6, 1929), 403–5.

11/7:5. "Dr. Johnson and Nature: English Poets in the Highlands," *TLS*, August 15, 1936, pp. 653–54.

11/7:6. Baker, Carlos. "The Cham on Horseback" [his appreciation of natural scenery], *Virginia Quarterly Review*, XXVI (Winter 1950), 76–90.

11/7:7. Ketton-Cremer, R. W. "Johnson and the Countryside," in item 10/6:329 (1965), pp. 65–75. See also item 6:23 (December 1961), pp. 33–41.

11/8. WOMEN AND MARRIAGE

11/8:1. Craig, W. H. *Dr. Johnson and the Fair Sex*. London: Sampson Low, Marston & Co., 1895.

11/8:2. Valbert, G. "Le docteur Samuel Johnson et les femmes," *Revue des Deux Mondes*, 4th ser., CXXXIV (March 1896), 205–16. Begins as review of item 11/8:1.

11/8:3. Hardy, Edward J. "Dr. Johnson and the Ladies" and "Johnson and Boswell as Husbands," *Love Affairs of Some Famous Men*, pp. 79–85 and 86–94. London: Fisher Unwin, 1897.

11/8:4. Molyneux, C. C. "Dr. Johnson as Lover and Husband," *Temple Bar*, CXX (August 1900), 532–37.

11/8:5. Reed, Myrtle (Mrs. James McCullough). "Samuel Johnson," *Love Affairs of Literary Men*, pp. 45–62. New York: G. P. Putnam's Sons, 1907.

11/8:6. Biron, Sir Chartres. "Dr. Johnson and Women," *Fortnightly Review*, n.s., CVI (August 1919), 308–20. Reprinted in *Pious Opinions*, pp. 96–115, London: Gerald Duckworth & Co., 1923.

11/8:7. Bell, Walter George. "Dr. Johnson's Womankind," *More About Unknown London*, pp. 174–88. London: John Lane, 1921.

11/8:8. Biron, Sir Chartres. [Dr. Johnson and women], *Lichfield Mercury*, September 22, 1922. Reprinted; see item 6:22.

11/8:9. McQuilland, Louis J. "Doctor Johnson as a Squire of Dames: The Great Samuel in Gallant Mood," *Book Notes* (Hartford, Conn.), II (June–July 1924), 162–64.

11/8:10. Emden, Cecil S. "Dr. Johnson's Attitude to Women," *Quarterly Review*, CCCIV (October 1966), 419–30.

11/9. JOHNSON'S THOUGHT

General intellectual history, including studies of his moral, psychological, and philosophical views. See also studies of specific works and, for religious views, Section 24.

11/9:1. Stephen, Leslie. *A History of English Thought in the Eighteenth*

Century. 2 vols. London: Smith, Elder, 1876. Often reprinted. Johnson is dealt with in Sec. X, "The Tories," pars. 80–82; Sec. XII, "General Literature," pars. 50–53; and *passim*.

*11/9:2. Courthope, William John. "Johnson and Carlyle: Common Sense versus Transcendentalism," *National Review*, II (November 1883), 317–32. A conservative interpretation of Johnson's thought and morality, attacking item 11/9:1.

11/9:3. Brownfield, Lilian B. *A Study in the Thought of Addison, Johnson and Burke*. Thesis, Indiana University, 1914. Privately printed, 1918.

11/9:4. Baumann, Arthur A. "The Cynicism of Dr. Johnson," *Fortnightly Review*, n.s., XCIX (January 1916), 134–40. Reprinted in *Living Age*, CCLXXXVIII (March 4, 1916), 609–14. See also *Nation* (London), XVIII (January 8, 1916), 537–38.

11/9:5. Houston, Percy H. *Doctor Johnson: A Study in Eighteenth Century Humanism*. Cambridge, Mass.: Harvard University Press, 1923. Reviewed by J. W. Tupper, *MLN*, XXXIX (March 1924), 191–92; Robert P. Utter, *University of California Chronicle*, XXVI (April 1924), 232–34; Bernhard Fehr, *Beiblatt zur Anglia*, XXXVI (January 1925), 9–12; Caroline F. Tupper, *JEGP*, XXIV (April 1925), 291–95.

11/9:6. Alexander, Samuel. "Dr. Johnson as a Philosopher," *Cornhill Magazine*, n.s., LV (October, November 1923), 385–92, 513–22. Reprinted in *Philosophical and Literary Pieces*, pp. 116–37, London: Macmillan, 1939.

11/9:7. Seeger, Oskar. "Die Auseinandersetzung Zwischen Antike und Moderne in England bis zum Tode Dr. S. Johnsons." Dissertation, Berlin-Humboldt University, 1927.

11/9:8. J., W. H. "Memory and Old Age" [Johnson on failing memory], *N&Q*, CLXVI (February 10, 1934), 103.

11/9:9. Charnwood, Lord (G. R. Benson). "Johnson What a Philosopher Should Be," *Lichfield Mercury*, September 28, 1934. Reprinted; see item 6:22.

11/9:10. Mays, Morley J. "Samuel Johnson: An Eighteenth Century Moralist" [abstract of thesis], *University of Pittsburgh Bulletin*, XXXIII (October 1936), 343–44.

*11/9:11. Brown, Stuart Gerry. "Dr. Johnson and the Old Order" [largely a discussion of the Soame Jenyns review, etc.], *Marxist Quarterly*, I (October–December 1937), 418–30. Reprinted in item 10/6:330 (1965).

11/9:12. Willey, Basil. "Soame Jenyns and Dr. Johnson," *The Eighteenth Century Background*, pp. 48–56. London: Chatto & Windus, 1940; New York: Columbia University Press, 1941.

11/9:13. Allodoli, Ettore. "Poliziano e Johnson" [and Johnson on some other Renaissance figures], *La Rinascita* (Florence), V (September 1942), 459–71.

11/9:14. W[ind], E[dgar]. " 'Milking the Bull and the He-Goat' " [Johnson's figure in the remark about Hume and skeptics], *Journal of the Warburg and Courtauld Institutes*, VI (1943), 225.

11/9:15. Keyl, Frieda. "Samuel Johnson und die Antike." Dissertation, University of Erlangen, 1945.

11/9:16. Hazard, Paul. *La pensée Européenne au XVIIIème stècle*, I, 301–6, etc. Paris: Boivin, 1946.

*11/9:17. Hallett, H. F. "Dr. Johnson's Refutation of Bishop Berkeley," *Mind*, LVI (April 1947), 132–47. Defends Johnson's position.

11/9:18. Davies, Godfrey. "Dr. Johnson on History," *Huntington Library Quarterly*, XII (November 1948), 1–21.

11/9:19. Leyburn, Ellen D. "Bishop Berkeley: Metaphysician as Moralist" [considers Johnson in relation to Berkeley], in item 10/6:273, pp. 319–28.

11/9:20. Moore, John Robert. "Dr. Johnson and Roman History," *Huntington Library Quarterly*, XII (May 1949), 311–14.

11/9:21. Hagstrum, Jean H. "The Nature of Dr. Johnson's Rationalism," *ELH*, XVII (September 1950), 191–205. Reprinted in *Studies in the Literature of the Augustan Age: Essays Collected in Honor of Arthur Ellicott Case*, ed. R. C. Boys, pp. 88–103. Ann Arbor, Mich.: George Wahr Publishing Co., 1952.

11/9:22. Keast, W. R. "Johnson and Intellectual History," in item 10/6:306 (1959).

11/9:23. Chapin, Chester F. "Dr. Johnson's Approval of a Passage in Rousseau," *N&Q*, November 1959, pp. 413–14.

11/9:24. Grange, Kathleen Mary. "Dr. Johnson and the Passions." Dissertation, University of California at Los Angeles, 1960.

11/9:25. Kaul, R. K. "Dr. Johnson and the Doctrine of Nature." Ph.D. thesis, Birkbeck College, University of London, 1961.

11/9:26. Lovejoy, Arthur O. *Reflections on Human Nature*, pp. 137–38. Baltimore, Md.: Johns Hopkins Press, 1961. Johnson on pride and love of praise.

11/9:27. Mitchell, Stephen Omer. "Samuel Johnson and the New Philosophy: The Effects of the New Philosophy on Johnson's Thought" (dissertation, Indiana University, 1961), *Dissertation Abstracts*, XXII (March 1962), 3203–4. Influence of Locke, Hume, Newton, etc.

*11/9:28. Voitle, Robert B., Jr. *Samuel Johnson the Moralist*. Cambridge, Mass.: Harvard University Press, 1961. Reviewed by Paul K. Alkon, *PQ*, XLI (July 1962), 603–5; Russell Kirk, *Sewanee Review*, LXXI (April–June 1963), 332–42.

11/9:29. Fleeman, J. D. "Johnson and the Truth" [importance of veracity about facts], in item 10/6:316 (1962), pp. 109–13.

11/9:30. Kaul, R. K. "Dr. Johnson on Matter and Mind," in item 10/6:316 (1962), pp. 101–8.

11/9:31. Noyes, Charles E. "Samuel Johnson: Student of Hume," *University of Mississippi Studies in English*, III (1962), 91–94.

*11/9:32. Grange, Kathleen M. "Samuel Johnson's Account of Certain Psychoanalytic Concepts," *Journal of Nervous and Mental Disease*, CXXXV (August 1962), 93–98. Reprinted in item 10/6:330 (1965), pp. 149–57.

11/9:33. Alkon, Paul Kent. "The Moral Discipline of the Mind: A Study of the Method and Intellectual Backgrounds of Dr. Johnson's Moral Writings." Dissertation, University of Chicago, 1963.

11/9:34. Littlejohn, David Thomas. "Johnson's Moral Thought." Dissertation, Harvard University, 1963.

11/9:35. Rhodes, Rodman D. "Samuel Johnson and the Problem of Evil." Dissertation, Harvard University, 1963.

11/9:36. Greene, Donald J. "Samuel Johnson and 'Natural Law,'" *Journal of British Studies*, II (May 1963), 59–75, 84–87. Comment by Peter Stanlis, pp. 76–83. See also Francis Oakley, *ibid.*, IV (November 1964), 1–5.

11/9:37. Sachs, Arieh. "Samuel Johnson on 'the Vacuity of Life,'" *Studies in English Literature* (Rice University), III (Summer 1963), 345–63.

11/9:38. Sachs, Arieh. "Generality and Particularity in Johnson's Thought," *Studies in English Literature* (Rice University), V (Summer 1965), 491–511.

*11/9:39. Shackleton, Robert. "Johnson and the Enlightenment," in item 10/6:329 (1965), pp. 76–92.

11/9:40. Sachs, Arieh. "Samuel Johnson and the Cosmic Hierarchy," *Scripta Hierosolymitana: Studies in English Language and Literature* [Hebrew University, Jerusalem], XVII (1966), 137–54.

11/9:41. Sachs, Arieh. "Johnson on Idle Solitude and Diabolical Imagination," *English Studies*, XLVII (June 1966), 180–89.

11/9:42. Sachs, Arieh. "Samuel Johnson on the Art of Forgetfulness," *SP*, LXIII (July 1966), 578–88.

11/9:43. McIntosh, Carey. "Johnson's Debate with Stoicism," *ELH*, XXXIII (September 1966), 327–36.

*11/9:44. Alkon, Paul Kent. *Samuel Johnson and Moral Discipline*. Evanston, Ill.: Northwestern University Press, 1967. Reviewed by Philip B. Daghlian, *PQ*, XLVII (July 1968), 390–91.

*11/9:45. Sachs, Arieh. *Passionate Intelligence: Imagination and Reason in the Works of Samuel Johnson*. Baltimore, Md.: Johns Hopkins Press, 1967. Reviewed by Donald Greene, *Studies in Burke and His Times*, IX (Winter 1968), 877–82; Ian Ross, *PQ*, XLVII (July 1968), 394–95.

11/9:46. Stanlis, Peter J. "Edmund Burke and the Scientific Rationalism of the Enlightenment" [contains a discussion of Johnson's attitude as compared to those of Swift and Burke], *Edmund Burke, the Enlightenment and the Modern World*, ed. Peter J. Stanlis, pp. 96–103. Detroit: University of Detroit Press, 1967.

11/9:47. Voitle, Robert. "Stoicism and Samuel Johnson," *Essays in English Literature of the Classical Period Presented to Dougald MacMillan*, ed. D. W. Patterson and A. B. Strauss, *SP*, Extra Series No. 4 (1967), pp. 107–27.

11/9:48. Austin, M. N. "The Classical Learning of Samuel Johnson," in *Studies in the Eighteenth Century: Papers Presented at the David Nichol Smith Memorial Seminar, Canberra, 1966*, ed. R. F. Brissenden, pp. 285–306. Canberra: Australian National University Press, 1968.

11/10. JOHNSON'S PERSONAL TRAITS AND HABITS

11/10:1. "Dr. Johnson as a Temperance Moralist," *Meliora*, VIII (1st quarter, 1865), 60–77.

11/10:2. D., H. W. "Was Dr. Johnson a Snuff-Taker?" *N&Q*, 4th ser., VIII (December 23, 1871), 534–35. Improbable story of an encounter between Johnson and William Beckford senior. See W. G., *N&Q*, IX, 87.

11/10:3. Axon, William E. A. "Dr. Johnson at Gwaenynog," *N&Q*, 4th ser., XI (May 31, 1873), 437–38. Johnson's "aversion to the canine race."

11/10:4. Burns, Dawson. *Dr. Samuel Johnson as a Temperance Witness and Moralist*. London: National Temperance Publicity Depot, [1885?].

11/10:5. Bouchier, Jonathan. "Dr. Johnson's Pronunciation," *N&Q*, 7th ser., VIII (July 13, 1889), 24–25.

11/10:6. Auld, Thomas. "Dr. Johnson and Tea-Drinking," *N&Q*, 9th ser., II (October 1, 1898), 265; III (March 18, 1899), 215. See also George Clulow, *ibid.*, II (November 19, 1898), 413; R. B., *ibid.*, III (April 8, 1899), 272–73.

11/10:7. Axon, William E. A. "Dr. Johnson's Sympathy for Animals," *Nation*, LXXXVII (September 10, 1908), 231.

11/10:8. "Dr. Johnson's Boots," *N&Q*, 11th ser., I (March 5, March 26, 1910), 184–85, 253.

11/10:9. Markland, Russell. "Was Dr. Johnson a Smoker?" *N&Q*, 12th ser., VI (May 15, 1920), 206–7. See also *ibid.* (June 5, June 12), pp. 279, 302.

11/10:10. Howard, Geoffrey. "The Early Rising of Dr. Johnson," *Cornhill Magazine*, n.s., LII (June 1922), 729–35.

11/10:11. Repplier, Agnes. *To Think of Tea!* Boston: Houghton Mifflin Co., 1932. Chap. V, "On a Tea-Drinker of England," pp. 59–77.

11/10:12. Coleman, A. M. "Johnson's Snuff-Taking," *N&Q*, CLXVII (November 10, 1934), 332. See also *ibid.*, CLXXXVI (March 25, 1944), 168.

11/10:13. C., T. C. "Johnson on Boots," *N&Q*, CLXXI (July 18, 1936), 43.

11/10:14. Miller, Clarence A. "Doctor Johnson and Tea," in *Johnsoniana*, pp. 44–76. Washington, D.C.: Privately printed, 1948.

11/10:15. Wilson, Ross. "Dr. Johnson and Gin," *New Rambler*, January 1966, pp. 7–12; (on Wine), January 1967, pp. 24–40.

12. JOHNSON'S PROSE STYLE

12:1. "An Apology for Obscure Writers," *London Chronicle*, XVII (February 23–26, 1765), 195. Feeble burlesque of *Rambler* style.

12:2. [Campbell, Archibald]. *Lexiphanes, a Dialogue Imitated from Lucian, and adapted to present times . . . Being an attempt to restore the English tongue to its ancient purity, and to correct, as well as expose, the affected style, hard words, and absurd phraseology of many later writers, and particularly of our English Lexiphanes, the Rambler*. London: J. Knox, 1767. 2nd ed., 1767. 3rd ed., London: R. Faulder, 1783.

12:3. Campbell, Archibald. *The Sale of Authors. A Dialogue, in Imitation of Lucian's Sale of Philosophers*. London: "Printed and sold by the booksellers," 1767. An attack on the prose style of Johnson, Garrick, and others.

12:4. "To the Author of Lexiphanes," *Lloyd's*, March 16–18, 1774. Attack on Johnson's prose style.

12:5. Anti-Empiricus. [Attack on Johnson's grammar], *Morning Chronicle*, October 11, 13, 16, 1779.

12:6. "An Idea of Dr. Johnson's Mode of Writing (From Dr. Blair's Lectures)," *London Magazine*, LII (June 1783), 289. Brief, hostile quotation. See item 12:40.

12:7. "A Tour to Celbridge, in Ireland (written in imitation of the style of Dr. Johnson)," *Scots Magazine* (October 1783), 517–20. Feeble.

12:8. Burrowes, Robert. "Essay on the Stile of Doctor Samuel Johnson," *Transactions of the Royal Irish Academy*, Vol. I (1787), pp. 27–56 of section "Polite Literature." Reprinted in *Port Folio*, 4th ser., XI (June 1821), 300–309; XII (September), 32–42.

12:9. Gleig, George. "Note C," in item 3:35, pp. 299–300. Analysis of Johnson's *Rambler* style.

12:10. G., O. [Echoes of Burton's *Anatomy* in Johnson's writings], *GM*, LXX (January 1800), 32–33.

12:11. Wallace, Thomas. *An Essay on the Variations of English Prose to the Present Time*. London, 1803. Not seen; review in *GM*, LXXIII (August 1803), 747–48, quotes passages favorable to Johnson.

12:12. Minto, William. "Samuel Johnson," *A Manual of English Prose Literature*, 3rd ed., pp. 413–28. Edinburgh: Blackwood, 1886.

12:13. Hunt, Theodore W. *Representative English Prose and Prose Writers*, pp. 310–33. New York: Armstrong, 1887.

12:14. Hill, George Birkbeck. "Dr. Johnson's Style," *Macmillan's Magazine*, LVII (January 1888), 190–94. Reprinted in *Living Age*, CLXXVI (February 4, 1888), 288–92.

12:15. Lewis, Edwin H. "Johnson," *The History of the English Paragraph*, pp. 115–17. Chicago: University of Chicago Press, 1894.

12:16. Auld, Thomas. "Dr. Johnson and Palfrey" [use of the word in his journal], *N&Q*, 9th ser., II (September 24, 1898), 245.

12:17. Clark, J. Scott. "Samuel Johnson," *A Study of English Prose Writers: A Laboratory Method*, pp. 236–81. New York: Charles Scribner's Sons, 1898.

12:18. Schmidt, Heinrich. *Der Prosastil Samuel Johnson's*. Dissertation, University of Marburg. Frankfort on the Main: Knauer, 1905.

12:19. Dawson, William J. *The Makers of English Prose*, pp. 23–48. New York: Fleming H. Revell Co., 1906.

12:20. Saintsbury, George. *A History of English Prose Rhythm*, pp. 265–72, etc. London: Macmillan, 1912.

12:21. Taylor, Warner. "The Prose Style of Johnson," in *Studies by Members of the Department of English*, University of Wisconsin, 1918, pp. 22–56.

12:22. Gosse, Edmund. "The Prose of Dr. Johnson," *Leaves and Fruit*, pp. 357–64. London: Wm. Heinemann, 1927.

12:23. Chandler, Zilpha E. *An Analysis of the Stylistic Technique of Addison, Johnson, Hazlitt, and Pater*. (University of Iowa Humanistic Studies, IV, no. 3.) Iowa City, January 1928.

12:24. Reynolds, W. Vaughan. "A Note on Johnson's Use of the Triplet" [his so-called triple tautology], *N&Q*, CLXV (July 15, 1933), 23–24.

12:25. Reynolds, W. Vaughan. "The Reception of Johnson's Prose Style," *RES*, XI (April 1935), 145–62.

*12:26. Wimsatt, William K., Jr. *The Prose Style of Samuel Johnson*. New Haven, Conn.: Yale University Press, 1941. Reprinted, 1966. See also Arthur Friedman, *PQ*, XXI (April 1942), 211–13, and reply by Wimsatt, *ibid.*, XXII (January 1943), 71–76. Reviewed by J. E. Congleton, *MLQ*, III (March 1942), 133–35; J. M. S. Tompkins, *MLR*, XXXVII (July 1942), 380–81; R. W. Chapman, *RES*, XX (January 1944), 84–86.

12:27. "The Style of Dr. Johnson," *N&Q*, CLXXXIV (March 27, 1943), 193–94.

12:28. Sutherland, James R. "Some Aspects of Eighteenth-Century Prose,"

Essays on the Eighteenth Century Presented to David Nichol Smith, pp. 94–110. Oxford: Clarendon Press, 1945.

12:29. Emden, Cecil S. "Rhythmical Features in Dr. Johnson's Prose," *RES*, XXV (January 1949), 38–54. Discussed by W. K. Wimsatt, Jr., *JNL*, IX, no. 3 (June 1949), 10–12.

12:30. Emden, Cecil S. "Dr. Johnson and Imagery," *RES*, n.s., I (January 1950), 23–38.

12:31. Krishnamurti, S. "Dr. Johnson's Use of Monosyllabic Words," *Journal of the University of Bombay*, XIX (September 1950), 1–12.

12:32. Morgan, Edwin. " 'Strong Lines' and Strong Minds," *Cambridge Journal*, IV (May 1951), 481–91. Browne's and Johnson's prose.

12:33. Krishnamurti, S. "Frequency-Distribution of Nouns in Dr. Johnson's Prose Works," *Journal of the University of Bombay*, XX (September 1951), 1–16. Application to Johnson of techniques described in G. Udny Yule, *The Statistical Study of Literary Vocabulary*.

12:34. Krishnamurti, S. "Vocabulary Tests Applied to (Dr. Johnson's) Authorship of the 'Misargyrus' Papers in *The Adventurer*," *Journal of the University of Bombay*, XXI (September 1952), 47–62.

12:35. Krishnamurti, S. "Vocabulary Tests: Applied to the Authorship of the 'New Essays' Attributed to Dr. Johnson," *Journal of the University of Bombay*, XXII (September 1953), 1–5. See item 25:43.

12:36. Watt, Ian. "The Ironic Tradition in Augustan Prose from Swift to Johnson," *Restoration and Augustan Prose*, pp. 19–46. Los Angeles: W. A. Clark Memorial Library, 1957.

12:37. Sherbo, Arthur. "The Case for Internal Evidence (5): The Uses and Abuses of Internal Evidence" [attributes to Johnson "An Essay on Elegies" in the *Universal Museum*, 1767], *Bulletin of the New York Public Library*, LXIII (January 1959), 5–22. Attacked by Ephim G. Fogel, *ibid.* (May, June), 223–36, 292–308. Reply by Sherbo, *ibid.* (July), 367–71. Reprinted in *Evidence for Authorship: Essays on Problems of Attribution*, ed. David V. Erdman and Ephim G. Fogel, pp. 6–14, Ithaca, N.Y.: Cornell University Press, 1966. Cf. E. G. Fogel, *ibid.*, pp. 88–90.

12:38. Bernard, F. V. "Two Errors in Boswell's *Life of Johnson*" [usage Johnson disapproved of], *N&Q*, July–August 1959, pp. 280–81.

12:39. Rockas, Leo. "The Description of Style: Dr. Johnson and His Critics" (dissertation, University of Michigan, 1960), *Dissertation Abstracts*, XXI (1960), 338–39.

12:40. Butt, John. "Blair on Johnson" [criticism of Johnson's style in students' notes of Blair's lectures], *JNL*, XX, no. 1 (March 1960), 9–10.

12:41. Kenney, William. "Addison, Johnson, and the 'Energetick' Style," *Studia Neophilologica*, XXXIII (1961), 103–14.

12:42. Sherbo, Arthur. "The Electronic Computer and I," *University Col-*

lege Quarterly (Michigan State University), March 1962, pp. 8–11. Describes project for statistical differentiation between Johnson's prose style and John Hawkesworth's. See item 12:45.

12:43. Greene, Donald J. "Is There a 'Tory' Prose Style?" *Bulletin of the New York Public Library*, LXVI (September 1962), 449–54.

12:44. Boulton, James T. *The Language of Politics in the Age of Wilkes and Burke.* (Studies in Political History.) London: Routledge and Kegan Paul, 1963. Chap. 3, "Samuel Johnson: *The False Alarm*," pp. 32–44; Chap. 4, "Junius and Johnson: The Falkland Islands Dispute," pp. 45–51.

12:45. Sherbo, Arthur. "The Electronic Computer and I: II," *University College Quarterly* (Michigan State University), IX (November 1963), 18 23. Plans for further computer analysis of style of *Parliamentary Debates.*

12:46. Bernard, F. V. "A Stylistic Touchstone for Johnson's Prose" [Johnson rarely uses "also"], *N&Q*, February 1964, pp. 63–64. See also E. G. Stanley, *ibid.*, August 1964, pp. 298–99.

12:47. Waywood, Pacificus. "Samuel Johnson's Conceptual Diction," *Greyfriars*, IX (1966), 12–18.

12:48. Milic, Louis T. *A Quantitative Approach to the Style of Jonathan Swift* [Johnson used as a control]. The Hague: Mouton, 1967.

12:49. Tucker, Susie I. *Protean Shape: A Study in Eighteenth-Century Vocabulary and Usage.* London: Athlone Press, 1967. *Passim.*

12:50. King, Lester S. "Style Analysis: Samuel Johnson" [Medical Writing, No. 10], *Journal of the American Medical Association*, CCIII (January 1, 1968), 41–42. Inept.

12:51. Hayes, Curtis W. "A Transformational-Generative Approach to Style: Samuel Johnson and Edward Gibbon," *Language and Style*, I (Winter 1968), 39–48.

12:52. McNally, James. "The Pithy Johnson," *University Review* (Kansas City), XXXV (Winter 1968), 113–18. Johnson's aphoristic style.

12:53. Thackrey, Donald Eugene. "The Uses of Argument in the Prose of Samuel Johnson." Dissertation, University of Michigan, 1969.

12:54. Sørensen, Knud. "Johnsonese in *Northanger Abbey*," *English Studies*, L (August 1969), 390–97.

13. THE *LIFE OF SAVAGE* AND OTHER EARLY BIOGRAPHIES
EDITIONS

13:1. *An Account of the Life of Mr. Richard Savage, Son of the Earl Rivers.* London: J. Roberts, 1744. 2nd ed., London: E. Cave, 1748. 3rd ed., "to which are added the Lives of Sir Francis Drake and Admiral Blake.

All written by the same author," London: Henry and Cave, 1767. 4th ed. [with lives of Drake and Blake], "All written by the Author of the Rambler," London: Newbery, 1769. First ed. reviewed (by James Ralph?) in *Champion*, February 21, 1744.

Included in item 22:1 (*Lives of the Poets*), 1781. For nineteenth-century reprints, see Courtney (item 1/1:19), p. 17.

Ed. Cyril Connolly, in *Great English Short Novels*, pp. 9–85. New York: Dial Press, 1953.

Ed. Richard Evan Lyon (dissertation, University of Chicago). Chicago: University of Chicago, Department of Photoduplication (microfilm), 1958.

*Ed. Clarence R. Tracy. Oxford: Clarendon Press (expected 1970). Will also form part of the Yale Edition of the Works of Samuel Johnson (item 2:8).

13:2. *A Memoir of Roger Ascham* [Johnson's life] . . . *with an introduction by James H. Carlisle*. Boston: Chautauqua Press, 1886. New ed., *Two Great Teachers: Johnson's Memoir of Roger Ascham; Stanley's Life and Correspondence of Thomas Arnold of Rugby. With an introduction by James H. Carlisle*, Syracuse, N.Y.: C. W. Bardeen, 1890.

13:3. Smith, Frederick M. [Selections from the life of Boerhaave], *Essays and Studies* [college textbook], pp. 289–93, 349–51. Boston: Houghton Mifflin Co., 1922.

13:4. *Sir Thomas Browne, Christian Morals* [with life by Johnson], ed. S. C. Roberts. Cambridge: Cambridge University Press, 1927.

COMMENTARY

13:20. Academicus (Oxford). [Attributes *Life of Cheynel* to Johnson; corrects attribution in item 1/1:1 of "Character of Collins" to Joseph Warton, and attributes it to Johnson], *GM*, XLIV (December 1774), 627.

13:21. Palmer, Samuel. Reprinting and comment on *Life of Cheynel*, in his edition of Edward Calamy, *The Nonconformist's Memorial; Being an Account of the Ministers Who Were Ejected or Silenced after the Restoration*, II, 467–68. London: W. Harris, 1775.

13:22. H., F. [Johnson's receipt for payment for *Life of Savage* and contract with Cave for a duodecimo edition of *The Rambler*], *GM*, LXXXII (April 1812), 313.

13:23. Whitehead, Charles. *Richard Savage: A Romance of Real Life*. London: Richard Bentley, 1842. Reprinted several times. A novel, based on Johnson's *Life*.

13:24. Chambers, Robert. "Johnson and Savage," *Chambers' Journal*, VII (January 30, 1847), 65–68.

13:25. "Richard Savage," *Dublin University Magazine*, LI (June 1858), 701–12.

13:26. Thomas, W. Moy. "Richard Savage," *N&Q*, 2nd ser., VI (November 6–December 4, 1858), 361–65, 385–89, 425–28, 445–48.

13:27. Ryley, Madeleine Lucette. *Richard Savage*. A play, given in New York, February 1901.

13:28. Makower, Stanley V. *Richard Savage: A Mystery in Biography*. London: Hutchinson & Co., 1909.

13:29. Jones, Gwyn. *Richard Savage*. London: Victor Gollancz, 1935.

13:30. McAdam, Edward L., Jr. "A Johnson Pamphlet" [life of Admiral Blake], *TLS*, March 14, 1936, p. 228.

*13:31. Hazen, Allen T. "Samuel Johnson and Dr. Robert James" [contributions to Dr. James's *Medicinal Dictionary*, etc.], *Bulletin of the Institute of the History of Medicine*, IV (June 1936), 455–65.

*13:32. Sutherland, James R. "Richard Savage," *TLS*, January 1, 1938, p. 12.

13:33. Hazen, Allen T. "Johnson's Life of Frederic Ruysch," *Bulletin of the Institute of the History of Medicine*, VII (March 1939), 324–34.

13:34. Lindsay, Jack. "Richard Savage, the First Poet of Colour" [a modern interpretation of his poetry], *Life and Letters Today*, XXII (September 1939), 384–93.

13:35. Johnson, Edgar. *A Treasury of Biography* [excerpts from the *Life of Savage* and Boswell's *Life*, with comments], pp. 148–201. New York: Howell, Soskin, 1941.

13:36. Atkinson, Edward R. "Samuel Johnson's 'Life of Boerhaave'" [short preface and text of life], *Journal of Chemical Education*, XIX (March 1942), 103–8.

*13:37. McAdam, Edward L., Jr. "Johnson's Lives of Sarpi, Blake, and Drake," *PMLA*, LVIII (June 1943), 466–76.

13:38. "Poet and Interloper, Richard Savage: 1698–1743," *TLS*, July 31, 1943, p. 368.

13:39. Carrigan, Edward. "Richard Savage" [Mrs. Oldfield's aid to poet], *TLS*, September 25, 1943, p. 463.

13:40. Jones, Gwyn. "Son of the Late Earl Rivers," *Welsh Review*, IV (June 1945), 114–25.

*13:41. Bergler, Edmund. "Samuel Johnson's 'Life of the Poet Richard Savage'—A Paradigm for a Type," *American Imago*, IV (December 1947), 42–63.

*13:42. Liebert, Herman W. *Johnson's Last Literary Project* [a life of John Scott of Amwell]. New Haven, Conn.: Privately printed, 1948.

13:43. Sherbo, Arthur. "Johnsoniana: An Obituary Notice and an 'Abstract' from the Life of Savage," *N&Q*, February 2, 1952, pp. 51–54.

*13:44. Tracy, Clarence R. *The Artificial Bastard: A Biography of Richard Savage*. Toronto: University of Toronto Press; Cambridge, Mass.: Harvard University Press, 1953. Reviewed by Benjamin Boyce, *PQ*, XXXIII (July 1954), 294–95; J. L. Clifford, *MLN*, LXX (May 1955), 373–74; M. J. C. Hodgart, *RES*, n.s., VI (July 1955), 323–24.

13:45. Schneck, Jerome. "Hermann Boerhaave and Samuel Johnson," *Journal of the American Medical Association*, CLXI, no. 14 (August 4, 1956), 1414–15.

*13:46. Boyce, Benjamin. "Johnson's *Life of Savage* and Its Literary Background," *SP*, LIII (October 1956), 576–98.

13:47. Wagley, Mary F. and Philip F. "Comments on Samuel Johnson's Biography of Sir Thomas Browne," *Bulletin of the History of Medicine*, XXXI (July–August 1957), 318–26.

13:48. Morgan, H. A. "Johnson's Life of Savage," *Contemporary Review*, CXCV (January 1959), 38–41.

13:49. Black, D. A. K. "Johnson on Boerhaave," *Medical History*, III (October 1959), 325–29.

*13:50. McHenry, Lawrence C., Jr. "Dr. Samuel Johnson's Medical Biographies" [in James's *Medicinal Dictionary* (see items 13:31, 13:33); also attributes life of Oribasius], *Journal of the History of Medicine and Allied Sciences*, XIV (1959), 298–310.

13:51. Hess, Walter C. "Samuel Johnson's Life of Boerhaave," *Georgetown Medical Bulletin*, XV (February 1962), 256–58.

13:52. Tracy, Clarence R. "Some Uncollected Authors—Richard Savage, d. 1743," *Book Collector*, XII (Autumn 1963), 340–49.

13:53. Brain, Lord. "Dr. Johnson or Dr. James?" Presidential address, Johnson Society, Lichfield, in item 6:23 (1963), pp. 19–27. James's *Medicinal Dictionary* and Johnson's contributions.

13:54. McHenry, Lawrence C., Jr. "Samuel Johnson's 'The Life of Dr. Sydenham,'" *Medical History*, VIII (April 1964), 181–87.

13:55. McHenry, Lawrence C. "Louis Morin, M.D., Botanist, and Dr. Johnson," *New England Journal of Medicine*, CCLXXIII (August 5, 1965), 323–34.

13:56. Abbott, John L. "Dr. Johnson, Fontenelle, Le Clerc, and Six 'French' Lives," *MP*, LXIII (November 1965), 121–27.

13:57. Abbott, John L. "Dr. Johnson and the Making of 'The Life of Father Paul Sarpi,'" *Bulletin of the John Rylands Library*, XLVIII (Spring 1966), 255–67.

13:58. Day, Robert A. "Richardson, Aaron Hill, and Johnson's 'Life of Savage,'" *N&Q*, June 1966, pp. 217–19.

13:59. Abbott, John L. "Samuel Johnson's 'A Panegyric on Dr. Morin,'" *Romance Notes*, VIII (Autumn 1966), 55–57.

13:60. Fleeman, J. D. "The Making of Johnson's *Life of Savage*, 1744," *Library*, 5th ser., XXII (December 1967), 346–52.

*13:61. Bernard, F. V. "A Possible Source for Johnson's Life of the King of Prussia," *PQ*, XLVII (April 1968), 206–15.

14. NONDRAMATIC POEMS
Editions

14:1. *Poetical Works. Now First Collected in One Volume.* London: Kearsley, 1785, and often reprinted (see Courtney, item 1/1:19, pp. 157–58). Editorship attributed to William Cooke; see Allen T. Hazen, *MP*, XXXV (February 1938), 289–95.

14:2. *Poems of Dr. Samuel Johnson. To Which Is Prefixed a Life of the Author by F. W. Blagdon.* London: W. Suttaby; Philadelphia: B. Johnson, J. Johnson, and R. Johnson, 1805.

14:3. *The Poetical Works of Johnson, Parnell, Gray, and Smollett. With Memoirs, critical, dissertative, and explanatory notes. The text edited by Charles Cowden Clarke.* London: J. Nichols, 1855. "Memoir" of Johnson by George Gilfillan, pp. [3]–16. Often reprinted.

14:4. *The Poems of Johnson, Goldsmith, Gray, and Collins,* ed. T. Methuen Ward. (Muses' Library.) London: George Routledge & Sons, 1905.

*14:5. *The Poems of Samuel Johnson,* ed. D. Nichol Smith and E. L. McAdam, Jr. Oxford: Clarendon Press, 1941. Reprinted, 1962. Reviewed in *Spectator*, November 14, 1941, p. 474; *TLS*, November 22, 1941, p. 582; by F. E. Hutchinson, *RES*, XVIII (April 1942), 242–45; F. R. Leavis, *Scrutiny*, XI (Summer 1942), 75–78; G. Tillotson, *MLR*, XXXVIII (April 1943), 149–54; A. Friedman, *PQ*, XXII (April 1943), 162–64; A. T. Hazen, *MLN*, LVIII (December 1943), 640–41; Raymond Mortimer, *New Statesman and Nation*, XXII (November 1, 1941), 394.

*14:6. *Poems,* ed. E. L. McAdam, Jr., with George Milne. New Haven, Conn.: Yale University Press, 1964. Vol. VI of Yale Edition of Johnson's Works, item 2:8. Reviewed by A. W. Rudrum, *English Language Notes*, III (December 1965), 139–42; Leicester Bradner, *MP*, LXIII (February 1966), 269–70; F. W. Bateson, *RES*, n.s., XVII (August 1966), 327–31; Bruce King, *Sewanee Review*, LXXVI (Winter 1968), 139–42.

14:7. *The Vanity of Human Wishes* (first published 1749).

Ed. E. J. Payne. Oxford: Clarendon Press, 1878. Often reprinted.

Ed. F. Ryland. London: Blackie & Son, 1893.

Ed. E. H. Blakeney. With Juvenal's Tenth Satire. London: Blackie & Son, 1925.

Type-facsimile. London: Oxford University Press, 1927.

Facsimile. With introduction by B. H. Bronson. Augustan Reprint Society, Publication No. 22, 1950.

Also included in numerous anthologies. See Section 2, above.

14:8. *London: A Poem and The Vanity of Human Wishes*, with introduction by T. S. Eliot. London: Etchells and Macdonald, 1930. Reviewed in *TLS*, November 20, 1930, p. 973.

14:9. *The Vanity of Human Wishes*, in *The Late Augustans: Longer Poems of the Later Eighteenth Century*, ed. Donald Davie, pp. xxii-xxiii, 14–24. London: Heinemann, 1958.

14:10. *Horace, Book 2nd, Ode 20th* [facsimile of English translation in Johnson's hand]. Buffalo, N.Y.: Privately printed for R. B. Adam, 1923.

*14:11. *The Vanity of Human Wishes* [facsimile of original manuscript in Hyde collection]. Privately printed for Donald and Mary Hyde, 1962.

14:12. *Selected Poems of Samuel Johnson and Oliver Goldsmith*, ed. Alan Rudrum and Peter Dixon. (English Texts Series.) London: Arnold, 1965.

COMMENTARY

14:40. D., J. "Translation of an Unpublished Latin Ode by the Late Dr. Johnson," *GM*, LIV (December 1784), 934. "To Dr. Lawrence," 1778.

14:41. [Seward, Anna]. [Earliest published version of the story of young Sam's "Epitaph on a Duckling"], *GM*, LV (February 1785), 100.

14:42. Seward, Anna. [Origin of "Verses on Receiving a Sprig of Myrtle from a Lady"], *GM*, LXIII (October 1793), 875. Reply by Boswell, (November), 1009–11. Rejoinder by Anna Seward, (December), 1098–1101. See also H. White, LXIV (March 1794), 196–97.

14:43. Protoplastides. [Affirms verses on Lovat's execution to be Johnson's; general defense of Johnson], *GM*, LXIV (July 1794), 623–25. Further remarks, LXV (January 1795), 6–8.

14:44. Aikin, John. [Criticism of Johnson's poetry], *Letters to a Young Lady on a Course of English Poetry*, pp. 273–78. London: J. Johnson, 1804.

14:45. Markland, J. H. "Dr. Johnson and Dr. Warton," *N&Q*, I (May 25, 1850), 481. Parallel between openings of *The Vanity of Human Wishes* and Thomas Warton the elder's *The Universal Love of Pleasure*. See also *N&Q*, II (June 8, 1850), 26.

14:46. Trench, Francis. "A Bull of Dr. Johnson," *N&Q*, 4th ser., III (January 30, 1869), 103. "Nor sell for gold what gold can never buy" (*London*). Controverted, *ibid.*, p. 203.

*14:47. "Johnsonese Poetry," *Spectator*, XLIX (May 13, 1876), 619–20. Reprinted in *Living Age*, CXXX (1876), 190–92. A general appreciation.

14:48. Courthope, William John. "Samuel Johnson," in *The English Poets*, ed. T. Humphry Ward, III, 245–47. London: Macmillan, 1880.

14:49. Hendriks, Frederick. [MS of verses written on a window of an inn at Calais], *N&Q*, 7th ser., XI (April 25, 1891), 329.

14:50. Neilson, George. "Johnson, Burton, and Juvenal" [Burton and Sir Edward Coke quote *Res angusta domi*—source of "Slow rises worth" in *London*], *N&Q*, 8th ser., IV (December 9, 1893), 465.

14:51. W[alford], E[dward]. "Dr. Johnson and Gwaenynog" [verses attributed to him], *N&Q*, 8th ser., VIII (December 21, 1895), 488. See also item 14:5, p. 400.

14:52. Craig, W. H. "Dr. Johnson and Miss Lucy Porter" [Hector vs. Anna Seward on the "Sprig of Myrtle" verses], *N&Q*, 8th ser., IX (March 14, 1896), 201–2.

14:53. Minchin, Harry C. "Dr. Johnson among the Poets," *Macmillan's Magazine*, LXXXV (December 1901), 98–105.

14:54. Hayes, James. "Lines Attributed to Dr. Johnson" [in copy of Murphy's *Life of Garrick*], *N&Q*, 9th ser., IX (April 26, 1902), 330.

14:55. Merritt, E. Percival. "Mrs. Thrale and Johnson's 'In Theatro,'" *N&Q*, 10th ser., III (March 4, 1905), 161–62.

14:56. Courthope, William J. *History of English Poetry*, V, 201–9. London: Macmillan, 1905.

14:57. Strachan, L. R. M. "Johnson's 'Vanity of Human Wishes'" [conjectures on opening lines], *N&Q*, 10th ser., V (January 13, 1906), 29. See also E. M. Layton, *ibid.* (January 27), p. 78.

14:58. "Johnson's Poems" [editions], *Athenaeum*, September 4, 1909, p. 267.

14:59. Lane, John. "Johnson's Poems" [bibliographical points], *Athenaeum*, No. 4272 (September 11, 1909), pp. 298–99. See also W. H. Grattan Flood, *ibid.*, No. 4273 (September 18, 1909), pp. 329–30.

14:60. Muir, John. "Poem Attributed to Dr. Johnson" [from *The Bee*, March 9, 1791], *N&Q*, 11th ser., X (October 17, 1914), 304–5. But see item 14:5, p. 398.

14:61. Goad, Caroline. "Samuel Johnson," *Horace in the English Literature of the Eighteenth Century*, pp. 233–70. (Yale Studies in English, No. LVIII.) New Haven: Yale University Press, 1918.

14:62. *Johnson and Goldsmith and Their Poetry*, ed. William Henry Hudson. (Poetry and Life Series.) London: George G. Harrap & Co., 1918.

14:63. Saintsbury, George. *A History of English Prosody*, 2nd ed., II, 460–63, etc. London: Macmillan, 1923.

14:64. N[eedham], F. R. D. "'A Slight Fault'" [Boswell's MS of a minor change in "The Vanity of Human Wishes"], *Bodleian Quarterly Record*, IV (3rd quarter, 1923), 50. See also *JNL*, December 1947, p. 7.

14:65. Quayle, Thomas. *Poetic Diction: A Study of Eighteenth Century Verse.* London: Methuen & Co., 1924.

14:66. Walker, Hugh. *English Satire and Satirists,* pp. 229–31. London: J. M. Dent & Sons, 1925.

14:67. Roberts, Sydney Castle. "On the Death of Dr. Robert Levet—A Note on the Text," *RES,* III (October 1927), 442–45. See also W. H. Grattan Flood, *ibid.,* IV (January 1928), 88–89.

14:68. Chapman, Robert William. "Dr. Johnson and Poetry," *219th Lichfield Birthday Celebration.* Lichfield: Mercury Press, 1928. See item 6:22. Reprinted in part in *SRL,* VI (August 17, 1929), 49–51, and in *TLS,* June 18, 1931, pp. 473–74.

14:69. Quiller-Couch, Sir Arthur. [On verses to Levet], *Studies in Literature,* Third Series, pp. 43–45. Cambridge: Cambridge University Press, 1929.

14:70. Chapman, R. W. "Hogarth's Epitaph" [Johnson's corrections], *TLS,* May 2, 1929, p. 362.

14:71. Tate, Allen. "Taste and Dr. Johnson" [largely a review of item 14:8], *New Republic,* LXVIII (August 19, 1931), 23–24.

14:72. Emperor, John B. "The Juvenalian and Persian Element in English Literature from the Restoration to Dr. Johnson." Dissertation, Cornell University, 1932.

*14:73. Eliot, T. S. Preface to item 14:8, reprinted in *English Critical Essays: Twentieth Century,* ed. Phyllis M. Jones, pp. 301–10. (World's Classics). London: Oxford University Press, 1933. Reprinted as "Poetry in the Eighteenth Century," in *The Pelican Guide to English Literature,* IV, 271–77, Penguin Books, 1957. An excerpt reprinted as "Eighteenth-Century Poetry" in Eliot, *Selected Prose,* ed. John Hayward, pp. 163–68. Penguin Books, 1953.

14:74. Sutherland, James R. *The Medium of Poetry,* pp. 86–87. London: Hogarth Press, 1934.

14:75. McAdam, E. L., Jr. "The Poems of Samuel Johnson." Dissertation, Yale University, 1935.

14:76. Moody, Dorothy. "Johnson's Translation of Addison's 'Battle of the Cranes and Pygmies,'" *MLR,* XXXI (January 1936), 60–65.

*14:77. Leavis, Frank Raymond. "English Poetry in the Eighteenth Century," *Scrutiny,* V (June 1936), 24–27. Largely reprinted in *Revaluation,* pp. 116–20, New York: Stewart, 1947.

*14:78. Smith, D. Nichol. "The Heroic Couplet—Johnson," *Some Observations on Eighteenth Century Poetry,* pp. 31–55. Toronto: University of Toronto Press, 1937. The Alexander Lectures.

14:79. Reading, J. "Poems by Johnson" [authenticity of poems published in *GM,* May 1747], *TLS,* September 11, 1937, p. 656.

14:80. Phelps, William Lyon. "Dr. Johnson and A. E. Housman" [resemblance of verses of Housman to Johnson's stanzas on Sir John Lade], *Spectator*, CLXI (July 1, 1938), 21.

*14:81. Pottle, Frederick A. *The Idiom of Poetry, passim.* Ithaca, N.Y.: Cornell University Press, 1941. Rev. ed., with added essay, 1946. Rev. ed. reprinted, Bloomington: Indiana University Press, 1963.

14:82. Chapman, Robert William. "Baretti's 'Carmen Seculare,'" *TLS*, August 16, 1941, p. 400.

14:83. Norman, Charles. "Dr. Johnson and *A Shropshire Lad*" [echoes of Johnson in Housman's verses], *Poetry*, LX (August 1942), 264–69.

14:84. L[oane], C[eorge] G. "Johnson on Banks's Goat," *N&Q*, CLXXXIII (November 21, 1942), 314.

*14:85. Smith, D. Nichol. "Samuel Johnson's Poems," *RES*, XIX (January 1943), 44–50. Reprinted in item 10/6:306 (1959) and in item 10/6:330 (1965).

14:86. Gregory, Horace. "Samuel Johnson in the Twentieth Century," *SRL*, XXVI (July 24, 1943), 4–6. Reprinted in *The Shield of Achilles*, pp. 3–20, New York: Harcourt, Brace & Co., 1944.

14:87. Howarth, R. G. "From China to Peru" [Aphra Behn's *Oroonoko* and Bacon's *New Atlantis* as possible sources], *N&Q*, CLXXXVII (October 21, 1944), 188–89.

14:88. Roussev, R. "Johnson and Juvenal," *Godishnik na Sofiisknia Universitet: Istoriko-filologicheski Fakultet* (*Annuaire de l'Université de Sofia: Faculté Historico-Philologique*), XLII (1945–46), 1–6 (separate pagination).

14:89. Eliot, T. S. "What Is Minor Poetry?" [mentions *The Vanity of Human Wishes*], *Sewanee Review*, LIV (Winter 1946), 1–18.

*14:90. Bronson, Bertrand H. "Personification Reconsidered" [contains analysis of Johnson's lines on Dr. Levet], *ELH*, XIV (September 1947), 163–77. See also Earl R. Wasserman, "The Inherent Values of Eighteenth-Century Personification," *PMLA*, LXV (June 1950), 435–63. Reprinted (rev.) in item 10/6:306 (1959), pp. 189–231, and in his *Facets of the Enlightenment*, pp. 119–52, Berkeley and Los Angeles: University of California Press, 1968.

14:91. Brown, Wallace Cable. "Johnson as Poet," *MLQ*, VIII (March 1947), 53–64. Rev. and reprinted as "Johnson: 'Pathos in Isolation,'" *The Triumph of Form*, pp. 67–86, Chapel Hill: University of North Carolina Press, 1948.

14:92. Moore, John Robert. "Johnson as Poet," *Boston Public Library Quarterly*, II (April 1950), 156–66.

14:93. Moore, John Robert. "Johnson's 'Falling Houses'" [a line in *London*], *N&Q*, CXCV (August 5, 1950), 342.

14:94. Jack, Ian. "The 'Choice of Life': Johnson and Matthew Prior" [influence of *Solomon* on *Vanity of Human Wishes* and *Rasselas*], *JEGP*, XLIX (October 1950), 523–30.

14:95. Williams, Harold. "China to Peru," *N&Q*, October 27, 1951, p. 479.

14:96. Springer-Miller, Fred. "Johnson and Boileau" [use of Boileau's *First Satire*—reference to George II in *London*], *N&Q*, November 10, 1951, p. 497.

*14:97. Davie, Donald. *Purity of Diction in English Verse*, pp. 45–47, 82–90, and elsewhere. London: Chatto and Windus, 1952.

*14:98. Jack, Ian. " 'Tragical Satire': *The Vanity of Human Wishes*," in *Augustan Satire*, pp. 135–45. Oxford: Clarendon Press, 1952.

*14:99. Leavis, F. R. "Johnson as Poet" [reprint of review in *Scrutiny* of item 14:5], in *The Common Pursuit*, pp. 116–20. London: Chatto and Windus; New York: George W. Stewart, 1952.

14:100. Mohr, Eugene V. "Dr. Johnson's Latin Poems: A Translation and Commentary." Master's thesis, Columbia University, 1952.

14:101. Sherbo, Arthur. "The Text of *The Vanity of Human Wishes*," *N&Q*, May 10, 1952, pp. 205–6.

14:102. Smith, D. Nichol. "A Boswell Fragment" [recovery of note recording emendation to *Vanity of Human Wishes*; see *Life*, III, 358, n. 1], *Meanjin*, XI (Spring 1952), 292–93.

14:103. Schoff, Francis G. "Johnson on Juvenal" [*Vanity of Human Wishes*], *N&Q*, July 1953, pp. 293–96.

14:104. Duggan, G. C. "Boulter's Monument: A Poem" [Samuel Madden], *Dublin Magazine*, XXIX (October–December 1953), 20–27.

14:105. Emslie, Macdonald. "Johnson's *The Vanity of Human Wishes*" [lines 23–26, 99–102, 137–40], *Explicator*, XII (November 1953), 1–2.

*14:106. Emslie, Macdonald. "Johnson's Satires and 'The Proper Wit of Poetry,'" *Cambridge Journal*, VII (March 1954), 347–60.

14:107. Greene, Donald J. "Johnson on Garrick?" [veiled slurs on Garrick in *London*?], *JNL*, XIV, no. 3 (September 1954), 10–12. See also Mary Lascelles, *JNL*, XV, no. 1 (March 1955), 11–12.

*14:108. Chapin, Chester F. *Personification in Eighteenth-Century English Poetry*, pp. 98–115. New York: Columbia University Press, 1955. Reviewed by A. D. McKillop, *PQ*, XXXV (July 1956), 254–55; E. R. Wasserman, *JEGP*, LV (October 1956), 651–54; B. H. Bronson, *MLN*, LXXI (November 1956), 533–41.

14:109. Gifford, Henry. "*The Vanity of Human Wishes*," *RES*, n.s., VI (April 1955), 157–65. See also Christopher Ricks, *RES*, n.s., XI (November 1960), 412–13.

14:110. Tucker, Susie I., and Henry Gifford. "Johnson's *On the Death of Dr. Robert Levet*," *Explicator*, XV (April 1957), 9.

14:111. Tucker, Susie I., and Henry Gifford. "Johnson's Latin Poetry," *Neophilologus*, XLI (July 1957), 215–21.

14:112. Fussell, Paul, Jr. "The Vanity of Human Wishes" [lines 15–20], *N&Q*, August 1957, pp. 353–54.

*14:113. Tucker, Susie I., and Henry Gifford. "Johnson's Poetic Imagination," *RES*, n.s., VIII (August 1957), 241–48.

14:114. Tucker, Susie I. "The Steeps of Fate" [line 125 of *Vanity of Human Wishes*], *N&Q*, August 1957, p. 354.

14:115. Bernard, F. V. "The Dreaded Spy of London" [allusion to Savage in *London*], *N&Q*, September 1958, pp. 398–99.

14:116. Ricks, C. B. "Wolsey in *The Vanity of Human Wishes*," *MLN*, LXXIII (December 1958), 563–68.

*14:117. Lascelles, Mary. "Johnson and Juvenal," in item 10/6:306, pp. 35–55.

14:118. Liebert, Herman W. " 'We Fell upon *Sir Eldred*' " [Johnson as reviser of Hannah More's verses], in item 10/6:306, pp. 233–45.

14:119. Kolb, Gwin J. "Johnson Echoes Dryden" [*The State of Innocence*], *MLN*, LXXIV (March 1959), 212–13.

*14:120. Butt, John. "Pope and Johnson in Their Handling of the Imitation," *New Rambler*, June 1959, pp. 3–14. Reprinted in item 10/6:306, pp. 19–34, as "Johnson's Practice in the Poetical Imitation."

*14:121. Jones, Marjorie. "Housman and Johnson: Some Similarities," in item 6:23, December 1959, pp. 12–36.

14:122. Earisman, Delbert L. "Samuel Johnson's Satire" (dissertation, Indiana University, 1960), *Dissertation Abstracts*, XXI (1960), 620.

14:123. Coffey, Warren J. "The Poetry of Samuel Johnson" (dissertation, University of Wisconsin, 1960), *Dissertation Abstracts*, XXI (1960), 615.

14:124. Ricks, Christopher. "Notes on Swift and Johnson," *RES*, n.s., XI (November 1960), 412–13.

14:125. Mell, Donald Charles, Jr. "Variations on Elegaic Themes: Dryden, Pope, Prior, Gray, Johnson." Dissertation, University of Pennsylvania, 1961.

14:126. Nagashima, Daisuke. "On Johnson's *London*" [in Japanese], *Studies in English Literature* (Tokyo), XXXVIII, no. 2 (1961), 165–79.

14:127. Aden, John M. "Pope's Horace in Johnson's Juvenal" [*Vanity*, lines 305–6], *N&Q*, July 1961, pp. 254–55.

14:128. Buckley, Vincent. "Johnson: The Common Condition of Men," *Melbourne Critical Review*, No. 6 (1963), 16–30. On *The Vanity of Human Wishes*.

14:129. Weinbrot, Howard D. "Imitation and Satire: A Study in the Tradition and Poetry of *London* and *The Vanity of Human Wishes*." Dissertation, University of Chicago, 1964.

14:130. Bernard, F. V. "A New Note on Johnson's 'London'" [Thales is Savage], *N&Q*, August 1964, pp. 293–96.

14:131. Rothenberg, Gunther E. "'The Fierce Croatian' in 'The Vanity of Human Wishes,'" *N&Q*, August 1964, pp. 296–98. See also F. V. Bernard, *ibid.*, November, pp. 432–33.

14:132. Hilles, F. W. "Johnson's Poetic Fire," in *From Sensibility to Romanticism*, ed. F. W. Hilles and Harold Bloom, pp. 67–77. New York: Oxford University Press, 1965.

14:133. Rawson, C. J. "'The Vanity of Human Wishes,' line 73: A Parallel from Swift," *N&Q*, January 1965, pp. 20–21.

14:134. Bloom, Edward A. *"The Vanity of Human Wishes*: Reason's Images," *Essays in Criticism*, XV (April 1965), 181–92.

14:135. Ricks, Christopher. "Johnson's Poetry," *New Statesman*, August 6, 1965, p. 190.

14:136. Hardy, John. "Johnson's *London*: The Country Versus the City," in *Studies in the Eighteenth Century: Papers Presented at the David Nichol Smith Memorial Seminar, Canberra 1966*, ed. R. F. Brissenden, pp. 251–68. Canberra: Australian National University Press, 1968.

14:137. Greene, Donald J. "'An Extempore Elegy,'" *JNL*, March 1966, pp. 11–12. Suggests change in order of stanzas of the impromptu by Johnson, Mrs. Thrale, and Fanny Burney.

14:138. Ricks, Christopher. "Johnson's 'Battle of the Pygmies and Cranes,'" *Essays in Criticism*, XVI (July 1966), 281–89.

14:139. Allen, Robert R. "Variant Readings in Johnson's *London*," *PBSA*, LX (2nd quarter, 1966), 214–15.

14:140. Sherbo, Arthur. "Samuel Johnson and Certain Poems in the May 1747 *Gentleman's Magazine*," *RES*, n.s., XVII (November 1966), 382–90.

14:141. Trickett, Rachel. "Johnson," *The Honest Muse: A Study in Augustan Verse*, pp. 224–94. Oxford: Clarendon Press, 1967.

14:142. O'Flaherty, Patrick. "Johnson as Satirist: A New Look at *The Vanity of Human Wishes*," *ELH*, XXXIV (March 1967), 78–91. Poem "must be judged finally a failure."

14:143. Grant, Douglas. "Samuel Johnson: Satire and Satirists," *New Rambler*, June 1967, pp. 5–17.

14:144. Weinbrot, Howard D. "Dr. Johnson's Poems: A New Version of 'Medea,' lines 193–203, and a New Translation of the Epitaph on Goldsmith" [in a volume of *Translations*, published in 1806 by Robert Bland and J. H. Merivale], *N&Q*, November 1967, pp. 410–11.

14:145. Spacks, Patricia Meyer. "From Satire to Description," *Yale Review*, LVIII (Winter 1969), 232–48. *The Vanity of Human Wishes* and Robert Lowell's recent rendering of Juvenal—a comparison.

14:146. Weinbrot, Howard D. *The Formal Strain: Studies in Augustan Imi-*

tation and Satire. Chicago: University of Chicago Press, 1969. "*London and the Proper Grounds of Satiric Failure,*" pp. 165–91; "*The Vanity of Human Wishes* and the Satiric Structure," pp. 193–217, and *passim.*

15. DRAMATIC WORKS

EDITIONS

15:1. *Prologue . . . Spoken at the Opening of the Theatre in Drury-lane, 1747.* London: M. Cooper and R. Dodsley, 1747. Reprinted in items 14:1, 14:5, 14:6, and elsewhere.

15:2. *Irene:A Tragedy. As It Is Acted at the Theatre Royal in Drury Lane. By Mr. Samuel Johnson.* London: R. Dodsley and M. Cooper, 1749. 2nd ed., 1754. Reprinted in the various editions of Johnson's *Works* (item 2:1 *et seq.*), in items 14:5 and 14:6, and elsewhere. Items 14:5 and 14:6 print important early drafts of *Irene.*

15:3. *Irene: A Tragedy. By Samuel Johnson, LL.D. Adapted for Theatrical Presentation. As performed at the Theatre-Royal, Drury-Lane. Regulated from the Prompt Book. . . .* London: G. Cawthorn, 1796 (British Library). Later Bell's British Theatre.

15:4. *Samuel Johnson's Prologue Spoken at the Opening of the Theatre in Drury-Lane in 1747 with Garrick's Epilogue* [facsimile of 1st ed.]. With preface by Austin Dobson and introduction and notes by A. S. W. Rosenbach. New York: Dodd, Mead & Co., 1902.

15:5. *The Drury-Lane Prologue by Samuel Johnson* [type-facsimile]. London: Oxford University Press, 1924.

15:6. *Johnson's Prologue to Comus* [type-facsimile]. London: Oxford University Press, 1925.

15:7. *Prologue Written by Samuel Johnson and Spoken by David Garrick at a Benefit Performance of Comus, April, 1750* [type-facsimile]. London: Oxford University Press, 1925.

15:8. *Eighteenth Century Tragedy,* ed. Michael R. Booth (*Irene,* pp. 67–154). (World's Classics, No. 603.) London: Oxford University Press, 1965.

COMMENTARY

15:20. B. "To the Author, etc." [praise of *Irene*], *General Advertiser,* February 18, 1749. Dated "Kent, Feb. 17."

15:21. *An Essay on Tragedy, with a Critical Examen of Mahomet and Irene.* London: R. Griffiths, 1749.

15:22. *A Criticism on Mahomet and Irene, in a Letter to the Author.* London: Reeve, 1749.

15:23. [Extract from *The Theatres, a Poetical Dissection*], *Whitehall*, December 14–17, 1771. Verse; includes attack on *Irene*.

15:24. Cook, Dutton. "*Irene* at Drury Lane," *Once a Week*, V (December 7, 1861), 651–56.

15:25. "Johnson's Irene," *Famous Plays*, ed. J. Fitzgerald Molloy, pp. 101–26. London: Ward and Downey, 1886, 1888, etc.

15:26. Brother Austin. *Dr. Johnson and the Drama* [paper read at Chingford, September 25, 1886]. Privately printed.

15:27. Lynn, W. T. "Johnson's 'Irene' and Astronomy," *N&Q*, 8th ser., IV (December 2, 1893), 446. See also W. F., *ibid.*, V (February 24, 1894), 156.

15:28. Radford, George H. "Johnson's 'Irene,'" *Shylock and Others*, pp. 95–115. London: Fisher Unwin, 1894.

15:29. Öftering, Michael. "Die Geschichte der Schönen Irene in der französischen und deutschen Literatur," *Zeitschrift für vergleichenden Literaturgeschichte*, n.s., XIII (1899), 27–45, 146–65. See also his Munich dissertation, *Die Geschichte der "Schönen Irene" in den modernen Literaturen*, Würzburg, 1897.

15:30. Archer, William. "About the Theatre: Dr. Johnson as a Playwright," *Tribune* [London], September 22, 1906, p. 2.

15:31. Loane, George G. "Time, Johnson and Shakespeare" [lines in the Drury-Lane prologue], *TLS*, August 9, 1917, p. 381; August 23, p. 406. See also J. W. Joynt, *ibid.*, August 16, p. 393; S. Butterworth, *ibid.*, September 13, p. 442; J. H. Jagger, *ibid.*, September 20, p. 454. See also *N&Q*, CLXXXIV (March 27, 1943), 184.

15:32. Walkley, Arthur B. "Johnson and the Theatre," *Fortnightly Review*, CV (April 1919), 578–87. Reprinted in item 6:28, pp. 199–217.

*15:33. Smith, D. Nichol. *Samuel Johnson's Irene*. Oxford: Clarendon Press, 1929. Reprinted from *Essays and Studies by Members of the English Association*, XIV (1929), 35–53. In part incorporated in item 14:5.

*15:34. Bronson, Bertrand H. "Johnson's 'Irene': Variations on a Tragic Theme," in item 10/6:254.

*15:35. Knapp, Mary E. "Prologue by Johnson" [for *Lethe*, 1740], *TLS*, January 4, 1947, p. 9.

15:36. Metzdorf, Robert F. "A Newly Recovered Criticism of Johnson's *Irene*," *Harvard Library Bulletin*, IV (Spring 1950), 265–68. A revision, "Johnson at Drury Lane," reprinted in item 10/6:306 (1959), pp. 57–64.

15:37. Lynch, James J. *Box, Pit, and Gallery*. Berkeley: University of California Press, 1953. Stage and society in Johnson's London.

15:38. Moran, Berna. "The Irene Story and Dr. Johnson's Sources," *MLN*, LXXI (February 1956), 87–91. Fails to use item 15:34.

15:39. Maxwell, J. C. "*Othello* and Johnson's *Irene*," *N&Q*, April 1957, p. 148.

15:40. Griffin, Robert J. "Dr. Johnson and the Drama," *Discourse: A Review of the Liberal Arts* (Concordia College, Moorhead, Minn.), V (Winter 1961–62), 95–101.

15:41. Waingrow, Marshall. "The Mighty Moral of *Irene*," in *From Sensibility to Romanticism*, ed. F. W. Hilles and Harold Bloom, pp. 79–92. New York: Oxford University Press, 1965.

15:42. Wolper, Roy S. "Samuel Johnson and the Drama" (dissertation, University of Pittsburgh, 1964), *Dissertation Abstracts*, XXVI (July 1065), 361.

15:43. Wolper, Roy S. "Johnson's Neglected Muse: The Drama," in *Studies in the Eighteenth Century: Papers Presented at the David Nichol Smith Memorial Seminar, Canberra 1966*, ed. R. F. Brissenden, pp. 109–17. Canberra: Australian National University Press, 1968.

16. PERIODICAL ESSAYS: *RAMBLER, ADVENTURER, IDLER*

EDITIONS

For the very numerous eighteenth- and early nineteenth-century editions of *The Rambler* (1750–52), *The Adventurer* (1752–54), and *The Idler* (1758–60), see Courtney, item 1/1:19, pp. 25–35, 39, 79–85. For two abortive series of weekly essays, "Observations" in the *Universal Chronicle*, and the *Weekly Correspondent*, see items 25:42 and 25:43. The *Rambler*, *Idler*, and *Adventurer* are routinely included in all collected editions of Johnson's works (item 2:1 *et seq.*); the two most recent complete editions are listed below, together with some of the more recent volumes of selections (for others, see Courtney).

*16:1. *The Idler and the Adventurer*, ed. Walter Jackson Bate, John M. Bullitt, and L. F. Powell. New Haven, Conn.: Yale University Press, 1963. Vol. II of the Yale Edition of Johnson's Works, item 2:8. Reviewed by R. P. Bond, *MLR*, LIX (April 1964), 275–76; (unfavorably) by Fredson Bowers, *MP*, LXI (May 1964), 298–309; W. B. Todd, *PQ*, XLIII (July 1964), 368–69; C. J. Rawson, *N&Q*, December 1965, 471–74.

*16:2. *The Rambler*, ed. W. J. Bate. Textual ed., Albrecht Strauss. New Haven, Conn.: Yale University Press, 1969. Vols. III, IV, and V of the Yale Edition of Johnson's Works, item 2:8.

16:3. *The Essays of Samuel Johnson*, ed. Stuart J. Reid. London: Walter Scott, 1888.

16:4. *Select Essays of Dr. Johnson*, ed. G. B. Hill, with etchings by Herbert Railton. 2 vols. London: J. M. Dent & Co., 1889.

16:5. *Essays from the Rambler and the Idler.* . . . (Little Masterpieces Series.) New York: Doubleday, Page, 1901.

16:6. *Selections from Dr. Johnson's "Rambler,"* ed. W. Hale White. (The Oxford Miscellany.) Oxford: Clarendon Press, 1907.

16:7. Dawson, W. J. and C. W., eds. *Great English Essayists*, pp. 49–55, 171–75. New York: Harper, 1909. *Rambler*, 117, excerpt from *Life of Milton*.

16:8. *Rambling Readings from "The Rambler,"* selected by R. B. Adam. [Buffalo, N.Y., n.d. (ca. 1920's).]

16:9. *Papers from the Idler*, ed. S. C. Roberts. Cambridge: Cambridge University Press, 1921, 1932.

16:10. *Essays by Samuel Johnson*, ed. Bergen Evans. Evanston, Ill.: Privately printed, 1940.

16:11. Facsimiles of *Ramblers* 5 and 60 in Augustan Reprint Society Publication No. 22 (1950), ed. B. H. Bronson (see item 14:7).

16:12. *The Rambler* [selections], with introduction by S. C. Roberts. London: J. M. Dent; New York: E. P. Dutton, 1953 (Everyman's Library).

16:13. *An Essay from the Rambler of April 3, 1750*. Privately printed by Ann and Leonard Bahr, 1965.

16:14. *Essays from the "Rambler," "Adventurer," and "Idler,"* ed. W. J. Bate. New Haven, Conn.: Yale University Press, 1968. 79 essays, 69 complete, from Vols. II–V of the Yale Edition of Johnson's Works.

Commentary

16:40. "To the Author of the Rambler. On Reading His Allegories," *Daily Advertiser*, August 24, 1750. Reprinted, *GM*, XX (October 1750), 465. Verse; high praise.

16:41. "To the Author of the Rambler," [Boddeley's] *Bath Journal*, August 27, 1750, p. 2. A highly complimentary 28-line poem.

16:42. [Smart, Christopher.] "On Gratitude," *The Student, or Oxford and Cambridge Miscellany*, II, no. 1 (October 2, 1750), 1–3. High praise of the style of *The Rambler*. See Arthur Sherbo, *JNL*, XIX, no. 2 (June 1959), 11. Reprinted *GM*, XX (October 1750), 465.

16:43. Thornton, Bonnell. "A Rambler, Number 99999," *Have at You All, or Drury Lane Journal*, January 30, 1752, no. 3, pp. 67–71. Extended burlesque.

16:44. Clément, Pierre. [Criticism of the *Rambler*], *Les Cinq Années Littéraires de M. Clément sur les ouvrages de littérature, qui ont paru dans les années 1748, 1749, 1750, 1751, et 1572*, II, 157, 368. The Hague: P. Gosse, jun., 1754; Berlin, 1755. Not seen; reprinted (from Berlin edition), *GM*, n.s., VII (February 1837), 138–39.

16:45. [Letter censuring *Idler* 26], *Grand Magazine*, I (September 1758), 471–72.

16:46. B., A. [Letter censuring *Idler* 65], *GM*, XXX (June 1760), 271–72. Defends Emlyn, editor of Hale's *Pleas of the Crown*.

16:47. Penny, Anne. *Anningait and Ajutt; a Greenland Tale. Inscribed to Mr. Samuel Johnson, M.A. Taken from the IVth Volume of His Ramblers, Versified by a Lady*. London: R. & J. Dodsley, 1761. Reprinted in her *Poems*, pp. 89–96, London: Dodsley, 1780.

16:48. [Review of 1st collected ed. of *The Idler*], *Critical Review*, XII (December 1761), 481.

16:49. "An Essay upon Versification," *London Chronicle*, XIV (July 14, 1763), 44–45. Disagrees with criticism of Pope in *Rambler* 92.

16:50. Seton, J. [Letter on *Idler* 89], *London Review*, I (April 1775), 313–16. Attacks the "frightful *caricatura*" of human nature found there and opposes to it the "amiable portrait" given by Rousseau.

16:51. *The Fatal Effects of Luxury and Indolence Exemplified in the History of Hacho, King of Lapland. A Tale of Lapland. A Tale of Dr. Johnson Versified*. Chesterfield: J. Bradley, 1778. From *Idler* 96, which is, however, by Warton, not Johnson.

16:52. Knox, Vicesimus. "Essay XXVIII. On the Periodical Essayists," *Essays, Moral and Literary*, I, 136–38. London: Dilly, 1782. Censures the style of *The Rambler*. The remarks on Johnson first appear in this edition and are reprinted in later editions of Knox's essays.

*16:53. Chalmers, Alexander. "Historical and Biographical Preface to the *Rambler*," Vol. XVI; ". . . the *Adventurer*," Vol. XIX; ". . . the *Idler*," Vol. XXVII, in *The British Essayists*. London: J. Johnson, etc., 1803. Often reprinted; volume numbers differ in different reprintings.

16:54. More, Hannah. *Hints Towards Forming the Character of a Young Princess*. 2 vols. London: Cadell and Davies, 1805. Chap. XXIX, "Of Periodical Essay Writers, Particularly Addison and Johnson."

16:55. Brydges, Sir Samuel Egerton. "The Ruminator, No. 58. On the Reception Originally Given to Dr. Johnson's Rambler," *Censura Literaria*, X, 71–77. London: Longman and Co., 1809.

*16:56. Drake, Nathan. *Essays, Biographical, Critical, and Historical, Illustrative of the Rambler, Adventurer, and Idler . . . and of the various periodical papers which . . . have been published between the close of the eighth volume of the Spectator and . . . 1809*. 2 vols. London: W. Suttaby, 1809. Contains "The Literary Life of Dr. Johnson," I, 111–488, and a bibliography, I, 489–99.

16:57. Montagu, Basil. "Enquiries respecting the insolvent debtor's bill, with the opinions of Dr. Paley, Mr. Burke, and Dr. Johnson, upon imprisonment for debt," *Pamphleteer*, V (May 1815), 513–42. Reprinted ("second edition") separately, 1816. Reprints *Idlers* 22 and 38.

16:58. Hazlitt, William. "Lecture V: On the Periodical Essayists," *Lectures on the English Comic Writers.* London: Taylor and Hessey, 1819; often reprinted. An unfavorable comparison of *The Rambler* with *The Spectator.*

16:59. Eisentraut, Ludwig. "Dr. Johnson as an Essayist," *Realschule erster Ordnung zu Nordhausen,* pp. 1–29. Nordhausen: Kirchner, 1879.

16:60. Hill, George Birkbeck. "On a Neglected Book" [*The Rambler*], *Macmillan's,* XLVIII (September 1883), 414–23.

16:61. "Johnson's *Rambler,*" *Saturday Review,* LVI (September 15, 1883), 333–34. Stresses its humor, said to be neglected by a writer in *Macmillan's* (presumably item 16:60).

16:62. Morris, Mowbray. "The Terrific Diction," *Macmillan's,* LIV (September 1886), 361–68. A slashing review of Swinburne's prose style in his *Miscellanies,* 1886, prefaced by a discussion of *Idler* 36.

16:63. H., F. "Dr. Johnson Self-Criticized" [revisions of *The Rambler*], *Nation,* LXIV (June 10, 1897), 434–35.

16:64. Bowen, Edwin W. "The Essay in the Eighteenth Century," *Sewanee Review,* X, no. 1 (January 1902), 12–27.

16:65. "Ranger." "The English Essayists, II. Johnson and Goldsmith," *Bookman* (London), XXVIII (July 1905), 124–26.

16:66. Marr, George S. "Johnson's Periodical Essay Work," *The Periodical Essayists of the Eighteenth Century,* pp. 116–38. London: James Clarke & Co., [1923].

16:67. Christie, O. F. *Johnson the Essayist.* London: Grant Richards, 1924.

16:68. "The Athletic Lady of the Eighteenth Century" [*Idler* 6], *Golden Book,* I (June 1925), 869–70.

16:69. Newmark, Leo. "Johnsoniana" [a German misapprehension about *The Rambler*], *N&Q,* CXLIX (August 15, 1925), 117.

*16:70. Powell, Lawrence F. "Johnson's Part in *The Adventurer,*" *RES,* III (October 1927), 420–29. Reprinted in item 1/4:19. A revised version appears in Vol. II of the Yale Edition of Johnson's Works, 1963 (item 16:1).

*16:71. Smith, D. Nichol. "Johnson's Revision of His Publications" [chiefly the essays], *Johnson and Boswell Revised by Themselves and Others,* pp. 7–18. Oxford: Clarendon Press, 1928.

16:72. Smith, D. Nichol. "The Contributors to *The Rambler* and *The Idler,*" *Bodleian Quarterly Record,* VII (4th quarter, 1934), 508–9.

16:73. Murphy, Mallie J. "*The Rambler,* No. 191," *PMLA,* L (September 1935), 926–28.

16:74. Pratt, Willis Winslow. "Leigh Hunt and *The Rambler,*" *University of Texas Studies in English, 1938,* pp. 67–84.

16:75. Bradford, Curtis B. "Johnson's Revision of *The Rambler,*" *RES,* XV (July 1939), 302–14. From dissertation, Yale University, 1937.

16:76. Bradford, Curtis B. "The Edinburgh 'Ramblers,' " *MLR*, XXXIV (April 1939), 241–44.

16:77. Leyburn, Ellen Douglass. "The Translations of the Mottoes and Quotations in the *Rambler*," *RES*, XVI (April 1940), 169–76.

*16:78. Green, Boylston. "Samuel Johnson's *Idler*: A Critical Study" (dissertation, Yale University, 1941], *Dissertation Abstracts*, XXV (December 1964), 3554.

16:79. R[endall], V[ernon]. "Johnson: A Slip in Latin Poetry" [*Adventurer* 58], *N&Q*, CLXXXI (August 23, 1941), 104.

16:80. [Johnson's idea of a submarine: *Rambler* 105], *N&Q*, CLXXXII (May 2, 1942), 239.

16:81. Chapman, Robert William. "The Sale of Johnson's 'Idler,' " *N&Q*, CLXXXIV (April 24, 1943), 256.

16:82. Elistratova, A. A. ["Samuel Johnson and the Essay in the Second Half of the Century,"] *Istoriya Angliskoi Literatury* [History of English Literature], I, pt. 2, 457–65. Moscow-Leningrad: Academy of Sciences of the USSR, 1945.

16:83. Dobrée, Bonamy. *English Essayists*, pp. 22–24. London: William Collins Sons & Co., 1946.

16:84. Greenough, Chester Noyes. *A Bibliography of the Theophrastan Character in English with Several Portrait Characters*, prepared for publication by J. Milton French. Cambridge, Mass.: Harvard University Press, 1947.

16:85. Davidson, Frank. "Hawthorne's Use of a Pattern from the *Rambler*," *MLN*, LXIII (December 1948), 545–48.

16:86. Sherbo, Arthur. "Father Lobo's *Voyage to Abyssinia* and *Ramblers* 204 and 205," *N&Q*, September 1, 1951, p. 388.

16:87. Sherbo, Arthur. "The Translation of the Motto for *The Adventurer* No. 126," *N&Q*, November 10, 1951, pp. 497–98.

16:88. Sherbo, Arthur. "The Translations of Mottoes and Quotations in Johnson's *Rambler*," *N&Q*, June 21, 1952, pp. 278–79. See also W. H. J., *N&Q*, July 19, 1952, p. 328.

16:89. Sherbo, Arthur. "The Making of *Ramblers* 186 and 187" [borrowings from Hans Egede, *A Description of Greenland*, 1745], *PMLA*, LXVII (June 1952), 575–80.

*16:90. Bloom, Edward A. "Symbolic Names in Johnson's Periodical Essays," *MLQ*, XIII (December 1952), 333–52.

16:91. Graham, W. H. "Dr. Johnson's *The Rambler*," *Contemporary Review*, CLXXXIV (July 1953), 50–53.

16:92. Cohen, B. Bernard. "Hawthorne's 'Mrs. Bullfrog' and *The Rambler*," *PQ*, XXXII (October 1953), 382–87.

16:93. Sherbo, Arthur. "The Mottoes to *Idlers* 88 and 101," *JNL*, XIII, no. 4 (December 1953), 10–11.

16:94. Sherbo, Arthur. "Two Notes on Johnson's Revisions" [*Adventurer* and Mary Masters's poems], *MLR*, L (July 1955), 311–15.

16:95. Watson, Melvin R. *Magazine Serials and the Essay Tradition, 1746–1820* [contains discussion of Johnson's periodical essays]. (Louisiana State University Studies, Humanities Series, No. 6.) Baton Rouge: Louisiana State University Press, 1956.

16:96. Sherbo, Arthur. "Translation of the Mottoes and Quotations in *The Adventurer*," in item 19:103, pp. 145–74.

16:97. Heinle, Edwin C. "The Eighteenth Century Allegorical Essay" (dissertation, Columbia University, 1957), *Dissertation Abstracts*, XVII (1957), 1763.

16:98. Fox, Robert C. "Dr. Johnson, Bishop Wilkins, and the Submarine" [*Rambler* 105], *N&Q*, August 1958, pp. 364, 368.

16:99. Greany, Helen T. "Johnson and the Institutes" [Quintilian's], *N&Q*, October 1958, p. 445.

16:100. Roberts, S. C. "The Author of the *Rambler*," *New Rambler*, January 1959, pp. 2–12.

16:101. Elder, A. T. "Irony and Humour in the *Rambler*," *University of Toronto Quarterly*, XXX (October 1960), 57–71.

16:102. Griffith, Philip M. "A Study of the *Adventurer* (1752–1754)" (dissertation, University of North Carolina, 1961), *Dissertation Abstracts*, XXII (1962), 3662–63.

16:103. Fox, Robert C. "The Imaginary Submarines of Dr. Johnson and Richard Owen Cambridge" [*Rambler* 105], *PQ*, XL (January 1961), 112–19.

16:104. Elder, A. T. "A Johnson Borrowing from Addison?" [*Rambler* 10 and *Spectator* 221], *N&Q*, February 1961, pp. 53–54.

16:105. Hamilton, Harlan W. "Boswell's Suppression of a Paragraph in *Rambler 60*," *MLN*, LXXVII (March 1961), 218–20.

16:106. Knieger, Bernard. "The Moral Essays of Dr. Samuel Johnson," *Personalist*, XLII (Summer 1961), 361–67.

16:107. Griffith, Philip Mahone. "The Authorship of the Papers signed 'A' in Hawkesworth's *Adventurer*: A Stronger Case for Dr. Richard Bathurst," *Tulane Studies in English*, XII (1962), 63–70. But see item 16:120.

16:108. Mayo, Robert D. *The English Novel in the Magazines, 1740–1815* [*Rambler*, *Adventurer*, etc.], pp. 93–117 and *passim*. Evanston, Ill.: Northwestern University Press, 1962.

16:109. Dubuque, Remi Gerard. "Samuel Johnson's *Idlers*: A Study of Satire, Humor, and Irony" (dissertation, Notre Dame, 1963), *Dissertation Abstracts*, XXIV (December 1963), 2461.

16:110. Fleeman, J. D. "The Reprint of *Rambler*, No. 1," *Library*, 5th ser., XVIII (December 1963), 288–94.

16:111. Carroll, Perry Alice Organ. "Samuel Johnson and the Art of Moralizing: A Study of the Periodical Essays and *Rasselas*." Dissertation, Harvard University, 1964–65.

*16:112. Strauss, Albrecht B. "The Dull Duty of an Editor: On Editing the Text of Johnson's *Rambler*," *Bookmark* (Friends of the University of North Carolina Library), No. 35 (June 1965), 8–22.

16:113. Elder, A. T. "Thematic Patterning and Development in Johnson's Essays," *SP*, LXII (July 1965), 610–32.

16:114. Howes, Victor. "Reading *The Rambler*," *Christian Science Monitor*, July 15, 1965, p. 6.

16:115. Strauss, Albrecht B. "Writer and Editor" [Johnson's revision of Richardson's *Rambler*], *TLS*, December 2, 1965, p. 1112.

16:116. Misenheimer, James B. "Dr. Johnson on the Essay," *New Rambler*, January 1966, pp. 13–17.

16:117. Rhodes, Rodman D. "*Idler* No. 24 and Johnson's Epistemology," *MP*, LXIV (August 1966), 10–21.

16:118. Levin, U. D. "Kto avtor 'vostochnoi' povesti 'Obidag'?" ["Who is the author of the 'eastern' tale 'Obidah'?"], *Izvestia Akademia Nauk USSR* (Serila literatury i iazyka), XXV (1966), 431–33. Demonstrates that this "tale," the authorship of which has puzzled Russian bibliographers, is an eighteenth-century translation of *Rambler* 65.

16:119. Liebert, Herman W. *Who Dropped the Copy for "Rambler" 109?* Printed to commemorate Johnson's birthday. New Haven, Conn., 1966.

*16:120. Lams, Victor J., Jr. "The 'A' Papers in the *Adventurer*: Bonnell Thornton, Not Dr. Bathurst, Their Author" [cites parallel passages in *Connoisseur* essays], *SP*, LXIV (January 1967), 83–96.

16:121. Corder, Jim W. "Ethical Argument and *Rambler* No. 154," *Quarterly Journal of Speech*, LIV (December 1968), 352–56.

*16:122. Wiles, R. M. "The Contemporary Distribution of Johnson's *Rambler*," *Eighteenth-Century Studies*, II (December 1968), 155–71.

16:123. Bullough, Geoffrey. "Johnson the Essayist," *New Rambler*, June 1968, pp. 16–33.

17. THE *DICTIONARY OF THE ENGLISH LANGUAGE*: JOHNSON
AS A STUDENT OF LANGUAGE

17:1. Johnson, Samuel. *A Dictionary of the English Language*. 2 vols., folio. London: Knapton, etc., 1755. Reviewed by Sir Tanfield Leman(?), *Monthly Review*, XII (April 1755), 292–324; by Adam Smith, *Edinburgh Review*, I (June 1755), 61–73; by M. Maty, *Journal Britannique*, XVII (July–August 1755), 217–44; in *Brittische Bibliothek* (Leipzig), III, pt. 2 (1758), 111–64. Facsimile reprint, New York: AMS Press, 1967. 2nd ed., 1756; 3rd ed., 1765; 4th ed. (heavily revised by Johnson), 1773. Abr. (by Johnson), 2 vols., 8vo, 1756. For the very many later eighteenth- and nineteenth-century editions, enlargements, and abridgements, see Courtney, item 1/1:19, pp. 54–72.

17:2. Chesterfield, Philip Dormer Stanhope, 4th Earl of. [Essays in praise of Johnson's *Dictionary*], *The World*, No. 100 (November 28, 1754); No. 101 (December 5, 1754).

17:3. Maxwell, John. *A Letter from a Friend in England to Mr. Maxwell complaining of his dilatoriness in the publication of his so-long-promised work: With a character of Mr. Johnson's English Dictionary, lately published.* . . . Dublin: Printed by S. Powell, 1755.

17:4. [Attack on the *Dictionary* and the pension], *North Briton*, No. 12 (August 21, 1762).

17:5. LL. B. "Remarks on Johnson's *Dictionary*," *Political Register*, III (October 1768), 209–13.

17:6. Lexiphanes [George Colman the elder]. [Mock "explications" of simple words in "Johnsonese"], *St. James's Chronicle*, No. 1526 (December 1–4, 1770). Reprinted in Colman's *Prose on Several Occasions*, II, 92–97. London: T. Cadell, 1787. A mock reply by "Academicus," *St. James's Chronicle*, December 11–13, in reality continues the attack.

17:7. [Maclaurin, John.] "On Johnson's Dictionary," *Weekly Magazine* (Edinburgh), XIX (January 14, 1773), 81. Verse.

17:8. Fergusson, Robert. "To Dr. Samuel Johnson. Food for a New Edition of His Dictionary," *Weekly Magazine* (Edinburgh), October 21, 1773, p. 114. Reprinted in his *Poems on Various Subjects*, II, 125–28, Edinburgh, 1779.

17:9. Tooke, John Horne. *A Letter to John Dunning, Esq.* London, 1778. Included in his Επεα πτεροεντα, *or, The Diversions of Purley*. London: J. Johnson, 1786. Often reprinted. Occasional criticism of Johnson's *Dictionary*.

17:10. Craig, Alexander. *The Mirror*, No. 89 (March 14, 1780). Laetitia Lappet, the milliner, is discouraged by the definition of "network."

17:11. R., J. "A Censure of Dr. Johnson's Dictionary, and of the Other Dictionaries of the English Language," *Westminster Magazine*, X (June 1782), 324–35.

17:12. Adelung, Johann Christoph. *Neues grammatisch-kritischen Wörterbuch der englischen Sprache für die Deutschen; vornehmlich aus dem*

grössern englischen Werke des Hrn. Samuel Johnsons nach dessen vier-
ten Ausgabe gezogen, und mit vielen Wörtern, Bedeutungen und Bey-
spielen vermehrt. Leipzig: Schwickert. Vol. I, 1783. Vol. II, 1796. Adelung's preface was translated by Anthony F. M. Willich and printed as
"On the relative merits and demerits of Johnson's English Dictionary,"
in Willich's *Elements of the Critical Philosophy . . . To which are*
added three philological essays translated from the German of John
Christopher Adelung, pp. cxxxi–cxxxii, London: T. N. Longman, 1798.

17:13. C., H. [Herbert Croft.] "Letter to the Editor from the Gentleman
employed upon a New Dictionary of the English Language," *GM*, LVII
(August 1787), 651–52. It will contain "5000 words which are not in the
wonderful, though very imperfect, Dictionary of my great friend and
master Johnson." See also A. B. D., *GM*, LVIII (January 1788), 7–8;
H[erbert] C[roft], (February), 91–92. See also Croft's *An Unfinished*
Letter to the Right Honourable William Pitt, Concerning the New Dic-
tionary of the English Language. London: "Printed in March, 1788, but
neither finished nor published." Discussed in Courtney, item 1/1:19, p.
69, and in item 17:173.

17:14. C., A. B. "Remarks on Dr. Johnson's Dictionary," *GM*, LVIII (November 1788), 948, 1152–54. Critical. Replied to by "Indignant," *ibid.*,
LIX (July 1789), 613–14.

17:15. Piozzi, Hester Lynch. *British Synonymy; or, an attempt at regulat-*
ing the choice of words in familiar conversation. London: G. G. J. and
J. Robinson, 1794. Occasional Johnsonian anecdotes. Excerpts reprinted
as "Piozziana" in *GM*, n.s., XXXI–XXXIV (January 1849–September
1850).

17:16. N., W. [Additions to Grose's account of Johnson in Gough Square
(item 3:30)], *GM*, LXIX (Supplement 1799), 1171–72. Francis Stuart, Johnson's amanuensis, and the making of the *Dictionary.*

17:17. G., O. G. [Attack on Johnson's *Dictionary* and style quoted and re-
butted], *GM*, LXX (April 1800), 335.

17:18. Mason, George. *A Supplement to Johnson's English Dictionary; of*
which the palpable errors are attempted to be rectified and its material
omissions supplied. London: J. White, etc., 1801. Reply by Philo-John-
son, *GM*, LXXIV (March 1804), 222–23.

17:19. Pegge, Samuel (the younger). *Anecdotes of the English Language;*
Chiefly Regarding the Local Dialect of London. London: Rivington,
1802. Criticism of Johnson as lexicographer, pp. 250–53, quoted in review, *GM*, LXXIII (February 1803), 148–49.

17:20. Webster, Noah. *A Compendious Dictionary of the English Lan-*
guage. Hartford, Conn.: Hudson and Goodwin; New Haven, Conn.: Increase Cooke, 1806. Preface is severely critical of Johnson's *Dictionary.*

Reviewed in *Monthly Anthology*, VII (October 1809), 246–64 (a sturdy defense of Johnson against Webster's strictures).

17:21. Webster, Noah. *A Letter to Dr. David Ramsay . . . respecting the errors in Johnson's dictionary and other lexicons.* New Haven, Conn.: Printed by Oliver Steele and Co., 1807.

17:22. Richardson, Charles. *Illustrations of English Philology; consisting of I. A Critical Examination of Dr. Johnson's Dictionary. . . .* London: Gale and Fenner, 1815.

17:23. Monti, Vincenzo. "Parallelo del Vocabolario della Crusca con quello della lingua inglese compilato da S. Johnson," *Proposta di Alcune Correzioni ed Aggiunte al Vocabolario della Crusca*, II, pt. 1, 1–52. Milan: Imprimeria Regia, 1819. Contains extensive passages translated from the preface to the *Dictionary*.

17:24. C., P. C. "Stray Thoughts" [against Johnson's *Dictionary*], *GM*, XCIX (August 1829), 120–24.

17:25. [Detailed comparison of Johnson's and Webster's dictionaries], *Westminster Review*, XIV (January 1831), 56–93.

17:26. Lawrence, Frederick. "A Few Words on Johnson's Dictionary," *Sharpe's London Journal*, X (1849), 227–30.

17:27. Trench, Richard Chenevix. *On Some Deficiencies in Our English Dictionaries.* London: J. W. Parker, 1857. 2nd ed., 1860. Various small strictures on Johnson's, *passim*.

17:28. [Report of presentation of Johnson's marked copies of Burton's *Anatomy of Melancholy* and Hale's *Pleas of the Crown* to the Philological Society planning the New English Dictionary], *Living Age*, LXXX (January–March 1864), 120. See item 17:147.

*17:29. Wheatley, Henry B. "Chronological Notices of the Dictionaries of the English Language," *Transactions of the Philological Society, 1865*, pp. 218–93. London: Asher & Co., [1865].

17:30. White, Richard Grant. "A Desultory Denunciation of English Dictionaries" [Johnson's included], *Galaxy*, VII (May 1869), 655–68.

17:31. Skeat, Walter W. "Dr. Johnson's Definition of 'Oats,'" *N&Q*, 4th ser., X (October 19, 1872), 309. Possible source in Burton's *Anatomy of Melancholy*.

17:32. [Tylor, Edward Burnett.] "English Dictionaries," *Quarterly Review*, CXXXV (October 1873), 235–54. Review of the 1866–70 Johnson-Todd-Latham *Dictionary* and others.

17:33. Solly, Edward. "Johnson's Dictionary," *N&Q*, 5th ser., V (March 4, 1876), 188. Particularly the definition of "excise." Continued, V, 355; VI, 157, 298, 339, 417, 545; and VII, 195.

17:34. Wheatley, Henry B. "The Story of Johnson's Dictionary," *Antiquary*, XI (January 1885), 11–17.

17:35. Stringer, George Alfred. *Leisure Moments in Gough Square, or The Beauties and Quaint Conceits of Johnson's Dictionary.* Buffalo, N.Y.: Ulbrich and Kingsley, 1886.

17:36. Saunders, Frederick. "Johnson's 'Dictionary,'" *The Story of Some Famous Books*, pp. 86–90. London: Elliot Stock, 1887.

17:37. Thompson, G. H. "Dr. Johnson and Oats," *N&Q*, 7th ser., III (January 8, 1887), 26. See also T. N. Brushfield, *ibid.*, IX (February 8, 1890), 107; Edward Marshall, *ibid.* (March 1, 1890), 172; Jonathan Bouchier, *ibid.*, 8th ser., IX (June 6, 1896), 451.

17:38. N., F. [Sale of Horne Tooke's annotated copy of the *Dictionary*], *N&Q*, 7th ser., IX (June 7, 1890), 456. See also C. A. Ward, in *N&Q*, May 24, 1890, p. 406.

17:39. Gennadius, Joannes. *Dr. Johnson as a Grecian.* Privately printed, 1898. Reprinted in item 6:16, pp. 19–48. For commentary, see *N&Q*, 9th ser., IV (December 2, 1899), 451–52; 9th ser., V (January 27, 1900), 71–72.

17:40. Radford, George H. "Johnson's Dictionary," in item 6:28, pp. 103–21.

*17:41. Murray, James A. H. *The Evolution of English Lexicography*, pp. 38–43. Oxford: Clarendon Press, 1900.

17:42. Dobson, Austin. "How Dr. Johnson Wrote His Dictionary," *Pall Mall Magazine*, XXXIV (December 1904), 517–22.

17:43. Skeat, W. W. "'Kidnapper'" [identifies Addison quotation in *Dictionary* entry for this word—*Spectator* 311], *N&Q*, May 4, 1907, pp. 345–46.

17:44. Long, Percy W. "English Dictionaries before Webster," *Bibliographical Society of America Papers*, IV (1910), 25–43.

17:45. Steger, Stewart A. *American Dictionaries*, pp. 14–17. Baltimore, Md.: Furst Co., 1913.

17:46. "'The Reader' and Dr. Johnson's Dictionary," *N&Q*, 11th ser., VIII (July 12, 1913), 36–37. See also W. P. Courtney, *ibid.* (July 26), 75; A. E. Bateman and Thomas White, *N&Q*, CLV (August 4, 1928), 84–85.

17:47. Kirkland, Winifred. "A Man in a Dictionary," *Outlook*, CXXI (February 12, 1919), 275.

17:48. Kirkland, Winifred. "Man in the Dictionary," *The View Vertical*, pp. 198–210. Boston: Houghton Mifflin Co., 1920.

17:49. Gilchrist, Marie Emilie. "A Dictionary to Read," *Poet Lore*, XXXI (June 1920), 291–96.

17:50. Parry, John J. "Doctor Johnson's Interest in Welsh," *MLN*, XXXVI (June 1921), 374–76.

17:51. Gordon, J. W. "The English Dictionary," *Quarterly Review*, CCXL (July 1923), 164–82.

17:52. Cox, Harold, and John E. Chandler. *The House of Longman*, pp. 10–11. London: Longmans, Green & Co., 1925.

17:53. Rypins, Stanley. "Johnson's Dictionary Reviewed by His Contemporaries," *PQ*, IV (July 1925), 281–86.

17:54. Collison-Morley, Lacy. "Dr. Johnson and the Modern Languages," *Cornhill Magazine*, n.s., LIX (November 1925), 572–77.

17:55. Pocock, Guy Noel. "Lexicographer's Chair," *The Little Room*, pp. 102–9. New York: E. P. Dutton & Co., [1926].

17:56. Chapman, Robert William. "Johnson's *Plan of a Dictionary*," *RES*, II (April 1926), 216–18.

17:57. Powell, Lawrence F. "Johnson and the *Encyclopédie*" [borrowings from Johnson], *RES*, II (July 1926), 335–37.

17:58. Bennett, James O. "The Dictionary," *Much Loved Books*, pp. 366–73. New York: Liveright Publishing Corp., 1927.

17:59. Cuming, A. "A Copy of Shakespeare's Works Which Formerly Belonged to Dr. Johnson" [used in making the *Dictionary*], *RES*, III (April 1927), 208–12. See also items 17:125 and 17:130.

17:60. Newton, A. Edward. "The Pathos and Humor of Dr. Johnson's Dictionary," *Atlantic Monthly*, CXXXIX (April 1927), 502–11. See also *World Review*, IV (April 25, 1927), 170. Reprinted in *This Book-Collecting Game*, pp. 309–32, Boston: Little, Brown & Co., 1928.

17:61. Burr, Charles W. "Some Medical Words in Johnson's Dictionary," *Annals of Medical History*, IX (June 1927), 183–89.

*17:62. Flasdieck, Hermann M. "Das Zeitalter Johnsons," *Der Gedanke einer englischen Sprachakademie in Vergangenheit und Gegenwart*, pp. 101–43. Jena: Verlag der Frommanschen Buchhandlung, 1928.

17:63. Stark, Eula Genevieve. "Samuel Johnson's Reading for the *Dictionary*." Master's thesis, University of Chicago, 1928.

17:64. [Corrected copy of 4th ed. in Rylands Library], *Bulletin of John Rylands Library*, XII (January 1928), 9–10.

17:65. Bensly, Edward. "Johnson's Dictionary: 'Excise,'" *N&Q*, CLIV (January 7, 1928), 14.

17:66. McGovern, J. B. "Johnson's Dictionary" [sale of proof sheets of 1st ed.], *N&Q*, CLIV (January 28, 1928), 62.

17:67. Wood, W. A. "The Preface to Dr. Johnson's Dictionary," *Lichfield Mercury*, May 4, 1928, p. 5.

17:68. Ingpen, Roger, and C. A. Stonehill. *A Relic of Dr. Johnson* [his copy of Bacon's *Works*]. London: Ingpen and Stonehill, [1929].

17:69. Winterich, John T. "Samuel Johnson and His *Dictionary of the English Language*," *Books and the Man*, pp. 230–50. New York: Greenberg, Publisher, 1929. Reprinted in *Carrousel for Bibliophiles*, ed. William Targ, pp. 193–207, New York: Duschnes, Crawford, 1947.

17:70. Vernon, Frederick. "Johnson's Dictionary" [quarto edition by Longmans, 1785], *TLS*, June 27, 1929, p. 514. See also J. Gordon Hayes, *ibid.*, July 11, p. 558.

17:71. Chapman, R. W. "Dr. Johnson, Dr. Bridges and the B.B.C." [Latinisms, etc.], *TLS*, August 15, 1929, p. 637.

17:72. Segar, Mary. "Dictionary Making in the Early Eighteenth Century," *RES*, VII (April 1931), 210–13.

17:73. Haight, Gordon S. "Johnson's Copy of Bacon's *Works*" [used in making the *Dictionary*], *Yale University Library Gazette*, VI (April 1932), 67–73.

17:74. Newmark, Leo. "Dr. Johnson Quoting Himself" [*London* and *Dictionary*], *N&Q*, CLXIII (July 2, 1932), 11–12.

17:75. Read, Allen Walker. "Furnivall's Review of Dr. Johnson," *Word Study*, VIII (September 1932), 2. His condemnation of the preface, under the mistaken impression it was by R. G. Latham.

17:76. Mathews, Mitford M. "From Cawdrey to Johnson," *A Survey of English Dictionaries*, pp. 18–33. London: Oxford University Press, 1933.

17:77. *The Preface to Johnson's Dictionary of the English Language 1755.* Cleveland: Rowfant Club, 1934.

17:78. Boddey, Margaret P. "Johnson and Burton" ["oats"], *TLS*, June 21, 1934, p. 443. See also Donald Dorian, *ibid.*, September 13, p. 620.

17:79. Read, Allen Walker. "The History of Dr. Johnson's Definition of 'Oats,'" *Agricultural History*, VIII (July 1934), 81–94.

17:80. Read, Allen Walker. "The Contemporary Quotations in Johnson's Dictionary," *ELH*, II (November 1935), 246–51.

17:81. J., W. H. "Johnson: Misquotations" [in *Dictionary*], *N&Q*, CLXX (June 6, 1936), 403.

17:82. MacDonald, Angus. "Johnson as Lexicographer," *University of Edinburgh Journal*, VIII (Summer 1936), 17–23.

17:83. Bennett, William W. "Dr. Samuel Johnson and Some Musical Definitions," *Choir*, XXVIII (April 1937), 90–91.

*17:84. Cooper, Lane. "Dr. Johnson on Oats and Other Grains," *PMLA*, LII (September 1937), 785–802. See also item 17:86.

17:85. McHale, Carlos F. *An Injustice of Human Memory: A Defense of the Greatest English Lexicographer.* New York: Privately printed, 1938.

17:86. Purcell, J. M. "Smollett on Oats as Food for Scots," *PMLA*, LIII (June 1938), 629.

17:87. Metzdorf, Robert F. "Notes on Johnson's 'Plan of a Dictionary,'" *Library*, XIX (September, December 1938), 198–201, 363.

17:88. C., T. C. "Johnson: Pedantry about Words," *N&Q*, CLXXVI (June 24, 1939), 437–38. See also *ibid.*, CLXXVII (July 15), 50.

17:89. "Philoscotus." "Johnson and Scott: A Greek Inscription" [sundial at Abbotsford], *N&Q*, CLXXVII (August 5, 1939), 96.

*17:90. Freed, Lewis M. "The Sources of Johnson's Dictionary" (dissertation, Cornell University), *Cornell University Abstracts of Theses, 1939*, pp. 31–34. Ithaca, N.Y.: Cornell University Press, 1940.

*17:91. Gove, Philip B. "Notes on Serialization and Competitive Publishing" [Johnson's and Bailey's dictionaries, 1755], *Proceedings of the Oxford Bibliographical Society*, V (1940), 305–22.

17:92. Hyde, Arnold. "Reading Johnson's Dictionary," *Papers, Manchester Literary Club*, LXV (1940), 82–88.

17:93. [Dodge, Norman L.] "A Plan That Hatched" [plan of the *Dictionary*, 1747], *Month at Goodspeed's Book Shop*, XI (January 1940), 122–25.

17:94. Allen, Harold B. "Samuel Johnson and the Authoritarian Principle in Linguistic Criticism." Dissertation, University of Michigan, 1941. Abstract included in *Microfilm Abstracts*, IV, no. 1 (1942), 34–35.

17:95. Wall, S. H. " 'Words Are the Daughters of Earth,' " *N&Q*, CLXXXII (April 25, 1942), 231. See also R. M. Hewitt, *ibid.* (June 27), 361; L. R. M. Strachan, *ibid.*, CLXXXIII (July 4), 27. Possible sources for Johnson's quotation in the preface to the *Dictionary*, including a line from Samuel Madden's *Boulter's Monument*.

17:96. Parker, Walter. "Johnson's Dictionary and Its Maker," *Congregational Quarterly*, XXI (July 1943), 219–22.

17:97. Stenberg, Theodore. "Quotations from Pope in Johnson's Dictionary," University of Texas *Studies in English, 1944*, pp. 197–210.

*17:98. Starnes, De Witt T., and Gertrude E. Noyes. *The English Dictionary from Cawdrey to Johnson, 1604–1755*. Chapel Hill: University of North Carolina Press, 1946.

17:99. Wimsatt, William K., Jr. "Johnson and Scots," *TLS*, March 9, 1946, p. 115. See also Vincent B. Hudson, *ibid.*, April 13, p. 175.

17:100. Leavitt, Robert K. *Noah's Ark: New England Yankees and the Endless Quest*, pp. 13–19, 105–6. Springfield, Mass.: G. & C. Merriam Co., 1947.

17:101. Wallis, John E. W. *Dr. Johnson and His English Dictionary* [see item 6:22]. Lichfield: The Johnson's Head, [1947]. Rev. ed., 1948. See also *TLS*, May 17, 1947, p. 239.

17:102. Wimsatt, William K., Jr. "Johnson on Electricity," *RES*, XXIII (July 1947), 257–60.

17:103. Speirs, James. "In Praise of Lexicographers," *Chambers's Journal*, 9th ser., I (July 1947), 413–15.

*17:104. Wimsatt, William K., Jr. *Philosophic Words: A Study of Style and Meaning in the "Rambler" and "Dictionary" of Samuel Johnson*. New Haven, Conn.: Yale University Press, 1948. Reprinted, Hamden, Conn.:

Archon Books, 1968. Reviewed by W. R. Keast, *PQ*, XXVIII (July 1949), 393–95. Reply by Wimsatt, *ibid.*, XXIX (January 1950), 84–88. Reviewed by Anna Granville Hatcher, *MLN*, LXVII (February 1952), 125–29. See also Donald Davie, "Berkeley and 'Philosophic Words,'" *Studies* (Dublin), XLIV (Autumn 1955), 319–24.

17:105. McCue, George S. "Sam Johnson's Word-Hoard," *MLN*, LXIII (January 1948), 43–45.

17:106. Wimsatt, William K., Jr. "Johnson's Treatment of Bolingbroke in the Dictionary," *MLR*, XLIII (January 1948), 78–80.

17:107. Wimsatt, William K., Jr., and Margaret H. Wimsatt. "Self-Quotations and Anonymous Quotations in Johnson's Dictionary," *ELH*, XV (March 1948), 60–68.

17:108. McAtee, W. L. "Johnson on the Letter 'H,'" *Word Study*, XXIV (December 1948), 6. See also reply by T. O. Mabbott, *ibid.* (May 1949), 7–8.

17:109. R[endall], V[ernon]. "Johnson and Scaliger on Dictionary-Making," *N&Q*, CXCIV (April 16, 1949), 161–62.

17:110. Atkinson, A. D. "Notes on Johnson's 'Dictionary,'" *N&Q*, CXCIV (October 15, 1949), 443–45; CXCV (January 21–June 10, 1950), 36–37, 55–56, 164–67, 249–50, 338–41, 516–19, 541–46, 561–63.

17:111. Greene, Donald J. "'Sooth' in Keats, Milton, Shakespeare, and Dr. Johnson" [crux in *Eve of St. Agnes* explained by definition in *Dictionary*], *MLN*, LXV (December 1950), 514–17. See also C. A. Luttrell, *N&Q*, September 15, 1951, pp. 405–7, and reply by Greene, May 10, 1952, pp. 204–5.

17:112. Greene, D. J. "Johnson's Definition of 'Network'" [echoes of Johnson's reading of Sir Thomas Browne's *Garden of Cyrus*], *N&Q*, CXCIV (December 10, 1949), 538–39.

*17:113. Wimsatt, William K., Jr. "Samuel Johnson and Dryden's *Du Fresnoy*" [use of translation of *The Art of Painting* in *Dictionary*], *SP*, XLVIII (January 1951), 26–39.

17:114. Hudson, Wilson M. "Whitaker's Attack on Johnson's Etymologies" [in his *History of Manchester*, 1775], *Huntington Library Quarterly*, XIV (May 1951), 285–97.

17:115. Michell, H. "Arrack" [in *Dictionary* and *Rambler* 16], *N&Q*, May 26, 1951, p. 237. See also A. D. Atkinson, July 7, p. 306, and T. O. Mabbott, July 21, p. 328.

17:116. Atkinson, A. D. "Dr. Johnson and Newton's *Opticks*," *RES*, n.s., II (July 1951), 226–37.

17:117. Atkinson, A. D. "Donne Quotations in Johnson's Dictionary," *N&Q*, September 1, 1951, pp. 387–88.

17:118. Sherbo, Arthur. "Dr. Johnson's *Dictionary*: A Preliminary Puff" [by

"W. S." (William Strahan?) in *Gentleman's Magazine*, 1749], *PQ*, XXXI (January 1952), 91–93.

17:119. Atkinson, A. D. "Dr. Johnson and Some Physico-Theological Themes" [use of Burnet's *Sacred Theory of the Earth*], *N&Q*, January 5, 1952, pp. 16–18; April 12, pp. 162–65; June 7, pp. 249–53.

17:120. Sherbo, Arthur. "Dr. Johnson Quotes One of His Amanuenses," *N&Q*, June 21, 1952, p. 276.

17:121. Gilbert, Vedder M. "Altercations of Thomas Edwards with Samuel Johnson" [over the *Dictionary*], *JEGP*, LI (July 1952), 326–35.

17:122. Sledd, James H., and Gwin J. Kolb. "Johnson's Definitions of *Whig* and *Tory*," *PMLA*, LXVII (September 1952), 882–85.

17:123. Sherbo, Arthur. "Dr. Johnson's Revision of His *Dictionary*" [more than 700 changes noted in words under "M" between 1755 and 1773 editions], *PQ*, XXXI (October 1952), 372–82.

17:124. Atkinson, A. D. "A Prospect of Words," *N&Q*, October 11, 1952, pp. 452–54; October 25, pp. 475–77.

17:125. Sherbo, Arthur. "Dr. Johnson Marks a Book List" [appended to Vol. VIII of Warburton's *Shakespeare*—see item 17:59], *N&Q*, November 22, 1952, p. 519.

*17:126. Keast, W. R. "The Preface to *A Dictionary of the English Language*: Johnson's Revision and the Establishment of the Text," *Studies in Bibliography* (University of Virginia), V (1952–53), 129–46. Reprinted in *Evidence for Authorship: Essays on Problems of Attribution*, ed. David V. Erdman and Ephim G. Fogel, pp. 294–305, Ithaca, N.Y.: Cornell University Press, 1966.

17:127. Keast, W. R. "Some Emendations in Johnson's Preface to the *Dictionary*," *RES*, n.s., IV (January 1953), 52–57.

17:128. Kolb, Gwin J., and James H. Sledd. "Johnson's *Dictionary* and Lexicographical Tradition," *MP*, L (February 1953), 171–94.

17:129. Boyce, Benjamin and Dorothy G. "Dr. Johnson's Definitions of 'Tory' and 'Whig,'" *N&Q*, April 1953, pp. 161–62.

17:130. Sherbo, Arthur. "Dr. Johnson's *Dictionary* and Warburton's *Shakespeare*" [further description of copy mentioned in item 17:59], *PQ*, XXXIII (January 1954), 94–96.

17:131. Fleming, Lindsay. "Dr. Johnson's Use of Authorities in Compiling His Dictionary of the English Language," *N&Q*, June 1954, pp. 254–57; July, pp. 294–97; August, pp. 343–47.

17:132. Keast, W. R. "Johnson's *Plan of a Dictionary*: A Textual Crux," *PQ*, XXXIII (July 1954), 341–47.

17:133. Fussell, Paul, Jr. "A Note on Samuel Johnson and the Rise of Accentual Prosodic Theory" [revised definition of "versification" in *Dictionary*, 1773], *PQ*, XXXIII (October 1954), 431–33.

17:134. *An Exhibition in Honor of the 200th Anniversary of the Publication of Johnson's Dictionary, 15 April 1755*, with introduction by John R. Turner Ettlinger. New York: Columbia University Libraries, 1955.

17:135. Liebert, Herman W. "Johnson's *Dictionary*, 1755–1955," *Yale Library Gazette*, XXX (1955), 27–28.

*17:136. Sledd, James H., and Gwin J. Kolb. *Dr. Johnson's Dictionary: Essays in the Biography of a Book*. Chicago: University of Chicago Press, 1955. Reviewed by D. T. Starnes, *MLN*, LXXI (April 1956), 309–11; D. J. Greene, *JEGP*, LV (April 1956), 331–34; W. K. Wimsatt, Jr., *PQ*, XXXV (July 1956), 308–10; J. C. Bryce, *RES*, n.s., IX (May 1958), 219–20.

*17:137. Wimsatt, William K., Jr. "Johnson's Dictionary: April 15, 1055," in item 10/6:306, pp. 65–90 (with facsimile of a page of Bacon's *Essays* marked by Johnson).

*17:138. Noyes, Gertrude E. "The Critical Reception of Johnson's *Dictionary* in the Latter Eighteenth Century," *MP*, LII (February 1955), 175–91.

17:139. Congleton, J. E. "Johnson's Dictionary, 1755–1955," *South Atlantic Bulletin* (South Atlantic Modern Language Association), XX (March 1955), 1–4.

*17:140. Kolb, Gwin J., and James H. Sledd. "The Reynolds Copy of Johnson's *Dictionary*," *Bulletin of the John Rylands Library*, XXXVII (March 1955), 446–75.

17:141. Clifford, James L. "Dr. Johnson's Dictionary: A Memorable Achievement of the Mind," *New York Times Book Review*, April 10, 1955, p. 7. Reprinted in item 17:134, pp. 3–6.

17:142. Tillotson, Geoffrey. "Johnson's Dictionary," *Spectator*, April 29, 1955, pp. 527–28. Reprinted in his *Augustan Studies*, pp. 224–28, London: Athlone Press, 1961.

17:143. Herzberg, Max J. "Johnson Bicentenary" [of *Dictionary*], *Word Study*, XXX (May 1955), 4–8.

17:144. Keast, W. R. "Self-quotation in Johnson's Dictionary," *N&Q*, September 1955, pp. 392–93. See also *ibid.*, June 1956, p. 262.

*17:145. Országh, Laszlo. "Johnson Lexikográfiai Modszere" [commemorates 200th annniversary of the *Dictionary*], *Filológiai Közlöny* (Magyar Tudományos Akadémia, Budapest), II (1956), 251–65. Summaries in Russian and English, p. 339.

17:146. Lehnert, Martin. "Das englische Wörterbuch in Vergangenheit und Gegenwart," *Zeitschrift für Anglistik und Amerikanistik* (Berlin), IV (June 1956), 265–323.

17:147. Fleming, Lindsay. "Johnson, Burton, and Hale" [copies of Burton and Hale used by Johnson], *N&Q*, April 1957, p. 154. See item 17:28.

17:148. Keast, W. R. "The Two *Clarissas* in Johnson's *Dictionary*" [quotations are from *A Collection . . . of Moral and Instructive Sentiments*, appended to Vol. VIII, 1751], *SP*, LIV (July 1957), 429–39.

17:149. Tucker, Susie I. "Dr. Watts Looks at the Language" [indebtedness to Watts in *Dictionary*], *N&Q*, July–August 1959, pp. 274–79.

17:150. Rawson, C. J. "Johnson's 'Bibliothèque,'" *N&Q*, February 1960, p. 71. Meaning of the word.

17:151. Balderston, Katharine C. "Dr. Johnson's Use of William Law in the Dictionary," *PQ*, XXXIX (July 1960), 379–88.

17:152. Arrieta, Rafael Alberto. "El Diccionario del Altillo," *La Prensa* (Buenos Aires), August 7, 1960.

17:153. Kolb, Gwin J., and James H. Sledd. "The History of the Sneyd-Gimbel and Pigott-British Museum Copies of Dr. Johnson's *Dictionary*," *PBSA*, LIV (4th quarter, 1960), 286–89.

17:154. Tucker, Susie I. "'Forsooth, Madam,'" *N&Q*, January 1962, pp. 15–16. Johnson's definition of the word "forsooth."

17:155. Reed, Joseph W., Jr. "Noah Webster's Debt to Samuel Johnson," *American Speech*, XXXVII (May 1962), 95–105.

17:156. Downes, Rackstraw. "Johnson's Theory of Language," *Review of English Literature*, III (October 1962), 29–41.

17:157. *Johnson's Dictionary: A Modern Selection*, ed. E. L. McAdam, Jr., and George Milne. New York: Pantheon Books, 1963. For some objections see George S. McCue, *PQ*, XLIII (July 1964), 369.

17:158. Osselton, N. E. "Formal and Informal Spelling in the 18th Century," *English Studies*, XLIV (August 1963), 267–75.

17:159. Nagashima, Daisuke. "Johnson's Dictionary Reconsidered," *Studies in English Literature* (Tokyo), XLI (August 1964), 35–57.

17:160. Illo, John. "The Polymathic Dictionary," *Western Humanities Review*, XVIII (Summer 1964), 265–73.

*17:161. Fleeman, J. D. "Some of Dr. Johnson's Preparatory Notes for His *Dictionary*, 1755" [in Bodleian Library], *Bodleian Library Record*, VII (December 1964), 205–10.

17:162. San Juan, E., Jr. "The Actual and the Ideal in the Making of Samuel Johnson's *Dictionary*," *University of Toronto Quarterly*, XXXIV (January 1965), 146–58.

17:163. Tucker, S. I. "Dr. Johnson Misread?" [the word "immaculate"], *N&Q*, June 1965, p. 218.

17:164. Todd, William B. "Variants in Johnson's *Dictionary*, 1755," *Book Collector*, XIV (Summer 1965), 212–13.

17:165. *The English Language: Essays by English and American Men of Letters, 1490–1839*, ed. W. F. Bolton. Cambridge: Cambridge University Press, 1966. Includes Johnson's preface to *Dictionary*, pp. 129–56.

17:166. *The English Dictionary*, ed. R. C. Alston [a bibliography], pp. 30–41, 70–71, plates XXIIA–XXVI. Leeds: E. J. Arnold and Son, 1966.

17:167. Nagashima, Daisuke. "An Historical Assessment of Johnson's *Dictionary*," *Anglica* (Anglica Society of Kansai University, Osaka, Japan), VI, nos. 1 and 2 (1966), 161–200; no. 4 (1968), 20–34 (not seen).

17:168. Elledge, Scott. "The Naked Science of Language, 1747–1786," in *Studies in Criticism and Aesthetics, 1660–1800: Essays in Honor of Samuel Holt Monk*, ed. Howard Anderson and John S. Shea, pp. 266–95. Minneapolis: University of Minnesota Press, 1967.

17:169. Griffith, Philip Mahone. "Dr. Johnson's 'Diction of Common Life' and Swift's *Directions to Servants*" [use of Swift's work in *Dictionary*], *Jonathan Swift: Tercentenary Essays*, pp. 10–30. (Monograph Series, No. 3.) Tulsa, Okla.: University of Tulsa, 1967.

17:170. Hardy, John P. " 'Dictionary' Johnson." Inaugural lecture at University of New England, Armidale, New South Wales. Armidale, N.S.W.: University of New England, 1967.

17:171. Nagashima, Daisuke. "The Mutual Debt Between Johnson and Lowth," *Studies in English Literature* (Tokyo), XLIV, no. 2 (1968), 221–32. In their treatment of English grammar.

17:172. Nagashima, Daisuke. "Backgrounds of Dr. Johnson's *Dictionary*," *Studies in the Foreign Languages and Literature* (Osaka University, Japan), No. 4 (1968), pp. 123–56 (not seen).

17:173. Congleton, J. E. "Sir Herbert Croft on Revising Johnson's *Dictionary*," *Tennessee Studies in Literature*, XIII (1968), 49–62.

17:174. Wilson, Ross. "The Dictionary and Drink," *New Rambler*, January 1969, pp. 24–43.

17:175. McCracken, David. "The Drudgery of Defining: Johnson's Debt to Bailey's *Dictionarium Britannicum*," *MP*, LXVI (May 1969), 338–41.

18. *RASSELAS* AND OTHER PROSE FICTION

Editions

Apart from the first edition, only a few of the more recent of the hundreds of editions and translations of *Rasselas* are listed here. Useful lists of older translations and editions are given in Courtney, item 1/1:19, pp. 87–97, supplemented by *Life*, II, 499–500. A full bibliography is in preparation (item 18:135).

18:1. Johnson, Samuel. *The Prince of Abissinia* [*Rasselas*]. 2 vols., 8vo. London: Dodsley, 1759. Reviewed in *Critical Review*, VII (April 1759), 372–75; by Owen Ruffhead, *Monthly Review*, XX (May 1759), 428–37 (severely critical); in *Annual Register*, II (1759), 477–79.

Ed. D. H. M. (Home and School Library.) Boston: Ginn and Co., [1886]. Often reprinted.

Ed. G. B. Hill. Oxford: Clarendon Press, 1887. Numerous reprints.

With introduction by William West. London: Sampson Low, Marston & Co., 1888. Reprint of an earlier edition.

With Voltaire's *Candide*. With introduction by Henry Morley. London: George Routledge & Sons, 1888 (3rd ed.).

Ed. Fred N. Scott. (Student's Series of English Classics.) Boston and New York: Leach, etc., [1891]. A good critical edition.

Boston: Howe Memorial Press, 1893. In raised letters for use of the blind.

Ed. Oliver F. Emerson. New York: Henry Holt & Co., 1895. Thorough, stimulating introduction.

Birmingham: Vincent Press, 1898.

Rendered in Benn Pitman phonography by J. Edmund Fuller. 3 vols. New York: Miner, 1899–1900.

Ed. Justin Hannaford. London: Greening and Co., 1900.

Wausau, Wis.: Van Vechten and Ellis, 1902.

Ed. R. Gibson. (Gibson's New Literary Reader, No. 5.) Glasgow, [1904].

Ed. Hannaford Bennett. (Carlton Classics.) London: John Lang, 1905.

With introduction by C. S. Fearenside. (Classic Tales.) London: George Bell & Sons, 1906.

Ed. A. J. F. Collins. (University Tutorial Series.) London: W. B. Clive, [1910].

With introduction by G. K. Chesterton and woodcuts by Douglas P. Bliss. London: J. M. Dent & Sons, 1926. Introduction reprinted in *G. K. C. as M. C.*, pp. 196–201, London: Methuen & Co., 1929.

Ed. R. W. Chapman. Oxford: Clarendon Press, 1927. Reviewed by R. S. Crane, *PQ*, VII (April 1928), 177–78.

Ed. Philip Henderson, in *Shorter Novels: Eighteenth Century*. (Everyman's Library.) London: J. M. Dent & Sons, 1930.

Reprinted (in full) in items 2:34, 2:40, 2:86, 2:87.

Ed. Warren L. Fleischauer. Great Neck, N.Y.: Barron's Educational Series, 1962.

Ed. Gwin J. Kolb. (Crofts Classics.) New York: Appleton-Century-Crofts, 1962.

Ed. J. P. Hardy. London: Oxford University Press, 1968.

18:2. *Rasselas*. Translations (Selective)

Tr. J. Bérard. (Baudry's European Library.) Paris, 1886. English and French texts.

Tr. with introduction and notes by Ch. Bastide. (English Classics.) Paris: H. Didier, 1905.

Tr. into Bengali by Tarasanker Tarkaratna. Calcutta: Chakravarty, 1907.

Tr. into Marathi by Krishna Shastir Chiplunkar. Poona: 'Chitra Shala' Press, 1900 (3rd ed.).

Tr. into Arabic by Sayyid Ahmad Fahmi. Cairo: Egyptian Printing Co., [1923].

Tr. into Japanese by Rokusuke Shibano. Tokyo: Dainippontosho-kabu-shiki-gaisha, 1905. Other translations in 1886 and 1909.

Rasselas, capitolo XLVIII [tr. for Feriani-Lampertico marriage, October 29, 1904]. Valdagno, 1904.

Tr. into French by J. Staquet. Brussels: Éditions La Boétie, 1946.

Tr. into Spanish, with introduction, by Mariano de Vedia y Mitre [*La Historia de Raselas, Principe de Abisinia*]. Buenos Aires: Guillermo Kraft, [1951].

Tr. into Arabic by Kamel el Mohandes and Magdi Wahba, with 50 illustrations by S. Diamantis [four reproduced in item 18:81]. Cairo: Anglo-Egyptian Bookshop, 1959. The illustrations have been separately reprinted.

Tr. into Japanese by Natsuo Shumuta. Tokyo: Azuma, 1962 (rev. of a 1948 ed.).

Tr. into German by Joachim Uhlmann. (Insel-Bücherei, No. 838.) Frankfort on the Main: Insel-Verlag, 1964.

18:3. *The Fountains: A Fairy Tale by Dr. Samuel Johnson.* With preface by H. V. M. London: Elkin Mathews, 1927. Reviewed in *TLS*, May 5, 1927, p. 314.

COMMENTARY

18:20. [Knight, Ellis Cornelia.] *Dinarbas, A Tale: Being a Continuation of Rasselas, Prince of Abyssinia.* London: C. Dilly, 1790. Often reprinted.

18:21. Smirke, Robert. *Proofs, from Pictures, Painted by Robert Smirke, R.A. and Engraved by A. Raimbach. The Subject Taken from the Rasselas of Dr. Johnson.* London: Printed by Savage and Easingwood, 1805.

18:22. Barbauld, Anna Letitia (née Aikin). "Johnson," *British Novelists, with . . . prefaces, biographical and critical,* XVI, i-viii. London: Rivington, etc., 1810. Chiefly a critique of *Rasselas.*

*18:23. M., J. [John Mitford.] [Letter attributing to Johnson Book IX, Chap. XI, of Charlotte Lennox's *The Female Quixote*], *GM*, n.s., XX (August 1843), p. 132.

18:24. Eirionnach. "*Rasselas* and The Happy Valley," *N&Q*, 4th ser., II (July 4, 1868), 1–2.

18:25. "Johnson's *Rasselas*," *Bibliographer*, III (May 1883), 173–75. Account of Dodsley's suit against Kennersley for reprinting extracts from *Rasselas* in the *Grand Magazine.*

18:26. *The Bibliography of Johnson's "Rasselas,"* comp. Elliot Stock. London: Elliot Stock, 1884.

18:27. "The Story of 'Rasselas'" [19th-century opinions of the book, with a bibliography of editions and translations], *Book-Lore*, I (December 1884), 5–11.

18:28. [The publisher of *Rasselas*], *Critic*, n.s., XIV (August 16, 1890), 85.

18:29. Raleigh, Walter A. "Rasselas," *The English Novel*, pp. 203–6. London: John Murray, 1894.

*18:30. Emerson, Oliver F. "The Text of Johnson's *Rasselas*" [revisions of text, etc.], *Anglia*, XXII (December 1899), 499–509.

*18:31. Whittuck, Charles. "Anti-Cant: *Candide; Rasselas*," in *The "Good Man" of the XVIII*th *Century*. London: George Allen, 1901. A thoughtful comparison.

18:32. "Hereabouts" [where Johnson wrote *Rasselas*—not Staple Inn], *Academy and Literature*, LXIV (May 23, 1903), 511–12.

*18:33. Conant, Martha P. *The Oriental Tale in England in the Eighteenth Century*, pp. 140–54. New York: Columbia University Press, 1908.

18:34. Piccioni, Luigi. "Per la fortuna del 'Rasselas' di Samuele Johnson in Italia: Una versione inedita di Giuseppe Baretti," *Giornale Storico della Letteratura Italiana*, LV (1910), 339–56.

18:35. Collison-Morley, Lacy. "'Rasselas': The First Italian Translation," *N&Q*, 11th ser., I (May 21, 1910), 404. See also Robert Pierpoint, *ibid*. (June 18), 497.

18:36. Saintsbury, George. *The English Novel*, p. 147. London: J. M. Dent & Sons, 1913.

18:37. Howells, W. D. "Editor's Easy Chair" [conversation about *Rasselas*], *Harper's*, CXXXI (July 1915), 310–13.

18:38. Markland, Russell. "Dr. Johnson and Shelley" [*Rasselas*, Chap. X, and the end of the *Defence of Poetry*], *N&Q*, 12th ser., IX (November 5, 1921), 368.

18:39. Armstrong, T. Percy. "Emerson and Dr. Johnson" [resemblances between *Rasselas* and *The American Scholar*], *N&Q*, 12th ser., X (March 4, 1922), 167.

18:40. Powell, Lawrence F. "Rasselas" [Voltaire's opinion of], *TLS*, February 22, 1923, p. 124.

18:41. Tinker, Chauncey B. "Rasselas in the New World" [concerning the first American edition and the Johnsonian recollections of William White of Philadelphia], *Yale Review*, XIV (October 1924), 95–107. Separately printed, New Haven, Conn.: Yale University Press, 1925.

18:42. Belloc, Hilaire. "Mrs. Piozzi's *Rasselas*," *SRL*, II (August 15, 1925), 37–38.

18:43. Belloc, Hilaire. "On *Rasselas*," *New Statesman*, XXV (September 5, 1925), 571–72. Reprinted in *Short Talks with the Dead*, pp. 173–83, London: Cayme Press; New York: Harper and Brothers, 1926. See also

Catholic World, CLXXI (June 1950), 212–13. Reprinted in *Hilaire Belloc: An Anthology of His Prose and Verse*, ed. W. N. Roughead, pp. 266–72, Philadelphia: J. B. Lippincott, 1951.

18:44. Palser, Ernest M. *A Commentary & Questionnaire on the History of Rasselas*. London: Sir Isaac Pitman & Sons, 1927.

18:45. Collins, Norman. *Facts of Fiction*, pp. 82–84. London: Victor Gollancz, 1932.

18:46. Warner, Oliver. "*Rasselas:* The Testament of a Romantic," *Bookman* (London), LXXXII (June 1932), 147–48.

18:47. Baker, Ernest A. "The Oriental Story from *Rasselas* to *Vathek*," *The History of the English Novel*, V, 55–76. London: H. F. & G. Witherby, 1934. Reprinted, New York: Barnes and Noble, 1957.

18:48. Barnouw, A. J. "*Rasselas* in Dutch," *TLS*, April 11, 1935, p. 244.

*18:49. Tillotson, Geoffrey. "*Rasselas* and the *Persian Tales*," *TLS*, August 29, 1935, p. 534. See also R. H. Griffith, *ibid.*, November 16, p. 752. Reprinted in *Essays in Criticism and Research*, pp. 111–16, Cambridge: Cambridge University Press, 1942.

18:50. Squire, Sir John C. "Johnson and Abyssinia," *Lichfield Mercury*, September 27, 1935. Reprinted; see item 6:22.

*18:51. Sewall, Richard B. "Rousseau's Second Discourse in England from 1755 to 1762" [shows satire on Rousseau's ideas in *Rasselas*], *PQ*, XVII (April 1938), 105–11.

*18:52. Jenkins, Harold D. "Some Aspects of the Background of *Rasselas*," *Studies in English in Honor of R. D. O'Leary and S. L. Whitcomb*, pp. 8–14. University of Kansas, 1940.

18:53. Cameron, Kenneth N. "A New Source for Shelley's *A Defence of Poetry*" [the discourse on poetry in *Rasselas*], *SP*, XXXVIII (October 1941), 629–44.

18:54. Cameron, Kenneth N. "*Rasselas* and *Alastor:* A Study in Transmutation" [Shelley's use of *Rasselas*], *SP*, XL (January 1943), 58–78.

18:55. Kolb, Gwin J. "A Commentary on Samuel Johnson's *Rasselas*." Dissertation, University of Chicago, 1949.

18:56. Kolb, Gwin J. "Johnson's 'Dissertation on Flying' and John Wilkins' *Mathematical Magick*," *MP*, XLVII (August 1949), 24–31. Reprinted in item 10/6:306 (1959).

18:57. Roddier, Henri. "Rousseau est-il visé dans Rasselas?" *J.-J. Rousseau en Angleterre au xviiie siècle*, pp. 49–52. Paris: Boivin, [1950].

18:58. Metzdorf, Robert F. "The Second Sequel to *Rasselas*" [by Elizabeth Pope Whately in 1835], *New Rambler*, No. 16 (January 1950), 5–7. Separately printed, Cambridge, Mass., 1950.

18:59. Guzzo, Orlando. *Il "Candide" Inglese: "Ras Selas" di Samuele John-*

son. (La Filosofia nella Letteratura, No. 3.) Turin: Edizioni di "Filosofia," 1951.

*18:60. Lascelles, Mary. "*Rasselas* Reconsidered," *Essays and Studies by Members of the English Association*, n.s., IV (1951), 37–52.

*18:61. Kolb, Gwin J. "The Structure of *Rasselas*," *PMLA*, LXVI (September 1951), 698–717.

18:62. Honig, Edwin. "Crusoe, Rasselas, and the Suit of Clothes," *University of Kansas City Review*, XVIII (Winter 1951), 136–42.

18:63. Moore, John Robert. "Conan Doyle, Tennyson, and *Rasselas*," *Nineteenth Century Fiction*, VII (December 1952), 221–23.

18:64. Kolb, Gwin J. "The Use of Stoical Doctrines in *Rasselas*, Chapter XVIII," *MLN*, LXVIII (November 1953), 439–47.

*18:65. Metzdorf, Robert F. "The First American 'Rasselas' and Its Imprint," *PBSA*, XLVII (4th quarter, 1953), 374–76.

18:66. Moore, John Robert. "*Rasselas* and the Early Travelers to Abyssinia," *MLQ*, XV (March 1954), 36–41.

18:67. Osgood, C. G. "Johnson and Macrobius" [Chap. VIII of *Rasselas*], *MLN*, LXIX (April 1954), 246.

18:68. Hovey, Richard B. "Dr. Samuel Johnson, Psychiatrist" [in *Rasselas*], *MLQ*, XV (December 1954), 321–35.

18:69. Leyburn, Ellen D. " 'No Romantick Absurdities or Incredible Fictions': The Relation of Johnson's *Rasselas* to Lobo's *Voyage to Abyssinia*," *PMLA*, LXX (December 1955), 1059–67.

18:70. Bredvold, Louis I. "*Rasselas* and the *Miscellanies* of John Norris," *JNL*, XVI, no. 1 (March 1956), 3–4.

18:71. Whitley, Alvin. "The Comedy of *Rasselas*," *ELH*, XXIII (March 1956), 48–70.

18:72. Barnett, George L. "*Rasselas* and *De Senectute*," *N&Q*, November 1956, pp. 485–86.

18:73. Pakenham, Thomas. "Gondar and the Mountain" [where Abyssinian princes were imprisoned], *History Today*, VII (March 1957), 172–81. See also his *The Mountains of Rasselas*, an account of the author's travels in Ethiopia, London: Weidenfeld and Nicolson; New York: Reynal and Co., 1959.

18:74. Barnett, George L. "*Rasselas* and *The Vicar of Wakefield*," *N&Q*, July 1957, pp. 303–5.

18:75. Kenney, William. "Johnson's *Rasselas* after Two Centuries," *Boston University Studies in English*, III (Summer 1957), 88–96.

18:76. Link, Frederick M. "*Rasselas* and the Quest for Happiness," *Boston University Studies in English*, III (Summer 1957), 121–23.

18:77. Joost, Nicholas. "Whispers of Fancy; or, the Meaning of *Rasselas*," *Modern Age*, I (Fall 1957), 166–73.

*18:78. Lockhart, Donald Merritt. "Father Jeronymo Lobo's Writings Concerning Ethiopia, Including Hitherto Unpublished Manuscripts in the Palmella Library." Dissertation, Harvard University (Department of Romance Languages), 1958. Discusses, pp. 70–79, Johnson's translation of Lobo-Legrand and, pp. 86–141, the sources of *Rasselas*. See item 18:111.

18:79. Fisher, Marvin. "The Pattern of Conservatism in Johnson's *Rasselas* and Hawthorne's *Tales*," *JHI*, XIX (April 1958), 173–96.

18:80. Kolb, Gwin J. "The 'Paradise' in Abyssinia and the 'Happy Valley' in *Rasselas*," *MP*, LVI (August 1958), 10–16.

18:81. *Bicentenary Essays on Rasselas*, ed. Magdi Wahba. Supplement to *Cairo Studies in English*, 1959. Individual essays are listed separately in this section. Reviewed by Gwin J. Kolb, *PQ*, XXXIX (July 1960), 336–39.

18:82. Clifford, James L. "Some Remarks on *Candide* and *Rasselas*," in item 18:81, pp. 7–14.

18:83. Dina Abdul-Hamid Al Aoun. "Some Remarks on a Second Reading of *Rasselas*," in item 18:81, pp. 15–20. Emphasizes its place in the tradition of tracts on a princely education.

18:84. Goodyear, Louis E. "Rasselas' Journey from Amhara to Cairo Viewed from Arabia," in item 18:81, pp. 21–29.

*18:85. Lombardo, Agostino. "The Importance of Imlac," in item 18:81, pp. 31–49. Trans. Barbara Arnett Melchiori.

18:86. Mahmoud, Fatma Moussa. "*Rasselas* and *Vathek*," in item 18:81, pp. 51–57.

18:87. Manzalaoui, Mahmoud. "*Rasselas* and Some Mediaeval Ancillaries," in item 18:81, pp. 59–73.

18:88. Metzdorf, Robert F. "Grand Cairo and Philadelphia: The Frontispiece to the 1768 Edition of Johnson's *Rasselas*," in item 18:81, pp. 75–80.

18:89. Moore, John Robert. "*Rasselas* in Retrospect," in item 18:81, pp. 81–84.

18:90. Rawson, C. J. "The Continuation of *Rasselas*" [Cornelia Knight's *Dinarbas*], in item 18:81, pp. 85–95.

18:91. Tillotson, Geoffrey. "Time in *Rasselas*," in item 18:81, pp. 97–103. Reprinted in his *Augustan Studies*, pp. 229–48, London: Athlone Press, 1961.

18:92. Wahba, Magdi. "A Note on the Manner of Concluding in *Rasselas*," in item 18:81, pp. 105–110.

18:93. Willard, Nedd. "*Zadig* and *Rasselas* Considered," in item 18:81, pp. 111–123.

18:94. Kenney, William. "*Rasselas* and the Theme of Diversification," *PQ*, XXXVIII (January 1959), 84–89.

18:95. Duncan-Jones, E. E. "Marvell, Johnson, and the First Sunset" [*Ras-*

selas, Chap. 35, and *The First Anniversary of the Government Under Oliver Cromwell*, lines 337–40], *TLS*, April 3, 1959, p. 193.

18:96. Clifford, James L. "Candide and Rasselas," *New York Times Book Review*, April 19, 1959, pp. 4, 14.

18:97. Johnson, J. W. "Rasselas and His Ancestors," *N&Q*, May 1959, pp. 185–88.

18:98. Alssid, Michael. "Man and the World in Johnson's *Rasselas*," *Thoth*, I (Spring 1959), 11–15.

18:99. Sherburn, George. "Rasselas Returns—To What?" *PQ*, XXXVIII (July 1959), 383–84.

18:100. Casini, Paolo. "Rasselas o il mito della felicità," *L'Approdo Letterario*, n.s., VI, no. 10 (1960), 37–45.

18:101. West, Paul. "Rasselas: The Humanist as Stoic," *English*, XIII (Summer 1961), 181–85.

18:102. Aden, John M. "*Rasselas* and *The Vanity of Human Wishes*," *Criticism*, III (Fall 1961), 295–303.

18:103. Kaul, R. K. "The Philosopher of Nature in *Rasselas* XXII," *Indian Journal of English Studies*, III (1962), 116–20.

18:104. Kolb, Gwin J. "*Rasselas*: Purchase Price, Proprietors, and Printings," *Studies in Bibliography*, XV (1962), 256–59.

18:105. Kolb, Gwin J. "Textual Cruxes in *Rasselas*," in item 10/6:316 (1962), 257–62.

18:106. Eddy, Donald D. "The Publication Date of the First Edition of *Rasselas*," *N&Q*, January 1962, pp. 21–22.

°18:107. Grange, Kathleen M. "Dr. Samuel Johnson's Account of a Schizophrenic Illness in *Rasselas* (1759)," *Medical History*, VI (April 1962), 162–69, 291. Episode of the astronomer often cited by later medical writers.

18:108. Leyburn, Ellen Douglass. "Two Allegorical Treatments of Man: *Rasselas* and *La Peste*," *Criticism*, IV (Summer 1962), 197–209.

18:109. Halsband, Robert. "*Rasselas*: An Early Allusion," *N&Q*, December 1962, p. 459. B. M. Add. MS. 6839, f. 138: letter of Robert Symmer to Andrew Mitchell, May 18, 1759.

18:110. Powell, L. F. "For Johnsonian Collectors" [Dutch translation of *Rasselas*], *TLS*, September 20, 1963, p. 712.

°18:111. Lockhart, Donald M. " 'The Fourth Son of the Mighty Emperor': The Ethiopian Background of Johnson's *Rasselas*," *PMLA*, LXXVIII (December 1963), 516–28.

18:112. McIntosh, Rustin Carey. "Samuel Johnson's Prose Fiction." Dissertation, Harvard University, 1964.

18:113. Price, Martin. *To the Palace of Wisdom*, pp. 316–19. Garden City, N.Y.: Doubleday, 1964.

18:114. Sacks, Sheldon. *Fiction and the Shape of Belief. A Study of Henry Fielding, With Glances at . . . Johnson.* Berkeley and Los Angeles: University of California Press, 1964. *Rasselas*, pp. 49–60, as a major example of the special demands of an apologue.

18:115. Adlard, John. "Blake and *Rasselas*" [general dislike of Blake to critical statements of Imlac], *Archiv für das Studium der Neueren Sprachen und Literaturen*, CCI (April 1964), 47.

18:116. Ebeling, Harry Alan. "The Allegorical Tales of Samuel Johnson" (dissertation, University of Kansas, 1965), *Dissertation Abstracts*, XXVI (December 1965), 3299–3300.

18:117. Fisher, S. T. "Johnson on Flying," *TLS*, November 4, 1965, p. 988. See also A. J. Meadows, *TLS*, December 2, 1965, p. 1112.

18:118. Hilles, F. W. "*Rasselas*, an 'Uninstructive Tale,'" in item 10/6:329 (1965), pp. 111–21.

18:119. Steeves, Harrison R. "Oriental Romance: Johnson and Beckford," *Before Jane Austen*, pp. 226–33. New York: Holt, Rinehart, and Winston, 1965.

18:120. Sutherland, W. O. S., Jr. "The Plot of *Rasselas*," *The Art of the Satirist*, pp. 92–104. Austin: University of Texas Press, 1965.

18:121. Einbond, Bernard. "Samuel Johnson's Allegories" (dissertation, Columbia University, 1966), *Dissertation Abstracts*, XXVII (October 1966), 1029A.

18:122. Manzalaoui, Mahmoud. "A Textual Crux in the Concluding Chapter of *Rasselas*," *Cairo Studies in English*, ed. Magdi Wahba, pp. 213–16. Cairo, 1966.

18:123. Reberdy, Mother Janet Louise. "William Law's *A Serious Call* and Samuel Johnson's *Rasselas*" (dissertation, Fordham University, 1966), *Dissertation Abstracts* XXVII (August 1966), 461A.

18:124. Suderman, Elmer F. "*Candide, Rasselas* and Optimism," *Iowa English Yearbook*, No. 11 (1966), 37–43.

18:125. Baker, Sheridan. "*Rasselas*: Psychological Irony and Romance," in *Essays in English Neoclassicism in Memory of Charles B. Woods, PQ*, XLV (January 1966), pp. 249–61.

18:126. Kallich, Martin. "Samuel Johnson's Principles of Criticism and Imlac's 'Dissertation upon Poetry,'" *Journal of Aesthetics and Art Criticism*, XXV (Fall 1966), 71–82. Imlac reflects Johnson, and both are "exemplars of neoclassical theory in England."

18:127. Tillotson, Geoffrey. "Imlac and the Business of a Poet," in *Studies in Criticism and Aesthetics, 1660–1800: Essays in Honor of Samuel Holt Monk*, ed. Howard Anderson and John S. Shea, pp. 296–314. Minneapolis: University of Minnesota Press, 1967.

*18:128. Jones, Emrys. "The Artistic Form of *Rasselas*," *RES*, n.s., XVIII (November 1967), 387–401.

18:129. Wimsatt, W. K. "In Praise of *Rasselas:* Four Notes (Converging)," in *Imagined Worlds: Essays on Some English Novels and Novelists in Honor of John Butt*, ed. Maynard Mack and Ian Gregor, pp. 111–36. London: Methuen, 1968.

18:130. Bernard, F. V. "The Hermit of Paris and the Astronomer in *Rasselas*," *JEGP*, LXVII (April 1968), 272–78.

18:131. Reichard, Hugo M. "The Pessimist's Helpers in *Rasselas*," *Texas Studies in Literature and Language*, X (Spring 1968), 57–64.

18:132. Weitzman, Arthur J. "More Light on *Rasselas:* The Background of the Egyptian Episodes," *PQ*, XLVIII (January 1969), 42–58.

*18:133. Preston, Thomas R. "The Biblical Context of Johnson's *Rasselas*," *PMLA*, LXXXIV (March 1969), 274–81.

18:134. Reed, Kenneth T. " 'This Tasteless Tranquility': A Freudian Note on Johnson's *Rasselas*," *Literature and Psychology*, XIX, no. 1 (1969), 61–62.

18:135. Metzdorf, Robert F. Complete bibliography of *Rasselas* in preparation (1970).

19. SHAKESPEARE (EDITING AND CRITICISM)

EDITIONS (SELECTED)

19:1. Johnson, Samuel. *The Plays of William Shakespeare, in eight volumes, with the corrections and illustrations of various commentators; to which are added notes by Sam. Johnson*. London: J. and R. Tonson, etc., 1765. Reviewed by William Kenrick in *Monthly Review*, XXXIII (October 1765), 285–301; (November) 374–89; in *Critical Review*, XX (November 1765), 321–32; (December), 401–11; XXI (February 1766), 81–88; *Annual Register*, VIII (1765), 311–18. Facsimile reprint, New York: AMS Press, 1968. Important revisions by Johnson in the 1773 and 1778 eds. (10 vols.). For other 18th- and 19th- century eds., see Courtney, item 1/1:19, pp. 108–10.

19:2. *Annotations by Sam. Johnson and Geo. Steevens and the Various Commentators* [on the individual plays of Shakespeare]. London: John Bell, 1787. A separate volume for each play. Reprinted, George Cawthorn, 1797; John Offor, 1819 (2 vols.).

19:3. *Doctor Johnson's "Short Strictures" on the Plays of Shakespeare* [selected passages of criticism]. London: Collins, Kew & Co., 1900.

*19:4. *Eighteenth Century Essays on Shakespeare*, ed. D. Nichol Smith.

Glasgow: MacLehose, 1903. 2nd ed. (completed by Herbert Davis and F. P. Wilson), Oxford: Clarendon Press, 1963.

*19:5. Raleigh, Walter, ed. *Johnson on Shakespeare*. London: Oxford University Press, 1908, and frequently reprinted. Contains Preface, 1756 Proposals, *Rambler* 168, and a selection of Johnson's notes. For a review by Lytton Strachey, see item 19:66.

19:6. *Johnson's Proposals for His Edition of Shakespeare, 1756* [type-facsimile]. London: Oxford University Press, 1923.

*19:7. *Johnson's Notes to Shakespeare*, ed. with introduction to each vol. by Arthur Sherbo. Los Angeles: Augustan Reprint Society. Vol. I, Comedies (Publications, Nos. 59–60), 1956. Vol. II, Histories (Nos. 65–66), 1957. Vol. III, Tragedies (Nos. 71–73), 1958.

19:8. *Preface to Shakespeare, with Proposals for Printing the Dramatic Works of William Shakespeare* (1756) [text "reprinted from *Johnson on Shakespeare*"—item 19:5]. London: Oxford University Press, 1957.

19:9. *Samuel Johnson: Preface to Shakespeare e Altri Scritti Shakespeariani*, ed. with introduction and notes by Agostino Lombardo. (Biblioteca Italiana di Testi Inglesi, Vol. IV.) Bari: Adriatica Editrice, 1960. Reviewed by Arthur Sherbo, *PQ*, XL (July 1961), 403. Contains *Miscellaneous Observations on Macbeth*, Drury Lane Prologue, *Rambler* 168, Proposals (1756), Preface, and selected notes.

19:10. *Samuel Johnson on Shakespeare*, ed. with introduction by W. K. Wimsatt, Jr. (Dramabook.) New York: Hill and Wang, 1960.

*19:11. *Johnson on Shakespeare*, ed. Arthur Sherbo with introduction by Bertrand H. Bronson. Vols. VII, VIII (1968) of the Yale Edition of Johnson's Works (item 2:8). Reviewed in *TLS*, May 22, 1969, pp. 545–47; see ensuing correspondence June 19, July 17, September 4, 18, 25, November 6, 13; reviewed by Shirley White Johnston, *Eighteenth-Century Studies*, III (Spring 1970).

COMMENTARY

19:40. [Colman, George, the elder]. "Extracts from the Preface to Mr. Johnson's Edition of Shakespeare (published this morning), with Remarks," *St. James's Chronicle*, No. 718 (October 8–10, 1765); No. 719 (October 10–12); No. 720 (October 12–15).

19:41. Fribble. "Fifty Words on Johnson's Edition of Shakespeare," *St. James's Chronicle*, No. 721 (October 15–17, 1765). The same writer, signing himself "Goodman Dull," continues the attack in No. 732 (November 9–12, 1765).

19:42. Wilbraham, C. [Criticism of Johnson's comment on Claudius's drinking in Hamlet], *Lloyd's Evening Post*, November 1, 1765.

19:43. Dennis, Christopher [George Colman the elder]. [Attack on Johnson's treatment of the text of *Henry V*], *St. James's Chronicle*, No. 730 (November 5–7, 1765).

19:44. "The Interview, or Shakespeare's Ghost. Occasioned by the Review of Dr. Johnson's Edition of that Poet," *St. James's Chronicle*, No. 787 (November 21–23, 1765). A hostile *jeu d'esprit* in verse; the "Review" is Kenrick's (item 19:46).

19:45. [Heath, Benjamin.] *A Revisal of Shakespear's Text*, pp. 374–409. London: Johnston, 1765.

19:46. [Kenrick, William.] *A Review of Doctor Johnson's New Edition of Shakespeare, in which the ignorance, or inattention of that editor is exposed, and the poet defended from the persecution of his commentators.* London: J. Payne, 1765. Reprinted, New York: AMS Press, 1968. Reviewed in *Critical Review*, XX (November 1765), 332–36 (a defense of Johnson); in *GM*, XXXV (December 1765), 529; by Ralph Griffiths in *Monthly Review*, XXXIII (December 1765), 457–67 (ostensibly critical of Kenrick, but actually intended to publicize his attack on Johnson?).

19:47. "Candour, Pens, Ink, and Paper, a Fable," *St. James's Chronicle*, No. 742 (December 3–5, 1765). A defense of Kenrick's *Review* (item 19:46) against attack in *GM*, November 1765.

19:48. "A Fragment," *St. James's Chronicle*, No. 765 (January 26–28, 1776). A discussion of Warburton, Johnson, and Edwards on Shakespeare.

19:49. Dramaticus. [Strictures on Johnson's reading of two passages in *Julius Caesar*], *St. James's Chronicle*, No. 773 (mistakenly printed "733") (February 13–15, 1766).

19:50. [Barclay, James.] *An Examination of Mr. Kenrick's Review of Mr. Johnson's Edition of Shakespeare.* London: W. Johnston, 1766.

19:51. R., R. [William Kenrick.] *A Defence of Mr. Kenrick's Review of Dr. Johnson's Shakespeare.* London: Bladon, 1766. Reprinted, New York: AMS Press, 1968.

19:52. [Attack on the Johnson-Steevens ed. of Shakespeare, 1773], *St. James's Chronicle.* No. 1981 (October 23–26, 1773).

19:53. [Ritson, Joseph.] *Remarks, Critical and Illustrative, on the Text and Notes of the Last Edition of Shakespeare* [Johnson-Steevens ed. of 1778]. London: J. Johnson, 1783.

19:54. Mason, John Monck. *Comments on the Last Edition of Shakespeare's Plays.* London: Dilly, 1785.

19:55. [Ritson, Joseph.] *The Quip Modest: A Few Words by Way of Supplement to Remarks, Critical and Illustrative on . . . the Last Edition of Shakespeare, occasioned by a republication of that edition, revised and augmented by the editor of Dodsley's Old Plays* [Isaac Reed, 1785]. London: J. Johnson, 1788.

19:56. Chedworth, John Howe, 4th Baron. *Notes upon some of the obscure passages in Shakespeare's plays: with remarks upon the explanations and amendments of the commentators* [Johnson and Steevens] *in the editions of 1785, 1790, 1793.* London: Bulmer, 1805.

19:57. Seymour, E. H. *Remarks, Critical, Conjectural, and Explanatory, upon the Plays of Shakespeare; resulting from a collation of the early copies with that of Johnson and Steevens* [i.e., 1785]. 2 vols. London: Lackington, Allen, 1805. Incorporates material by Lord Chedworth (see item 19:56).

19:58. Hazlitt, William. "Preface," *Characters of Shakespear's Plays.* London: R. Hunter and C. and J. Ollier, 1817. Often reprinted. A violent onslaught on Johnson.

19:59. Stendhal [Marie-Henri Beyle]. "Des Unités de Temps et de Lieu," in Appendix III, "Qu' Est-ce que le Romanticisme?" *Racine et Shakespeare, No. II, ou Réponse au Manifeste Contre le Romantisme Prononcé par M. Auger.* . . . Paris: A. Dupont et Roret, 1825. Often reprinted. A free translation (i.e., plagiarism) of Johnson's discussion of the unities in the Preface. Cf. Doris Gunnell, *Stendhal et l'Angleterre* (Paris, 1909), pp. 340–51.

19:60. Zetes. "A Word with Dr. Johnson," *Hood's Magazine,* VI (August 1846), 113–23; (September), 209–23; (October), 317 (printed "371")– 336. An attack on the Shakespeare criticism.

19:61. Pollock, Walter H. "Shakespearian Criticism" [typical Victorian point of view], *Nineteenth Century,* XI (June 1882), 923–26, etc.

19:62. Norris, J. Parker. "The Editors of Shakespeare: Dr. Johnson," *Shakespeariana,* III (January 1886), 25–30.

19:63. James, Ralph N. "Shakespeare and Johnson" [sale of copy of 2nd folio owned by Theobald, with MS notes by Johnson], *N&Q,* 7th ser., V (February 25, 1888), 146.

19:64. Walder, E. *Shaksperian Criticism Textual and Literary from Dryden to the End of the Eighteenth Century.* Bradford, 1895.

19:65. Warner, Beverley. "Samuel Johnson," *Famous Introductions to Shakespeare's Plays,* pp. 110–70. New York: Dodd, Mead & Co., 1906.

19:66. Strachey, Lytton. "Shakespeare on Johnson," *Spectator,* CI (August 1, 1908), 165. A review of item 19:5. Reprinted in his *Spectatorial Essays,* pp. 59–65, London: Chatto and Windus, 1964; New York: Harcourt, Brace, 1965.

19:67. Johnson, Charles F. *Shakespeare and His Critics,* pp. 113–26. Boston: Houghton Mifflin Co., 1909.

19:68. Wheatley, Henry B. "Johnson's Edition of Shakespeare" [documents concerned with the financial arrangements with Tonson], *Athenaeum*, No. 4272 (September 11, 1909), p. 298.

*19:69. Raleigh, Walter. "Johnson on Shakespeare," in item 10/6:146, pp. 75–97.

19:70. Richter, Helene. "Die Wiederbelebung Shakespeares und der Volk-poesie," *Geschichte der englischen Romantik*, I, 79–159, *passim*. Halle: Niemeyer, 1911.

19:71. Wheatley, Henry B. "Shakespeare's Editors, 1603—to the Twentieth Century," *Transactions of the Bibliographical Society*, XIV (October 1915–March 1917), 164–66, etc.

19:72. Young, Karl. "Samuel Johnson on Shakespeare: One Aspect," *University of Wisconsin Studies in Language and Literature*, No. 18 (1923), 146–226.

19:73. Mason, Eugene. "Dr. Samuel Johnson and the Shakespearean Drama," *Considered Writers Old and New*, pp. 1–26. London: Methuen, 1925.

19:74. Raysor, Thomas M. "The Downfall of the Three Unities," *MLN*, XLII (January 1927), 1–9.

*19:75. Smith, D. Nichol. *Shakespeare in the Eighteenth Century*. Oxford: Clarendon Press, 1928. See also item 19:4.

19:76. Small, Miriam R. "The Source of a Note in Johnson's Edition of *Macbeth*," *MLN*, XLIII (January 1928), 34–35.

19:77. Hastings, William T., ed. [Preface to Shakespeare], *Essays from Five Centuries*, pp. 115–27. Boston: Houghton Mifflin Co., [1929].

19:78. Babcock, Robert W. *The Genesis of Shakespeare Idolatry, 1766–1799*, pp. 49 ff. and *passim*. Chapel Hill: University of North Carolina Press, 1931.

19:79. Pillai, V. K. Ayappan. *Shakespeare Criticism from the Beginnings to 1765*, pp. 73–85. London and Glasgow: Blackie & Son, 1932.

19:80. Ralli, Augustus. *A History of Shakespearian Criticism*, I, 57–62. London: Oxford University Press, 1932.

19:81. Robinson, Herbert S. "Samuel Johnson," *English Shakespearian Criticism in the Eighteenth Century*, pp. 121–46. New York: H. W. Wilson Co., 1932.

19:82. McKerrow, Ronald B. "The Treatment of Shakespeare's Text by His Earlier Editors, 1709–1768," *Proceedings of the British Academy 1933*, XIX, 89–122.

19:83. Wohlers, Heinz. *Der persönliche Gehalt in den Shakespeare-Noten Samuel Johnsons*. Dissertation, University of Hamburg. Bremen: Wohlers & Brickwedde, 1934.

19:84. Paul, Henry N. "Johnson's Shakespeare, 1765," *University of Pennsylvania Library Chronicle*, II (March 1934), 1–3.

19:85. Lovett, David. "Shakespeare as a Poet of Realism in the Eighteenth Century," *ELH*, II (November 1935), 267–89.

19:86. Bronson, Bertrand H. *Joseph Ritson: Scholar-at-Arms*, II, 429–54, etc. [discussion of Johnson's Shakespeare]. Berkeley: University of California Press, 1938.

19:87. Hart, C. W. "Dr. Johnson's 1745 Shakespeare Proposals," *MLN*, LIII (May 1938), 367–68.

19:88. Hazen, Allen T. "Johnson's Shakespeare: A Study in Cancellation," *TLS*, December 24, 1938, p. 820.

19:89. "Cancels in Johnson's Shakespeare," *Bodleian Library Record*, I (February 1939), 42–43.

19:90. Saer, H. "A Note on Dr. Johnson and Sebastien Mercier" [Mercier indebted to Johnson's Preface], *MLR*, XXXVI (January 1941), 109–12.

19:91. Wilson, J. Dover. "Introduction: Back to Johnson," *The Fortunes of Falstaff*, pp. 1–14. Cambridge: Cambridge University Press, 1944.

19:92. Conklin, Paul S. *A History of "Hamlet" Criticism, 1601–1821*, pp. 49, 61–62, etc. New York: Columbia University Press, 1947.

*19:93. Eastman, Arthur M. "Johnson's Shakespearean Labors in 1765," *MLN*, LXIII (December 1948), 512–15. From dissertation, Yale University, 1947.

19:94. Evans, G. Blakemore. "The Text of Johnson's *Shakespeare* (1765)," *PQ*, XXVIII (July 1949), 425–28.

19:95. Eastman, Arthur M. "The Texts from Which Johnson Printed His Shakespeare," *JEGP*, XLIX (April 1950), 182–91.

*19:96. Eastman, Arthur M. "Johnson's Shakespeare and the Laity: A Textual Study," *PMLA*, LXV (December 1950), 1112–21.

19:97. Fleischauer, Warren L. "Dr. Johnson's Editing and Criticism of Shakespeare's Lancastrian Cycle." Dissertation, Western Reserve University, 1951.

19:98. Sherbo, Arthur. "Dr. Johnson on *Macbeth*: 1745 and 1765," *RES*, n.s., II (January 1951), 40–47.

*19:99. Sherbo, Arthur. "The Proof-Sheets of Dr. Johnson's Preface to Shakespeare," *Bulletin of the John Rylands Library*, XXXV (September 1952), 206–10.

19:100. "Johnson's Shakespeare Folios," *JNL*, XIII, no. 4 (December 1953), 10. Letter of George Steevens, wanting to get rid of leaves in his First Folio "scribbled on" by Johnson.

19:101. Monaghan, T. J. "Johnson's Additions to His *Shakespeare* for the Edition of 1773," *RES*, n.s., IV (July 1953), 234–48. See also Arthur Sherbo, *PQ*, XXXIII (July 1954), 283–84.

19:102. Liebert, Herman W. "Proposals for Shakespeare, 1756," *TLS*, May 6, 1955, p. 237.

*19:103. Sherbo, Arthur. *Samuel Johnson, Editor of Shakespeare, with an Essay on The Adventurer.* (Illinois Studies in Language and Literature, Vol. 42.) Urbana: University of Illinois Press, 1956. Reviewed by H. K. Miller, *PQ*, XXXVI (July 1957), 378–79; Arthur M. Eastman, *Shakespeare Quarterly*, VIII (Autumn 1957), 548–49; G. A. Bonnard, *Erasmus*, XI (January 1958), 43–45; M. R. Ridley, *RES*, n.s., IX (February 1958), 91–93; W. K. Wimsatt, Jr., *MLN*, LXXIII (March 1958), 214–17. See also Arthur M. Eastman, "In Defense of Dr. Johnson," *Shakespeare Quarterly*, VIII (Autumn 1957), 493–500, and reply by Sherbo, IX (Summer 1958), 433.

19:104. Sherbo, Arthur. "Johnson and a Note by Warburton" [on *King Lear*, reprinted as Johnson's by Raleigh and others], *JNL*, XVI, no. 1 (March 1956), 11–12.

19:105. Tucker, Susie I. "Johnson and Lady Macbeth" [connotations of "blanket," "dun," "knife," etc.], *N&Q*, May 1956, pp. 210–11.

19:106. Bernard F. V. "Johnson and *Lear*" [quoted copiously in *Dictionary* despite Johnson's disclaimer of having reread it], *JNL*, XVII, no. 1 (March 1957), 7–8.

19:107. Sherbo, Arthur. "Sanguine Expectations: Dr. Johnson's *Shakespeare*," *Shakespeare Quarterly*, IX (Summer 1958), 426–28.

19:108. Badawi, M. M. "The Study of Shakespearian Criticism," *Cairo Studies in English* (1959), pp. 98–117.

19:109. Donner, H. W. "She Should Have Died Hereafter," *English Studies*, XL (October 1959), 385–89.

19:110. Adler, Jacob H. "Johnson's 'He That Imagines This'" [in Preface to Shakespeare], *Shakespeare Quarterly*, XI (Spring 1960), 225–28.

*19:111. Scholes, R. E. "Dr. Johnson and the Bibliographical Criticism of Shakespeare," *Shakespeare Quarterly* XI (Spring 1960), 163–71.

19:112. Greene, Donald. "Shaw on Johnson," *JNL*, XXI, no. 3 (September 1961), 11. Shaw "restated Johnson's conclusions" on Shakespeare.

19:113. Kaul, R. K. "The Unities Again: Dr. Johnson and Delusion" [Johnson follows Farquhar rather than Kames], *N&Q*, July 1962, pp. 261–64. Cf. John Hardy, *N&Q*, September 1962, pp. 350–51; and Gunnar Sorelius, December, pp. 466–67, and April 1963, p. 156.

19:114. Eddy, Donald D. "Samuel Johnson's Editions of Shakespeare (1765)," *PBSA*, LVI (4th quarter, 1962), 428–44.

19:115. Maxwell, J. C. "Prescriptive," *N&Q*, July 1962, p. 268.

19:116. Hardy, John. "Shakespeare—'The Poet of Nature' and 'Intellectual Nature,'" *New Rambler*, January 1963, pp. 10–19.

19:117. Robinson, William Henry, Jr. "Samuel Johnson as a Critic of Shakespeare." Dissertation, Harvard University, 1964.

19:118. Siegel, Paul N. "Johnson," *His Infinite Variety: Major Shakespear-*

ean Criticism Since Johnson, pp. 6–12. Philadelphia and New York: J. B. Lippincott, 1964.

19:119. Barnes, G. "Johnson's Edition of Shakespeare," in item 6:23, December 1964, pp. 16–39.

19:120. Gardner, Helen. "Johnson on Shakespeare," *New Rambler,* June 1965, pp. 2–12.

19:121. Clifford, James L. "Johnson, Samuel," in *The Reader's Encyclopedia of Shakespeare,* ed. O. J. Campbell, pp. 403–5. New York: Thomas Y. Crowell, 1966.

19:122. Hardy, John. "Johnson and *Don Bellianis*" [quotations from this old romance in *Observations on Macbeth*], *RES,* n.s., XVII (August 1966), 297–99.

19:123. Stock, Robert Douglas. "The Intellectual Background of Dr. Johnson's Preface to Shakespeare" (dissertation, Princeton University, 1967), *Dissertation Abstracts,* XXVIII, no. 9 (March 1968), 3649–50A.

19:124. Fleischmann, Wolfgang Bernard. "Shakespeare, Johnson, and the Dramatic 'Unities of Time and Place,'" *SP,* Extra Series, No. 4 (January 1967), 128–34.

19:125. Hardy, John. "The 'Poet of Nature' and Self-Knowledge: One Aspect of Johnson's Moral Reading of Shakespeare," *University of Toronto Quarterly,* XXXVI (January 1967), 141–60.

19:126. Grover, P. R. "The Ghost of Dr. Johnson: L. C. Knights and D. A. Traversi on *Hamlet,*" *Essays in Criticism,* XVII (April 1967), 143–57.

19:127. Bronson, Bertrand H. "Johnson's Shakespeare," *Facets of the Enlightenment,* pp. 241–65. Berkeley and Los Angeles: University of California Press, 1968. A reprint of Bronson's Introduction to Vols. VII and VIII of the Yale Edition of Johnson's Works (item 19:11).

19:128. Eastman, Arthur M. "Chaper 2. Johnson," *A Short History of Shakespearean Criticism,* pp. 20–34. New York: Random House, 1968.

20. POLITICAL AND ECONOMIC WRITINGS AND VIEWS

No attempt is made here to list all of the very large number of pieces of writing by Johnson with a political reference; for such a list, see item 20:83, pp. xii–xix.

20:1. "Debates in the Senate of Lilliput [i.e., the Parliament of Great Britain]." These appeared originally in the *Gentleman's Magazine,* beginning in June 1738 and continuing throughout the early 1740's. On the problem of identifying Johnson's share in these, see items 20:68, 20:77, 20:95, 20:100, 25:76. Debates by Johnson were reprinted in the next four items:

20:2. ["Chandler."] *The History and Proceedings of the House of Commons from the Restoration to the Present Time.* Vol. XII. London: Richard Chandler, 1742. *The History and Proceedings of the House of Commons during the Third Parliament of . . . King George II. Held in the Years 1741 and 1742.* London: Richard Chandler, 1743. *The History and Proceedings of the House of Commons during the Third Parliament of . . . King George II. Held in the years 1742 and 1743.* London: Printed and sold by William Sandby. 1744.

20:3. ["Timberland."] *The History and Proceedings of the House of Lords, from the Restoration . . . to the Present Time.* Vol. VII. London: Ebenezer Timberland, 1742. *The History and Proceedings of the House of Lords, during the Third Parliament of King George II. Held in the years 1741 and 1742.* London: Ebenezer Timberland, 1743.

20:4. ["Torbuck."] *A Collection of the Parliamentary Debates in England from the Year MDCLXVIII to the Present Time.* 13 vols. London: John Torbuck, 1739–42. *An Impartial History of the Proceedings and Debates in Both Houses of Parliament* [from December 1, 1741, to July 15, 1742]. London: B. Cowse, 1743.

20:5. ["Parliamentary History"; "Cobbett"; "Hansard."] *[Cobbett's] Parliamentary History of England from the Norman Conquest to the Year 1803,* [ed. John Wright]. Vol. XI, 1739–41. Vol. XII, 1741–43. London: Printed by T. C. Hansard, 1812.

20:6. [Johnson, Samuel.] *The False Alarm.* London: T. Cadell, 1770. Reviewed in *Critical Review,* XXIX (January 1770), 54–57; *Monthly Review,* XLII (January 1770), 62–66.

20:7. No Jacobite. "On the Notorious Ingratitude of Pensioner J——n," *Middlesex Journal,* February 3–6, 1770.

20:8. Anti-Leviathan. "An Enquiry Whether the Principles of Hobbs Are Not Adopted by the Present Administration," *Political Register,* VI (June 1770), 315–18. Johnson is censured as a Hobbesian.

20:9. [Attack on *The False Alarm*], *North Briton* [Bingley's Continuation], No. 190 (November 13, 1770).

20:10. *The Crisis. In Answer to the False Alarm.* London: Murray, 1770. Attributed to Philip Rosenhagen.

20:11. *The Remonstrance. A Poem.* London: J. Wheble, W. Davenhill, etc., 1770. Anti-Wilkes, pro-Johnson. Sometimes attributed to Percival Stockdale.

20:12. [Scott, John.] *The Constitution Defended, and Pensioner Exposed; in Remarks on the False Alarm.* London: Dilly, 1770.

20:13. [Wilkes, John.] *A Letter to Samuel Johnson, L.L.D.* London: Almon, 1770.

20:14. [Johnson, Samuel.] *Thoughts on the Late Transactions Respecting*

Falkland's Islands. London: T. Cadell, 1771. Reviewed (hostilely) in *Political Register*, VIII (May 1771), 313–18. For a reprint, see item 20:74.

20:15. "The Censor, No. 10," *Oxford Magazine*, VI (May 1771), 153–56. Chiefly a political attack on Johnson.

20:16. *A Refutation of a Pamphlet called Thoughts on the Late Transactions Respecting Falkland's Islands.* London: Evans, 1771.

20:17. "The School of Reason, an Allegory," *Oxford Magazine*, VIII (January 1772), 9–13. A general condemnation of Johnson (called "the Idler"), but principally political.

20:18. [Attack on Johnson as author of "Tullius" letters in *Public Advertiser*], *London Evening Post*, May 8–11, 1773.

20:19. [Anecdote of Lord Lyttelton and Johnson], *London Evening Post*, September 4–7, 1773. Lyttelton, wanting to help Johnson, recommended that he write a history of the House of Brunswick. Johnson indignantly refused.

20:20. [Johnson, Samuel.] *The Patriot.* London: T. Cadell, 1774. Reviewed in *London Magazine*, XLIII (October 1774), 502; *Monthly Review*, LI (October 1774), 298–304.

20:21. "Causes of the Present Discontents and Commotion in America," *GM*, XLIV (November 1774), 514–16. Attacks *The Patriot*.

20:22. -F-. "Strictures on the Patriot," *Edinburgh Magazine and Review*, III (January 1775), 18–23.

20:23. Macaulay, Catherine. *An Address to the People of England.* London: Dilly, 1775. Mainly an attack on *The Patriot*; Johnson entered a riposte to it in *Taxation No Tyranny*.

20:24. [Scott, John.] *Remarks on the Patriot.* London: Richardson & Urquhart, 1775.

20:25. [Johnson, Samuel.] *Taxation No Tyranny: An Answer to the Resolutions and Address of the American Congress.* London: T. Cadell, 1775. Reviewed in *GM*, XLV (March 1775), 134–36; in *London Magazine*, XLIV (March 1775), 147; in *Monthly Review*, LII (March 1775), 253–61; in *London Review*, I (March 1775), 228–30.

20:26. A Bostonian. "To Samuel Johnson, LL.D." [comment on *Taxation No Tyranny*], *Public Advertiser*, March 13, 1775.

20:27. Denuder. [Attack on political pamphlets], *St. James's Chronicle*, April 1–4, 1775.

20:28. Columbus. [Letter attacking *Taxation No Tyranny*], *Whitehall*, April 6–8, 1775.

20:29. Tribunus. [Attack on *Taxation No Tyranny*], *London Evening Post*, April 11–15, 1775.

20:30. Regulus. "General Remarks on the Leading Principles of *Taxation*

No Tyranny" [attack], *London Evening Post*, April 29–May 2, 1775; continued May 2–4.

20:31. Franklyn. [Attack on *Taxation No Tyranny*], *Public Advertiser*, May 1, 1775.

20:32. "Casca's Epistle to Lord North," *Crisis*, No. XVIII (May 20, 1775). Verse. Includes a long reply to *Taxation No Tyranny*.

20:33. [Mock news report of Johnson's being hanged in effigy at Salem, Mass., after receipt of *Taxation No Tyranny*], *St. James's Chronicle*, No. 2235 (June 10–13, 1775).

20:34. *An Answer to a Pamphlet, entitled Taxation no Tyranny. Addressed to the Author and to Persons in Power.* London: Almon, 1775.

20:35. [Baillie, Hugh.] *An Appendix to a Letter to Dr. Shebbeare. To which are added, Some Observations on a Pamphlet, entitled, Taxation no Tyranny: In which the Sophistry of that Author's Reasoning is detected.* London: Donaldson, 1775.

20:36. *A Defence of the Resolutions and Address of the American Congress, in Reply to Taxation no Tyranny. By the Author of Regulus.* London: Williams, 1775.

20:37. [Johnson, Samuel.] *Marmor Norfolciense. . . . A new edition, with notes, and a dedication to Samuel Johnson, LL.D., by Tribunus.* London: J. Williams, 1775. Intended to embarrass Johnson in his current political activities. Reviewed (savagely; by William Kenrick?) in *London Review*, II (July 1775), 76–79; in *Monthly Review*, LII (October 1775), 360.

20:38. *The Pamphlet, entitled "Taxation no Tyranny," Candidly Considered, and it's [sic] Arguments, and Pernicious Doctrines, Exposed and Refuted.* London: Davis, 1775.

20:39. *Resistance no Rebellion: in Answer to Doctor Johnson's Taxation no Tyranny.* London: Bell, 1775.

20:40. *Resistance no Rebellion. In which the Right of the British Parliament to tax the American Colonies is fully considered.* London: Maud, 1775.

20:41. "Sincerus." *Plain English. A Letter to the King.* N.p., n.d., but preface dated "1775." In part, a reply to *Taxation No Tyranny*.

20:42. *Taxation, Tyranny. Addressed to Samuel Johnson, L.L.D.* London: Bew, 1775.

20:43. Towers, Joseph. *A Letter to Dr. Samuel Johnson: Occasioned by His Late Political Publications. With an Appendix, Containing Some Observations on a Pamphlet Lately Published by Dr. Shebbeare.* London: Printed for J. Towers, 1775. Reprinted in his *Tracts on Political Subjects*, I, 145–232, London: T. Cadell, 1796.

20:44. *Tyranny Unmasked. An Answer to a Late Pamphlet entitled Taxation No Tyranny.* London: Flexney, 1775.

20:45. Wesley, John. *A Calm Address to the American Colonies.* London: B. Hawes, [1775]. Largely "cribbed" from *Taxation No Tyranny.*

20:46. [Toplady, Augustus Montague.] *An Old Fox Tarr'd and Feather'd. Occasion'd by what is called Mr. John Wesley's Calm Address to our American Colonies. By an Hanoverian.* London: J. French, 1775. Discloses Wesley's unacknowledged borrowing from Johnson's *Taxation No Tyranny.*

20:47. *Political Tracts. Containing, The False Alarm. Falkland's Islands. The Patriot; and, Taxation No Tyranny.* London: W. Strahan and T. Cadell, 1776. Edited by Johnson (with some revision).

20:48. *The Sixteenth Ode of the Third Book of Horace Imitated. With a dedication to . . . the Lord N——h* [North]. London: J. Almon, 1776. A political satire; the dedication is signed "S——l J——n."

20:49. Stevenson, John Hall. *An Essay upon the King's Friends, with an account of some discoveries made in Italy, and found in a Virgil, concerning the Tories. To Dr. S——l J——n* [a burlesque of *Marmor Norfolciense*]. London: Almon, 1776. Reprinted in Stevenson's *Works,* I, 249–85, London: Debrett and Becket, 1795.

20:50. [Report of John Wilkes's speech in House of Commons attacking Johnson and other pensioned writers], *St. James's Chronicle,* No. 2514 (April 19–22, 1777).

20:51. A Plain Dealer. [Attack on Johnson's politics], *London Evening Post,* December 16–18, 1779.

20:52. Towzer. "A Chapter of Bears," *Courant,* August 17, 1780. Attack on Sandwich, Shebbeare, Johnson, etc.

20:53. [Badini, Joseph.] *The Flames of Newgate; or, the New Ministry.* London: Southern, 1782. Badini's authorship is stated in *European Magazine,* II (July 1782), 51–53.

20:54. [Attribution of "A Speech Dictated by Dr. Johnson . . . after the Expedition to Rochfort, in September, 1757 . . ."], *GM,* LV (October 1785), 764–65.

20:55. "The Collector. No. VI. Doctor Johnson and the Coronation," *London Magazine,* VI (July 1820), 56–58. Applies Johnson's strictures on the expense of George III's coronation to that of George IV. Reprints Johnson's *Weekly Correspondent* No. III (1760), "On the Coronation of George the Third" (see item 25:43.)

20:56. C., B. [Johnson's views on slavery contrasted with Boswell's], *Christian Observer,* XXV (March 1825), 158–59. See also "An Abolitionist," *ibid.* (May 1825), 293.

20:57. Sheridan, Richard Brinsley. [Notes and fragments of an unpublished reply to *Taxation No Tyranny*], in Thomas Moore, *Memoirs of the Life of the Right Honourable Richard Brinsley Sheridan*, I, 150–55. London: Longmans, 1825. Additional extracts from the MS given in Walter Sichel, *Sheridan*, I, 472–74, London: Constable; Boston: Houghton Mifflin, 1909.

*20:58. Duyckinck, Evert A. and George L. [Report by Thomas Cooper, of South Carolina, of a conversation with Johnson concerning his political views], *Cyclopaedia of American Literature*, II, 333. New York: Scribner, 1855. See item 5:363.

*20:59. Hill, George Birkbeck. "Dr. Johnson as a Radical," *Contemporary Review*, LV (June 1889), 888–99.

*20:60. Sargeaunt, John. "Dr. Johnson's Politics," *Bookman* (New York), VI (January 1898), 420–22. Reprinted in item 6:16, pp. 193–200.

20:61. Lee, Sir Sidney. "Dr. Johnson and Current Affairs," *Lichfield Mercury*, September 19, 1919. Reprinted; see item 6:22.

20:62. Kent, William. "Dr. Johnson" [as a pacifist, etc.], *Socialist Review*, XVII (October–December 1920), 345–52.

20:63. Haynes, E. S. P. "Dr. Johnson on Liberty," in item 6:28, pp. 57–64.

20:64. Russell, Sir Charles. "Johnson the Jacobite," *Fortnightly Review*, CXI (February 1922), 229–40.

20:65. O'Brien, George. "Dr. Samuel Johnson as an Economist," *Studies*, XIV (March 1925), 80–101.

20:66. Langenfelt, Gösta. "Patriotism and Scoundrels" [Johnson's political beliefs], *Neophilologus*, XVII (October 1931, January 1932), 32–41, 117–25.

20:67. Stiles, Robert E. "Doctor Samuel Johnson's 'Taxation No Tyranny' and Its Half Title," *American Book Collector*, I (March 1932), 155–56.

*20:68. Evans, Medford. "Johnson's Debates in Parliament." Dissertation, Yale University, 1933.

*20:69. Orlovich, Robert B. *Samuel Johnson's Political Ideas and Their Influence on His Works*. Abstract of thesis. Urbana: University of Illinois, 1941.

20:70. Ransome, Mary. "The Reliability of Contemporary Reporting of the Debates of the House of Commons, 1727–1741," *Bulletin of the Institute of Historical Research*, XIX (May 1942), 67–79.

20:71. Sypher, Wylie. *Guinea's Captive Kings*, pp. 58–61, etc. [Johnson's attitude toward slavery]. Chapel Hill: University of North Carolina Press, 1942.

20:72. C., P. "Johnson on Subordination," *N&Q*, CLXXXVI (March 25, 1944), 159.

*20:73. Kilbourne, H. R. "Dr. Johnson and War," *ELH*, XII (June 1945), 130–43.

20:74. *Thoughts on the Late Transactions Respecting Falkland's Islands.* With preface by F. N. B. London: Thames Bank Publishing Co., 1948.

*20:75. Bloom, Edward A. "Johnson on a Free Press: A Study in Liberty and Subordination," *ELH*, XVI (December 1949), 251–71.

20:76. "Un Siècle avant Solférino" [Johnson's ideas adumbrate those of Henri Dunant, inspirer of the Geneva Convention and the Red Cross], *Revue Internationale de la Croix Rouge* (Geneva), XXXIII (December 1951), 969–71. Contains a French translation, by J. C. de Watteville, of Johnson's Introduction to *Proceedings of the Committee . . . for Cloathing French Prisoners of War.*

*20:77. Hoover, Benjamin B. *Samuel Johnson's Parliamentary Reporting.* (University of California Publications, English Studies, No. 7.) Berkeley and Los Angeles: University of California Press, 1953. Reviewed by Arthur Sherbo, *JEGP*, LIII (October 1954), 640–41; Benjamin Boyce, *MLQ*, XVII (March 1956), 75–76; John Butt, *RES*, n.s., VII (October 1956), 433–35.

*20:78. Todd, William B. "Concealed Editions of Samuel Johnson" [*The False Alarm* and *Taxation No Tyranny*], *Book Collector*, II (Spring 1953), 59–65.

20:79. Metzdorf, Robert F. "Samuel Johnson in Brunswick" [early German translation of *Taxation No Tyranny*], *MLN*, LXVIII (June 1953), 397–400.

20:80. Graham, W. H. "Dr. Johnson and Royalty," *Contemporary Review*, No. 1081 (January 1956), 36–38.

20:81. Sidney, Joseph. "The Political Thought of Samuel Johnson" (dissertation, University of Chicago, 1957). Chicago: University of Chicago Department of Photoduplication [microfilm], 1957.

*20:82. Miner, Earl R. "Dr. Johnson, Mandeville, and 'Publick Benefits,'" *Huntington Library Quarterly*, XXI (February 1958), 159–66.

*20:83. Greene, Donald J. *The Politics of Samuel Johnson.* New Haven, Conn.: Yale University Press, 1960. Reviewed by Medford Evans, *National Review* (New York), May 7, 1960, pp. 306–7; Milton Hindus, *New Leader*, August 29, 1960, pp. 26–27; in *Economist*, September 24, 1960, pp. 1190, 1195; by John A. Rycenga, *Modern Age*, V (Winter 1960–61), 95–98; by W. R. Ward, *Parliamentary Affairs*, XIV (Winter 1960–61), 125–26; by Asa Briggs, *Science & Society*, XXV (1961), 285–87; by Caroline Robbins, *Journal of Modern History*, XXXIII (1961), 322–23; by E. L. McAdam, Jr., *PQ*, XL (July 1961), 401–2; by C. H. Peake, *RES*, XIV (August 1963), 305–6. Revision of Columbia University dissertation, 1954.

20:84. Greene, Donald J. "*The False Alarm* and *Taxation No Tyranny:*

Some Further Observations" [variant issues; see item 20:78], *Studies in Bibliography* (University of Virginia), XIII (1960), 223–31.

20:85. Lyles, Albert M. "The Hostile Reaction to the American Views of Johnson and Wesley," *Journal of the Rutgers University Library*, XXIV (December 1960), 1–13.

*20:86. Middendorf, John H. "Dr. Johnson and Mercantilism," *JHI*, XXI (January–March 1960), 66–83.

20:87. Kirk, Russell. "Samuel Johnson the Statist" [largely an attack on item 20:83], *Kenyon Review*, XXII (Autumn 1960), 679–86.

20:88. Greene, Donald. "Lord Campbell on Johnson's 'Debates,'" *JNL*, XXIII, no. 2 (June 1963), 11–12. His praise, in *Lives of the Lord Chancellors*, of the report of Lord Hardwicke's speech, February 13, 1741.

20:89. *Political Writers of Eighteenth-Century England*, ed. Jeffrey Hart, pp. 23–24, 287–96. New York: Knopf, 1964.

20:90. Sullivan, Gerald J. "Politics and Literature of Samuel Johnson" [concentrates on *Irene*, allegories, and *Rasselas*] (dissertation, University of Oklahoma, 1964), *Dissertation Abstracts*, XXV (October 1964), 2501.

20:91. Lustig, Irma S. "Boswell on Politics in *The Life of Johnson*," *PMLA*, LXXX (September 1965), 387–93.

20:92. Boyle, Sir Edward. "Johnson's Attitude to the American Colonies," presidential address, in item 6:23, December 1965, pp. 30–40.

20:93. McAdam, E. L., Jr. "Johnson, Walpole, and Public Order," in item 10/6:329, pp. 93–98.

20:94. Middendorf, John H. "Johnson on Wealth and Commerce" in item 10/6:329, pp. 47–64.

20:95. Bernard, F. V. "Johnson and the Authorship of Four Debates," *PMLA*, LXXXII (October 1967), 408–19.

20:96. *The Political Writings of Dr. Johnson*, ed. John P. Hardy. London: Routledge and Kegan Paul, 1968. A selection.

20:97. Davie, Donald. "Politics and Literature: John Adams and Doctor Johnson," in *Politics and Experience: Essays Presented to Professor Michael Oakeshott on the Occasion of His Retirement*, pp. 395–408. Cambridge: Cambridge University Press, 1968.

*20:98. Butler, James A. "Samuel Johnson: Defender of Admiral Byng," *Cornell Library Journal*, no. 7 (Winter 1969), 25–47.

20:99. Johnson, Samuel. *Political Writings*, ed. Donald J. Greene. A forthcoming volume (perhaps in 1971) in the Yale Edition of Johnson's Works (item 2:8).

20:100. Johnson, Samuel. *Debates in Parliament*, ed. Benjamin B. Hoover. Forthcoming volumes in the Yale Edition of Johnson's Works (item 2:8).

21. *JOURNEY TO THE WESTERN ISLANDS,* AND TRAVEL GENERALLY

EDITIONS

21:1. Johnson, Samuel. *A Journey to the Western Islands of Scotland.* London: W. Strahan; T. Cadell, 1775. Reviewed in *Critical Review,* XXXIX (January 1775), 33–44; in *GM,* XLV (January, February), 35–38, 83–86; in *London Review,* I (January), 32–42; by Ralph Griffiths in *Monthly Review,* LII (January, February), 57–65, 158–62; in *Town and Country Magazine,* VII (January), 27–29; in *London Magazine,* XLV (February), 88–89; in *Edinburgh Magazine and Review,* III (March), 154–62. For eighteenth- and nineteenth-century editions, see Courtney (Item 1/1:19), pp. 122–25.

Ed. E. J. Thomas. London: University Tutorial Press, 1904.

Ed. D. T. Holmes. Paisley: A. Gardner, 1906.

*Ed. (with item 4:12) R. W. Chapman. London: Oxford University Press, 1924.

Ed. John Freeman. London: Chapman and Dodd, 1924; Boston (Abbey Classics): Small, Maynard, 1925.

Ed. Philip B. M. Allan. (Pilgrim Books.) London: Philip Allan & Co., 1925.

Ed. John Bailey. (Abr.; Teaching of English Series, No. 80.) London: Thomas Nelson & Sons, 1926.

Ed. D. L. Murray. (Traveller's Library.) London: Jonathan Cape, 1931.

Ed. (with item 4:12) Allan Wendt. (Riverside Editions.) Boston: Houghton Mifflin, 1965.

Ed. Mary Lascelles. (Yale Edition of the Works of Johnson, item 2:8.) New Haven, Conn.: Yale University Press (forthcoming).

21:2. *Diary of a Journey into North Wales in the Year 1774; by Samuel Johnson, LL.D.,* ed. Richard Duppa. London: Jennings, 1816. Included in many later editions of Boswell's *Life,* e.g., item 4:14 (1934–50), Vol. V (2nd ed., 1964), and in item 2:8, Vol. 1 (1958).

*21:3. Tyson, Moses, and Henry Guppy. *The French Journals of Mrs. Thrale and Dr. Johnson.* Manchester: John Rylands Library, 1932. Johnson's also included in item 2:8, Vol. I (1958).

COMMENTARY

21:20. "Notes of Mr. Samuel Johnson's Tour to Scotland and the Western Isles," *London Magazine,* XLIII (January 1774), 26–27. "Offered to our readers as a *whet.*" Reprinted (in part) *Aberdeen Journal,* February 19,

1774, p. 3. See also *Gentleman and Lady's Weekly Magazine* (Edinburgh), April 22, May 11, 1774.

21:21. "The Critic, No. 1. On the Journey to the Western Islands of Scotland, by the Author of the Rambler, in letters to a friend," *London Packet*, No. 827 (February 3–6, 1775).

21:22. Ixion. "To Dr. Samuel Johnson, on His Tour through Scotland" [hostile], *Weekly Magazine* (Edinburgh), XXVII (February 9, 1775), 204–6.

21:23. A Hater of Impudence, Pedantry and Affectation. [Attack on *Journey*], *Weekly Magazine* (Edinburgh), XXVII (February 16, 1775), 225–28; (February 23), 257–60.

21:24. Whackum. "A Cure for Dr. J—s–n" [verse], *Weekly Magazine* (Edinburgh), XXVII (February 16, 1775), p. 256.

21:25. Staffa. "Anecdote of the Last Hebridean Traveller," *St. James's Chronicle*, No. 2191 (February 28–March 2, 1775). Satire on Johnson's alleged attitude toward the Scots.

21:26. Philoaletheios. [Attack on *Journey*], *Weekly Magazine* (Edinburgh), XXVII (March 2, 1775), 289–92.

21:27. A Recruiting Officer. [Attack on *Journey*], *London Evening Post*, March 4–7, 1775.

21:28. Urbanus. "Remarks on Some Passages in a Late Performance, Intitled A Journey Through Scotland. Letter I. Containing Some Strictures on Dr. Johnson's Characters and a Vindication of the Scots Reformers," *Weekly Magazine* (Edinburgh), XXVII (March 9, 16, 1775), 320–25, 353–56. Attributed in BM copy to "Dr. Geddes."

21:29. An Impartial Observer. [Defense of James Macpherson], *Public Advertiser*, March 10, 1775.

21:30. Druid, The. [Attack on *Dictionary* and *Journey*], *Weekly Magazine* (Edinburgh), XXVII (March 22, 1775), 385–87.

21:31. Henderson, Andrew. *A Letter to Dr. Samuel Johnson on His Journey to the Western Isles.* London: Henderson, 1775.

21:32. Henderson, Andrew. *A Second Letter to Dr. Samuel Johnson. In which his wicked and opprobrious Invectives are shown, etc.* London: Henderson, 1775.

21:33. *Remarks on a Voyage to the Hebrides, in a Letter to Samuel Johnson, L.L.D.* London: Kearsley, 1775.

21:34. A Lover of Scots Manufactures. "Strictures on Travellers, and Observations on Some Scots Manufactories Lately Established," *Weekly Magazine* (Edinburgh), XXXI (February 1, 1776), 165–67. Censures Johnson for ignoring them.

21:35. Brace, Miss. "On Reading Dr. Johnson's Tour to the Western Islands of Scotland," *Weekly Magazine* (Edinburgh), XXXIII (August 22, 1776), 272.

21:36. Cameron, Ewen. *The Fingal of Ossian, an Ancient Epic Poem in Six Books. Translated from the original Galic language, by Mr. James Macpherson; and now rendered into heroic verse.* Warrington: William Byres, 1776. Preface (pp. [3]–90) is a detailed reply to Johnson's strictures on Macpherson.

21:37. Topham, Edward. *Letters from Edinburgh; Written in the Years 1774 and 1775.* London: Dodsley, 1776.

21:38. [Hanway, Mary Ann.] *A Journey to the Highlands of Scotland. With Occasional Remarks on Dr. Johnson's Tour.* London: Fielding and Walker, 1777.

21:39. M'Nicol, Donald. *Remarks on Dr. Samuel Johnson's Journey to the Hebrides.* London: Cadell, 1779. Reprinted 1817, together with the *Journey.*

21:40. M'Nicol, Donald. *Da Oran Oirdheirc, do'n Olla Shasgumnach; agus son Oran do Mhinisdeir Liosmoir, Mr. Domhnul Macneacail, le fior Gaidheal Albannach.* Glasgow, 1781. Contains "Oran do'n olla Shasgunnach, Samuel Johnson [A Song to the English Doctor, Samuel Johnson]," pp. 5–9; "Oran Connsachaidh no Riasanachaidh ris an Olla Shasgunnach [Ratiocinating Song with the English Doctor]," pp. 12–17.

21:41. Shaw, William. *An Enquiry into the Authenticity of the Poems ascribed to Ossian.* London: Murray, 1781. 2nd ed., 1782.

21:42. Knox, John. *Extracts from the Publications of Mr. Knox, Dr. Anderson, Mr. Pennant, and Dr. Johnson; Relative to the Northern and Northwestern Coasts of Great Britain.* London: C. Macrae, 1787. Proposals for the Scottish fish industry.

21:43. Sinclair, A. G. *The Critic Philosopher; or Truth Discovered,* pp. 15–16, 86–91. London: Strahan and Kearsley, 1789. Attack on *Journey.*

21:44. R., H. P. "Dr. Johnson's Tour," *N&Q,* 4th ser., V (May 28, 1870), 505. Four lines of a contemporary verse satire on the Scottish tour.

*21:45. Hill, George Birkbeck. *Footsteps of Dr. Johnson.* With illustrations by L. Speed. London: Sampson Low, Marston & Co., 1890.

21:46. Glover, Arnold. "A Johnson Manuscript" [MS of journal of French trip in 1775], *Athenaeum,* No. 3693 (August 6, 1898), pp. 191–92. See also *ibid.,* No. 3694 (August 13), pp. 226–27, and No. 3696 (August 27), p. 291. See also item 21:3.

21:47. Whale, George. "Dr. Johnson as a Traveller," in item 6:16, pp. 259–70.

21:48. Scott, H. Spencer. "Mr. Janes of Aberdeenshire," *N&Q,* 10th ser., II (July 16, 1904), 54–55. See also P. J. Anderson, *ibid.* (August 20), 155–56.

21:49. Hadden, J. Cuthbert. "Johnson and Boswell in Scotland," *GM,* CCXCVIII (June 1905), 597–605.

21:50. Marks, Jeannette. "Dr. Johnson's Cambrian Experience" [the Welsh tour of 1774], *Atlantic Monthly*, CV (January 1910), 53–61.

21:51. J., D. "Dr. Johnson in Scotland" [apocryphal anecdote from *Memoirs of Bishop Bathurst*, 1853], *N&Q*, 11th ser., IV (August 5, 1911), 105.

21:52. Marks, Jeannette. "Dr. Johnson's Tour of North Wales," *Gallant Little Wales*, pp. 59–85. Boston: Houghton Mifflin Co., 1912.

21:53. Couper, W. J. *Dr. Johnson in the Hebrides: A Bibliographical Paper.* Glasgow: Privately printed, 1916.

21:54. Bell, A. Montgomerie. "Scotland's Debt to Johnson" [his encouragement of the Gaelic translation of the Scriptures, etc.], *Spectator*, CXXI (July 13, 1918), 40.

*21:55. Chapman, Robert William. "Johnson in Scotland," *TLS*, October 3, 1918, pp. 461–62. Reprinted in *The Portrait of a Scholar*, pp. 127–40, London: Oxford University Press, 1920.

21:56. Bell, A. Montgomerie. "Johnson in Scotland," *Cornhill Magazine*, n.s., XLVIII (January, February 1920), 106–20, 244–56.

21:57. McDowall, Arthur. "Johnson and Wordsworth: A Contrast in Travel," *London Mercury*, III (January 1921), 269–78. Reprinted in *Ruminations*, pp. 141–61, Boston: Houghton Mifflin Co., 1925.

21:58. Roscoe, Edward Stanley. "Johnson and Wordsworth in the Highlands," *North American Review*, CCXIV (November 1921), 690–96. Reprinted in item 10/6:204, pp. 97–112.

21:59. Chapman, R. W. "Notes on Eighteenth-Century Bookbuilding" [cancels in Johnson's *Journey*, etc.], *Library*, 4th ser., IV (December 1923), 165–80.

21:60. Knox, David H. "Dr. Johnson in Scotland," *Proceedings of the Royal Philosophical Society of Glasgow*, LII (1924), 46–57.

21:61. Birrell, Augustine. "Johnson's 'Journey' and Boswell's 'Journal' " [chiefly a review of 21:1, ed. Chapman], *Nation-Athenaeum*, XXXV (August 9, 1924), 591–92.

21:62. Matheson, Percy E. [Johnson as a traveler], *Lichfield Mercury*, September 26, 1924. Reprinted; see item 6:22.

21:63. Maclean, Catherine M. "Dr. Johnson in the Highlands," *English Review*, XXXIX (November 1924), 686–90.

21:64. Harries, Frederick J. "Dr. Johnson," *Famous Writers and Wales*, pp. 23–32. Pontypridd: Glamorgan County Times, 1925.

*21:65. Elias, C. F. "Dr. Samuel Johnson as Traveller," *Proceedings of the Liverpool Philomathic Society*, LXXIII (1928), iii–xxxiv. Separately printed, Liverpool: D. Marples, 1927.

21:66. Mackenzie, William C. "Dr. Johnson and the Western Isles," *Transactions of the Gaelic Society of Inverness*, XXXI (1927), 31–58.

21:67. McKinlay, Robert. "Scottish Ministers as Seen by Dr. Johnson," *Records Scottish Church Historical Society*, III, Pt. II (1928), 146–58.

21:68. Gatenby, E. V. "Johnson and Boswell in Scotland," *Studies in English Literature* (Tokyo), IX (1929), 341–54.

21:69. Sutherland, D. S. "Samuel Johnson in Inverness-shire," *Caledonian Medical Journal*, XIV (1929), 114–33.

21:70. Rendall, Vernon. "Johnson and a Latin Psalm Heading," *N&Q*, CLVI (January 5, 1929), 7–8. A note on an entry in the *Diary of a Journey to North Wales*.

21:71. Lovat-Fraser, J. A. "Ghosts in the Isle of Coll," *Contemporary Review*, CXXXV (April 1020), 478–85.

21:72. Roscoe, Edward Stanley. "A Journey to the Western Islands" [where Johnson first thought of writing it], *TLS*, June 6, 1929, p. 454.

21:73. McKinlay, Robert. "Some Notes on Dr. Johnson's Journey to the Western Islands," *Records of Glasgow Bibliographical Society*, VIII, pt. II (1930), 144–50.

21:74. Lovat-Fraser, J. A. *Johnson in the Isle of Skye* [reprinted from the *Inverness Courier*, December 26, 30, 1930]. Inverness: Robert Carruthers & Sons, 1931.

21:75. Lovat-Fraser, J. A. *Doctor Johnson in the Isle of Mull* [reprinted from the *Inverness Courier*]. Inverness: Robert Carruthers & Sons, 1931.

21:76. Hindle, C. J. "Dr. Johnson at Tobermory," *N&Q*, CLXI (August 22, 1931), 133.

*21:77. Cox, Edward G. "The Case of Scotland vs. Dr. Samuel Johnson" [M'Nicol's attack on Johnson], *Transactions of the Gaelic Society of Inverness*, XXXIII (1932), 49–79.

21:78. Chapman, R. W. "Johnson's *Journey*, 1775," *RES*, VIII (July 1932), 315–16.

21:79. Watkin-Jones, A. "While Dr. Johnson Toured Scotland," *Cornhill Magazine*, n.s., LXXIII (August 1932), 193–98.

21:80. Bracey, Robert. "To Paris with Dr. Johnson," *Blackfriars*, XIV (April 1933), 281–88. Review article based on item 21:3.

21:81. Pearson, Hesketh, and Hugh Kingsmill. *Skye High* [record of a modern tour following Johnson and Boswell]. London: Hamilton, 1937.

21:82. Gray, W. Forbes. "Dr. Johnson in Edinburgh," *Quarterly Review*, CCLXIX (October 1937), 281–97.

21:83. R[endall], V[ernon]. "Johnson and Scotland: Early Prejudice," *N&Q*, CLXXIII (October 30, 1937), 315–16.

21:84. Robertson, James D. "The Opinions of 18th Century English Men of Letters concerning Scotland." Dissertation, University of Cincinnati, 1939.

21:85. "The Doctor, via Bozzy, to the Laird" [copy of *Journey* sent to

Laird of Raasay], *Month at Goodspeed's Book Shop*, IX (March 1938), 195–99.

21:86. Ferguson, James. " 'Worthy Nairne' " [William Nairne, met in 1773], *Cornhill Magazine*, CLIX (January 1939), 101–15.

21:87. Murray, John. "Notes on Johnson's Movements in Scotland: Suggested Attributions to Boswell in the *Caledonian Mercury*," *N&Q*, CLXXVIII (January 6, March 16, 1940), 3–5, 182–85.

*21:88. Powell, Lawrence F. " 'The History of St. Kilda,' " *RES*, XVI (January 1940), 44–53.

21:89. Pleadwell, F. L. "Samuel Johnson at Edinburgh" [possible dinner with Joseph Black], *N&Q*, CLXXIX (October 19, 1940), 278–79.

*21:90. Hazen, Allen T. "The Cancels in Johnson's *Journey*, 1775," *RES*, XVII (April 1941), 201–3.

21:91. De Blácam, A. S. "Behold the Hebrides!" *Irish Monthly*, LXIX (September 1941), 455–64.

21:92. Chapman, R. W. "Johnson's 'Journey,' " *TLS*, March 27, 1943, p. 156.

21:93. Hetherington, John. *The Tour to the Hebrides: Its Value to the Social Historian* [see item 6:23]. Lichfield: The Johnson's Head, 1948.

21:94. Mossner, Ernest C. "Dr. Johnson 'in partibus Infidelium?' " [Boswell not in Hume's house in 1773], *MLN*, LXIII (December 1948), 516–19.

21:95. Cornu, Donald. "Dr. Johnson at Fort Augustus: Captain Lewis Ourry," *MLQ*, XI (March 1950), 27–49.

21:96. Brain, W. Russell. "Dr. Johnson and the Kangaroo" [he imitated one in an inn at Inverness], *Essays and Studies by Members of the English Association*, n.s., IV (1951), 112–17. Reprinted in item 3:744, pp. 48–54.

21:97. Lindsay, Lilian. "Dr. Johnson and Scotland," *New Rambler*, July 1951, pp. 5–8.

21:98. Cornu, Donald. "The Historical Authenticity of Dr. Johnson's 'Speaking Cat' " [incident mentioned in *Life*, III, 246], *RES*, n.s., II (October 1951), 358–70.

21:99. Osbaldeston-Mitford, Mrs. "Skye as Johnson Saw It," *New Rambler*, January 1952, pp. 5–8.

21:100. Sherbo, Arthur. "The Text of Johnson's *Journey to the Western Islands of Scotland*: 'Bayle' or 'Boyle' ?" *N&Q*, April 26, 1952, pp. 182–84.

21:101. Fletcher, Edward G. "Mrs. Piozzi on Boswell and Johnson's Tour" [annotations on copy at Harvard], *Texas Studies in English*, XXXII (1953), 45–58.

*21:102. Todd, William B. "The Printing of Johnson's *Journey* (1775)," *Studies in Bibliography* (University of Virginia), VI (1953–54), 247–54.

21:103. McLaren, Moray. *The Highland Jaunt*. London: Jarrolds, 1954; New York: William Sloane, 1955. See also his "Dr. Johnson's Island" [Coll], *New Statesman and Nation*, January 24, 1953, pp. 88–89.

21:104. Greene, Donald J. "Yeats's Byzantium and Johnson's Lichfield" [echo in Yeats of Johnson's "monuments of sacred magnificence"?], *PQ*, XXXIII (October 1954), 433–35.

21:105. Stucley, Elizabeth. *A Hebridean Journey with Johnson and Boswell.* London: Christopher Johnson, 1956.

21:106. Graham, W. H. "Dr. Johnson in Scotland," *Contemporary Review*, CXCIII (February 1958), 78–82.

21:107. Quaintance, Richard E., Jr. "A Johnson Anecdote," *JNL*, XVIII, no. 4 (December 1958), 9–10. Comment on Henry Mackenzie, at a visit to the Blacklocks' in Edinburgh.

21:108. Hart, Jeffrey. "Johnson's *A Journey to the Western Islands:* History as Art," *Essays in Criticism*, X (January 1960), 44–59. See items 21: 109, 21:115, 21:124, 21:128, 21:130.

21:109. Greene, Donald J. "Johnsonian Critics," *Essays in Criticism*, X (October 1960), 476–80. Largely an attack on item 21:108.

21:110. Curwen, H. Darcy. "In Search of Johnson" [account of his trip to the Hebrides], *Harvard Alumni Bulletin*, LXIII (November 5, 1960), 146, 148.

21:111. Lascelles, Mary. "Some Reflections on Johnson's Hebridean Journey," *New Rambler*, June 1961, pp. 2–13.

21:112. Fleeman, J. D. "Dr. Johnson in the Highlands," *TLS*, September 29, 1961, p. 645. Cf. G. F. Sleigh, December 15, p. 897.

21:113. Fleeman, J. D. "A Dr. Johnson Mystery" [just where he decided to write *Journey*], *Scots Magazine*, LXXVI (November 1961), 120–25.

21:114. Mitchell, Stephen O. "Johnson and Cocker's *Arithmetic*," *PBSA*, LVI (1st quarter, 1962), 107–9.

*21:115. Kaul, R. K. "*A Journey to the Western Isles* Reconsidered," *Essays in Criticism*, XIII (October 1963), 341–50.

21:116. Lasser, Michael L. "Johnson in Scotland: New Life amid the 'Ruins of Iona,'" *Midwest Quarterly*, IV (Spring 1963), 227–34.

21:117. Durkee, Elizabeth. "The Barren Years: A Further Consideration of Johnson's Prejudice against Scotland," *Journal of the Rutgers University Library*, XXVII (December 1963), 1–18.

21:118. Hoyt, Charles A. "On Samuel Johnson Who Wrote against Scotland," *American Book Collector*, XIV (February 1964), 21–24.

21:119. Fleeman, J. D. "Johnson's 'Journey' (1775) and Its Cancels," *PBSA*, LVIII (3rd quarter, 1964), 232–38.

21:120. Kendall, Lyle H., Jr. "A Note on Johnson's *Journey* (1775)," *PBSA*, LIX (3rd quarter, 1965), 317–18.

*21:121. Lascelles, Mary. "Notions and Facts: Johnson and Boswell on Their Travels," in item 10/6:329, pp. 215–29.

21:122. Skipp, Francis E. "Johnson and Boswell Afloat," *New Rambler*, January 1965, pp. 21–28.

21:123. Jemielity, Thomas John. "Philosophy as Art: A Study of the Intellectual Background of Samuel Johnson's *Journey to the Western Islands of Scotland*" (dissertation, Cornell University, 1965), *Dissertation Abstracts*, XXVI (April 1966), 6022–23.

21:124. Sherbo, Arthur. "Johnson's Intent in the *Journey to the Western Islands of Scotland*," *Essays in Criticism*, XVI (October 1966), 382–97.

21:125. Jemielity, Thomas J. " 'Savage Virtues and Barbarous Grandeur': Johnson and Martin in the Highlands," *Cornell Library Journal*, No. 1 (Winter 1966), 1–12.

21:126. Moore, Thurston Maxwell. "Samuel Johnson and the Literature of Travel" (dissertation, University of Michigan, 1966), *Dissertation Abstracts*, XXVIII, no. 1 (July 1967), 237A–238A.

21:127. Schalit, Ann E. "Literature as Product and Process: Two Differing Accounts of the Same Trip" [Johnson's *Journey* and Boswell's *Tour*], *Serif* (Kent State University), IV (March 1967), 10–17.

21:128. Tracy, Clarence. "Johnson's *Journey to the Western Islands of Scotland*: A Reconsideration," *Studies on Voltaire and the Eighteenth Century* (Institut et Musée Voltaire, Geneva), LVIII (1967), 1593–1606.

21:129. Meier, Thomas K. "Pattern in Johnson's *A Journey to the Western Islands*," *Studies in Scottish Literature*, V (January 1968), 185–93.

21:130. Meier, Thomas K. "Johnson on Scotland," *Essays in Criticism*, XVIII (July 1968), 349–52. A reply to item 21:115.

21:131. Rauter, Herbert. "Johnsons Kritik des Primitivismus in *A Journey to the Western Islands of Scotland*," *Germanisch-Romanische Monatsschrift*, n.s., XVIII (July 1968), 257–73.

21:132. Hodgart, Matthew. "Johnson the Traveller," in item 6:23 (1969), pp. 41–47.

22. *THE LIVES OF THE POETS*

For general studies of Johnson as a biographer, see Section 10/2, and of Johnson as a critic, see Section 10/1.

EDITIONS

22:1. *Prefaces, Biographical and Critical, to the Works of the English Poets.* *By Samuel Johnson.* London: C. Bathurst, J. Buckland, etc., Vols. I–IV, 1779; Vols. V–X, 1781. Reviewed in *London Review*, IV (April 1779), 257–67 (hostile); *Critical Review*, XLVII (May 1779), 354–62; (June), 450–53; LII (August 1781), 81–92; *Westminster Magazine*, VI (May

1779), 265; *GM*, XLIX (June 1779), 312–13; (July), 362–64; September), 453–57; (October), 505–7; LI (May 1781), 224–27 (June), 271–76; by Edmund Cartwright in *Monthly Review*, LXI (July 1779), 1–10; (August), 81–92; (September), 186–91; LXV (August 1781), 100–12; (November), 353–62; (December), 408–11; LXVI (February 1782), 113–27; in *Annual Register*, XXV (1779), 179–84.

Many eds. in next few decades under titles such as *The Lives of the English Poets, and a Criticism of Their Works*; *The Lives of the Most Eminent English Poets, with Critical Observations on Their Works*; *The Lives of the Most Eminent English Poets*; *The Lives of the English Poets*. See Courtney (item 1/1:19), pp. 140–47.

Ed. Peter Cunningham. 3 vols. London: John Murray, 1854. Reviewed in *Athenaeum*, October 28, 1854, pp. 1297–98; November 25, p. 1430; *Bentley's Miscellany*, XXXVI (1854), 445–46; and see items 22:79 and 22:80.

Ed. (and continued) by William Hazlitt, Jr. London: Nathaniel Cooke, 1854.

(Cassell's National Library.) London: Cassell, 1886–88.

Ed. Robina Napier (Mrs. A. Napier). With introduction by J. W. Hales. (Bohn's Standard Library.) London: Bohn, 1890.

Ed. W. E. Henley. With introduction by John Hepburn Millar. London: Methuen, 1896.

Ed. Arthur Waugh. London: Kegan, Paul, 1896; World's Classics, London: Oxford University Press, 1906.

*Ed. G. B. Hill. 3 vols. Oxford: Clarendon Press, 1905. Facsimile reprint, New York: Octagon Press, 1967. For reviews see items 22:87, 22:88.

Ed. C. H. Firth. Oxford: Clarendon Press, 1907.

Ed. L. Archer-Hind. (Everyman's Library.) London: Dent, [1925].

2 vols., paperbound. (Dolphin Books.) New York: Doubleday, n.d. [1950's].

22:2. Selections

The Six Chief Lives of Johnson's "Lives of the Poets," with Macaulay's "Life of Johnson" [Milton, Dryden, Swift, Addison, Pope, and Gray], ed. Matthew Arnold. London: Macmillan, 1878. Reprinted 1892, etc. Arnold's introduction separately printed in *Macmillan's Magazine*, XXXVIII (June 1878), 153–60.

Selections from the Lives of the Poets, ed. Warren L. Fleischauer [lives of Savage, Pope, Collins, Gray; excerpts from Cowley, Milton, Dryden, Addison]. Chicago: Henry Regnery Co., 1955. Rev. ed., 1964.

Lives of the Poets, selected and introduced by S. C. Roberts. (Fontana Library.) London: Collins, 1963.

22:3. *Life of Addison*

Ed. F. Ryland. London: George Bell & Sons, 1893.

Ed. Grace E. Hadow. Oxford: Clarendon Press, 1915.

22:4. [*Life of Cowley*] *Critical Remarks on the Metaphysical Poets* [by Johnson], ed. Horace Gregory. With line drawings by Kurt Roesch. Mt. Vernon, N.Y.: Golden Eagle Press, 1945.

22:5. *Life of Dryden*

Ed. F. Ryland. (Bell's English Classics.) London, 1895.

Ed. Peter Peterson. London: Macmillan, 1899.

Ed. Alfred Milnes. Oxford: Clarendon Press, 1913 (first published 1885).

Ed. Adrian J. F. Collins. London: University Tutorial Press, 1914.

Ed. G. S. Dickson. London: Thomas Nelson & Sons, 1937.

22:6. "Life of Gay," in *The Plays of John Gay*, Vol. I. London: Chapman & Dodd, [1923].

22:7. *Life of Gray*

(Plain Texts.) Oxford: Clarendon Press, 1915.

In *Gray, Poetry and Prose*, ed. J. Crofts. Oxford: Clarendon Press, 1926.

Also in item 2:75 and other anthologies.

22:8. *Life of Milton*

Ed. K. Deighton. London: Macmillan, 1892.

Ed. F. Ryland. London: George Bell & Sons, 1894.

Ed. T. W. Berry and T. P. Marshall. Berry's P. T. Series. London: Simpkin, Marshall, [1900].

Ed. John W. Duff. (Blackwood's English Classics.) Printed with the Life of Addison. Edinburgh, 1900.

Ed. C. H. Firth. Oxford: Clarendon Press, 1907 [1888].

Ed. S. E. Goggin. London: University Tutorial Press, 1907.

In *Milton, Poetry and Prose*, selected by Beatrice G. Madan. Oxford: Clarendon Press, 1920.

22:9. *Life of Pope*

Ed. Alfred Milnes. Oxford: Clarendon Press, 1885.

Ed. Kate Stephens. New York: Harper and Brothers, 1897.

Ed. Peter Peterson. London: Macmillan, 1899.

Ed. F. Ryland. London: George Bell & Sons, 1906, 1920.

Ed. A. R. Weekes. London: W. B. Clive, 1917.

In Barrett H. Clark, *Great Short Biographies*, pp. 731–86. New York: Robert M. McBride, 1928.

In *Oxford Anthology of English Prose*, ed. A. Whitridge and J. W. Dodds, pp. 278–300. New York: Oxford University Press, 1935.

Also in items 2:29 and 2:34, and excerpts in other anthologies.

22:10. *Lives of Prior and Congreve*, ed. F. Ryland. London: George Bell & Sons, 1897.

22:11. *Life of Swift*, ed. F. Ryland. London: George Bell & Sons, 1894.

22:12. *Life of Watts*, ed. Samuel Palmer. "With notes containing animadversions and additions." London: Rivington, 1785. See item 24:47, 2nd ed., 1791.

COMMENTARY

22:40. "Anecdote Concerning the Celebrated Dr. J——n," *Town and Country*, I (September 1769), p. 463. Johnson said that Swift was "a very shallow fellow."

22:41. Eugenio. "Remarks on Pope's Epitaphs Examined," *GM*, XLVIII (December 1778), 574–75. On the essay appended to Johnson's *Life*.

22:42. Eugenio. [Additional information concerning lives of Hammond, Prior, etc.], *GM*, XLIX (May 1779), 231–32.

22:43. B., W. [Critique of Johnson's treatment of Milton's religious position in *Life of Milton*], *London Packet*, No. 1489 (June 28–30, 1779).

22:44. T., T. [Comment on Johnson's account of Milton's being whipped at Cambridge], *GM*, XLIX (August 1779), 395. Further discussion by Verax, (October), p. 493; by J. Boerhadem, (October), pp. 492–93, (December), pp. 595–96.

22:45. "A New Correspondent," *London Review*, X (November 1779), 350–52. Criticism of *Lives* of Milton and Dryden.

22:46. R., B. S. [Attack on Johnson's *Life of Smith*], *Westminster Magazine*, VII (November 1779), 591–92.

22:47. Scrutator. "Strictures on Dr. Johnson's Prefaces to the English Poets," *GM*, XLIX (December 1779), 593–95; L (February 1780), 64–65.

22:48. [Blackburne, Francis.] *Remarks on Johnson's Life of Milton. To which are added Milton's Tractate of Education and Areopagitica*. London: Dilly, 1780. The *Remarks* are reprinted from Blackburne's *Memoirs of Thomas Hollis*, II, 538*–582*. London: J. Nichols, 1780.

22:49. Potter, Robert. "Remarks on Dr. Johnson's Lives of the Poets," *GM*, LI (October 1781), 463–67; (November), 506–10; (December), 561–64; LII (January 1782), 24–26; (March), 116–18. Reprinted (expanded) as *The Art of Criticism as exemplified in Dr. Johnson's Lives of the Most Eminent English Poets*, London: T. Hookham, 1789. Includes "A Dream" (item 9:46).

22:50. D., J. "Lines Occasioned by the Perusal of Dr. Johnson's *Lives of the Poets*, wherein the Characters of Contemporary Statesmen Are Occasionally Handled," *London Courant*, October 2, 1781. Verse; political, not critical.

22:51. [Fitzthomas, William Windsor.] *A Cursory Examination of Dr. Johnson's Strictures on the Lyric Performances of Gray*. London: Crowder, 1781.

22:52. [Beville, William.] *Observations on Dr. Johnson's Life of Hammond.* London: W. Brown, 1782.

22:53. "A Yorkshire Freeholder." *Remarks on Dr. Johnson's Lives of the Most Eminent English Poets.* York: Ward, 1782. Attributed to "Rev. Dr. Beilby, incumbent of Ferriby, near Hull."

22:54. Newton, Thomas. *The Works of the Right Reverend Thomas Newton, D.D. . . . with Some Account of His Life,* I, 130–31. London: Rivington, 1782. Severe censure of the *Lives.*

22:55. [Tindal, William.] *Remarks on Dr. Johnson's Life, and Critical Observations on the Works of Mr. Gray.* London: Fielding, 1782.

22:56. D., J. [Attack on essay on Pope's epitaphs and Johnson's politics], *London Courant,* January 1, 1782.

22:57. Potter, Robert. *An Inquiry into Some Passages in Dr. Johnson's Lives of the Poets: Particularly His Observations on Lyric Poetry, and the Odes of Gray.* London: Dodsley, 1783.

22:58. Young, John. *A Criticism on the Elegy written in a Country Church Yard. Being a continuation of Dr. J——n's Criticism on the Poems of Gray.* London: G. Wilkie, 1783. Little about Johnson, except a vague imitation of his style.

22:59. "Memoirs of the Life of William Shenstone, Esq; with some strictures on the biographical criticisms of Dr. Johnson, on the writings on that ingenious poet," *Universal Magazine,* LXXIII (December 1783), 289–95.

22:60. Sheridan, Thomas. "The Life of the Reverend Dr. Jonathan Swift" [attack on Johnson's *Life of Swift*], in Swift, *Works,* I, 520–39. London: Hathurst, 1784.

22:61. *A Dialogue between Dr. Johnson and Dr. Goldsmith, in the shades, relative to the former's strictures on the English poets, particularly Pope, Milton and Gray.* London: Debrett, 1785.

22:62. Hoole, John. "An Account of the Life and Writings of John Scott, Esq.," in John Scott [of Amwell], *Critical Essays on Some of the Poems of Several English Poets,* pp. i–lxxxix. London: J. Phillips, 1785. Replies to Johnson's critiques of *Lycidas, Cooper's Hill,* etc.

22:63. Turner, Daniel. *Devotional Poetry Vindicated, in Some Occasional Remarks on the Late Dr. S. Johnson's Animadversions upon That Subject in His Life of Waller.* Oxford: J. Buckland, etc., [1785].

22:64. Wakefield, Gilbert, ed. *The Poems of Mr. Gray, with Notes.* London: Kearsley, 1786. Professes to provide an "antidote" to the "severity of Dr. Johnson's strictures." The notes contain much detailed reply to Johnson's comments on individual poems.

22:65. Wright, J. *Elegia Scripta in Sepulchreto Rustico . . . Latine red-*

dita. To which other poems are added. London: Lewis, 1786. The preface defends Gray against Johnson.

22:66. Nemesius. "Strictures on Dr. Johnson's Criticism on Milton's Latinity," *GM*, LVI (July 1786), 557–59.

22:67. "Strictures upon Dr. Johnson's Remarks on the Poetry of Gray," *Poems Written While the Author Was at College*, pp. 31–54. London, 1787.

22:68. Amerus. [Johnson's own character revealed in *Lives of the Poets*], *GM*, LVIII (April 1788), 300–303. By Alexander Chalmers?

22:69. Brydges, Sir Samuel Egerton. Comment in his ed. of Edward Phillips, *Theatrum Poetarum Anglicanorum.* Canterbury: J. White, 1800. Pp. liii–lvi, correction to account of Cibber's *Lives of the Poets* in Boswell's *Life*; pp. lvi–lviii, criticism of Johnson's *Lives*.

22:70. Stockdale, Percival. *Lectures on the Truly Eminent English Poets.* 2 vols. London: Printed for the author, 1807. Frequent references to Johnson's *Lives*, especially in Lectures XIX and XX on Gray.

22:71. Hill, T. "Hypercritical Remarks on Dr. Johnson," *European Magazine*, LIV (July 1808), 22–24. Strictures on his criticism of Pope's epitaphs.

22:72. "Milton's Religion," *Monthly Repository*, IV (August 1809), 432–33, Challenges Johnson's view.

22:73. D'Israeli, Isaac. "Johnson's Hints for the Life of Pope," *Curiosities of Literature*, First Series, III, 479–83. London: J. Murray, 1817. With facsimile of Johnson's notes.

22:74. White, Thomas Holt. *A Review of Johnson's Criticism on the Style of Milton's English Prose; with strictures on the introduction of Latin idioms into the English language.* London: R. Hunter, 1818.

22:75. Cary, Henry Francis. "Continuation of Dr. Johnson's Lives of the Poets" [long series of short lives], *London Magazine*, IV (August 1821), *et seq.* Reprinted as *Lives of English Poets from Johnson to Kirke White, designed as a continuation of Johnson's Lives*, London: H. G. Bohn, 1846. See also item 3:65.

22:76. Channing, William Ellery. [Review of Milton's *Treatise on Christian Doctrine*], *Christian Examiner*, III (January 1826), 29–77. Attacks Johnson's *Life of Milton*, pp. 54–56. Reprinted in Channing's *Works*, pp. 118–92, London: E. Rainford, 1829.

22:77. Ivimey, Joseph. "Animadversions upon Dr. Johnson's Life of Milton," *John Milton, His Life and Times*, pp. 349–82. London: Effingham Wilson, 1833. A blistering attack.

22:78. Vectis. "Dr. Johnson's Recommendation of Burnet's Life of Rochester," *Christian Observer*, XLIII (January 1843), 31–32.

22:79. Dilke, Charles Wentworth (the elder). [On the *Life of Pope*, osten-

sibly a review of Peter Cunningham's ed. of *Lives of the Poets*, 1854],
Athenaeum, III (April 14, 1855), 424–25. Reprinted in his *Papers of a
Critic*, [ed. Sir Charles W. Dilke], I, 160–64, 2 vols., London: Murray,
1875. Many other references to Johnson's *Life, passim*.

22:80. "Literary Leaflets. By Sir Nathaniel. No. XXVII. Johnson's Lives of
the Poets," *New Monthly Magazine*, 2nd ser., CIII (January 1855), 18–
27. Review article based on Cunningham's ed., 1854.

22:81. J., D. "Johnson's *Life of Dryden*," *N&Q*, XII (August 4, 1855), 83–
84. Criticism of biographical details.

22:82. Reed, Henry. "Burns, with notices of Johnson's *Lives of the Poets*,"
Lectures on the British Poets, II, 16–24 (Lecture X). Philadelphia: Parry
and McMillan, 1857. Extremely hostile.

22:83. De Quincey, Thomas. "Prefatory Memoranda" to "Life of Milton,"
The Logic of Political Economy and Other Papers, pp. 221–32. Boston:
Ticknor and Fields, 1859 (Vol. XXI of the first American collected ed.
of De Quincey's *Works*; also in Vol. XI of his *Works*, Edinburgh: J. Hogg,
1859.) Retitled "Postscript Respecting Johnson's Life of Milton," in
Works, ed. D. Masson, London: A. and C. Black, 1897 (IV, 104–7). Extremely hostile. The essay on Milton itself contains some hostile references to Johnson; it was first published 1838 in the same work as item
3:76. But the "Prefatory Memoranda" seem to have been added by De
Quincey to the 1859 *Works*. There are numerous other references (generally hostile) to Johnson in De Quincey's writings—e.g., in the essay
"Dr. Samuel Parr, or, Whiggism in Its Relation to Literature," 1831.

22:84. Symonds, John Addington. "The Blank Verse of Milton," *Fortnightly Review*, n.s., XVI (December 1, 1874), 767–81. Contains a
lengthy criticism of Johnson's views.

22:85. Vaughan, C. E. "Samuel Johnson" [on the metaphysical poets], *English Literary Criticism*, pp. lv–lxx, 87–104. London: Blackie & Son, 1896.

22:86. Curry, John T. [A passage in the *Life of Cowley*], *N&Q*, 9th ser.,
XII (October 31, 1903), 342.

22:87. Strachey, Lytton. "The Lives of the Poets," *Books and Characters*,
pp. 71–80. London: Chatto & Windus, 1922. Reprinted in *Literary Essays*, pp. 94–99, London: Chatto and Windus, 1948; New York: Harcourt, Brace, 1949. First printed in *Independent Review*, X, July 1906,
as a review of item 22:1, ed. G. B. Hill, 1905.

22:88. Trent, William P. "Dr. Birkbeck Hill and His Edition of Johnson's
'Lives of the Poets,'" *Forum*, XXXVII (April 1906), 540–51.

*22:89. Collins, J. Churton. "Dr. Johnson's 'Lives of the Poets,'" *Quarterly
Review*, CCVIII (January 1908), 72–97.

22:90. Bayne, Thomas. "Dr. Johnson and Edmund Smith," *N&Q*, 10th ser.,
XI (February 27, 1909), 166–67.

22:91. [Errors in *Lives of the Poets*], *N&Q*, 10th ser., XI (May 22, 1909), 401.

*22:92. Raleigh, Walter. "Johnson's Lives of the Poets," in item 10/6:146, pp. 128–76.

22:93. Williams, J. B. "Dr. Johnson's Accusation against Milton" [re *Eikon Basilike*], *British Review*, IX (March 1915), 431–40.

22:94. [Birrell, Augustine.] *Aphorisms on Authors and Their Ways; with some general observations on the humours, habits, and methods of composition of poets—good, bad, and indifferent. Diligently collected from Johnson's Lives, by A. B.* Privately printed, 1917.

22:95. Nethercot, Arthur H. "The Term 'Metaphysical Poets' before Johnson," *MLN*, XXXVII (January 1922), 11–17.

22:96. Nethercot, Arthur H. "The Reputation of the 'Metaphysical Poets' during the Age of Johnson and the 'Romantic Revival,'" *SP*, XXII (January 1925), 81–132.

22:97. Bridges, Robert S. "Poetic Diction in English" [Johnson on *Lycidas*], *Collected Essays, Papers, &c*, III, 59–70. London: Oxford University Press, 1928.

22:98. Garrod, H. W. "Cowley, Johnson, and the 'Metaphysicals,'" *The Profession of Poetry*, pp. 110–30. Oxford: Clarendon Press, 1929.

22:99. Quiller-Couch, Sir Arthur. [Concerning criticism of *Lycidas*], *Studies in Literature*, Third Series, pp. 1–22. Cambridge: Cambridge University Press, 1929.

22:100. Metcalf, John Calvin. *The Stream of English Biography* [excerpts from the *Life of Pope* and Boswell's *Life*, with critical introduction], pp. 19–26, 102–45. New York: Century Co., 1930.

22:101. Longaker, John Mark. "Johnson's Lives of the Poets," *English Biography in the Eighteenth Century*, pp. 314–406. Philadelphia: University of Pennsylvania Press, 1931.

22:102. Beckingham, C. F. "Johnson on Swift and Fuller on De Dominis" [similarity between two sentences], *N&Q*, CLXIX (October 19, 1935), 276.

22:103. More, Paul Elmer. "How to Read 'Lycidas'" [Johnson's criticism analyzed], *American Review*, VII (May 1936), 140–58.

22:104. Osborn, James M. "Lord Hailes and Dr. Johnson," *TLS*, April 16, 1938, p. 262; April 23, p. 280.

*22:105. Lam, George L. "Johnson's *Lives of the Poets*" [their origin, text, and history], *Cornell University Abstracts of Theses for 1938*, pp. 36–38. Ithaca, N.Y.: Cornell University Press, 1939.

*22:106. Osborn, James M. "Samuel Johnson" [biographical method exemplified in *Life of Dryden*], *John Dryden: Some Biographical Facts and*

Problems, pp. 22–38. New York: Columbia University Press, 1940. Rev. ed., Gainesville: University of Florida Press, 1965.

22:107. Chapman, Robert William. "An Afterthought in Johnson's Life of Addison," *N&Q*, CLXXXIV (February 13, 1943), 103.

22:108. Ames, Alfred Campbell. *English Criticism of Pope's Poetry, 1744–1793*. Abstract of thesis. Urbana: University of Illinois, 1943.

22:109. Carver, George. "Samuel Johnson and 'The Lives of the Poets,'" *Alms for Oblivion*, pp. 123–36. Milwaukee: Bruce Publishing Co., 1946.

22:110. "Life of Cowley" [selections], in *Abraham Cowley: Poetry and Prose*, ed. L. C. Martin. Oxford: Clarendon Press, 1949.

*22:111. Williams, Harold. "Swift's Early Biographers," in *Pope and His Contemporaries*, ed. J. L. Clifford and Louis A. Landa, pp. 114–28. Oxford: Clarendon Press, 1949.

*22:112. Tate, Allen. "Johnson on the Metaphysicals," *Kenyon Review*, XI (Summer 1949), 379–94. Reprinted in *The Forlorn Demon*, pp. 112–30, Chicago: Henry Regnery, 1953; in his *Collected Essays*, Denver: Alan Swallow, 1959; and in item 10/6:330.

*22:113. Keast, William R. "Johnson's Criticism of the Metaphysical Poets," *ELH*, XVII (March 1950), 59–70.

22:114. Tillotson, Kathleen. "Arnold and Johnson" [echoes of *Lives* in Arnold's thought], *RES*, n.s., I (April 1950), 145–47.

22:115. Horsman, E. A. "Dryden's French Borrowings" [Johnson's charge in *Life of Dryden* is correct], *RES*, n.s., I (October 1950), 346–51.

*22:116. Hart, Edward. "Some New Sources of Johnson's *Lives*," *PMLA*, LXV (December 1950), 1088–1111.

22:117. Carroll, Richard A. "Johnson's *Lives of the Poets* and Currents of English Criticism, 1750–1779" (dissertation, University of Michigan, 1950), *Microfilm Abstracts*, X, no. 4 (1950), 208–9.

22:118. Darbishire, Helen. *Milton's Paradise Lost*, pp. 7 ff. [concerned with Johnson's criticism of Milton]. London: Oxford University Press, 1951.

22:119. Liebert, Herman W. "Johnson's Revisions" [in the character of Collins, 1763, for the *Life of Collins*], *JNL*, XI, no. 2 (April 1951), 7–8.

22:120. Allison, James. "Joseph Warton's Reply to Dr. Johnson's *Lives*" [Warton's *Essay on Pope*, Vol. II, 1782], *JEGP*, LI (April 1952), 186–91.

22:121. Rowan, D. F. "Johnson's *Lives*: An Unrecorded Variant and a New Portrait," *Book Collector*, I (Autumn 1952), 174.

*22:122. Johnson, Maurice. "A Literary Chestnut: Dryden's 'Cousin Swift'" [Johnson's part in the legend], *PMLA*, LXVII (December 1952), 1024–34. Discussion, with J. R. Moore, *PMLA*, LXVIII (December 1953), 1232–39.

*22:123. Perkins, David. "Johnson on Wit and Metaphysical Poetry," *ELH*, XX (September 1953), 200–217.

22:124. Shibasaki, Takeo. "Johnson on *Lycidas*" [in Japanese], *The Rising Generation* (Tokyo), C (1954), 470–72.

*22:125. Boyce, Benjamin. "Samuel Johnson's Criticism of Pope in the *Life of Pope*," *RES*, n.s., V (January 1954), 37–46.

22:126. Grenander, M. E. "*Samson's* Middle: Aristotle and Dr. Johnson" [Johnson's critique of Milton's *Samson Agonistes*], *University of Toronto Quarterly*, XXXIV (1955), 377–89.

22:127. Carnie, R. H. "Lord Hailes's Notes on Johnson's *Lives of the Poets*," *N&Q*, February–November, 1956, pp. 73–75, 106–8, 174–76, 343–46, 486–89.

22:128. Hill, D. M. "Johnson as Moderator" [in *Life of Milton*], *N&Q*, December 1956, pp. 517–22.

22:129. Hilles, Frederick W. *Johnson on Dr. Arbuthnot* [alterations in the *Life of Pope*]. New Haven: Privately printed for The Johnsonians [George Grady Press], 1957. Facsimiles of a page from Johnson's MS and two pages of his proof sheets.

*22:130. Hilles, Frederick W. "The Making of *The Life of Pope*," in item 10/6:306, pp. 257–84. Facsimile of a page from Johnson's MS—a different page from that in item 22:129.

22:131. Keast, W. R. "Editing Johnson's *Lives*," *New Rambler*, June 1959, pp. 15–29.

22:132. Crossett, John. "Did Dr. Johnson Mean 'Paraphysical'?" *Boston University Studies in English*, IV (Summer 1960), 121–24.

22:133. Lucas, F. L. "Johnson's Bête Grise" [Thomas Gray], *New Rambler*, June 1960, pp. 15–28.

*22:134. Fleischauer, Warren. "Johnson, *Lycidas*, and the Norms of Criticism," in item 10/6:316 (1962), pp. 235–56.

*22:135. Leicester, James H. "Johnson's Life of Shenstone: Some Observations on the Sources," in item 10/6:316 (1962), pp. 189–222.

22:136. Fleeman, J. D. "Some Proofs of Johnson's *Prefaces to the Poets*," *Library*, XVII (September 1962), 213–30.

22:137. Keast, W. R. "Johnson and 'Cibber's' *Lives of the Poets*, 1753," in *Restoration and Eighteenth-Century Literature*, ed. Carroll Camden, pp. 89–101. Chicago: University of Chicago Press for Rice University, 1963.

22:138. Schulz, Max F. "Coleridge's 'Debt' to Dryden and Johnson," *N&Q*, n.s., X (May 1963), 189–91. Their similar view of metaphysical poetry.

22:139. Johnston, Arthur. "Dr. Johnson, John Dyer, and *The Ruins of Rome*" [Johnson's criticism of the poem], *New Rambler*, January 1964, pp. 11–21.

22:140. Watson, Tommy G. "Johnson and Hazlitt on the Imagination in Milton," *Southern Quarterly*, II (January 1964), 123–33.

22:141. Leicester, James H. "Dr. Johnson and Isaac Watts," *New Rambler*, June 1964, pp. 2–10.

22:142. Hardy, John. "Johnson and Raphael's Counsel to Adam," in item 10/6:329, pp. 122–36.

22:143. Meyers, Jeffrey. "Autobiographical Reflections in Johnson's 'Life of Swift,' " *Discourse: A Review of the Liberal Arts* (Concordia College, Moorhead, Minn.), VIII (Winter 1965), 37–48.

22:144. Battersby, James Lyons, Jr. "Samuel Johnson's 'Life of Addison': Sources, Composition and Structure" (dissertation, Cornell University, 1965), *Dissertation Abstracts*, XXVI (March 1966), 5409.

22:145. Fogle, Richard H. "Johnson and Coleridge on Milton," *Bucknell Review*, XIV (March 1966), 26–32.

*22:146. Hamilton, Harlan W. "The Relevance of Johnson's 'Lives of the Poets,' " *English Studies Today*, Fourth Series, pp. 339–55. Rome: Edizioni di Storia e Letteratura, 1966.

22:147. Fox, Adam. "Johnson's Strictures upon Pious Poetry," *New Rambler*, January 1967, pp. 4–13.

22:148. Spencer, Lois M. G. "Johnson and Cowley," *New Rambler*, June 1967, pp. 18–32.

22:149. Hardy, John. "Stockdale's Defence of Pope," *RES*, n.s., XVIII (November 1967), 49–54.

*22:150. Sigworth, Oliver F. "Johnson's *Lycidas*: The End of Renaissance Criticism," *Eighteenth-Century Studies*, I (Winter 1967), 159–68. See comment by Victor Milne and reply by Sigworth, *ibid.*, II (Spring 1969), 300–2.

22:151. Dussinger, John A. "Richardson and Johnson: Critical Agreement on Rowe's *The Fair Penitent*," *English Studies*, XLIX (February 1968), 45–47.

22:152. Bell, Vereen M. "Johnson's Milton Criticism in Context," *English Studies*, XLIX (April 1968), 127–32.

22:153. Warncke, Wayne. "Samuel Johnson on Swift: The *Life of Swift* and Johnson's Predecessors in Swiftian Biography," *Journal of British Studies*, VII (May 1968), 56–64.

22:154. Taira, Zensuke. "Dr. Johnson's View of the Metaphysical Poets" [in Japanese], *Studies in English Literature* (Tokyo), XLV (September 1968), 25–38.

22:155. Uhlman, Thompson Potter. "The Reputation of Samuel Johnson's *The Lives of the Poets* in England and America" (dissertation, University of Southern California, 1968), *Dissertation Abstracts*, XXIX, no. 9 (March 1969), 3160A.

22:156. Battersby, James L. "Patterns of Significant Action in the 'Life of Addison,' " *Genre*, II (March 1969), 28–42.

22:157. Battersby, James L. "Johnson and Shiels: Biographers of Addison," *Studies in English Literature* (Rice University), IX (Summer 1969), 522–37.

23. LETTERS

Many individual first publications of letters by Johnson (e.g., in the *Gentleman's Magazine* and *European Magazine*) have been omitted. These are recorded in R. W. Chapman's edition, item 23:14.

Editions

23:1. *Letters to and from the Late Samuel Johnson, LL.D. To which are added some poems never before printed. Published from the original MSS. in her possession. By Hester Lynch Piozzi.* 2 vols. London: Strahan and Cadell, 1788. An analysis of some of Mrs. Piozzi's omissions and changes may be found in items 23:91 and 23:94.

23:2. *The Celebrated Letter from Samuel Johnson, LL.D. to Philip Dormer Stanhope, Earl of Chesterfield; Now First Published, with Notes, by James Boswell, Esq.* London: Charles Dilly, 1790.

*23:3. *Letters of Samuel Johnson,* ed. G. B. Hill. 2 vols. Oxford: Clarendon Press, 1892. Reviewed in *Quarterly Review,* CLXXV (October 1892), 394–422.

23:4. *Eighteenth Century Letters* [selections from Johnson and Chesterfield], ed. R. Brimley Johnson. With introduction by G. B. Hill. London: Innes, 1897.

23:5. *Dr. Samuel Johnson: Some Unpublished Letters,* ed. Clement Shorter. Privately printed (20 copies), 1915.

23:6. *Selected Letters of Samuel Johnson,* ed. R. W. Chapman. London: Oxford University Press, 1925.

23:7. *Samuel Johnson's Celebrated Letter to the Earl of Chesterfield and His Interview with King George III as Published in 1790 by James Boswell* [facsimile]. Buffalo, N.Y.: Privately printed for R. B. Adam, 1927.

23:8. *Forty-four Letters from Samuel Johnson,* annotated by L. D'O. Walters. Chelsea: Swan Press, 1931.

23:9. [Letter to Chesterfield.] Warlington: J. M. Shelmerdine, 1931.

*23:10. *Johnson and Queeney* [letters from Johnson to Hester Maria Thrale], ed. Marquis of Lansdowne. London: Cassell & Co., 1932. Reviewed by R. W. Chapman, *TLS,* March 17, 1932, p. 192. See also item 23:11.

*23:11. *The Queeney Letters: Being Letters Addressed to Hester Maria Thrale by Doctor Johnson, Fanny Burney and Mrs. Thrale-Piozzi,* ed.

Marquis of Lansdowne. London: Cassell & Co., 1934. Includes letters in item 23:10.

23:12. *English Letters of the XVIII Century*, ed. James Aitken, pp. 69–87. (Pelican Books.) London: Penguin Books, 1946.

23:13. *Selected Letters of Samuel Johnson*, ed. R. W. Chapman. (World's Classics.) London: Oxford University Press, 1951. A revision of item 23:6.

*23:14. *The Letters of Samuel Johnson, with Mrs. Thrale's Genuine Letters to Him*, ed. R. W. Chapman. 3 vols. Oxford: Clarendon Press, 1952. Reviewed by Sir Harold Williams, *MLR*, XLVIII (July 1953), 339–41; in *TLS*, September 18, 1953, pp. 589–91; by Mary Lascelles, *RES*, n.s., V (January 1954), 88–93; E. L. McAdam, Jr., *PQ*, XXXV (July 1956), 304–6; Robert Wieder, *Études Anglaises*, IX (October–December 1956), 350–52.

23:15. *Dr. Johnson: His Life in Letters*, selected and ed. by David Littlejohn. Englewood Cliffs, N.J.: Prentice-Hall, 1965.

COMMENTARY

23:40. Baretti, Joseph. "On Signora Piozzi's Publication of Dr. Johnson's Letters. Stricture the First," *European Magazine*, XIII (May 1788), 313–17; "Stricture the Second," (June), 393–99; "Stricture the Third," XIV (August), 89–99. Reprinted in his *Prefazioni e Polemiche*, ed. Luigi Piccioni, pp. 333–82, Bari: G. Laterza & Figli, 1933.

23:41. Eboracensis. [Condemnation of Johnson's epistolary style], *GM*, LXIV (June 1794), 508–10.

*23:42. Simeon, Sir John. "Original Letters of Dr. Johnson" [to John Taylor], *Miscellanies of the Philobiblon Society*, Vol. VI (separately paged 1–43). London: [Philobiblon Society], 1860–61.

23:43. D., E. A. "Dr. Johnson and the Shepherd in Virgil," *N&Q*, 5th ser., I (March 14, 1874), 213. See also *ibid.* J. H. I. Oakley. Source and meaning of the allusion in the letter to Chesterfield.

23:44. Merydew, J. T. "Samuel Johnson," *Love Letters of Famous Men and Women*, pp. 254–64. London: Remington, 1888.

23:45. Fitzgerald, Percy. *Dr. Birkbeck Hill's Edition of Johnson's Letters Examined and Criticised. Part I.* Privately printed pamphlet, n.d. [ca. 1892].

23:46. "Dr. Johnson's Letters," *Church Quarterly Review*, XXXIV (July 1892), 295–312. Reprinted in *Living Age*, CXCV (October 8, 1892), 67–77.

23:47. Mayor, John E. B. "Johnson's 'Letters': Apperley of Oriel" [Thomas Apperley], *N&Q*, 8th ser., IV (November 4, 1893), 365.

23:48. Birrell, Augustine. "Dr. Johnson" [largely a review of item 23:3], *Essays about Men, Women, and Books*, pp. 38–46. London: Elliot Stock, 1894.

23:49. Bailey, John C. "Johnson," *Studies in Some Famous Letters*, pp. 142–90. London: T. Burleigh, 1899.

23:50. West, Alfred. "Dr. Johnson as a Correspondent," in item 6:16, pp. 219–35.

23:51. Schomberg, J. "Dr. Johnson: Letter and Seal" [to Charles Congreve], *Athenaeum*, May 23, 1908, pp. 637–38. Another letter described, *ibid.*, May 8, 1909, pp. 559–60. One to Gilbert Repington, *ibid.*, September 4, 1909, pp. 205–06.

23:52. *Sotheby Sale Catalogue* [listing letters to Mrs. Thrale], January 30, 31, February 1, 1918. Other sales of letters, December 14, 1901; December 6, 1904; January 22, 1907; June 4, 1908.

23:53. *Letter to Robert Chambers, April 11, 1772* [facsimile of unpublished letter]. R. B. Adam Christmas Greeting, 1922.

23:54. [Letter to Robert Chambers, April 19, 1783.] R. B. Adam Christmas Greeting, [1923?].

23:55. *The Decision upon the Court of Sessions* [Boswell] . . . *And a Letter from Dr. Samuel Johnson to William Strahan upon the Subject, March 7, 1774* [facsimile]. Buffalo, N.Y.: Privately printed for R. B. Adam, 1925.

23:56. Chapman, R. W. "Johnson's Letters to Perkins," *RES*, II (January 1926), 97–98.

23:57. Chapman, R. W. "Johnson's Letters to Taylor," *RES*, II (January 1926), 86–92; *ibid.* (October 1926), 466; *TLS*, August 16, 1934, p. 565; *RES*, XV (January 1939), 81–84; *ibid.*, XVI (July 1940), 317.

23:58. Cline, Thomas L. "Samuel Johnson," *Critical Opinion in the Eighteenth Century English Personal Letter* (dissertation, University of Virginia, 1923), pp. 96–112. Ann Arbor, Mich.: Edwards Bros., 1926.

*23:59. Chapman, R. W. "Proposals for a New Edition of Johnson's Letters," *Essays and Studies by Members of the English Association*, XII (1926), 47–62.

23:60. Longman, C. J. *A Letter of Dr. Johnson and Some Eighteenth-Century Imprints of the House of Longman* [letter to Thomas Longman, ca. 1746]. London: Printed for private circulation, 1928.

23:61. Chapman, R. W. *Johnson, Boswell, and Mrs. Piozzi: A Suppressed Passage Restored.* London: Oxford University Press, 1929. See also *TLS*, January 24, 1929, p. 62.

23:62. Chapman, R. W. "Time's Whirligig" [reading suppressed passage in letter to Mrs. Thrale; see item 23:61], *TLS*, January 24, 1929, p. 62.

23:63. Roscoe, Edward Stanley. "Letters of Dr. Johnson to Sir Robert Chambers," *Cornhill Magazine*, n.s., LXVII (October 1929), 407–21.

23:64. Gurn, Joseph. "Dr. Johnson Makes a Plea," *Columbia* (Knights of Columbus), March 1930, pp. 18–19, 48. Johnson's letter to Charles O'Conor, April 9, 1757 about ancient Irish culture.

*23:65. Wright, J. D. "Some Unpublished Letters to and from Dr. Johnson," *Bulletin of the John Rylands Library*, XVI (January 1932), 32–76.

23:66. Wright, J. D. "Johnson Letters" [puzzling reference in a letter to Mrs. Thrale, November 30, 1782], *TLS*, January 21, 1932, p. 44. See also L. F. Powell, *ibid.*, June 2, 1932, p. 408.

23:67. Chapman, R. W. "Johnson's Letters," *TLS*, April 13, 1933, p. 261. For other miscellaneous references see *TLS*, October 26, 1922, p. 687; *ibid.*, October 1, 1925, p. 639; *ibid.*, July 29, 1939, p. 460; *N&Q*, CLXXXVI (April 22, 1944), 205; *ibid.*, CXC (June 1, 1946), 235–36; etc.

23:68. Metzdorf, Robert F. "An Unpublished Johnson Letter concerning Percy's *Reliques*," *MLN*, L (December 1935), 509–13.

23:69. Clifford, James L. "Further Letters of the Johnson Circle" [from Mrs. Piozzi's collection], *Bulletin of the John Rylands Library*, XX (July 1936), 268–85.

23:70. Tucker, William J. "Great English Letter Writers," *Catholic World*, CXLIII (September 1936), 697–98.

*23:71. Chapman, R. W. "Johnson's Letters" [a check list], *RES*, XIII (April 1937), 139–76; *ibid.*, XVI (January 1940), 66–68; *TLS*, December 6, 1934, p. 875; *ibid.*, April 13, 1933, p. 261.

23:72. Chapman, R. W. "Johnson's Letters to Percy," *TLS*, January 22, 1938, p. 60.

23:73. Wecter, Dixon. "Letter from Dr. Johnson" [to Mrs. Edmund Burke on death of her father], *TLS*, July 2, 1938, p. 449.

23:74. Charles, B. G. "A Dr. Johnson Discovery at National Library" [Margaret Owen papers at Aberystwyth], *Western Mail and South Wales News*, August 1, 1938, p. 9.

23:75. Ettinger, Amos A. "A Note on Dr. Johnson's Letter No. 34 to the Rev. Dr. Taylor," *RES*, XV (January 1939), 80–81.

23:76. Chapman, R. W. "Dr. Johnson's Letters: Notes on Boswell's Text," *TLS*, February 25, 1939, p. 128; March 4, p. 140.

23:77. "Dr. Johnson Bows to a Bishop" (letter from Johnson to Dr. Robert Lowth], *Bodleian Library Record*, I (December 1940), 199–201.

23:78. Wecter, Dixon. "Dr. Johnson, Mrs. Thrale, and Boswell: Three Letters," *MLN*, LVI (November 1941), 525–29.

23:79. Chapman, R. W. "Emendations in Johnson's Letters," *N&Q*, CLXXXII (March 28, April 11, 1942), 174–76, 201–2, etc.

23:80. Chapman, R. W. "Johnson's Letters to Boswell" [a calendar of the letters], *RES*, XVIII (July 1942), 323–28.

23:81. Chapman, R. W. "Confusion of T and N" [in Johnson's handwriting], *N&Q*, CLXXXIII (September 12, 1942), 165.

23:82. Chapman, R. W. "The Text of Johnson's Letters" [classifying various misreadings of Johnson's hand], *TLS*, September 26, 1942, p. 480.

23:83. Chapman, R. W. "Johnson's Letters to Mrs. Thrale" [conjectural emendations, etc.], *N&Q*, CLXXXV (July 3, 1943), 18.

23:84. Chapman, R. W. "The Johnson-Boswell Correspondence," *N&Q*, CLXXXV (July 17, 1943), 32–39; CLXXXVI (January 15, 1944), 45–47.

23:85. Chapman, R. W. "Did Johnson Destroy Mrs. Thrale's Letters?" *N&Q*, CLXXXV (August 28, 1943), 133–34.

23:86. Chapman, R. W. "Piozzi on Thrale" [her attempts to restore suppressions in Johnson's letters], *N&Q*, CLXXXV (October 23, 1943), 242–47. See also *PQ*, XXIII (April 1944), 172–73.

23:87. Chapman, R. W. "The Formal Parts of Johnson's Letters," in *Essays on the Eighteenth Century Presented to David Nichol Smith in Honour of His Seventieth Birthday*, pp. 147–54. Oxford: Clarendon Press, 1945. See also *N&Q*, CXC (February 23, 1946), 74.

23:88. Vulliamy, C. E. *English Letter Writers*, pp. 21–22. London: William Collins Sons & Co., 1945.

23:89. "To Tetty from Sam" [letter, January 31, 1740], *Month at Goodspeed's Book Shop*, XVI (January–February 1945), 91–99.

23:90. Chapman, R. W. "Doodle" [a passage in the letter to Mrs. Thrale of August 3, 1771], *N&Q*, CLXXXVIII (March 10, 1945), 101–2.

23:91. Chapman, R. W. "Mrs. Piozzi's Omissions from Johnson's Letters to Thrales," *RES*, XXII (January 1946), 17–28.

23:92. "Designs and Failures of Doctor Johnson" [letter to Mrs. Thrale, August 3, 1771], *Month at Goodspeed's Book Shop*, June 1946, pp. 295–98.

23:93. Jones, Claude E. "Johnson and Mrs. Montagu: Two Letters" [addressed to Herbert Croft], *N&Q*, CXCI (September 7, 1946), 102–3.

23:94. Chapman, R. W. "Mrs. Thrale's Letters to Johnson Published by Mrs. Piozzi in 1788," *RES*, XXIV (January 1948), 58–61.

23:95. Thrale, Hester Lynch. *An Unrecorded Thrale Letter*, [ed. George H. Tweney]. [Ferndale, Mich.]: Privately printed, 1949. Possibly to Johnson.

23:96. Liebert, Herman W. "New Letters from Dr. Johnson to Dr. Taylor," *Harvard Library Bulletin*, III (Winter 1949), 143–47.

23:97. Sherbo, Arthur. "Dr. Johnson and 'Topsel on Animals': A Conjecture" [Chapman No. 11; 'Topsel' used for *Marmor Norfolciense*?], *N&Q*, March 15, 1952, pp. 123–24.

23:98. Clifford, James L. "A New Johnson Correspondent" [Mrs. Way of Denham Place], *TLS*, May 30, 1952, p. 368.

23:99. Sherbo, Arthur. " 'Impransus' " [Chapman No. 10], *JNL*, XIII, no. 2 (May 1953), 12.

23:100. Graham, W. H. "Dr. Johnson's Letters," *Contemporary Review*, CLXXXV (January 1954), 26–28.

23:101. Viets, Henry R. "Johnson and Cheyne" [identification of quotations in Chapman Nos. 338, 426, 493], *TLS*, February 5, 1954, p. 89.

23:102. "The Indulgence of Children" [Johnson's letters to Queeney Thrale], *TLS*, November 19, 1954, pp. i–ii of Children's Book Supplement.

23:103. Irving, William H. "Johnson and the Johnsonian Tinge," *The Providence of Wit in the English Letter Writers*, pp. 286–306. Durham, N.C.: Duke University Press, 1955.

23:104. [Liebert, Herman W.] *To Honor the Two Hundred and Eighteenth Anniversary of the Departure of Samuel Johnson and David Garrick to Try Their Fortunes in the Great Metropolis, 2 March 1737* [with facsimile of letter to George Huddesford, February 26, 1755 (Chapman No. 63)]. New Haven, Conn.: Privately printed for Dorothy and Halsted Vander Poel [Yale University Press], 1955.

23:105. McAdam, E. L., Jr. *Dr. Johnson and the King's Library* [Johnson's letter to F. A. Barnard, May 28, 1768 (Chapman No. 26); facsimile]. New York: Privately printed for The Johnsonians [Harvard University Printing Office], 1955.

23:106. Kolb, Gwin J. "The Address of Dr. Johnson's Last Letter to William Windham," *N&Q*, May 1957, p. 213.

23:107. Kolb, Gwin J. "Notes on Four Letters by Dr. Johnson: Addenda to Chapman's Edition," *PQ*, XXXVIII (July 1959), 379–83.

23:108. Comyn, J. R. G. "Two Letters of Dr. Johnson" [to Dr. Burney], *TLS*, August 26, 1960, p. 545.

23:109. Eaves, T. C. Duncan. "Dr. Johnson's Letters to Richardson," *PMLA*, LXXV (September 1960), 377–81.

23:110. Sherbo, Arthur. "Dr. Johnson's Letters" [additional notes to item 23:14], *JNL*, XX, no. 3 (September 1960), 10–11.

23:111. Halsband, Robert. *Dr. Johnson and "The Great Epistolick Art"* [with facsimile of letter to Mrs. Thrale, October 27, 1777]. Privately printed for the annual dinner of The Johnsonians, New York, 1961.

23:112. Fleeman, J. D. "A Letter of Dr. Johnson" [of September 22, 1783, in Pembroke College], *TLS*, June 22, 1962, p. 461.

23:113. Knox, T. M. "Notes on R. W. Chapman's Edition of Johnson's Letters," *N&Q*, July 1962, pp. 264–66.

23:114. Ryskamp, Charles. "A Letter and a Portrait of Dr. Johnson," *Princeton University Library Chronicle*, XXIV (Autumn 1962), 32–35.

23:115. Link, Frederick M. "A New Johnson Letter" [to Taylor, March 26, 1774], *N&Q*, February 1964, pp. 64–65.

23:116. Sherbo, Arthur. "The Date of Johnson's Letter [Chapman No.] 1154," *JNL*, XXIV, no. 1 (March 1964), 10–11.

23:117. Osborn, James M. "Johnson to Taylor No. 90" [Chapman No. 1156], *TLS*, December 24, 1964, p. 1171.

23:118. Irwin, George. "Plump and Prospering Printer" [letter 1006.1 probably not to Strahan], *TLS*, April 1, 1965, p. 255.

*23:119. Isles, Duncan E. "Unpublished Johnson Letters" [Charlotte Lennox collection], *TLS*, July 29, 1965, p. 666.

23:120. Daghlian, Philip B. "Dr. Johnson in His Letters: The Public Guise of Private Matter," in *The Familiar Letter in the Eighteenth Century*, ed. Howard Anderson, Philip B. Daghlian, and Irvin Ehrenpreis, pp. 108–29. Lawrence: University of Kansas Press, 1966.

*23:121. Hyde, Mary C. " 'Not in Chapman,' " in item 10/6:329 (1965), pp. 286–319.

23:122. Fleming, Kent. "Samuel Johnson as Letter Writer: Some Versions of His Personae," *San Francisco Quarterly*, V, no. 3 (Spring 1969), 12–14.

23:123. Hilles, Frederick W. "Johnson's Correspondence with Nichols: Some Facts and a Query," *PQ*, XLVIII (April 1969), 226–33. Corrections to Chapman's account.

24. DIARIES, PRAYERS, SERMONS

Includes discussions of Johnson's religious beliefs.

EDITIONS

24:1. Dodd, William [actually by Samuel Johnson]. *The Convict's Address to his unhappy brethren, delivered in the chapel of Newgate on Friday, June 6, 1777*. Salisbury, 1777. Reviewed in *London Review*, VI (August 1777), 152.

24:2. *Prayers and Meditations, composed by Samuel Johnson, LL.D. and published from his manuscripts, By George Strahan*. . . . London: T. Cadell, 1785. 2nd to 5th eds., 1785–1817. With preface by Rev. William Gresley, Lichfield: T. G. Lomax, 1860.

*Ed. G. B. Hill, *Johnsonian Miscellanies*, I, 3–124. Oxford: Clarendon Press, 1897.

Ed. William A. Bradley. New York: McClure, Philips, 1902–3.

Ed. Hinchcliffe Higgins. With preface by Augustine Birrell. London: Elliot Stock, [1904].

Ed. William Stead, with Conversations, etc. (Little Masterpieces Series.) 1905.

Ed. H. C. London: H. R. Allenson, 1906.

Ed. Henry Edwin Savage. Lichfield: The Johnson's Head, 1927.

Ed. S. A. Jacobs. Mt. Vernon, N.Y.: Golden Eagle Press, 1937.

Ed. D. Elton Trueblood. Stanford University, Calif.: J. L. Delkin, 1945; New York: Harper and Brothers, 1947; London: Student Christian Movement Press, 1948.

See also item 24:7.

24:3. *A Sermon, Written by the Late Samuel Johnson, LL.D. for the Funeral of His Wife. Published by the Rev. Samuel Hayes.* . . . London: T. Cadell, 1788.

24:4. *Sermons on Different Subjects, Left for Publication by John Taylor, LL.D. Published by the Rev. Samuel Hayes.* London: T. Cadell. Vol. I, 1788, Vol. II, 1789. 2nd to 5th eds., 1790 to 1812. Reprinted in *British Prose Writers,* Vol. XV, London: John Sharpe, 1819. Reprinted in item 2:6 (Vol. IX). See also item 24:8.

24:5. *Selections from Johnson's Diary and Other Papers* [facsimile]. Buffalo, N.Y.: Privately printed for R. B. Adam, 1926.

24:6. Aston, Henry Hervey [actually Samuel Johnson]. *A Sermon Preached at the Cathedral Church of Saint Paul, Before the Sons of the Clergy* [1745], ed. with introduction by James L. Clifford. Los Angeles: Augustan Reprint Society, 1955 (Publication No. 50). See item 24:116.

*24:7. *Diaries, Prayers, and Annals,* ed. E. L. McAdam, Jr., with Donald and Mary Hyde. New Haven, Conn.: Yale University Press, 1958. Vol. I of the Yale Edition of the Works of Samuel Johnson (item 2:8). 2nd ed., 1960. Reviewed by Fredson Bowers, *JEGP,* LVIII (January 1959), 132–37; in *TLS,* March 6, 1959, pp. 121–22; by Margery Bailey, *PQ,* XXXVIII (July 1959), 331–33; by Maurice J. Quinlan, *MLQ,* XX (September 1959), 287–88.

*24:8. *Sermons,* ed. Jean H. Hagstrum and James Gray. In the Yale Edition of the Works of Samuel Johnson (item 2:8). New Haven, Conn.: Yale University Press (forthcoming).

COMMENTARY

24:40. B., A. Letter to "Mr. Urban," *GM,* LV (September 1785), 675. Praise of Dr. Johnson's *Prayers and Meditations* in *Norwich Chronicle* attributed to Dr. Samuel Parr.

24:41. Green, M. [i.e., John Nichols.] Letter to "Mr. Urban," *GM*, LVII (July 1787), 557–58. Prints "Thoughts on the Soul" found among Anna Williams's MSS, "which, I believe, you will have no difficulty in pronouncing to have been formed in the Johnsonian school."

24:42. Fordyce, James. "Address VI. On the Death of Dr. Samuel Johnson," *Addresses to the Deity*, pp. 209–32. London: T. Cadell, 1785. Reprinted in item 3:75.

24:43. Agutter, William. *On the Difference between the Deaths of the Righteous and the Wicked, illustrated in the instance of Dr. Samuel Johnson and David Hume. A Sermon, preached before the University of Oxford, at St. Mary's Church, July 23, 1786.* London: Philanthropic Society, 1800.

24:44. I., E. O. "Candid Thoughts on the Prayers and Meditations of Dr. Johnson," *GM*, LVII (November 1787), 979–81. A defense against Benvolio's attack (item 10/6:11).

24:45. Taylor, John. *A Letter to Samuel Johnson, LL.D., on the Subject of a Future State.* London: Cadell, 1787. Includes three letters from Johnson to Taylor.

24:46. R., R. G. [Richard Greene?] Letter to "Mr. Urban," *GM*, LVIII (January 1788), 39. Johnson's "doubts and fears" before his death.

24:47. Palmer, Samuel. *A Vindication of the Modern Dissenters . . . Intended as a Supplement to Dr. Johnson's Life of Dr. Watts, with notes.* London: J. Johnson, 1790. 2nd ed., 1791. A reply to criticism of his edition of the *Life of Watts*, 1785 (item 22:12).

24:48. *Reflections on the Last Scene of the Late Doctor Johnson's Life: as exhibited by his biographer Sir John Hawkins; shewing the real goodness of his state; and that his friends had no just ground to be shocked at expressions arising from a truly broken and contrite heart. . . .* London: Printed for the author and sold by C. Dilly and J. Matthews, 1791.

24:49. Foster, John. *Essays in a Series of Letters.* London: Longmans, 1805 (frequently reprinted). Letter IX of Essay IV, "On Some of the Causes by Which Evangelical Religion Has Been Rendered Unacceptable to Persons of Culture and Taste," contains strictures on Johnson's writings.

24:50. "On the Character of Dr. Johnson as a Moralist," *Monthly Anthology or Boston Review*, II (June 1805), 292–94.

24:51. Angelus. "Dr. Johnson on the Propagation of the Gospel," *Christian Observer*, VII (May 1808), 303–4. Calls attention to his letters to William Drummond advocating a Gaelic translation of the Bible.

24:52. "Dr. Johnson's Dispute with Mrs. Knowles," *Monthly Repository*, VI (August 1811), 519–24. Reprints Anna Seward's version (from her *Letters*, I, 97–103 [Letter XXII]) and item 5:17.

24:53. "Protestant Purgatory," *Monthly Repository,* IX (March 1814), 156–59. Includes comment on Johnson's views on purgatory.

24:54. Wilks, Samuel Charles. "True and False Repose in Death," *Christian Essays,* I, 236–64. 2 vols. London: Baldwin, 1817. On Johnson's conversion and death. Reprinted in *Methodist Magazine,* XLIII (2nd ser., XVII), (September 1820), 660–71; *Methodist Magazine* (New York; later *Methodist Review*), IV (July 1821), 287–98; *Christian Observer,* XXVII (October 1827), 581–92; (November), 649–57. Further comment by Christian Ignatius La Trobe, *Christian Observer,* XXVIII (January 1828), 32–33, and by II.R.X., *ibid.* (March 1828), 177–78.

24:55. An Admirer of the Liturgy. "On a Prevailing Mode of Reading Certain Passages of the Liturgy" [page headline], *Christian Observer,* XXVII (October 1827), 608–9. Dubious about Johnson's emphasis on "not" in the Ten Commandments. Johnson defended by Liturgicus, *ibid.,* XXVIII (January 1828), 30–32. See also *ibid.,* XXXIV (May 1834), 535–42.

*24:56. L., J. "Original Memorials of Dr. Johnson's Religious Friends," *Christian Observer,* XXXI (January 1831), 1–13. Hill Boothby and the Fitzherbert circle. Continued in "Original Letters of Archbishop Secker and Mrs. Fitzherbert," *ibid.* (August 1831), 449–55, and "On the Letters of Miss Hill Boothby to Dr. Johnson," *ibid.,* XXXII (January 1832), 6–10.

24:57. L., J. "The Last Days and Religious Character of Dr. Johnson," *Christian Observer,* XXXII (January 1832), 1–5, 344–47. Replies to Croker's strictures in item 4:14 (1831).

24:58. La Trobe, John Antes. "Croker and La Trobe on Dr. Johnson's Deathbed," *Christian Observer,* XXXII (May 1832), 344–47. Rebuts John Wilson Croker's strictures in item 4:14 (1831) on the account given in item 24:54.

24:59. T., E. "Religious Principles of Dr. Johnson," *Wesleyan-Methodist Magazine* [later *Methodist Magazine*], 3rd ser., XII (February 1833), 92–97.

24:60. L., J. "Last Days of Dr. Johnson—The *Quarterly Review* and Hannah More," *Christian Observer,* XXXV (January 1835), 51–62. Controverts *Quarterly Review's* strictures on item 5:53. See also *ibid.* (October 1835), 620–29.

24:61. Wilberforce, William. "The Last Days of Dr. Johnson," *Christian Observer,* XXXVII (January 1837), 35–36. Letter from Wilberforce affirming tradition of Johnson's "death-bed conversion."

24:62. Zenas. "Dr. Johnson's 'Conversion,'" *Christian Observer,* XXXVII (November 1837), 683–85. Supplemented by G. C. G., *ibid.* (Appendix 1837), 813–16, and by Zenas, *ibid.,* XXXVIII (February 1838), 81.

24:63. H., J. M. "Desultory Thoughts on Religious Poetry," *Christian Observer*, XXXVIII (January 1838), 34–37, 114–19. Attacks Johnson's views on sacred poetry.

24:64. T., D. M. "On the Last Days of Dr. Johnson," *Christian Observer*, XXXIX (April 1839), 219–20.

24:65. Armitage, Robert. *Doctor Johnson: His Religious Life and His Death*. London: R. Bentley; New York: Harper, 1850. (Misattributed in Lowndes, *Bibliographer's Manual* to J. T. Hewlett.) 2nd ed., rev., 1851. Reviewed (savagely) by J. W. Croker ("Dr. Johnson and Dr. Hookwell"), *Quarterly Review*, LXXXVII (1850), 59–68; (favorably) in *Bentley's Miscellany*, XXVII (1850), 397–99; (with mild praise) in *Dublin University Magazine*, XXXVI (1851), 477–89.

24:66. "Shades of the Departed: Johnson," *Leisure Hour*, I (November 18, 1852), 737–42. Largely on his religious attitudes.

24:67. [Slashing review of *The Letters of James Boswell to William Johnson Temple*, 1857, with much reference to Johnson's religious position], *Christian Observer*, LVIII (January 1859), 9–21. Reprinted in *Living Age*, LX (1859), 353–60. See item 4:16.

24:68. "The Last Days of Dr. Johnson," *Leisure Hour*, XIII (April 23, 1864), 268–70. (Accounts of Johnson's death were frequently printed as single-sheet "tracts" by religious organizations.)

24:69. Ryder, Charles E. "Dr. Johnson's Opinions on Religion," *The Month*, XIX (XXXVIII) (March 1880), 418–36. A Roman Catholic view.

24:70. Van Dyke, Henry J., Jr. "A Sturdy Christian" [Johnson], *Andover Review*, V (May 1886), 490–96.

24:71. Gloag, Paton J. "Last Days of Dr. Johnson," *Sunday at Home*, December 1898, pp. 114–18.

24:72. Hunt, Theodore W. "Samuel Johnson," *Treasury of Religious Thought*, XIII (February 1896), 793–96.

24:73. Ringwalt, Roland. "Samuel Johnson; Churl, Champion and Churchman," *Church Eclectic: An Anglo Catholic Monthly* (Milwaukee), XXVI (September 1898), 496–504.

24:74. Fitzgerald, Percy H. "Dr. Johnson's Catholic Tendencies," *The Month*, XCIII (January 1899), 64–74.

24:75. Burns, J. "Dr. Johnson as a Writer of Prayers," *Puritan*, III (August 1900), 651.

24:76. Potts, R. A. "Johnson's Prayer ['Summe Pater']," *N&Q*, 9th ser., XII (December 26, 1903), 516.

24:77. Hutton, William H. "The Religion of Dr. Johnson," *Burford Papers*, pp. 277–81. London: Constable & Co., 1905.

24:78. Waters, Charles T. "Dr. Johnson's Catholic Tendencies," *Irish Monthly*, XXXIV (July 1906), 361–72.

24:79. Hughes, H. G. "Dr. Johnson at His Prayers," *Irish Monthly*, XXXIV (November 1906), 601–11. Reprinted from *Ave Maria*, July 14, 1906.

*24:80. Walsh, Edmund A. "An Eighteenth Century Witness to Catholicism," *American Catholic Quarterly*, XXXIII (April 1908), 253–74.

24:81. Beeching, H. C. *Johnson and Ecclesiastes* [sermon preached in Lichfield Cathedral]. London: Hugh Rees, 1909. Reprinted from *Guardian*, September 22, 1909, p. 1478.

24:82. "Samuel Johnson, 1709–1784," *Christian*, September 16, 1909, pp. 17–18.

24:83. May, George Lacey. "The Religion of Dr. Johnson," *Treasury*, XXV (April 1915), 62–66.

24:84. Gilbert, Richard H. "Samuel Johnson—Preacher," *Methodist Review*, CI (March 1918), 241–50.

24:85. Russell, Sir Charles. "Dr. Johnson and the Catholic Church," *Studies*, VIII (March 1919), 95–107. Reprinted in item 6:28, pp. 139–56.

24:86. May, George Lacey. "Samuel Johnson," *Some Eighteenth Century Churchmen*, pp. 13–32. London: Society for Promoting Christian Knowledge; New York: Macmillan, 1920.

24:87. *A Leaf from the Private Note Book of Samuel Johnson, LL.D. 1773*. With comment by Robert William Rogers. Princeton, N.J.: Privately printed, 1922.

24:88. Inge, Dean W. R. "Dr. Johnson's Religious Faith," *Lichfield Mercury*, September 23, 1921. Reprinted; see item 6:22.

24:89. Van Dyke, Henry. "Sturdy Believer," *Companionable Books*, pp. 307–31. New York: Charles Scribner's Sons, 1922.

24:90. Bracey, Robert. "Dr. Johnson's Catholic Friends" and "Dr. Johnson as a Preacher," *Eighteenth Century Studies and Other Papers*, pp. 1–9 and 10–19. New York: Appleton, 1925.

24:91. Bremond, Henri, Jean, and André. "Un Socrate Chrétien: Le Docteur Johnson," *Le charme d'Athènes et autres essais*, pp. 264–95. Paris: Bloud and Gay, 1925.

24:92. Primrose, C. L. "A Study of Dr. Johnson's Religion," *Theology*, XII (April 1926), 207–16.

24:93. Esdaile, Arundell. *The Religion of Reality* [see item 6:32]. London: Garden City Press, 1926. Reprinted in *Contemporary Review*, CXXX (December 1926), 751–56, and in item 10/6:243.

24:94. Silvester, James. *Samuel Johnson: A Man of Faith*. Stirling, Scotland: Drummond's Tract Depot, [1926].

24:95. Mackay, H. F. B. "The Religion of Dr. Johnson," *Saints and Leaders*, pp. 163–79. London: Philip Allan & Co., 1928.

24:96. Roberts, Sydney Castle. *Samuel Johnson, Christian* [address delivered at St. Clement Danes; see item 6:32]. London: Privately printed, 1928.

24:97. Paull, H. M. "Some Unidentified Writings of Dr. Johnson" [the sermons, etc.], *Fortnightly Review*, CXXIV (October 1928), 570–73.

24:98. Roscoe, Edward Stanley. "Johnson's Religion," in item 10/6:204, pp. 32–41.

24:99. Kingdon, Frank. "Dr. Johnson and the Methodists," *Methodist Review*, CXII (November 1929), 884–89.

24:100. Westlake, F. T. B. *Fame and Faith.* London: Skeffington, [1930]. Visits of Goldsmith and Johnson to vicarage of Easton Maudit, and a discussion of their religious views.

24:101. Glover, T. R. "Serviendum et Lactandum" [prayers, Easter 1777], *TLS*, March 6, 1930, p. 190. See also J. J. B., *ibid.*, March 13, p. 214.

24:102. "Dr. Johnson on 'The Old Religion,'" *Catholic World*, CXXXII (November 1930), 217–19.

24:103. Scott, R. McNair. "A Note on Dr. Johnson and Death," *Life and Letters*, VI (January 1931), 45–49.

24:104. Pillans, T. D. "Dr. Johnson and Catholicism," *Truth*, XXXV (September 1931), 21–22.

24:105. Chapman, Robert William. "Sermon by Dr. Johnson? MS. for Yale," *Times* (London), September 29, 1933, pp. 13–14.

24:106. Wallace, Archer. *The Religious Faith of Great Men*, pp. 94–113. New York: Round Table Press, 1934.

24:107. Matthews, A. G., and G. F. Nuttall. "Dr. Johnson and the Nonconformists," *Transactions of the Congregational Historical Society*, XII (August 1936), 330–36.

24:108. Stockley, J. J. G. *Johnson Memorial Sermon* [December 13, 1936]. See item 6:32.

24:109. Brown, Stuart Gerry. "Dr. Johnson and the Christian Tradition" (dissertation, Princeton University, 1937). Ann Arbor, Michigan: University Microfilms, [1952].

24:110. [Discovery of Johnson's diary by Col. Ralph Isham], *N&Q*, CLXXII (April 3, 1937), 235.

24:111. Smith, Neil G. "The Piety of Doctor Johnson," *Queen's Quarterly*, XLIV (Winter 1937), 477–82.

24:112. May, George Lacey. *Samuel Johnson.* (Little Books on Religion, No. 153.) London: Society for Promoting Christian Knowledge, 1938.

24:113. Quintus Quiz [Edward Shillito]. "Dr. Samuel Johnson's Prayer [for April 6, 1777], *Christian Century*, LV (January 5, 1938), 9.

*24:114. Brown, Stuart Gerry. "Dr. Johnson and the Religious Problem," *English Studies*, XX (February, April 1938), 1–17, 67.

24:115. Baker, H. Arthur. "Dr. Johnson and Spiritual Diaries" [diary of the

Quaker, John Rutty, etc.], *Contemporary Review*, CLIV (August 1938), 183–89.

*24:116. Powell, Lawrence F. "Dr. Johnson and a Friend" [sermon for Henry Hervey Aston], *Times* (London), November 25, 1938, pp. 15–16.

24:117. Rogers, Clement F. *Dr. Johnson.* Sermon, December 11, 1938; see item 6:32.

*24:118. Gove, Philip B. "Dr. Johnson and the Works of the Bishop of Sodor and Man," *RES*, XVI (October 1940), 455–57.

24:119. Drummond, E. J. "For the Night Cometh" [Johnson as moral teacher and religious man], *Catholic World*, CLV (July 1942), 454–59.

*24:120. Hagstrum, J. H. "The Sermons of Samuel Johnson," *MP*, XL (February 1943), 255–66. See also Hagstrum's unpublished dissertation, Yale University, 1941.

24:121. Belshaw, Harry. "The Influence of John Wesley on Dr. Johnson's Religion," *London Quarterly and Holborn Review*, CLXVIII (July 1943), 226–34.

24:122. Williamson, Edward W. "Cheerfulness Breaks In," *Theology*, XLVIII (March 1945), 50–55.

24:123. Cairns, William T. "The Religion of Dr. Johnson," *The Religion of Dr. Johnson and Other Essays*, pp. 1–23. London: Oxford University Press, 1946. Reprinted from *Evangelical Quarterly*, January 1944, pp. 53–70. Reviewed by M. Quinlan, *Review of Religion*, XI (March 1947), 299–302; J. L. Clifford, *PQ*, XXVI (April 1947), 124.

24:124. Kirchhofer, K. Hermann. "Dr. Johnson's Religion." Dissertation, Syracuse University, 1947.

24:125. "Mental Vellications" [Johnson's prayers], *British Weekly*, May 8, 1947.

*24:126. Hagstrum, J. H. "On Dr. Johnson's Fear of Death," *ELH*, XIV (December 1947), 308–19. See also M. Quinlan, *PQ*, XXVII (April 1948), 146–47.

*24:127. Quinlan, Maurice. "The Rumor of Dr. Johnson's Conversion," *Review of Religion*, XII (March 1948), 243–61. See item 24:157.

24:128. *The Prayer* [Johnson's last prayer], set to music by Arthur B. Plant. London: A. Weekes & Co., n.d. [before 1950].

*24:129. Hyde, Donald and Mary. "Johnson and Journals," *New Colophon*, III (1950), 165–97. See also E. L. McAdam, Jr., *PQ*, XXX (July 1951), 275–76.

24:130. Stamm, Israel S. "Some Aspects of the Religious Problem in Haller," *Germanic Review*, XXV (February 1950), 5–12. Contrasts religious thought of Albrecht von Haller, 1708–77, with that of his contemporary, Johnson.

24:131. Williamson, Bishop Edward. "Dr. Johnson and the Prayer Book," *Theology*, LIII (October 1950), 363–72.

24:132. De Vedia y Mitre, Mariano. "El Doctor Johnson y la Obsesion de la Muerte," *La Nacion* (Buenos Aires), January 21, 1951, 2nd section, p. 1.

24:133. Joost, Nicholas. "Poetry and Belief: Fideism from Dryden to Eliot," *Dublin Review*, No. 455 (1st quarter, 1952), 35–53.

*24:134. Quinlan, Maurice J. "The Reaction to Dr. Johnson's *Prayers and Meditations*," *JEGP*, LII (April 1953), 125–39.

24:135. May, George Lacey. "Religious Letters of Dr. Johnson," *Church Quarterly Review*, CLIV (April–June 1953), 168–75.

24:136. South, Helen P. "Dr. Johnson and the Quakers," *Bulletin of Friends Historical Association*, XLIV (Spring 1955), 19–42.

24:137. Roberts, S. C. "Dr. Johnson as a Churchman," *Church Quarterly Review*, CLVI (October–December 1955), 372–80. Reprinted in item 10/6:302.

24:138. De Beer, E. S. "Johnson's θ ϕ" [in *Prayers and Meditations*], *N&Q*, December 1955, pp. 537–38.

*24:139. [McAdam, E. L., Jr., Mary C. and Donald F. Hyde, and George Milne], *The Johnsons Photographed* [restoration of passages in Johnson's diaries erased by George Strahan; facsimiles]. New York: Privately printed for The Johnsonians, 1956.

*24:140. Sutherland, Raymond C. "Dr. Johnson and the Collect," *MLQ*, XVII (June 1956), 111–17.

24:141. Graham, W. H. "Dr. Johnson and Law's *Serious Call*," *Contemporary Review*, CXCI (February 1957), 104–6.

24:142. Broderick, James H. "Dr. Johnson's Impossible Doubts," *South Atlantic Quarterly*, LVI (April 1957), 217–23.

24:143. North, Richard. "The Religion of Dr. Johnson," *Hibbert Journal*, LVI (October 1957), 42–46.

24:144. Wand, Bishop J. W. C. "Dr. Johnson, Devout Wit and Critic," *True Lights: Talks on Saints and Leaders of the Christian Church*, pp. 112–22. London: A. R. Mowbray, 1958.

24:145. Bennett, Hiram R. "Samuel Johnson, Churchman," *Anglican Theological Review*, XL (October 1958), 301–9.

*24:146. Williams, Philip. "Samuel Johnson's Central Tension: Faith and the Fear of Death," *Tohoku Gàkuin Daigaku Ronshu* [Journal of Literary Studies, North Japan College, Sendai], Nos. 33–34 (September 1958), pp. 1–35.

24:147. Greene, Donald J. "Johnson and Newman" [parallels between a Latin verse prayer of Johnson and "Lead, Kindly Light"], *JNL*, XVIII, no. 3 (October 1958), 4–6. See also Sister M. Jean Clare, *JNL*, XX, no. 1 (March 1960), 12.

24:148. Finnerty, Sister M. Jean Clare. "Johnson the Moralist: Friend and Critic of the Clergy and Hierarchy." Dissertation, Fordham University, 1959.

24:149. Doubleday, F. N. "The Prayers and Meditations of Samuel Johnson," *New Rambler*, June 1960, pp. 43–54.

24:150. Balderston, Katharine C. "Doctor Johnson and William Law," *PMLA*, LXXV (September 1960), 382–94.

24:151. Quinlan, Maurice. "Johnson's Sense of Charity," *New Rambler*, January 1961, pp. 21–22.

24:152. Chapin, Chester F. "Johnson's Prayer for Kitty Chambers," *MLN*, LXXVI (March 1961), 216–18.

24:153. Chapin, Chester F. "Johnson and the 'Proofs' of Revelation," *PQ*, XL (April 1961), 297–302.

24:154. Bloom, Edward A. "Johnson's 'Divided Self,'" *University of Toronto Quarterly*, XXXI (October 1961), 42–53.

24:155. Chapin, Chester F. "Samuel Johnson's 'Wonderful' Experience," in item 10/6:316 (1962), 51–60.

24:156. Doubleday, F. N. "The Religion of Dr. Samuel Johnson," in item 10/6:316 (1962), 93–100.

*24:157. Greene, Donald J. "Dr. Johnson's 'Late Conversion': A Reconsideration," in item 10/6:316 (1962), 61–92.

24:158. Humphreys, A. R. "Dr. Johnson, Troubled Believer," in item 10/6:316 (1962), 37–49.

24:159. Seamans, Arthur Frederick. "The Phenomenon of Religious Distress in Cowper and Johnson and Its Relationship to Their Theological Milieu" (dissertation, University of Maryland, 1963), *Dissertation Abstracts*, XXIV (June 1964), 5417.

24:160. Matthews, Dean W. R. "William Law," *New Rambler*, January 1963, pp. 2–9.

24:161. Angèle, Sister M. "Samuel Johnson's View of the Roman Catholic Church," *New Rambler*, January 1963, pp. 29–37.

*24:162. Quinlan, Maurice J. *Samuel Johnson: a Layman's Religion*. Madison: University of Wisconsin Press, 1964. Reviewed by D. J. Greene, *Canadian Journal of Theology*, XI (June 1965), 207–16; Robert Voitle, *JEGP*, LXIV (April 1965), 322–24; Chester F. Chapin, *MP*, LXIII (May 1966), 359–61.

24:163. Chapin, Chester F. "Samuel Johnson's Religious Development," *Studies in English Literature* (Rice University), IV (Summer 1964), 457–74.

24:164. Sachs, Arieh. "Reason and Unreason in Johnson's Religion," *MLR*, LIX (October 1964), 519–26.

24:165. Matthews, Dean W. R. "The Formation of Johnson's Religious Beliefs," in item 6:23 (December 1964), pp. 42–51.

24:166. Meyers, Jeffrey. "The Sermons of Swift and Johnson," *Personalist*, XLVII (January 1966), 61–80.

24:167. Alkon, Paul K. "Robert South, William Law, and Samuel Johnson," *Studies in English Literature* (Rice University), VI (Summer 1966), 499–528.

24:168. Chapin, Chester F. "Samuel Johnson's Earliest Instruction in Religion," *Papers of the Michigan Academy*, LII (1967), 357–68.

*24:169. Chapin, Chester F. *The Religious Thought of Samuel Johnson*. Ann Arbor: University of Michigan Press, 1968.

*24:170. Fleeman, J. D. "Some Notes on Johnson's Prayers and Meditations," *RES*, n.s., XIX (May 1968), 172–79. New MS readings, supplementary to item 24:7.

24:171. Johnson, Samuel. *A Meditation, 8 August 1784*. Privately printed for the Johnsonians, September 20, 1968.

24:172. Griffith, Philip Mahone. "The Faith of Samuel Johnson: 'From Curiosity to Conviction,'" *Literature and Theology*. University of Tulsa English Department Monograph Series, No. 7 (1969), pp. 3–11.

25. MISCELLANEOUS WRITINGS

25:1. [Dedication of George Adams's *Treatise on the Globes* attributed to Johnson on authority of Edmund Allen], *GM*, LV (March 1785), 188.

25:2. Green, M. [i.e., John Nichols.] [Attributes to Johnson letters from Zachariah Williams to the Admiralty, concerning his method of determining the longitude], *GM*, LVII (September 1787), 757.

25:3. "Johnsoniana," *European Magazine*, XVI (July 1789), 4–5. Miscellaneous small attributions.

25:4. A., E. E. [Dubious attribution of essays in *Common Sense*, 1737], *GM*, LXIV (May 1794), 426–27.

25:5. G. [Attributes "Foreign History," *GM*, November 1747, to Johnson], *GM*, LXIV (November 1794), 1001.

25:6. Corney, Bolton. "On Authors and Books, No. 5," *N&Q*, I (February 23, 1850), 259–60. Attributes dedication to Payne's *An Introduction to Geometry*.

25:7. Davis, Wm. "Johnson's Prefaces and Dedications," *N&Q*, 2nd ser., XI (March 16, 1861), 207–8. Suggests they be collected and attributes dedication of Baretti's *Italian Dictionary*.

25:8. Este. "Dr. Johnson and Birmingham Newspapers," *N&Q*, 4th ser., II (August 15, 1868), 167. Only one copy (May 21, 1733) of early *Birmingham Journal* preserved.

25:9. A *Voyage to Abyssinia by Father Jerome Lobo. Translated from the French by Samuel Johnson*, ed. Henry Morley. London: Cassell & Co., 1887. See item 2:1 (1789).

25:10. Wheatley, Henry B. "Dr. Johnson's Dedications," *The Dedication of Books*, pp. 175–85. London: Elliot Stock, 1887.

25:11. "An Essay on the Origin and Importance of Small Tracts and Fugitive Pieces by Dr. Samuel Johnson" [from *Harleian Miscellany*], *Literary Pamphlets*, ed. Ernest Rhys, I, 41–54. London: Kegan Paul, 1897.

25:12. Hutton, Arthur W. "Dr. Johnson and the 'Gentleman's Magazine,'" *English Illustrated Magazine*, XVII (September 1899), 663–69. Reprinted in item 6:16, pp. 95–113.

25:13. Axon, William E. A. [*Occasional Papers by the Late William Dodd*], *Nation*, XCV (October 24, 1912), 381–82.

25:14. Oliver, John W. "Johnson, Goldsmith and 'The History of the Seven Years' War,'" *TLS*, May 18, 1922, p. 324. Goldsmith's indebtedness to Johnson's *Literary Magazine* essays.

25:15. Chapman, R. W. "Occasional Papers by William Dodd," *TLS*, December 7, 1922, pp. 789–90. See also items 25:19 and 25:25.

25:16. Bracey, Robert. "Dr. Johnson's First Book" [Father Lobo], *Eighteenth Century Studies and Other Papers*, pp. 20–27. New York: Appleton, 1925.

25:17. Chapman, R. W. "Johnson and the Longitude" [Williams's work, 1755], *RES*, I (October 1925), 458–60.

25:18. Powys, A. R. "Dr. Johnson on a Thames Bridge" [letters in *Gazetteer*, 1759–60, about designs by John Gwynn for Blackfriars Bridge], *London Mercury*, XIII (December 1925), 199.

*25:19. *Papers Written by Dr. Johnson and Dr. Dodd in 1777, Printed from the Originals in the Possession of A. E. Newton*. With introduction by R. W. Chapman. Oxford: Clarendon Press, 1926. See also item 25:25.

25:20. *Proposals for Printing . . . Bibliotheca Harleiana* [1742]. Facsimile with introductory note by R. W. Chapman. Oxford: Clarendon Press, 1926.

25:21. Walsh, James J. "Father Jerome Lobo Missionary to Abyssinia by Samuel Johnson," *These Splendid Priests*, pp. 201–19. New York: Sears, 1926.

25:22. Squire, Sir John C. "Johnson's Contributions to Other People's Works," *London Mercury*, XVII (January 1928), 273–85. See also Matt. Richardson, *ibid.* (March), 575. Reprinted in *Reflections and Memories*, pp. 211–38, London: Wm. Heinemann, 1935.

*25:23. Powell, Lawrence F. "Percy's Reliques" [discusses Johnson's connection], *Library*, 4th ser., IX (September 1928), 113–37.

25:24. Roberts, Sydney Castle. "Johnson in Grub Street," *Cornhill Magazine*, n.s., LXV (October 1928), 440–51. Reprinted in item 10/6:216.

25:25. "Unique Dr. Johnson Item" ["Occasional Papers" by Dr. Dodd], *British Museum Quarterly*, IV, no. 3 (1929), 78–79.

25:26. Chapman, Robert William. "Bennet's *Ascham*" [Johnson as editor], *RES*, V (January 1929), 69–70.

25:27. *Proposals for the Publisher 1744 Now Reprinted in Facsimile and for the First Time Ascribed to Samuel Johnson* [note by R. W. Chapman]. London: Oxford University Press, 1930. See also item 25:28.

*25:28. Chapman, R. W. "Johnson's Works: A Lost Piece and a Forgotten Piece" [proposals for *The Publisher* and the life of Pearce], *London Mercury*, XXI (March 1930), 438–41.

25:29. [Johnsoniana—selections from Vol. IV of item 1/4:19]. Buffalo, N. Y.: Privately printed for R. B. Adam, 1930. Discussed in *TLS*, January 29, 1931, p. 84.

25:30. Hazen, Allen T. "A Johnson Preface" [du Fresnoy's *Chronological Tables*], *TLS*, June 28, 1934, p. 460.

25:31. Chapman, R. W. "Johnson and Burney" [two dedications written by Johnson for Burney], *RES*, X (July 1934), 329–31.

25:32. Balderston, Katharine C. "Dr. Johnson and Burney's *History of Music*," *PMLA*, XLIX (September 1934), 966–68.

*25:33. Hazen, Allen T. "Crousaz on Pope" [Johnson's translation], *TLS*, November 2, 1935, p. 704. See also R. W. Chapman, "Crousaz on Pope," *RES*, n.s., I (January 1950), 57, and L. F. Powell, *Life*, IV, 127, 494–96.

*25:34. Churchill, Irving L. "William Shenstone's Share in the Preparation of Percy's *Reliques*" [discusses Johnson's help], *PMLA*, LI (December 1936), 960–74.

*25:35. Hazen, Allen T. *Samuel Johnson's Prefaces and Dedications*. New Haven, Conn.: Yale University Press, 1937. Reviewed in *N&Q*, CLXXIII (September 18, 1937), 215–16; by P. Meissner, *Beiblatt zur Anglia*, XLIX (January 1938), 52–53; Clarissa Rinaker, *JEGP*, XXXVII (April 1938), 316–18; R. W. Chapman, *RES*, XIV (July 1938), 359–65.

25:36. Bonnard, George A. "Note on the English Translations of Crousaz' Two Books on Pope's 'Essay on Man,'" *Recueil de Travaux*, University of Lausanne, June 1937, pp. 175–84.

25:37. Wright, Reginald W. M. "A Johnsonian Find," *Bath Chronicle and Herald*, December 23, 1937, p. 13. Unlikely attribution to Johnson of an essay in Boddely's *Bath Journal*, December 20, 1762.

25:38. Carlson, Carl Lennart. *The First Magazine: A History of the Gentleman's Magazine* [with account of Dr. Johnson's editorial activity]. Providence, R.I.: Brown University Press, 1938. See also D. Bond, *MP*, XXXVIII (August 1940), 85–100.

25:39. Lewis, Frank R. "The Book Dr. Johnson Did Not Write" [*Concise Account* of the Society of Arts], *TLS*, January 28, 1939, p. 57.

25:40. Botting, Roland B. "Johnson, Smart, and the *Universal Visiter*," *MP*, XXXVI (February 1939), 293–300.

*25:41. McAdam, Edward L., Jr., and A. T. Hazen. "Dr. Johnson and the Hereford Infirmary," *Huntington Library Quarterly*, III (April 1940), 359–67.

*25:42. Green, Boylston. "Possible Additions to the Johnson Canon," *Yale University Library Gazette*, XVI (April 1942), 70–79. "Observations" in *Payne's Universal Chronicle* in 1758.

*25:43. McAdam, Edward L., Jr. "New Essays by Dr. Johnson" ["Weekly Correspondent" essays in *Public Ledger*, etc.], *RES*, XVIII (April 1942), 197–207.

*25:44. Powell, Lawrence F. "An Addition to the Canon of Johnson's Writings" [Preface to first index of *GM*, 1753], *Essays and Studies by Members of the English Association*, XXVIII (1943), 38–41. See also *JNL*, III (December 1943), 1.

25:45. Sigerist, Henry E. "A Literary Controversy over Tea in 18th Century England," *Bulletin of the Institute of the History of Medicine*, XIII (February 1943), 185–99.

25:46. Chapman, R. W. "Johnson: A Literary Project" [possible help with George A. Grierson's literary remains], *N&Q*, CLXXXVII (August 12, 1944), 78.

25:47. Yates, Frances A. "Paolo Sarpi's 'History of the Council of Trent,'" *Journal of the Warburg and Courtauld Institutes*, VII (July–December 1944), 123–43.

25:48. Hazen, Allen T., and T. O. Mabbott. "Dr. Johnson and Francis Fawkes's *Theocritus*," *RES*, XXI (April 1945), 142–46.

25:49. Mabbott, Thomas O. "The Text of Dr. Johnson's Dedication of Hoole's 'Tasso,'" *N&Q*, CLXXXIX (November 3, 1945), 187–88.

25:50. Hennig, John. "Young Johnson and the Jesuits" [Father Lobo], *The Month*, CLXXXII (November–December 1946), 440–49.

25:51. Bloom, Edward A. *Samuel Johnson as Journalist* [abstract of thesis]. Urbana: University of Illinois, 1947.

25:52. *Portuguese Voyages, 1498–1663*, ed. C. D. Ley, pp. 291–330. (Everyman's Library.) London: J. M. Dent & Sons, 1947. Contains selections from Johnson's translation of Father Lobo.

25:53. Liebert, Herman W. "An Addition to the Bibliography of Samuel Johnson," *Papers of the Bibliographical Society of America*, XLI (3rd quarter, 1947), 231–38. Some revisions of Henry Lucas's tragedy *The Earl of Somerset*.

25:54. Greene, D. J. "The Johnsonian Canon: A Neglected Attribution,"

PMLA, LXV (June 1950), 427–34. "Observations" in *Literary Magazine or Universal Review*, June 1756.

*25:55. Liebert, Herman W. "Dr. Johnson's First Book: An Account of the Variant Issues of the First Edition of *A Voyage to Abyssinia*, with a Facsimile of Their Title-Pages," *Yale University Library Gazette*, XXV (July 1950), 23–28.

25:56. McLeod, A. L. "Notes on John Gay" [letter by Pamphilus, *GM*, October 1738], *N&Q*, January 20, 1951, p. 32. See items 25:57 and 25:71.

25:57. Liebert, Herman W. "Johnson and Gay" [Pamphilus letter, October 1738], *N&Q*, May 12, 1951, p. 216. See items 25:56 and 25:71.

25:58. McCutcheon, Roger P. "Johnson and Dodsley's *Preceptor*, 1748," *Tulane Studies in English*, III (1952), 125–32.

25:59. Greene, Donald J. "Was Johnson Theatrical Critic of the *Gentleman's Magazine?*" *RES*, n.s., III (April 1952), 158–61.

*25:60. McAdam, E. L., Jr. "Dr. Johnson and Saunders Welch's *Proposals*," *RES*, n.s., IV (October 1953), 337–45.

25:61. Sherbo, Arthur. "Two Additions to the Johnson Canon," *JEGP*, LII (October 1953), 543–48. Letter to *Daily Advertiser*, April 1739, and "Foreign History," *GM*, November 1747.

25:62. [Hanson, L. F.] "Johnson, Percy, and Sir William Chambers," *Bodleian Library Record*, IV (December 1953), 291–92. Annotation by Percy on Johnson's connection with Chambers's writings on China.

25:63. Kolb, Gwin J. "A Note on the Publication of Johnson's 'Proposals for Printing the *Harleian Miscellany*,'" *PBSA*, XLVIII (2nd quarter, 1954), 196–98.

*25:64. Ruhe, Edward. "The Two Samuel Johnsons," *N&Q*, October 1954, pp. 432–35. Translations of Sarpi's *History of the Council of Trent*.

25:65. Sherbo, Arthur. "A Possible Addition to the Johnson Canon," *RES*, n.s., VI (January 1955), 70–71. Review of Keysler's *Travels* in *Literary Magazine*, 1756.

25:66. McAdam, E. L., Jr. "Johnson, Percy, and Warton," *PMLA*, LXX (December 1955), 1203–4. Relation between Johnson's work with Percy on *Reliques* and his edition of Shakespeare.

25:67. Braham, Lionel. "Johnson's Edition of Roger Ascham," *N&Q*, August 1956, 346–47.

*25:68. Greene, Donald J. "Johnson's Contributions to the *Literary Magazine*," *RES*, n.s., VII (October 1956), 367–92.

25:69. Bloom, Edward A. *Samuel Johnson in Grub Street* [as journalist]. (Brown University Studies, No. XXI.) Providence, R.I.: Brown University Press, 1957. Reviewed by C. R. Tracy, *PQ*, XXXVII (July 1958), 337–38; S. C. Roberts, *MLR*, LIII (October 1958), 567–68; D. J. Greene, *MLN*, LXXIV (February 1959), 169–72; Henry Gifford, *RES*, n.s., X

(May 1959), 201–2; Georges A. Bonnard, *English Studies*, XLIII (June 1962), 194–98.

25:70. Leed, Jacob. "Samuel Johnson and the *Gentleman's Magazine*, an Adjustment of the Canon" [*Account of the Conduct of the Duchess of Marlborough*, 1742], *N&Q*, May 1957, pp. 210–13.

*25:71. Leed, Jacob. "Two New Pieces by Johnson in the *Gentleman's Magazine?*" [letters by Pamphilus, 1738], *MP*, LIV (May 1957), 221–29. See items 25:56 and 25:57.

25:72. Greene, Donald J. "Dr. Johnson and 'An Authentic Account of the Present State of Lisbon'" [not written by Johnson], *N&Q*, August 1957, p. 351.

25:73. Kolb, Gwin J. "Dr. Johnson and the *Public Ledger*: A Small Addition to the Canon," *Studies in Bibliography* (University of Virginia), XI (1958), 252–55.

*25:74. Leed, Jacob. "Samuel Johnson and the *Gentleman's Magazine*: Studies in the Canon of His Miscellaneous Prose Writings, 1738–1744" (dissertation, University of Chicago). Chicago: University of Chicago Department of Photoduplication [microfilm], 1958.

*25:75. Greene, Donald J. "Johnson and the *Harleian Miscellany*," *N&Q*, July 1958, pp. 304–6. Attributes ten short prefaces signed "J."

*25:76. Greene, Donald J. "Some Notes on Johnson and the *Gentleman's Magazine*," *PMLA*, LXXIV (March 1959), 75–84.

25:77. Sherbo, Arthur. "Dr. Johnson and Joseph Warton's Virgil," *JNL*, XVIII, no. 4 (December 1958), 12; XIX, no. 1 (March 1959), 10. Various critical remarks extracted from Johnson's works and inserted in Warton's notes; also discusses Johnson's part in Fawkes's *Theocritus*.

25:78. Gibbs, F. W. "Dr. Johnson's First Published Work?" *Ambix*, VIII (February 1960), 24–34. Attribution of a translation of Boerhaave's *Elementa Chemiae* (1732). See Arthur Sherbo, *ibid.*, XIII (June 1966), 108–15, and reply by Gibbs.

25:79. Leed, Jacob. "Two Notes on Johnson and *The Gentleman's Magazine*," *PBSA*, LIV (2nd quarter, 1960), 101–10. Attributes "Foreign Books," 1741–43, and "The Art of Deciphering," 1742.

25:80. Haley, Sir William. "Dr. Samuel Johnson: Journalist," in item 6:23 (December 1960), pp. 29–39.

25:81. Kolb, Gwin J. "More Attributions to Dr. Johnson," *Studies in English Literature* (Rice University), I (Summer 1961), 77–95. Short items in *GM* and elsewhere.

25:82. Gold, Joel J. "Samuel Johnson's 'Epitomizing' of Lobo's *Voyage to Abyssinia*" (dissertation, Indiana University, 1962), *Dissertation Abstracts*, XXIII (May 1963), 4357.

25:83. Sherbo, Arthur. "Samuel Johnson and the *Gentleman's Magazine*,

1750–1755," in item 10/6:316 (1962), 133–59. Attributes many short items.

25:84. Abbott, John L. "Dr. Johnson's Translations from the French" (dissertation, Michigan State University, 1963), *Dissertation Abstracts*, XXV (July 1964), 449.

25:85. Kolb, Gwin J. "Johnson's 'Little Pompadour': A Textual Crux," in *Restoration and Eighteenth-Century Literature*, ed. Carroll Camden, pp. 125–42. Chicago: University of Chicago Press for Rice University, 1963.

*25:86. Chapple, J. A. V. "Samuel Johnson's *Proposals for Printing the History of the Council of Trent* [1738]," *Bulletin of the John Rylands Library*, XLV (March 1963), 340–69. See also *TLS*, May 25, 1962, p. 373.

25:87. Bernard, F. V. "A Note on Two Attributions to Johnson" [in *GM*], *N&Q*, February 1964, p. 64; May 1964, pp. 190–91.

25:88. Bernard, F. V. "New Evidence on the Pamphilus Letters," *MP*, LXII (August 1964), 42–44. See item 25:71.

*25:89. Gold, Joel J. "Johnson's Translation of Lobo," *PMLA*, LXXX (March 1965), 51–61.

25:90. Abbott, John L. "Dr. Johnson and the Amazons" [translation of essay by Guyon], *PQ*, XLIV (October 1965), 484–95.

25:91. Bernard, F. V. "Johnson's Address 'To The Reader'" [*GM*, May 1739], *N&Q*, December 1965, p. 455.

25:92. Spector, Robert Donald. *English Literary Periodicals and the Climate of Opinion during the Seven Years' War* [Johnson and the *Literary Magazine*, etc.], pp. 288–92 and *passim*. The Hague: Mouton, 1966.

25:93. Sambrook, A. J. "Dr. Johnson—Civil Engineer," *New Rambler*, January 1966, pp. 18–23. The "Plans for Blackfriars Bridge."

25:94. Leed, Jacob. "Johnson, Du Halde, and the Life of Confucius," *Bulletin of the New York Public Library*, LXX (March 1966), 189–99.

*25:95. Abbott, John L. "Dr. Johnson and the Making of 'The Life of Father Paul Sarpi,'" *Bulletin of the John Rylands Library*, XLVIII (Spring 1966), 255–67.

25:96. Sherbo, Arthur. "Samuel Johnson's 'Essay' on Du Halde's *Description of China*," *Papers on Language and Literature*, II (Fall 1966), 372–80.

*25:97. Abbott, John L. "No 'Dialect of France': Samuel Johnson's Translations from the French," *University of Toronto Quarterly*, XXXVI (January 1967), 129–40.

25:98. Bernard, F. V. "Common and Superior Sense: A New Attribution to Johnson" [in *GM*, December 1738], *N&Q*, May 1967, pp. 176–80.

25:99. Goodson, Lester. "Samuel Johnson's Review of Soame Jenyns's *A Free Enquiry into the Nature and Origin of Evil*: A Re-examination," *New Rambler*, January 1968, pp. 19–23.

25:100. Sherbo, Arthur. "Samuel Johnson and Giuseppe Baretti: A Question of Translation," *RES*, n.s., XIX (November 1968), 405–11. Johnson's share in Baretti's *Introduction to the Italian Language*.

25:101. Philip, Ian G. "Doctor Johnson and the Encaenia Oration," *Bodleian Library Record*, VIII (February 1969), 122–23. Johnson probably the author of last public speech of Dr. William King, Principal of St. Mary Hall, Oxford, on July 8, 1763.

INDEX

INDEX

Abbreviations: J = Samuel Johnson; B = James Boswell. Page references are to pages in the "Survey of Johnsonian Studies;" other references are to item numbers in the bibliography. Generally, works by or attributed to Johnson are listed separately by title; for others, see Johnson, Samuel.